One Drop

ALSO BY BLISS BROYARD

My Father, Dancing

One Drop

MY FATHER'S HIDDEN LIFE —
A STORY OF RACE AND FAMILY SECRETS

Bliss Broyard

LITTLE, BROWN AND COMPANY

New York Boston London

Little, Brown and Company
Hachette Book Group USA
237 Park Avenue, New York, NY 10017
Visit our Web site at www.HachetteBookGroupUSA.com

First Edition: September 2007

"The Man with the Blue Guitar," from *The Collected Poems of Wallace Stevens* by Wallace Stevens, copyright 1954 by Wallace Stevens and renewed 1982 by Holly Stevens. Used by permission of Alfred A. Knopf, a division of Random House, Inc.

Library of Congress Cataloging-in-Publication Data
Broyard, Bliss.
    One drop : my father's hidden life—a story of race and family secrets / Bliss Broyard.—
1st ed.
        p. cm.
    Includes bibliographical references and index.
    ISBN-13: 978-0-316-16350-7
    ISBN-10: 0-316-16350-3
    1. Broyard, Bliss—Family.   2. Authors, American—20th century—Biography.   I. Title.
    PS3552. R79154Z46 2007
    813'. 54—dc22   2007006973

10 9 8 7 6 5 4 3

Q-FF

Printed in the United States of America

for my newfound family,
the Broyards,

and

for my daughter, Esme Broyard Israel

The words of a dead man
Are modified in the guts of the living.
—W. H. Auden, "In Memory of W. B. Yeats"

Contents

Etienne BROYARD
b. 1729, in La Rochelle, France
d. 1791, in New Orleans
French soldier sent to Louisiana Territory

Louisa BUQUOY
b. circa 1734, in New Orleans
d. June 5, 1790, in New Orleans

Pierre COUSIN
b. 1710, in Lille, France
d. 1747, in Unknown
Helped to settle St. Tammany Parish

Henry BROYARD
b. circa 1770, in New Orleans
d. Feb. 22, 1818, in New Orleans
Owned at least three slaves

Adelaide HARDY
b. Dec. 25, 1769, in New Orleans
d. Dec. 26, 1799, in New Orleans

Jean François COUSIN
b. Sep. 7, 1745, in New Orleans
d. Oct. 31, 1819, in New Orleans
Ran a brickmaking operation in St. Tammany Parish

Gilbert BROYARD
b. Oct. 11, 1795, in New Orleans
d. Dec. 21, 1851, in Baratoria, LA
Also had 5 children with a free woman of color

Marie PANQUINET
b. Apr. 1, 1806, in New Orleans
d. Unknown

Pierre BONEE
b. circa 1807, in Baracoa, Cuba
d. Aft. 1860, in New Orleans

Henry Antoine BROYARD
b. Jul. 18, 1829, in New Orleans
d. Feb. 5, 1873, in New Orleans
"Passed" as colored to marry a free woman of color

Marie Pauline BONEE
b. Jan. 24, 1833, in New Orleans
d. May 18, 1915, in New Orleans
Descended from St. Domingue refugees

Paul BROYARD
b. Jul. 21, 1856, in New Orleans
d. Nov. 25, 1940, in New Orleans
"Belhomme"

✳ *The Central Figures of ONE DROP*

Marie Françoise RENARD
b. Unknown, in New Orleans
d. Unknown

Catherine PECHE
b. Unknown
d. Bef. 1800

Marie Adelaide BELHOMME
b. circa 1800, in St. Domingue
d. circa 1860, in New Orleans

François COUSIN
b. Jan. 24, 1786, in
St. Tammany Parish
d. Jul. 11, 1863, in
St. Tammany Parish
*Had pied-à-terre in New Orleans across
from Xavier family home*

Eugenie JUDISSE
b. Bef. 1817, in Unknown
d. circa 1841, in St. Tammany
Parish
Part Choctaw Indian

François XAVIER
b. circa 1802, in Havana,
Cuba
d. Aug. 27, 1839, in
New Orleans
St. Domingue refugee

Marie Claire L'HERRISSE
b. Bef. 1802, in St. Domingue
d. Aft. 1861, in New Orleans
St. Domingue refugee

Anatole Laurent COUSIN
b. Oct. 31, 1830, in St. Tammany Parish
d. Jan. 30, 1887, in St. Tammany Parish
*Had 11 children with Margaret Ducré,
daughter of ex-slave*

Marie Evaline XAVIER
b. Dec. 5, 1824, in New Orleans
d. Sep. 2, 1908, in New Orleans
*Free woman of color whose parents owned
slaves*

Rosa COUSIN
b. Dec. 3, 1852, in St. Tammany
Parish
d. Jul. 4, 1921, in New Orleans

Charles MILLER
b. Apr. 5, 1872, in
New Orleans
d. Bet. 1909–1920,
in Unknown

Louise SOULE
b. Aug. 18, 1878, in
New Orleans
d. Oct. 31, 1945, in
Jackson, LA

Paul Anatole BROYARD
b. Jan. 21, 1889, in New Orleans
d. Mar. 11, 1950, in Brooklyn, NY
"Nat"

Edna MILLER
b. Dec. 18, 1895, in New
Orleans
d. Sep. 1978, in Bronx, NY

Lorraine BROYARD
b. Feb. 20, 1919, in New Orleans
d. Aug. 29, 1992, in New York,
NY

Shirley BROYARD
b. Jan. 3, 1923, in
New Orleans

Anatole Paul BROYARD
b. Jul. 16, 1920, in New Orleans
d. Oct. 11, 1990, in Cambridge,
MA

Alexandra NELSON
b. Dec. 12, 1937, in Mamaroneck,
NY

Todd BROYARD
b. Jul. 26, 1964, in Greenwich, CT

Bliss BROYARD
b. Sep. 5, 1966, in Greenwich, CT

I.

Love at Last Sight

~ 1 ~

Two months before my father died of prostate cancer, I learned about a secret, but I had always sensed that there was something about my family, or even many things, that I didn't know. As a child, when I was left alone in the house, I would search through my mother's file cabinets and my father's study for elaboration, clarification, some proof...

Of what? I couldn't exactly say.

My mother kept files on each of us, and I rifled through their contents: my father's passport, a small cellophane envelope containing a lock of hair, a doctor's report about my brother's childhood dyslexia. In my own file, I ran my finger across the raised seal on my birth certificate, read again the story about an escaped tiger that I once recited to a babysitter and a comment I made about a dance performance that my mother jotted down, examined my report cards and class photos. While these artifacts made me understand that, as young as I was, I already had my own history and in some way that I couldn't articulate was always looking for myself too, they weren't the evidence I sought.

In my father's study, I shuffled through the items in the wooden box on his desk: a small red vinyl address book, bills to be paid, scraps of papers and old envelopes with scrawled phone numbers and phrases: "Their joy is a kind of genius."

I stood on a chair and peered at a cardboard box on the back of a shelf in his closet. The box was square, a little smaller than a cake box, and unadorned. Sometimes I took it into my arms and felt its surprising heft. The mailing label listed a return address for the United States Crematorium, a Prince Street address in Greenwich Village for Anatole Broyard, my father, and a 1950 postmark. Sometime during the year I was twelve, a second cardboard box appeared. This one was a little lighter. Here were my grandparents, whom I never knew.

Neither box had ever been opened. At each seam the original packing tape remained intact. But I knew better than to think I'd find anything useful inside. These boxes held only ashes of answers, and all their presence meant was more mysteries, and a worry that someday something else might explode.

At times I knew what my father was going to say before he said it. I could tell you whether a movie, song, or woman was likely to suit his tastes. When I'd see him crouch for a low forehand playing paddleball on the beach, I could feel in my own body what the movement felt like to him — the crunch-clamp of his stomach, the scoop-snap of his arm. I knew my father like you know a room that you've lived in for a long time — his frequencies, scent, and atmosphere were all familiar to me — but I didn't know anything *about* him, his history or how he came to be.

And I felt that because I'd come from my mother and father — been made up by their parts — that I had a right to know *everything* about them. I *was* them. And they were mine, for better or worse. Not even death could part us.

In August of 1990, my parents, my brother, Todd, and I gathered on Martha's Vineyard, where my family had a summer home, for the annual Chilmark Road Race, which Todd ran in every year. We were also trying to spend time together, because the rate at which my father was deteriorating from his cancer had suddenly sped up. He'd been diagnosed a year earlier, just after my parents moved from Fairfield, Connecticut, where I was raised, to Cambridge, Massachusetts.

The move was supposed to mark a new, carefree phase of their lives. They'd sold their house in Fairfield at a nice profit, so they had money in the bank for the first time. After eighteen years as a daily book critic and editor at the Sunday book review, my father had retired from the *New York Times* and was happily at work on a memoir about life in the Greenwich Village of the 1940s. My brother and I had just finished college and had jobs at which we were finally making our own livings.

My parents planned trips to Europe, longer stretches on Martha's Vineyard, leisurely days fixing up their cozy Victorian, which would eventually resemble, in my father's words, a "perfect doll's house." Above all, they would enjoy Cambridge, which, they imagined, offered a comparable atmosphere to the café life and highbrow conversation of Greenwich Village that my father was now recounting.

Twelve months later he was on the verge of becoming someone I didn't recognize. He weighed about 115 pounds, 40 pounds lighter than the trim figure I'd admired throughout my childhood, running for a Frisbee on a beach or strutting onto a dance floor. His face, which had always appeared youthful, looked even more so. With large staring eyes and a round greedy mouth, his countenance had lost the guise of adulthood, leaving the shocks to his flesh and spirit in plain view. In recent weeks I'd felt compelled to keep him in my sight, as if my constant vigilance and memory of the "old" him might prevent any further transformation.

The last time our family had been together on the Vineyard, two months before, although my dad had been very sick and all the treatment options available through Western medicine had been exhausted, we had felt that there were still things that could be done: a special vitamin cure to try, phone calls about other alternative treatments to make, marijuana to smoke to curb his constant queasiness, the beach to stroll on, friends to come over and distract us from thinking about what was next.

But since then he'd pushed off for more rocky shores. His prostate made him prostrate, a pun that he might have appreciated in better days. Months earlier the cancer had traveled up from that innocent-seeming gland into his bones, where it bit down now with a death grip that knocked him off his feet. He lay on the couch upstairs in the living room and flipped through the television channels. He lay on the couch downstairs while nearby in the kitchen my mother cooked things that he might eat—rye toast, scrambled eggs, chicken broth. "No, no, no." He'd wave his hand in front of his face. "Even the smell makes me nauseous." He lay awake in bed, too uncomfortable to read or sleep.

On Sunday, though, the day of the Chilmark Road Race, he got up. Since my brother had begun running competitively, my father seemed to concentrate all his ambitions and concerns for his son on his races, as if life really were a footrace and Todd's standing in this 5K today could predict how he would fare after our father was gone. In my own life there was no equivalent focus of my father's attentions. He often said that he didn't worry about me, which I was meant to take as a compliment.

He insisted that we watch the race from our regular spot: about a third of a mile from the finish line. His theory was that the location was close enough to the end for us to feel the excitement of the finish but far enough away that our encouragement of Todd could still make some difference.

The walk there fatigued him, and while we waited for my brother to appear, he had to sit on a beach chair that I'd brought. The day was hot and still. Across the road, some cows stood motionless in a field. Beyond them, in the distance, the ocean was flat. A motorboat made slow progress across the horizon. I looked down at my father, who was wearing long sleeves and pants to cover his skinny limbs. Behind him, down the hill, some other spectators walked toward us, but the heat trapped any noise they made, and their feet fell silently on the pavement. *My father's dying,* I had an urge to yell to them. *He's dying!*

Some runners rounded the curve and began the ascent, and then there was Todd, pumping up the hill. His blond curls bounced on his sweaty forehead. I helped my dad to his feet. We cheered and yelled, my mother snapped pictures, and my brother flashed my father a huge grin. The thought passed through my mind that this race was probably the last one my father would see his son run, and I wondered if Todd was thinking the same thing.

My dad was holding on to my arm. The lightness of his weight on my elbow made me tremble.

He turned to me and said, "Did you see the way that Todd smiled at me? He's not using all of his energy if he has the reserve for that smile."

Todd ran well, placing ninth overall out of 1,500 runners, but my dad estimated that he had 10 percent of his energy left over and told him so when we met up at the finish.

I hated how my father was changing from the cancer, and at the same time, I wanted to shake him by his bony shoulders and say, *Aren't you ever going to change, for God's sake? There isn't much time.*

Most of Chilmark turned out for the race, and as we made our way to the car, we kept bumping into people we knew. While he chatted with someone, my father would have to sit down in the beach chair, which he would apologize for, and the friend would sit down too, right there in the dirt or on the roadside. Before my dad lost his strength, he would greet women friends with a bear hug that lifted them off their feet. With his male friends, he'd throw an arm around their shoulder and draw them away a few steps, asking, "How are you?" and "What's been on your mind?"

Recently he had published a number of articles in the *Times* on the experience of being ill that mentioned his own prognosis. Most of the people we encountered that day had an idea of how sick my father was, but I could tell from the way they would startle briefly that they were shocked by the sight of him.

If my dad noticed this response, he ignored it. In one of the essays, "Toward a Literature of Illness," he wrote that for those who are critically ill, "it may not be dying we fear so much, but the diminished self." He reasoned that by developing a style for their illness, a stance that incorporated it into the ongoing narrative of their lives, sick people could "go on being themselves, perhaps even more so than before." And then their friends and loved ones might put away their expressions of "grotesque lovingness" and other false behaviors and go back to being themselves too.

My father's energy for these summer friends surprised me. His conversation was witty, vibrant, enthusiastic. "It's still me," he seemed to be saying. That seated figure in the baggy clothes was the same Anatole they'd always known. And he was asking them, "Please, still be you."

When we got home, my mother called us into the family room. She said that we needed to talk. My father lay on his side on the couch. I sat down on one end and put his feet in my lap. My mother and my brother sat in two captain's chairs facing us. I rubbed my father's feet and calves, because physical contact helped him to focus on some other sensation than his pain and nausea.

His skin was shiny with illness, luminescent from it, reminding me of the veneer inside a clamshell that, if you touch it too roughly, can flake away in your hands. I'd never before been on such intimate terms with my father's body, and I was by turns moved and disgusted.

My mother is a psychiatric social worker by profession, and I could see that she was retreating into her therapist mode to get a conversation going. This kind of gathering was out of character for us. We were a family that did things together, played tennis, went dancing, took walks. We knew best how to relate to each other on the move.

She asked Todd what the experience of my father's illness was like for him.

"It's tough, of course. But I know you're tough, Dad." Todd wasn't looking at any of us when he answered. He was scratching our Labrador retriever's back.

"What about Daddy's pain? Does that scare you?"

"Well, sure. I don't want to see him in pain." Todd was still looking down at the dog. He cooed at her, "Good girl, Georgie. Who's a good dog?"

"What about you, Bliss?" My mother turned to me. "How does the pain make you feel?"

Georgie started her high-pitched whine in response to my brother's attentions. I can remember the rage boiling up inside me: at Todd for eliciting this noise, at my mother for her stilted effort to get us talking, and, most of all, at the foreignness of this shiny fragile limb, my father's foot, in my lap.

I mumbled that I was afraid of the pain.

"There are things they can do for the physical pain, but there's psychological pain too, and that's harder to deal with." My mother talked about a family therapist my parents began seeing when my father refused to go along with the vitamin cure. She mentioned the need for a dialogue and getting things out into the open.

My brother, having finally turned his attention away from the dog, was nodding along, but I was wary of this heart-to-heart business. My family made jokes. We suffered privately. We didn't go around the room and share our feelings. Why wasn't my father — who loathed the way illness could distort people's behavior — raising any objections?

"Is there anything you'd like to say to your children, Anatole?"

"Sandy." There was warning in his voice.

"Anatole," my mother persisted. "What would you want to say to your children if you were dying?"

My mother's tone seemed to suggest that my father had something to tell us. I already knew about his two other daughters—one from his first marriage, when he was nineteen, and the other from a short-lived relationship when he was a bachelor—but my dad hadn't seen either of them in years. I wondered what else it could be. My mother's elliptical phrasing seemed to catch my father off guard.

"I would say that I hope you'll be all right, that you will be happy." He raised himself up on his elbow. "My only regret is that we didn't confide in each other more." He looked at my brother. "Especially with you, Todd. I wish I knew better what makes Todd Broyard happy in his life, what gets him excited. My father and I never learned how to talk to each other as friends, and I always wanted that with my own son."

"I have simple tastes, Dad. You know what makes me happy. We talk."

It occurred to me that what my father wanted was for my brother to have different tastes, more like his own. Todd's passions were mostly solitary: running, karate, reading history, drawing, playing the harmonica. He was like my mother in this way, while my dad and I were extroverted. We became restless easily; we liked team sports and parties. We needed a lot of attention from people.

"Well, I wish we could have found an easier way to talk," my father said. "I suppose I could have shared more of myself too."

"What would you have wanted the kids to know?" my mother prodded. "You can tell them right now."

"I don't want to go into that today."

Todd and I looked at each other. "Go into what?" I asked.

"Your father has lived with a secret for a long time. Something from his childhood." My mother gripped the arms of the captain's chair.

"Goddamn it, Sandy."

"In some ways this secret is more painful than the cancer." She looked back and forth from my brother to me. "It will help to explain a lot about your father."

"I said I didn't want to talk about it today."

"When else are we going to talk about it? We're all together now. We're here now."

"I don't feel well. I've been horribly nauseous all day. A person can't concentrate when he's nauseous. It's like someone is constantly tugging at your sleeve."

"You don't need to concentrate, Dad." I rubbed his leg to reassure him. "Just tell us what you want to tell us."

"Yeah, Dad." Todd leaned forward in his chair. "We're your family."

"Anatole, talk to your children."

"We want to know you," I said. And I did, but of course at twenty-three years old, I was also intensely curious to know myself — as a grown-up, not my parents' child. I thought, conveniently, of identity as a kind of board game, where solving the mystery of my father would allow me to move forward onto the next level of discovery. Years later I'd understand that a mark of adulthood is the ability to live with uncertainty. But back then I wanted to figure everything out, myself most of all. I hoped to discover that I was a complicated person, which I equated with being an interesting person, and since I was too young to feel I'd earned my own complications, I'd happily take some from my father.

At the moment he appeared all out of defenses. He'd removed his legs from my lap and curled them into his body. Half sitting up, propped on his elbow with a cushion wedged under his arm at the far end of the couch, he looked uncomfortable and cornered. If he were stronger, if he were as he used to be, he would have just gotten up and left the room, saying he wasn't going to talk about it, end of discussion.

He told us he didn't believe that we really wanted to know him. If we did, he wondered, why didn't we read more of his writing?

Todd laughed sourly. "I'm supposed to understand my father by knowing his opinion on the latest Philip Roth novel."

"I read your writing, Dad," I broke in. "And you wrote that the most important thing for a dying man is to be understood." He looked at me and nodded faintly. Yes, he did write that. I continued: "But how can I understand you without knowing where you came from? You've never talked about your parents or your sisters. We barely know anything about them."

All these years later, I can still recall the feeling of control I had over my father as he listened to me, perhaps because it was so unusual. All my life he'd appeared a powerful and assured figure. Of course many children are inclined to see their father as an important man in the world, but my dad's job as a daily book critic for the *Times* caused some other people to see him that way too. In Fairfield, or in the summer on Martha's Vineyard, people would recognize his name and further ratify his authority in my eyes.

"You've got to give me something to write about," I said reflexively to lighten the moment.

Now his expression changed again, flashing with understanding: that I would write about this day on Martha's Vineyard, that this secret—whatever it was—wouldn't remain secret forever, that his story would continue after he wasn't around to narrate it.

"I will tell you, but I'm not going to talk about it today," he said more firmly. "I need to think about how to present things. I want to order my vulnerabilities so they don't get magnified during the discussion."

Todd and I argued that a father shouldn't need a prepared text to speak to his children, but no amount of cajoling would convince him to change his mind. And he was so beleaguered and exhausted that it began to seem unkind to continue. We set a date a few weeks later to meet at my parents' house in Cambridge to try the discussion again. Then my mother helped my father upstairs, because he wanted to lie down. I wonder now what he was thinking as he lay in his bed alone. His children said that they wanted to know him. Was he considering what he might say when we met again? Was he worrying about how a single conversation might accomplish what being our father for more than twenty years apparently had not?

At the time, though, I was too occupied with the question of what the secret was to consider my father's experience of revealing it. Todd and I both guessed that it had something to do with sex or death, but neither of us had any specific ideas. Years later Todd confided that he felt very apprehensive about what we might discover: that our father had been abused as a child or been involved in some horrible crime.

For my part the existence of a secret made me feel strangely elated. My childhood suspicions were confirmed, and I welcomed the new variation in the routine of my father's illness — the chance to feel something else. For the past twelve months, my family's life had been filled with decisions about hormone treatments and radiation, midnight trips to the hospital because of huge blood clots in my father's urine, coffee enemas, incontinence, and diapers. I muddled through this world of corporeal intimacy, feeling embarrassed and clumsy, and fretted that there was never going to be energy or time for a familial closeness of any other type.

Here was at last our chance for true intimacy, the kind that confessions and forgiveness might bring. Besides, I could do secrets much better than I could do scared-daughter-standing-by-her-father's-hospital-bed. The betrayals and danger they involved, the mix of self-interest, protection, and cowardice at their core — for these dramas, I felt much better equipped.

Before we had our family meeting, another emergency sent my father back to Brigham and Women's Hospital, in Boston. Over Labor Day weekend, he was transferred into Dana-Farber Cancer Institute across the street, where, the doctors said, they were better prepared to treat cases like his. What kind were they? I wondered. Hopeless ones?

Any talk of alternative treatments was forgotten. The focus now was on what work my father could accomplish in the time he had left. There was no mention of the secret.

My twenty-fourth birthday was a few days later. My best friend, Chinita, came up from New York, and we had a small celebration in my father's hospital room. But my dad couldn't stay awake. My mother kept having to rouse him, saying, "Honey, Blissy's blowing out the candles now," and "Look, she's unwrapping her present."

On the weekend, Todd came up from Hartford, where he was living at the time, and met my mother and me at Dana-Farber. Michael Vincent Miller—Mike to us—my father's closest friend, was there too. My dad was particularly energized. This hospital stay was nearing the end of its second week, and he couldn't get enough news about the outside world. He seemed desperate for distraction, asking us over and over, "What else is going on? Tell me something else." Then he began to shake.

"Shit, Sandy. Shit. It's starting again."

I looked at my mother for a clue about what was happening. My dad only swore blasphemously—goddamn it and Jesus Christ.

"Okay, Anatole, breathe," my mother said. She explained that he'd been having these waves of pain all morning. "Stay focused on us."

I was sitting in a chair by the head of his bed. I took his hand and told him to squeeze my fingers.

Todd stood at the end of the bed and began to talk. "I made a big sale this week, Dad."

"Yes?" My father locked eyes on his son. I could see his jaw muscle trembling.

Todd nodded vigorously. "Yeah, a big sale, so it looks like I'll make my quota and then I'll start earning commission on top of my salary."

"That's great. Good work. Oh Christ, it's getting worse. Keep talking." His fingers tightened around mine.

"And, uh, I've got another race coming up on the Vineyard."

"Shit. Fucking Christ." Under the blanket, his legs bounced against the mattress.

"This one's a 10K, about a thousand runners."

The tremor moved up his body, and his shoulders shook. "Good, Todd. You in shape for it?" The pitch of his voice shot up. "Oh God, please. I can't stand another one."

He tried to pull his hand away from mine. "I'm going to hurt you, Bliss."

"I'm fine. It's fine." I put my other hand on top of his and pressed down.

"I'm going to squeeze too hard." He jerked free of my grasp. His head quivered and his pupils narrowed.

"Hold on, honey." My mother crouched at my father's side.

"Come on, Buddy." Mike reached a hand forward toward the bed.

My father struggled to sit up. He began to yell: "Help! Someone. Help me! Please, help."

I remember that we all froze for a moment, pinned down into ourselves by the terror of this anguish. Then Todd was moving toward the door, and I thought that he intended to close it, an impulse, it's strange to admit now, that made sense to me. What was happening in that hospital room felt too raw and private. It seemed wrong for strangers to overhear us.

But Todd was going out the door. He was running down the hallway, calling for a nurse, and he quickly returned with one in tow. My mother's calm demeanor was rapidly fading. She'd been engaged in an ongoing battle with the hospital staff because they wouldn't give my father enough painkillers to actually kill his pain for fear that he would become addicted to them. Which forced my mother to point out the obvious: given the imminence of my father's death, what did it matter? Now she turned on the nurse, spittle gathered in the corners of her mouth. "For God's sake, can't you see this level of morphine is not enough? Give him more!"

The nurse mumbled something about needing to get the pain management team back in there, but she fiddled with the morphine drip and upped the dosage. Then, as suddenly as the episode of pain had begun, it stopped. My father lay back in the bed, panting shallow breaths. His face was white, and his eyes were very wide. He seemed to be staring at nothing, or everything. Then he closed his eyes and he was asleep, or more likely the narcotic had knocked him out.

We headed outside to get some fresh air. Mike left for home, and Todd, my mother, and I sat on a stone wall across the street. With my eyes I counted the floors of the building and the windows in from the corner until I located my father's room. I wondered if other families were engaged in similar dramas behind the drawn curtains of the neighboring windows. During the six weeks that I regularly visited the Dana-Farber Cancer Institute, I looked for people who were going through the same ordeal as we were. But it always seemed like we were the only ones crying in the hallway, the only ones struggling to talk in calm voices as the doctors asked us to make decisions so vital to another person's well-being as to feel ludicrous and wrong, the only ones who walked around with shocked and stricken faces because the knowledge that all people must die one day had in no way prepared us for the death of this man. Our spot on the stone wall was in the sunshine, but I was shivering with cold. I rubbed my hands up and down my arms.

"I think I better tell you what this secret is," my mother said. She was sitting between Todd and me. We caught eyes behind her back. Inexplicably we both began to grin.

"Well." She took a breath and let it out. "Your father's part black."

I burst out with a laugh. "That's the secret? Daddy's part black?"

"That's all?" Todd asked.

"That's it," my mother said, allowing herself a smile.

We asked a few questions: How black was he? After all, he didn't look black. Neither did his sister Lorraine or his mother, whom we'd seen once or twice when we were little. My mother explained that my father had "mixed blood," and his parents were both light-skinned Creoles from New Orleans, where race-mixing had been common. She said that his parents had to pass for white in order to get work in

1930s New York, which confused my father about what their family was, or was supposed to be. He was the lightest child out of the three siblings, and the fact that his two sisters lived as black was one of the reasons that we never saw them. My mother said that when my father was growing up in Brooklyn, where his family had moved when he was six, he'd been ostracized by both white and black kids alike. The black kids picked on him because he looked white, and the white kids rejected him because they knew his family was black. He'd come home from school with his jacket torn, and his parents wouldn't ask what happened. My mother said that he didn't tell us about his racial background because he wanted to spare his own children from going through what he did.

"So this means that we're part black too," I said, taking in the news. I had always bought into the idea of the American "melting pot," and now I was an example of it. The idea thrilled me, as though I'd been reading a fascinating history book and then discovered my own name in the index. I felt like I mattered in a way that I hadn't before.

Todd was pleased too. "What a great pickup line," he said. "'I may look white, but I'm really Afro-American where it counts.' The guys in my office are always giving me such a hard time about being so white-bread."

"Todd," my mother said, alarmed. "This isn't something you should be telling everyone. Anyway, you kids aren't black. You're white."

Two days later a tumor burst through the wall of my father's bladder, although the doctors didn't realize it until they got him into the operating room. All my mother understood when she called me at work was that there was an unexpected crisis and the nurses told her to tell her children to come to the hospital as quickly as they could.

I was at Scudder, Stevens & Clark, a mutual funds company, where I worked answering letters from shareholders with complaints or questions. I sat in an open room the size of a football field, lined with rows and rows of low-walled cubicles filled with hundreds of other customer service representatives, also answering calls and letters from shareholders. It took me a moment to understand what my mother was actually saying. After I hung up the phone, I closed out all the documents open on my computer and shut it down. I straightened up the letters and papers on my desk and then gathered together my things and put them in my purse. I got up, put on my sweater, and slowly walked around the row of cubicles to my boss's cubicle. Sheila looked up and raised her eyebrows.

"Hi, uh, I've got to go, um, my mother called from the hospital, and—"

Sheila had lost her brother to brain cancer a few years earlier. She knew better than I did what kind of phone call I'd just received. She stood up and took me in her arms briefly. I was shaking. I wasn't ready for this to happen yet.

She called another customer service rep up to her desk, gave her twenty dollars, and told her to take me in a taxicab over to the hospital. I resisted briefly, saying I could take the subway, I'd be fine on my own. Their fussing underlined the direness of the situation, and I didn't want to understand, in fact I couldn't understand, what was happening.

When I arrived at Dana-Farber, my mother was talking with the oncologist and urologist in my father's room about scheduling an emergency surgery. He'd been moved to the room in front of the nurses' station reserved for crisis patients. The doctors had some forms for my mother to complete, and as she left with them, I started to follow, but she pointed behind her and told me, "Stay with your father." I turned and headed back into his room. At the moment, my father was terrifying to me.

He was laid out flat except for his head, which was propped up at an unnatural angle by too many pillows. A blanket covered him completely, pulled up to his chin. But underneath I could see that his body was motionless, rigid, as though he were in shock. His expression looked shocked too. His eyebrows were raised, and his eyes were unblinking. His mouth was opened in a small "O," and his breath panted in and out fast, like a dog's. He hadn't acknowledged me yet.

His gaze was focused on an invisible spot before him. I thought perhaps that he was staring down a tunnel to the end of his life and that I should try to ease his mind by reassuring him that he'd arrived there valiantly. I pulled a chair to the head of his bed and leaned in close and whispered to my father that I loved him, that he'd been a great dad, that because of him, I'd never be able to lead an ordinary life. These words were true, but saying them made me feel uncomfortable, following as I was some borrowed notion of how to act at a loved one's deathbed. I chose not to mention the secret. It wasn't a subject we had any history with, and I didn't want to say anything that might upset him.

His eyes glanced in my direction, which encouraged me to continue. I told him that I was proud of him, of all that he'd accomplished, and that he'd had a successful life. He looked at me again and spoke in a hoarse whisper: "Blissy, enough with your bromides. I'm trying to concentrate. You have no idea how difficult this is."

Many times since, I've chastised myself for resorting to such conventional language. I should have spoken of his favorite poet, Wallace Stevens, or offered an observation about the world—something quirky and funny and true—to wrap him more firmly in humanity's grip.

Less frequently I've wondered how my father could have rebuked me for trying to tell him, as clumsy as it might have been, that I loved him and that he hadn't lived in vain.

His surgery would take place over at Brigham and Women's Hospital. While he was transported in an ambulance the short distance between the two buildings, my mother did her best to answer his questions about what was happening. But she didn't know much beyond what the surgeon told her when they were deciding whether to operate: Your husband's chances of surviving a lengthy surgery are slim.

Just as he was going into the operating room, my father called out, "What's happened to my voice? Listen. It's lost its timbre. What's happened to my voice?" Then the doors swung closed behind him.

My father did survive to live another month, but for the first time in my life, he didn't make sense. After he came out of intensive care, he moved in and out of lucidity, and never regained it completely.

In his journal, my father wrote that a sick person needs to guard against the disfigurement of illness because "at the end, you're posing for eternity." Throughout my father's writing ran the theme that a person's identity was an act of will and style. In a review of Ernest Becker's *Denial of Death*, a book that my father greatly admired, he wrote about Becker's idea that we can defend ourselves against the fear of death "by becoming so insistently and inimitably ourselves, or by producing something so indelibly our own, that we may be said, as a poet put it, to have added forever to the sum of reality." Achieving this kind of immortality, in Becker and my father's view, was not a passive act.

After the surgery my dad was stunned to realize, despite his cloudy mind, that he'd almost died. He told my mother in a childlike voice: "I'm not the golden boy anymore. I'm not that beautiful boy. I have to find a new way to think of myself." With bags to collect his waste hanging from his body, tubes and machinery crowding his bedside, his brain short-circuited and unreliable, he needed to find some aspect of himself to latch onto so that he might remain "insistently and inimitably" Anatole. This was necessary both for him and for those who loved him, because, as he also wrote in his journal, "the final view for survivors, the family and friends, would be, in the philosopher Walter Benjamin's phrase, 'love at last sight.'"

There were still flashes of his old self. He would startle us with an observation: "The color of this blanket is institutional yellow," or

"The breadth of that doctor's shoulders gives him false confidence." But as the days wore on, these came less and less frequently.

And then the tug of his failing body finally won out. He roamed from stranger to father to man-child to madman. There wasn't much talking with him, just listening, and deciphering.

He put his hand over his eyes, as if he was staring at something. "I'm standing on the rocks looking out over a promontory. But I can't see the shoreline. Will I like it there?"

"Yes," we told him.

"Are you sure?" he asked, grabbing my mother's arm. "This isn't a time for lying."

"I promise," she said.

"Okay then." He looked around at the friends and family assembled in his room. "Who wants to join me?" He patted the mattress next to him. "Blissy?"

I lowered the bed's railing and stretched my body alongside his, resting my head lightly on his shoulder. He draped his thin arm across my back. We could have been home on the couch, watching TV.

"Sandy?" he said, lifting his head. "David?" He called to a friend. "Come join us." He raised his hands, the magnanimous host. "I invite all of you, anyone who'd care to, to come join me in my bed. Why not?" My mother spread herself out on the other side of my father. He smiled and patted his wife and daughter.

"We'll go down in history as the family with the least affection for each other," he said.

"No!" we all protested.

He shook his head, exasperated. "It's a joke."

Another time, when I was helping him to eat, he became agitated suddenly and took the fork out of my hand. Then he took my hand and pressed it to his lips several times, kissing it over and over again. "I had to do that because you're my daughter," he said.

"And you're my father," I answered.

* * *

We camped out in that hospital room for days, keeping him company. We ordered in pizza and brought back ice-cream sundaes. A steady stream of people came to say good-bye. On some nights the atmosphere was like a party.

While my father drifted in and out of consciousness, we talked about the story of the secret. Friends visiting shared what details they knew and told of the secrets their own families harbored: Illegitimate children. Adopted children. Jewish ancestry.

It's said that the hearing is the last sense to go when someone is dying. Maybe my father heard us. He beckoned to me one evening: "Lorraine. Lorraine." His sister's name. Another time he told me, "You've got to listen to more Afro-Cuban music."

There were no final words that anyone agreed on. The last to me were on the phone one afternoon during a brief flash of clearheadedness. I told him that I'd be at the hospital soon. "Okay, sweetie pie," he said. "See you then." My brother remembers a conversation about a road race coming up. My mother didn't offer what final words she and my father shared, and I've never asked.

One day he fell into a coma. And then, a week or so later, very early one morning, he died.

His death certificate indicates that he was born in New Orleans, Louisiana, on July 16, 1920, to Edna Miller and Paul Anatole Broyard and that he died in Cambridge, Massachusetts, on October 11, 1990, as the husband of Sandy Broyard. His race is identified as white.

~2~

My father used to say that he'd come from nothing. While he'd been raised with modest means in New Orleans and Brooklyn, and his parents only had eighth grade educations, I knew that by "nothing" he meant the existential kind. With no ancestors that he spoke of, no legacy that could explain his habits and tastes, he seemed, as he later wrote, to have "sprung from my own brow, spontaneously generated the way flies were once thought to have originated." Where some people had parents and siblings, a history and hometown, my father had the literature of his favorite authors: Franz Kafka, Wallace Stevens, Charles Baudelaire, and D. H. Lawrence. In his memoir about living in Greenwich Village in the 1940s — which was published posthumously as *Kafka Was the Rage* — he explained that these writers were "all the family I had now, all the family I wanted."

But after twenty years of bachelorhood in New York City, my father married my mother, they moved to Connecticut, and my brother and I were born. He still had his writers — they lined the shelves of the study where he spent his days, alternately reclined in a Barca-Lounger chair with a book balanced in his large palm or hunched over a wooden desk, writing on a long yellow legal pad with a very sharp number one pencil — and we became all the family that my father wanted. Or so I'd been led to believe.

When I asked him why we didn't see his relatives — his father died before I was born, but his mother and two sisters lived an hour away in New York for much of my childhood—my dad would say that they didn't interest him. "You know, Blissy, just because you share blood with someone doesn't mean you have to like them," he'd explain. The implication was that he liked—*loved*—us by choice, as long as we remained interesting.

My mother didn't have much family either. Her parents were both dead by the time she was twenty, and her brother and sister lived very different lives in faraway places. On vacations, at school graduations, and on Christmas mornings, it was usually just my mother, my father, my brother, and me. Our tribe of four made us seem alternately special and forsaken, the last survivors of a dying colony or the founding members of an exclusive club. We were fragile. We were definitive. We were the platonic ideals of father, mother, daughter, son.

On holidays, without the buffer of other relatives, our home life grew even more concentrated. There were elaborate meals, abundant presents, roaring fires in the hearth. Looking back now, I wonder if these efforts were a celebration of what we had or compensation for the people we were missing. While my mother's relatives were absent by circumstance, my father's had been banished—although never quite completely. Occasional stories, artifacts buried in closets, photos tucked into old albums, kept their spectral presences in the air. Then, every so often, one of them would burst into life, unexpectedly fracturing the calm surface of our existence, and, as if I'd spied a ghost, everything that I believed about the natural order of my world would be called into question.

It was Mother's Day 1979, and I was twelve years old. For some reason he didn't share with me, my father decided to get my mother something extra special that year—a pair of gold earrings shaped like sea urchins, from Tiffany. My dad considered himself a connoisseur of many things in life, but he was most discriminating when it came to women. He would hold forth about their varieties of beauty and the fashions that suited each type as if he were a gardener discussing the preferred growing conditions of heirloom roses. My mother— who my father often said grew more beautiful every year—had classic Nordic looks that were best complemented by modern twists on traditional designs. (I, on the other hand, was told I should stick to dark blues and earth tones that didn't overwhelm my "subtle appeal.") My dad showed me the earrings he had chosen and explained why they were perfect for my mom. Then he confided that he'd spent nearly $300 on them.

On the evening of Mother's Day, my father came into the kitchen to present his gift. I was already in there with my mother, who was making dinner, and I remember that she was in a rather bad mood. No doubt her foul humor was owed to the fact that despite its being *her day*, she still had to tend to all of us. My father placed the blue Tiffany box in the middle of the kitchen table and sat down. "Sandy, come over here," he said, throwing a wink toward me.

My mother was stirring a pot on the stove, and she delayed, saying something to the effect that, *couldn't he see she was busy?* She hadn't turned around, so she didn't know about the present on the table. My father tried again, suggesting that the meal wouldn't be ruined by turning off the burner for a minute. And my mother—who still hadn't turned around—started to explain why the meal *would* be ruined, when my father abruptly stood up and flung the earring box across the room.

"Fine!" he yelled. "Happy Mother's Day!"

After it was too late, I recognized the strained quality of my father's entreaties: "She works so hard, Mommy does," he'd appealed to me when trying to get her to sit down. He was at his worst when he was supposed to act a certain way. He seemed to have been reaching for the kind of moment that an advertisement for Tiffany might promise—a message from a man to his wife of love and appreciation as uncomplicated and unmistakable as that bright blue box.

My father's outburst snapped my mother to attention. I watched her face cloud in confusion as she scrambled, playing catch-up, trying to figure out what in the world had gotten into her husband. I made some comment scolding my father for ruining his nice surprise and promptly fled the room. His rages didn't scare me so much—the same way a child's temper tantrum wasn't scary—but I didn't like to hear my parents argue, especially when I'd heard similar versions of the same fight many times before. I knew that my mother would complain about getting stuck with all the work around the house, and that my father would say that taking care of the home was her job, just as making the money was his job, and she didn't hear him complaining about it all the time. And then my mother would point out all the things she had to do herself because there wasn't enough money, such as weed the gardens or make the curtains, and my father would say that no one had asked her to plant all those flower beds and redecorate all those rooms, and it would go back and forth like this for a while, until my father stormed out of the room, yelling, "You're going to nag me to death one day!" And then sometime later, my father would take my brother and me aside and tell us how we had to help out more around the house, and for the next few days, he would even go as far as clearing his own plate from the dinner table and placing it in the dishwasher himself.

I avoided my parents for the rest of the night and eventually went to bed. I'd been asleep for an hour or two when my mother came bursting in and shook my shoulder to wake me.

"What? What?" I said.

She was in her bathrobe, a hunched shadow in the doorway. Despite my grogginess and the dark, I could see that she was panicked. I started to sit up, my body getting ready to leap out of bed and run with the announcement of fire.

"Blissy," she said. "Where did you put the bologna?"

"What?"

"The bologna. Your father can't find his bologna."

Every night before my father went to bed, he ate a bologna and cheddar cheese sandwich on rye bread, washed down with a single beer. That afternoon I'd helped my mother put away the groceries.

"I don't know," I said, still confused. She'd woken me for bologna? "It's somewhere in the fridge."

"Where in the fridge, Blissy? Do you remember where?"

"I don't know." Now I was irritated. "In the meat drawer probably."

And then she was gone, running — from the sound of it — down the hallway to the back stairs.

I lay down again, but I couldn't fall back to sleep. After a half hour or so, I got up and went down to the kitchen. After rounding the stairwell, I found my mother kneeling on the floor in front of the open refrigerator door, sweeping pieces of broken glass and globs of mayonnaise and jelly into a dustpan. She was crying, and my father was nowhere in sight. Bottles of ketchup and jars of pickles and tomato sauce were scattered across the kitchen floor like bowling pins after someone has thrown a strike. I leaned past her and saw that every single one of the shelves from the fridge's door had been pulled off.

I remember thinking to myself, or perhaps even saying out loud, "Wow, Daddy did this?" The idea of his lashing out in anger this way was certainly frightening, but more than that, it surprised me and even impressed me a tiny bit. I'd never seen him totally lose control before.

"The bologna was right there in the drawer," my mother said. "Right in front of him. He just didn't look. He never looks."

"I'm sorry, Mom." It struck me as particularly unfair that she was stuck with cleaning up his mess on Mother's Day. "Do you want some help?"

"No, you don't have any shoes on. You'll cut your foot."

I stood in the doorway as my mother cried and cleaned and began to talk in a despairing way about not being able to put up with my father anymore. He was so unreasonable at times, and she was tired of his craziness. "He just went crazy!" she said, gesturing at pieces of the disassembled shelf on the floor.

This kind of talk—although I'd heard it before—struck me mute with fear. To my mind, my mother ridding my father from her life was as good as ridding him from my brother's and my lives too. As much as I believed that my father loved us—telling us so was his daily ritual, like a sort of unorthodox prayer—I couldn't picture how we'd fit into the world of Greenwich Village, bachelorhood, and books where my mother had found him. I knew that other family members had lost him to those pursuits before.

"What's his problem, anyway?" I managed finally. "I mean, it's Mother's Day, and he got you a nice present and everything. He just ruined the whole thing."

My mother looked up at me. Her face cleared for a moment, and I could see that she actually had an answer for the question of what my father's problem might be. "Well, his mother died," she said hesitantly. "And I think he feels guilty."

"Daddy's mother died?" I repeated. "Grandma died? When?"

"Back in September." Now my mother sounded apologetic.

That was eight months ago. "How come nobody told me?" I asked.

My mother shrugged. "You didn't really know her."

I couldn't help laughing. "As if that was my fault."

But my mother had said enough. "It's late," she said. "You should go to bed." I stood there for a minute, unsure what to think about this news. My mom sighed and sat back on her heels, planting her hands on her thighs. "Listen, honey, don't worry. Your father can be irrational sometimes, but he loves us. There's nothing to worry about. Go to bed, okay?"

I climbed back up the stairs to my room, feeling the hot stab of tears gathering at the corners of my eyes, but when I lay down in bed, clutching my pillow tightly to my chest, they refused to come. Grandma's dead, Grandma's dead, I whispered to myself, trying to help things along. Shouldn't I feel something?

I'd heard kids at my school, back in class after an absence, explaining how they'd been at a grandparent's funeral—their voices quivering as they tried not to cry. I'd nod along sympathetically with my other classmates, as if I too was grief-stricken at the thought of losing a grandparent. But in truth, I had no idea what that might feel like. My father's mother was my only living grandparent, and I'd met her only once that I could remember, shortly after my seventh birthday. The thought that I'd never know what that relationship was like sent a shot of self-pity sputtering through me.

Her death, however, didn't come as a complete surprise. My dad had mentioned in passing that he'd been to visit his mother in the nursing home where she lived, which prompted me to ask if I could join him the next time. He shook his head, saying that he doubted there would be a next time. His mother's mind was gone, and she no longer recognized him. "She didn't know her own son," my dad said again, as if he couldn't quite believe it. The visits were sad and very hard on him.

"But can't I go just one time?" I pressed. "I barely know her, and she's my only grandparent." I felt a sudden desperation that this representative figure in my life was slipping through my fingers, without my even realizing that she'd been so close at hand.

My father looked resolved and plaintive. "But you wouldn't be getting to know her, not the real her," he said. "She's nothing like she used to be. And I wouldn't want you to form your impressions about her now."

This made sense to me. But, I wanted to ask my father, why hadn't my brother and I gotten a chance to know her any earlier? How had it suddenly become too late? Something, though, made me drop my line of questioning. While my father could be very tender with Todd and me, and my mother too at times, it was rare to hear him talk about his own family in this way. It was as if I'd stumbled on a scene of two deer grooming each other in the woods, and I was afraid of moving or making any noise that might scatter them.

As I lay in bed that night on Mother's Day, trying to cry about the death of my grandmother Edna, what finally moved me to tears was this fresh evidence of the boundaries around my father's personal life. I hadn't even been invited to his mother's funeral! I wondered about the tenacity of our connection, of his love for me.

Our family wasn't bound by duty and obligation: children didn't attend their grandparents' funerals; aunts and uncles didn't visit their nieces and nephews. In our house, we didn't love each other because we were supposed to. Rather my father and I reknitted our ties every day—throwing a softball in the backyard after school, showing him what I'd learned in ballet class that afternoon, answering his nightly question when he carried me upstairs after I'd fallen asleep in front of the TV: *Who loves you, Blissy?* You do, Daddy....You do....You do.

I had almost drifted off to sleep, but a thought jerked me back awake, and kept me tossing and turning for much of the night. Hadn't my father once loved his parents and siblings too? What had they done to make his feelings change? Or was it what they hadn't done—read enough, accomplished enough, remained interesting?

The next morning, my brother and I were watching cartoons and eating cereal when I told him what I'd learned the night before.

"Yeah, Grandma's dead," Todd said, without lifting his eyes from the TV set. "That stinks."

"Wait a minute. How did you know?"

"I saw another box of ashes in the closet in Daddy's study." Now Todd glanced at me and a look of understanding passed between us. So he searched through our father's things too.

"Well, did you know that she died back in September? Eight months ago?" My voice was full of affront.

"I figured from the postmark on the box." Todd frowned. "And I remember that Dad seemed kind of down around then, which was weird, since usually he's pretty happy. And I figured that it must have been about his mom."

Our father had been sad? Normally he was happy? I was too close to my father—too caught up in the ebb and flow of his affections—to notice the changing weather of his moods. What else had I been missing? But I didn't ask. For the most part, Todd and I carried on our family's pact of secrecy. To have discussed the mysteries in our household would have entailed trying to solve them, which seemed like an impossible, or at least dangerous, task. As the saying goes, what you don't know can't hurt you.

And so for the next dozen years, these questions stayed in the closet along with the ashes of my grandparents. But after my father died, we had to start going through his things.

~3~

The village of Southport, where my family lived before moving to Cambridge, has been described as the jewel in the crown of the town of Fairfield, a town that is located in Fairfield County, the richest county in Connecticut, the richest state in the United States, the richest country in the world.

Southport is a historic village, which means that we couldn't alter or renovate our home without permission from the committee in charge of zoning. There are rules that dictate the style of your shutters, how high you may build your fence, the types of windows you may add to your family room. Unwritten rules dictate that your grass be clipped, your hedges shorn, and any dead limbs promptly cut down and carted away. As a result the village is breathtakingly beautiful in a uniform, wedding-cake-decoration kind of way.

At the edge of the village center, at the end of a narrow inlet, sits the Pequot Yacht Club. Twin brick buildings constitute the club — both tall, rectangular, and imposing. Ivy covers the front façade of the one that serves as clubhouse, and a large wooden porch extends from its back to overlook the harbor. On the first floor is a dining room where members can have burgers and club sandwiches for lunch year-round.

In 1987 Phil Donahue and Marlo Thomas tried to join the yacht club after buying a mansion on Long Island Sound a few miles down the road. After initially voting to admit them, the membership committee reversed its position and denied the Donahues' application. The reasons were unclear: that the family weren't serious sailors but wanted to dock a large motor yacht, or some objection to the subjects covered on Phil's talk show, or a general disdain for celebrities. My family had joined a year earlier, and my mother, who moored an eighteen-foot Cape Cod catboat there, had learned these details from some people on the membership committee with whom she'd become friendly.

My family's application was approved without incident. Anatole Broyard, the erudite, politically conservative literary critic for the *New York Times,* was their kind of guy. Of course nobody knew about his racial background. In 1986 the club had never had a black member. When I spoke to a former commodore in 2000, the club still had not, although one member offered my father, whose racial identity had since become public knowledge, as evidence of the club's history of integration. According to the former commodore, the Pequot Yacht Club had never denied a black person either—none had ever applied. Sailing, he observed, isn't typically a black sport. Another explanation might be the demographics of the town: 0.5 percent of the population, or twenty-four out of the town's five thousand people are African American, according to the 2000 census. I asked some residents and the local librarian if they knew who these two dozen black people were or where they lived, but nobody could think of any African American families in Southport. They did remember, however, seeing some black nannies pushing strollers down its cobblestone streets.

Back in 1986 it wasn't the yacht club's policies or politics that interested my mother, but sailing. She was not yet a serious sailor—her experience was mostly a few summers as a kid—and she was eager to learn. My father didn't like being on the water. He spent too much time cooped up on ships during World War II, he'd explain. But he enjoyed having lunch at the yacht club, and on the days that he worked from home, he would walk over there at noon, eat a hamburger, and chat with the retirees and the men whose family trusts were such that they had never had to work.

As my mother was casting about for a location for the reception following my father's memorial service, the yacht club had seemed like the perfect choice. My dad once wrote that "dying should be like a birthday party to end all birthday parties." We imagined that he would have approved of his final celebration's being held in a setting he'd found so beautiful.

My father particularly admired the view from the porch. From there you can see the harbor filled with freshly painted boats; the rolling green of the golf course across the inlet and the tall umber reeds along its edge that ripple in the wind like water; the high hill above the curving shoreline, banked by massive oaks and maples through which peek the tops of turrets, widow's walks, and chimneys of the mansions; the great blue-green swath of the Sound; and in the distance, the smudged brown line that is Long Island, and the horizon, and the sky.

This view has always made me think of the scene in *The Great Gatsby* when Jay Gatsby stands in front of his mansion and stares at the green light of Daisy Buchanan's dock across the bay. My father greatly admired Fitzgerald's novel about American self-invention. It's tempting to think of my dad standing on the porch while reflecting to himself how far he, like Gatsby, had traveled in his life — from a young colored boy in New Orleans to this! But I can't actually imagine him indulging in that kind of sentimental, self-congratulatory moment. It never seemed to occur to him that someone might want to keep him out. And I don't think he would view his version of the American dream as being as hollow and ultimately tragic as Gatsby's.

Anyway, I wasn't ready yet in the weeks after his death to consider what it meant to my father to live in this town and belong to this club, or, more significantly, why he rejected his black ancestry in the first place. There was still too much information to absorb, and his family to meet.

The service itself was held in a Congregational church up the street. In the church's back hallway, I saw my father's older sister, my aunt Lorraine, for the first time in seventeen years, and finally met his younger sister, my aunt Shirley, and her son, my cousin Frank Jr.

I noticed first how tall Frank was—he didn't look like a Broyard to me; from my limited contact with them (my father and my brother), the men were of medium height and wiry—and then I noticed how, unlike Lorraine and my father's mother, he and Shirley actually looked black, despite being light-skinned.

I knew who they were before my mother introduced us. Out of the more than three hundred people who showed up that day, they were the only black people there, except for one colleague from my father's office.

And Lorraine felt familiar, like family even. She looked like my father's sister; I recognized the shape of her face, her full cheeks and round jaw, from some pictures in our family album of a trip to Europe she took with my parents before I was born. When I was growing up, she used to call the house occasionally. I would answer the phone, and after she identified herself, I'd say, "Oh hi, Aunt Lorraine," and then yell up the stairs for my father. "Dad, phone for you. It's Aunt Lorraine." Sometimes she even chatted with me briefly, asking about school or what sports I liked. As we said hello again, even though I was twenty-four and she was seventy-two and we didn't know anything about each other, those words, "Aunt Lorraine," didn't feel funny in my mouth.

After I graduated from college, I moved to New York and had my first apartment with my own phone number. I looked up my name in the huge Manhattan phone book, "Bliss Broyard," and saw right below me "Lorraine Broyard." We were the only Broyards listed. I put my finger on her listing and thought to myself, *That's my aunt, I could call her up right now.* But I never did.

I knew growing up that my father didn't speak to his other sister, Shirley. Over the years I would become curious about her and her family. They lived in Manhattan, too, on the Upper West Side. Whenever I asked my father about why we didn't see them, he would say that he wasn't interested in politics and that Shirley was married to a politician. In fact her husband, Franklin Williams, who died a few months before my father did, was a civil rights lawyer who worked under Thurgood Marshall in the NAACP in the 1940s. He started the Constitutional Rights Division in California in the early sixties and had served as the U.S. ambassador to Ghana in the seventies. The speakers at his funeral included New York City mayor David Dinkins and the South African independence leader Bishop Desmond Tutu.

While it's true that my father wasn't political — as far as I know, he never once voted in an election — it might be more accurate to say that it was Frank Williams's particular politics that didn't interest him. When I pushed my father further, he offered another excuse: one of Shirley's two sons suffered from schizophrenia, a condition that made it sad for the family to be around other families.

Frank and Shirley were the secret brought to life. There weren't any tears or long embraces. We all shook hands, and they offered their condolences. I can remember thinking, *This is my father's family and they are black,* as I sought to confirm with my own eyes what before I had taken on faith. *It's really true!* I thought.

Then we hurried into the sanctuary, because the service was scheduled to start. My mother motioned for my father's family to join us in the front row. There was plenty of room, given that his survivors numbered only six: my mother, my brother, me, his two sisters, and a nephew.

Years later, at a dinner party with some old friends, I told the story about meeting my relatives. A man at the party who had been at the memorial service commented that he'd thought to himself, when he saw these three light-skinned black people sit down in the family row, that he hadn't realized the Broyards had so much help.

One by one my father's friends took their place at the pulpit and briefly brought him back to life. The man who emerged took many forms: an eloquent literary critic and ironic observer of life, a purveyor of high culture and dispenser of common sense, an unsurpassed enthusiast of literature and a writer whose "intolerable perfectionism" kept him from finishing a long-awaited novel, an eager playmate and graceful athlete, a doting father and attentive friend, someone who worried that the world wouldn't live up to the beauty and substance described by his favorite writers and so was forever searching out and celebrating those moments when people and life didn't disappoint him.

Michael Vincent Miller described three decades of strolls through Greenwich Village, Paris, Rome, Florence, over Connecticut country roads, and down imagined literary landscapes as my father lay dying. Another friend, the playwright David Epstein, recounted the start of their nearly forty-year friendship on a beach in Fire Island, when David was a chubby eight-year-old and my dad was a popular bachelor in his early thirties. The anthropologist Richard Shweder remembered my father's emphasis on style—how a person walked, the precision of his language, the flourish with which he caught the football—as "the best defense against the materialism of a dreary world." Everyone commented on his youthfulness, the immediacy of his presence, and his unapologetic, idiosyncratic take on the world. He didn't seem like someone who had regrets about how he'd lived his life.

When it was my turn at the pulpit, my gaze kept returning to my father's family. I'd lost my dad and found them. They were the consolation prize that I hadn't been expecting. I had the urge to address them, to ask them to rise before the congregation as if they were some kind of miracle that had been conjured up out of our collective grief. Anatole lives on, their presence said to me. His semblance, his flesh, blood, and DNA, his history exists beyond my brother and myself. There was more to him that I could still discover. Perhaps they could start by explaining why my father had kept us apart.

It's hard to imagine what was going through their minds as they listened to my father's friends and family talk about this man who had become lost to them years before he died. It must have been sad, and maddening, for my father's sisters and nephew to learn at his funeral about what he meant to the people in his life. Were they thinking, That's only half the story? Did they wonder why he'd chosen South-port, that jewel in the crown of Fairfield, where in the 1980s a black family would have stood out as baldly as a purple house? Shirley's husband, Frank, served as the NAACP's regional director for the western part of the country in the 1950s and worked intensely to integrate residential neighborhoods; their lives were spent fighting against communities like ours.

After the service was over, everyone poured outside onto the church's lawn. It was a mild, beautiful day at the end of October, and the early afternoon light was sparkling and clear. I stood with my aunts and cousin. People were swarming all around us, and I stopped everyone who passed by to introduce them. "This is my aunt Shirley and my aunt Lorraine and my cousin Frank." My enthusiasm, it seemed, was a little bewildering; Shirley looked overwhelmed.

The uncanny exhilaration that can follow funerals buzzed in the air. Anatole might be dead, but we were not, and after hearing the vivid recounting of his life, we were determined to be as alive as we could. Then I was surrounded by friends. We started down the stone steps to the street, heading toward the yacht club. A little boy in a blue blazer ran past, yelling for his mother. I looked around, panicked because I'd lost track of my father's family, but they'd assured me that they were going to the reception, so I expected to catch up with them there.

I pulled aside my friend Jennifer from Martha's Vineyard, whom I'd known since I was eight. Our parents were also close friends.

"I found out what the secret was," I said. I had already told her about that day on the Vineyard. "That was my dad's sisters and his nephew back there. He was really black, but he didn't want Todd and me to know."

"Well, *I* knew he was black."

"What?" I stopped walking. "How?"

"I don't remember. I just did. I've known forever."

Perhaps my mother, who had known about my dad's ancestry since before she got married, had told Jennifer's parents. In the hospital I discovered that many of her and my father's friends knew about his heritage, but that was different: I was accustomed to adults having access to information that I didn't.

She shrugged her shoulders. "I always thought that you just didn't want to talk about it."

"No. I had no idea."

"It wasn't like it was a big deal," she assured me. "I hardly ever thought about it."

I was upset, because I felt that who I was had been misunderstood. I was not a girl who knew her father was black but didn't want to talk about it. Had my friend been treating me like I was that girl? Was there any time when some racist joke was made that she shot me a glance, looking for my reaction, and saw none, or worse, laughter?

I felt slow-witted and exposed.

"It's just weird that you knew something like that about me when I didn't know it myself," I said.

"But it didn't make any difference. I didn't even think of you as black," she said.

"Well, why not? If you knew my father was black?"

"I don't know. I guess I didn't think of him as being black either."

But he was. Or at least his two sisters and his nephew were. And if my father was black, what did that make me?

I don't remember seeing my aunts and my cousin at the yacht club. I never saw anything beyond the circle of sympathetic faces waiting for their turn to offer me their condolences.

Over and over: "Thank you for coming." "Yes, he would have liked the service." "I can't believe it either."

At the end my family and some close friends were slumped in the chairs on the front porch, exhausted. The talk turned to the events of the day: who came, who didn't, what conversations people had, how everyone looked, how the service went, what my father would have thought.

The only scandal anyone heard mention of throughout the afternoon was not the presence of Anatole's secret black family, but the fact that Martha Stewart, who lived in the next town over and had known my parents for years, had shown up wearing jeans and a suede fringed jacket.

-4-

I had hoped to meet up with my father's family at the reception following his memorial service, because I still had so many unanswered questions. Why would my father keep his racial identity a secret in the first place? How black was he? How black was I? A quarter? An eighth? Were we descended from slaves? But even the thought of raising these subjects could make my heart beat faster. I worried that I was going to say something to my father's family that would be considered ignorant or racist, and we would become estranged all over again.

The problem was, I'd never had a conversation about race. In the world I was raised in, it was considered an impolite subject. The people I knew lowered their voices when referring to a black person. I didn't know anything about African American history, nor had I ever known anyone black well enough to call them a friend. I don't remember issues such as affirmative action or busing, which dominated racial politics in the 1970s and 1980s, ever coming up for discussion in my house. Although I grew up within an hour's drive of three of the poorest black communities in the United States—Bridgeport, New Haven, and Hartford—those neighborhoods seemed as distant as a foreign country. I'd make jokes with my brother about getting lost in "Father Panic Village," infamous as the worst section of neighboring Bridgeport, but I never gave any thought to the people who lived there. I couldn't have imagined their lives even if I had tried.

Yet conspicuous among my childhood memories were encounters with African Americans, which stood out perhaps because they were so rare and because the pervasiveness of racism — in my sheltered life and in me — had lent them a special charge. I grew up believing, without exactly realizing I believed it or knowing where this belief had come from, that blacks were different from whites, probably inferior, and possibly had even brought on some of their own ill treatment. If you asked me if I thought this way, I would have objected vigorously. As a well-off white kid with artsy parents growing up in the 1970s and 1980s just outside New York City, I gave lip service to principles like justice and equal rights and considered myself immune to racial prejudice. Nevertheless, when I encountered African Americans, the racist belief arose, like a word on the tip of my tongue, at once concentrating my mind and distracting me with its relentless agitation.

The first black person that I remember meeting was Leroy — yes, that really was his name — the head of a cleaning crew that visited our house once every few weeks when I was about seven years old. He was a small, energetic, medium-brown man with a surprisingly deep voice for his size and an aura of intense masculinity that belied my notion that cleaning was woman's work. He performed the job double-time, with lots of sweat and heavy lifting.

I liked it when Leroy and his crew of black men were at our house, the whirlwind way they would turn everything upside down — moving furniture and rolling up rugs to wax the floors — and then set it right again, a faint lemon scent lingering in their wake. I liked the way our house would become alive with the noise of their vacuum cleaner and floor buffer and conversation that to my ears was more waves of sound than words — notes that dipped and sprang, repeating and overlapping, interrupted by round soft laughter and high-pitched exclamations.

My father would talk to Leroy in a familiar way, saying *Hey man!* and *What's happening?*, which made it seem as if they knew each other from somewhere. I was impressed that my dad seemed to know how to talk to our cleaning man in what I construed to be Leroy's particular way of speaking. I imagined that he'd learned to do this when he lived in Manhattan, a loud, fast place where my mother occasionally took my brother and me.

Manhattan lay at the end of a long car ride that led us over iron bridges and elevated highways from which, with my nose pressed against the window, I peered down onto vacant lots strewn with rusted appliances and old mattresses, apartment buildings with sheets tacked over their windows and the occasional Jesus on the Cross dangling against a pane, and scruffily dressed children, black and Puerto Rican kids, whose parents let them play in the street; after which we barreled down a stretch of tunneled roadway and then popped up into the city, our arrival punctuated with my mother's instruction to lock our doors.

After parking the car, we took public transportation to get around. On the subways and buses, over my mother's arm that pulled me tight against her, I stared at the other riders, many of whom, with their strange clothes and thick accents, their dark skin, the unusual caps and hairstyles they wore, I took to be visitors from other countries.

Both my parents had lived in the city, but while my mother gave off the impression that she'd lived beside these foreign inhabitants, my father seemed to have lived among them and, as a result, had learned their ways and means.

Leroy and his crew stopped cleaning our house after one of his men broke a decorative plate and hid the remains rather than confessing the accident. When I asked why he didn't come anymore, my father, sounding regretful, explained that this dishonesty had left no choice but to fire him.

When I remember this conversation now, I can picture my seven-year-old self nodding to indicate that I understood what my father was saying, and with that nod, plucking from the atmosphere the vague notion that black people lived by a different — lesser — code of behavior and embedding it more firmly in my brain. At the same time, I can imagine my child self feeling sorry for Leroy and his men, because I would view this moral shortcoming as an affliction rather than a choice, rather like a character in a fairy tale who's been turned— through no fault of his own—into a frog.

A few years ago, my mother ran into Leroy at the home of the woman who had originally recommended him. My mother reintroduced herself, explaining that Leroy's crew had cleaned her house some twenty years earlier. I remember you, he told her. And then my mom asked something that she had always wondered: Had Leroy known about her husband's background?

"Sure. I knew," he said.

I asked my mother to describe his response. Had he seemed tickled, resentful, enraged, admiring, about the fact that the guy in the big house on the hill in the Waspiest part of Fairfield with the white wife and the white kids was really a brother? But her memory refused to supply any inflection. "They used to do this thing together." She waved her hands back and forth, like she was describing dance moves or a boxing match. What she meant was, they used to be black together. I knew that behavior of my father's. I'd seen it at the bar on Martha's Vineyard where we'd go listen to a funk band. I knew it from parties at home when my dad told a story about his army days as the (white) captain of a black unit or about the time he took his Greenwich Village buddies up to Spanish Harlem to hear Afro-Cuban music. He grew animated, his voice stretched and preened, his body was looser and lighter on his feet. But it never occurred to me to think of this behavior as "black"; it was just my dad telling stories about his life.

The first black person that I remember touching and being touched by was Uncle Pete. He drove the afternoon school bus when I was in the sixth grade. All of the kids loved him, in no small part because he seemed to love all of us so much, starting with his insistence that we call him Uncle. Pete made an immense effort to keep us entertained, filling the forty-five-minute route with more frivolity and celebration than the best birthday party. As Christmas approached he strung the cards that we gave him the length of the bus and draped the windows with garland and Christmas balls, and then one afternoon he showed up wearing a red felt cap with a black pompom hanging from some tassel and a fake white beard and mustache.

This was around the time of the TV series *Roots*, and Pete began referring to himself as Kunta Claus, encouraging us to do the same. He was in his midtwenties, with a plump-cheeked, boyish face, dark brown skin, and a short Afro. It was the first time I had heard some-one call attention to his own racial identity—I was used to other people pointing out this fact—and to joke about himself in this way struck me at first as embarrassing and then hilarious.

I was the last kid that Uncle Pete dropped off. When we were alone, he would invite me to sit on the seat next to him. He would tell me to put my hand on the wheel, and then, on the straightaways, he would take his own hand away so that I was the only one steering. Barreling down those country roads, feeling the great length of the bus swaying heavily behind me in response to the slightest movement of my hand on the oversized wheel, I was more exhilarated and scared than I had ever been. If Pete spotted an approaching car, he would re-claim the wheel and tell me to duck out of sight. I would lean forward with his hand resting on my back until he tapped my shoulder, signal-ing that the coast was clear.

I remember my surprise at the roominess of the bus driver's seat—almost as wide as the bench seats we students filled two by two behind him—but not so roomy that as I settled my narrow eleven-year-old frame next to him our legs didn't touch. I was acutely con-scious of the left side of my body where I rested against him—the pressure and warmth. I felt that we were doing something that we shouldn't, a feeling that was connected in my mind with our close proximity, and the fact that he was black and male and older than me but not so old that, despite his nickname, he actually seemed avuncular.

Sometimes I resisted the invitation to join him on his seat. I wasn't specifically worried that our game was a prelude to his touching me in an inappropriate way, and even now in these more puritanical times, I'm not sure that's where he was headed. But I was afraid of getting into trouble, and I thought it was reckless to even pretend that I was driving the bus.

I was nervous, too, because I wondered if the difference between us, his blackness and my whiteness, rendered him unknowable to me on an essential level, and out of politeness or ignorance, I might over-look any hidden motives on his part. I was not unaware that black people could resent white people. The guy on Leroy's cleaning crew might have broken the plate on purpose. Maybe Pete wanted to hurt me. These worries didn't present themselves in such concrete terms, but as a vague fear, as if I were trying to navigate across a room in the dark.

"That's okay," I would say. "I don't really feel like driving today."

"Then come sit next to me to keep me company."

"That's okay," I would say again as cordially as I could, because I also didn't want to hurt his feelings, since I knew that black people had had their feelings hurt plenty already.

After we came back from Christmas break, we learned that Uncle Pete had been fired. The teachers at my school were concerned about how to explain his dismissal to a white girl named Kathy who had been especially close to him. I knew, in the way that children know things about what people are capable of, that he had done something wrong to someone—something not terribly wrong, probably nothing worse than inviting someone to share his seat—but the someone, likely a girl, had told her parents. This was 1977 in Fairfield, Con-necticut, on a bus route that serviced Greenfield Hill, which next to

Southport was the most exclusive area in town. The fact that Pete was black mattered.

For high school I attended Greens Farms Academy, a local prep school housed in a converted estate overlooking Long Island Sound. Some descendants of the Vanderbilt family had built the Tudor-style stone mansion in the early twentieth century. The property featured formal gardens, ivy-covered stone gates, an apple orchard, and a great lawn. It was said that the train station a quarter of a mile up the road had been added specifically for the Vanderbilts' convenience. The station was now used by students from neighboring towns whose families could afford the $6,000 tuition. (As of 2006, it has topped $26,000 a year.) In the mornings girls in plaid skirts and knee socks and boys in navy blue blazers could be seen trudging up the long driveway, beside the mothers driving car pool in their Volvo station wagons or Mercedes sedans and the harried-looking teachers — many of whom had long commutes since they couldn't afford to live nearby — vying for a parking spot for their secondhand Subarus.

During my first year at Greens Farms, I joined the drama club, where I met a girl named Dawn in the grade above me who was black. So far in my schooling, I'd never gotten to know a black schoolmate; there had been one African American student apiece in my elementary and junior high schools, both boys and in different classes from me. I was curious about Dawn, in part because she was black, but also because of her spunky nature and a poise that made her stand out among her fellow tenth graders.

One day when we were talking, I asked her if she liked it at Greens Farms. She looked at me for a long moment, perhaps trying to decide how interested I really was in her experience at the school. Finally she said, "Well, you know, there aren't many chips in this cookie." I nodded solemnly. "But it's all right, I guess." And that was it, the closest I ever came to having a conversation about race. Race, however, did sometimes come up in conversation. One day during my junior year, my friends and I were exchanging jokes over lunch, while another of the black students, I'll call him Bob, sat unnoticed at the far end of the table.

Here are two that I remember telling:

What do you call a black kid with a bicycle?

A thief.

If a black person, a spic, and a Chink fell out of an airplane, who would hit the ground first?

Who cares?

I remember the giddiness that came with daring to be offensive and my laughter—nervy and full of theatrical mortification. (I don't remember using the word "nigger," although the symmetry of the second joke calls for it. For a long time, I maintained that I had never used that word, and then one night someone took a sip from my beer bottle and handed it back with the rim all wet, and the term "nigger-lip" sprang to my mind, and I recalled my days of teenage smoking and realized that, in fact, I had used it, often.)

Whispers traveled down the table to my end, saying that Bob had gotten up and left the lunchroom. *Oh shit. Bob heard us. I didn't see him. Why didn't someone say he was there?* He was well liked: smart, handsome, fun, a good athlete, and a nice guy. Nobody wanted to intentionally hurt his feelings. I vaguely recall a friend named Chris, who at age seventeen had a more developed sense of decency than the rest of us, going after him.

After an embarrassed silence, more whispers: *It's cool. Bob's cool. He knows that we didn't mean anything by it.* The implication was that Bob would understand that we knew he was different from the butts of our racist jokes. He was one of us, at private school, with wealthy parents and a nice house. He was cut from the same cloth, just a darker color. We trusted that Bob would realize that these jokes were the continuation of a groove that started with amputees and blondes and ratcheted up in offensiveness from there, and that we didn't mean him. We weren't thinking about him.

I wanted to apologize many times, but I never did. I couldn't face Bob, or rather, I couldn't face what he must have thought of me. That was my only real concern — how I now looked in his eyes.

Fifteen years later, as part of an effort to attract more "students of color" to the school, a friend who currently teaches at Greens Farms spoke to some of the handful of minority alumni about what it had been like for them. Bob didn't particularly want to talk about it, but he told my friend that he'd had a difficult time.

The subject of race started coming up at home too toward the end of my father's life. African American culture had always been a part of our household: it was the music that we listened to, the athletes and entertainers that we admired on TV, but I don't remember my parents ever discussing race, or making overtly racist comments for that matter. Neither did they instill in Todd and me a belief that all people were created equal. Whatever I came to believe about the difference between blacks and whites grew up in that void, fed by the racism in the world at large.

After my father got sick, he became more outspoken. One night over dinner, he praised David Dinkins, the mayor of New York at the time, the first (and to date only) African American to hold the job. My dad approved of the fact that Dinkins, in his opinion, didn't make excuses for black people. "Finally, someone who doesn't just want to give them handouts and encourage their laziness and dependence," he said.

Armed with my youthful well-meaningness, I suggested to my father that what he called laziness was really a lack of opportunity, and any dependence could be blamed on the legacy of slavery. My response was mostly of the knee-jerk liberal variety, as I'd never given these issues a lot of thought. But my dad wasn't particularly interested in arguing with me.

"Dinkins can say it," he continued, "because he's black, and people will have to listen."

About six months later, shortly before my father died, he made a more pointed outburst. He had got it into his head that he and my mother needed to sell their "perfect doll's house" and move to a better neighborhood. The house itself was elegant enough: a Victorian with four fireplaces and a front and back stair (which, according to my mother, used to be the definition of a mansion), but the block had an apartment building for low-income housing on one end, and some of our neighbors looked too down-at-the-heels for my father's taste. He would regularly walk up and down the block, dragging a trash barrel behind him and picking up any garbage from the street. (He had done this in Connecticut too.) My dad believed, superstitiously, that a tonier address might protect him from getting any sicker. At least he would be less depressed, and as he regularly said, depression was bad medicine.

One morning when some prospective buyers were due to make a second visit, my dad returned from one of his street cleaning missions, tight-lipped and angry. He sat down at the dining room table, where I was having my breakfast.

"What's wrong?" I asked him.

"What's wrong?" he repeated. "There's some black kids playing outside down the street. That's what's wrong. These people aren't going to want to buy this house when they see that!"

Shocked, I answered with an outburst of my own. "Jesus Christ, Dad," I said. "You sound like a goddamned racist." Part of what surprised me was that my father loved children indiscriminately: fat, thin, funny, serious, and in all colors, or so I thought. I couldn't believe that he would speak so harshly against them.

I can still remember his expression as he sat across from me, his hands laid flat against the tabletop as if he were about to dart up and run away. He looked angry, hurt, confused, defenseless. Mostly I viewed his behavior through the lens of his cancer. I knew he felt trapped by it, and by extension, the narrowing circumstances of his life.

I was also suddenly, painfully, aware of his age—almost seventy by this time—and his obsolete attitudes that were shaped during a distant era. He was forty-three, after all, when Dr. King made his famous "I Have a Dream" speech in the March on Washington in the summer of 1963.

In the years to come, I would revisit the expression on my father's face in light of what I had learned about his racial identity. I would wonder anew about the circumstances that my father felt trapped by; whether he worried that he'd ended up back in the sort of place that he'd spent so many years trying to escape.

-5-

When I was about twelve years old, I received a letter inviting me to apply to the Daughters of the American Revolution, the organization for female descendants of the colonial settlers. At that age, it was rare for me to receive a piece of mail, and I was thrilled to open the letter and read *Dear Bliss Broyard, You may be eligible for membership...* My mother, who seemed amused by the letter, said that since I wasn't actually descended from any colonial settlers (my ancestors came later, from Norway and France, or so I was told), I needn't bother replying. In retrospect I realize that the offering was probably from a genealogy company trying to entice customers with the suggestion of illustrious backgrounds, but I interpreted it as recognition that I came from good stock, someone who could be mistaken for a member of an old prominent family. In other words, a Wasp. I liked the idea that an anonymous person out there might be keeping track of who was who and that I hadn't escaped his or her notice.

When I described our family as Wasps in front of my mother, she corrected me, saying, "Your father's Catholic." (Of course, she didn't mention the other reason he couldn't be a Wasp.)

"He's lapsed," I said. "Anyway, we're not Catholic." Todd and I had no religion, having never been baptized.

"Doesn't matter," my mother said.

"But you're a Wasp."

"I'm Presbyterian and Norwegian. That's different."

"Close enough," I said.

I wasn't concerned with exact definitions — I could never even remember if the *W* of the acronym stood for white or wealthy.

Besides, my mother and my brother certainly looked Waspy: blond
with strong jaws, high foreheads, and lips that disappeared when they
smiled. (I have the same angular, thin-lipped features with my father's
darker coloring.) And my mother's family had money — her maternal
grandparents owned lumber mills in Minnesota — but an uncle secretly transferred the bulk of it into his name, robbing her of her inheritance. Even this story, with the ne'er-do-well relative, seemed
classically Wasp to me.

If my family didn't fit the bill genetically, we did by association. To
my mind, where we lived, how we lived, and who we lived next to
made us Wasps, which I un-
derstood to be a combina-
tion of habits, wealth, and
taste rather than a matter of
birthright, unless a person
was Jewish, a practicing Catholic, or African American, in
which case they couldn't be a
Wasp nor a member of cer-
tain local country clubs.

In the sixth grade, I received my first pair of white gloves, to wear to
Miss Sadler's ballroom dancing class, held once a week in the community room of the Pequot Library in Southport. We learned to waltz,
fox trot, and cha-cha, steps that would be forgotten and have to be
relearned five years later for the holiday cotillions and coming-out
parties that populated our junior and senior years.

In the winter my schoolmates skied at Killington, Aspen, and the Bugaboos in Canada, which were accessed by helicopter; a class trip headed to the French Alps over Christmas break. In the summer my friends rode horses, played tennis, and learned to sail on Block Island, Cape Cod, or at one of the country clubs at home. My family spent July and August on Martha's Vineyard, taking with us our two black Labrador retrievers (Smudge and Pepper), a friend each for Todd and me, and a babysitter, whom we referred to as the au pair.

Largely true to the Connecticut stereotype, the local mothers dressed sensibly in slacks and knee-length skirts, pumps by Pappagallo and tennis shoes. They cleaned their own houses, tended their own gardens, ran the dogs, darned the socks, cooked their husbands gourmet meals. They had their hair styled every six weeks. They kept their nails short and their lipstick bright. Their manner was cheery and charming or steely and polite. In their free time, they donated their considerable skills to beautifying the local private schools or raising money for the arts.

The fathers worked in Manhattan in law or investment firms, banks and insurance companies. They ran IBM and Stanley Tools. They took the 7:10 train in every morning and the 5:47 train home every night. They read the *Wall Street Journal*, the *New York Times*, and biographies of historical figures. They talked about the stock market, and they didn't talk about money.

Some of them drank too much or pushed around their kids or had affairs. Some of their wives were cold or crazy or desperately sad. Occasionally a couple got divorced; more often they stayed together, for the sake of the children. These families weren't exempt from tragedy: a classmate's sister was killed in a car accident one year, and the following year two other classmates tried to kill themselves; one of them succeeded.

But there were many people who seemed happy, in their beautiful homes set on big tracts of land, among the family heirlooms, prized peonies, and boxwood hedges, with their attractive, athletic children, their purebred dogs, and German cars. Many of them couldn't imagine a better or different life. Polo matches and pool parties, fox hunts and antique fairs—this was the way it had always been, the way it would always be.

I can't remember when or why I first began to question how well my family fit into this world. Maybe it was the way we kept moving all the time. (My mother would tell people, in a sort of self-deprecating brag, that we'd moved six times in less than twenty years without ever changing our phone number.) Or how unmoored we were to the community. My parents kept mostly to themselves, importing their friends on the weekends from New York City, or disappearing up to Martha's Vineyard for months at a time. What Connecticut people they did socialize with tended to be other writers or the (mostly) single women and gay men that my mom knew from her previous career as a modern dancer.

But the main difference between us and our neighbors was that everyone else seemed to have a lot more money. By working at the *Times* and writing various freelance articles, my father was able to cover the mortgage and most of the crucial bills, but his annual salary never made it to six figures and wasn't nearly enough to afford our family's lifestyle.

One night over dinner, my brother asked my dad if our family was middle class or upper middle class, a distinction that nobody makes anymore. Our family's situation was confusing because, on the one hand, the succession of elegant houses in Connecticut, the vacation home on Martha's Vineyard, and my dad's pied-à-terre in New York made it seem as though we belonged in the upper reaches; but then, on the other hand, we rented out our home in Fairfield while we moved to the Vineyard for the summer, my mother cut coupons, we shopped mostly off the sale racks or at outlet stores, and, as a rule, we never ate out at restaurants.

And my parents worried about money constantly. Sometimes on the desk in my father's study, I would spy pages from a yellow legal pad filled with columns of numbers, labeled "mortgage," "taxes," "electric," "tuition," added up over and over as if they could be made to total a different sum. My parents had managed—through luck and good timing—to continually trade up in real estate as they bought and sold their various homes, but they ended up house-poor in the process. One year there was talk of a lien being placed on our home, which filled the air with such tension that I began to imagine a physical force actually leaning against our walls and nearly toppling them.

Every fall my parents scrambled to come up with my brother's and my school tuition. At the start of my junior year at Greens Farms, my mother met with my headmaster to inquire if, given that I'd ranked among the top students in my class the previous year, I might qualify for a scholarship. The headmaster explained that financial aid was reserved for those with financial need. Was he mistaken or didn't we own two homes and three cars? That's right, my mother told him, and that's why we don't have any cash for the tuition.

The disparity between how my family lived and how much money we had was a constant source of unease and uncertainty. I was never sure if my parents were exaggerating our money problems or if we were simply living beyond our means. The moments they chose to splurge or the reason behind a sudden switch from feast to famine always felt arbitrary and slightly unfair. Nevertheless, I did my own share of keeping up appearances. Over one spring break, as my classmates headed off to various islands and mountain ranges, I lay in our backyard in my bikini. For nine days straight, I shivered in the cool mid-April air so that when school resumed, I'd fit in among the newly bronzed student body.

Of course not everyone I knew was rich. (My perspective didn't extend enough beyond our zip code to consider that our family was far richer than most everyone else in the country and the world.) There were kids at Greens Farms who were raised by a single working parent, and others whose families made great sacrifices to afford the steep tuition. But they didn't seem like they were trying to pretend they were rich people, as we were.

When you have class, you don't need money, my mother would say in response to the question of our family's standing. By class she meant good taste—which she had in abundance, as evidenced by the people who flocked to our home during the annual house tour to benefit the Young Women's League—and polished manners, which my parents tried to instill in Todd and me, mostly during dinner (served always in the dining room), making it near impossible to complete a story without some interruption. *Raise the food to your mouth, don't lower your face to your plate like a beggar. Don't stab at your meat like that; it's already dead. "May you," not "can you" have some more.*

How can we be upper class? I'm just a newspaperman, was my father's ironic reply, which summed up the truth of my family's place in society. My dad may not have earned as much as our neighbors, but his job as a widely read critic made up for it in clout. And cachet was almost as good as cash when it came to buying certain things: like admission to the Pequot Yacht Club or my acceptance to my prep school, although I'd applied after the deadline. A series of phone calls to the right people, along with a signed copy of one of my father's books, usually did the trick.

My parents' bohemian, artistic edge also made them "cool." People, even my friends, wanted to be around them. When I was young, they threw dance parties instead of cocktail parties. They would roll up the rug in the living room and play Patti LaBelle's "Lady Marmalade" on the record player, the Isley Brothers' "It's Your Thing," and anything by James Brown. When I was sixteen, they started taking my brother and me along when they went out dancing at the Seaview Lounge on Martha's Vineyard. Todd, who had just turned eighteen, could get in legally, since those were the days before the drinking age was raised, but I had to be sneaked past the bouncer by my father, who'd pretend to be my date. "She's with me," he'd say, jerking his head in my direction, and I would saunter by in my best cool-girl impersonation.

The house band, Kitch 'n Sync, played covers from War, the Commodores, and Santana. My mother, with her Martha Graham dance training, favored abstract gestures and contractions. My dad, who grew up on jazz and Afro-Cuban music, asserted his rhythmic sophistication by dancing off the beat, either double time or half. With one leg in front of the other, he'd switch his weight forward and back and twitch his hips in a funked-up salsa. He'd tweak his pant leg, kick his foot out Michael Jackson–style, and spin around, caressing an invisible partner. Nearby, my parents' friends stomped, shuffled, and swung to the music. One of the women might venture over to my father, where she'd try to match his prowess, spicing up her steps with some sexy moves.

The tempo would increase, and someone would start spinning. Arms flailed, heads snapped, and long hair waved back and forth overhead. One friend, Morgan, would drop to the floor, lie on his back, and wiggle his arms and legs in the air—he called this "doing the lobster"—which was the signal for the band and the dancers to kick it up a notch, and for the owner, Loretta (who was said to have been a cigarette girl at New York's Savoy Hotel in the 1950s), to bang a baseball bat on the wooden bar and yell, "Turn it down!" But the band would loudly jam on to the finish, sweating, hunched over their instruments, to the last harmonized chords, strummed again, and once more, and once more. Then everyone poured onto a side porch and pressed cold beers to necks and foreheads, sipped ice waters and fanned themselves, or stepped away a few paces to smoke a quick joint before the last set.

I would take my own turn across from my dad, trying to mimic his complicated rhythms, abandoning myself to the funk in the sea of familiar faces, welcoming the break from the constant self-consciousness of being sixteen. When I caught the rhythm, when it was moving through me so that my steps came without thought or effort, my father would smile and nod. And when I added an extra bit of shine, he would clap and call out, "Do it, Bliss," making me dance harder, and when I finished, with a dip, a stomp, or a pose right on cue with the end of the song, he'd yell, "*¡Fenómeno!*" like the dancers did at the nightclubs in Spanish Harlem he used to frequent.

On those nights I felt distinctly like a Broyard in a way that expanded the identification beyond my happening to carry this particular last name. The Broyards were graceful, cool, and confident on the dance floor; sensual, witty, social, earthy, and fun; a center of attention while at the same time remaining one step removed. Mostly it was my father who was all of these things, but nevertheless on that wooden floor I formed a sense of our collective identity—complete with my mother's abstractions and my brother's reluctance to be out rock dancing with his parents and their friends. At the end of the night, the four of us rode home in the car, the island dark and shadowy with twisted scrub oaks and low pine trees on either side, the high beams cutting a misty path in the fog before us, my mother driving, tapping her thumbs on the wheel to a melody still echoing in her head, my father quiet except for a comment about the band being really on tonight, didn't we think so?, and Todd and me in the backseat, leaning into our separate corners but not yet fully retreated into our secret teenage worlds, the spell of our coming together lasting until we reached the house, the barking dogs, the question of who would walk them, and our respective beds.

On nights like these, I reveled in the ways that my parents were different. None of my friends back in Connecticut went out dancing with their folks. By the end of high school, I came to think of my family as our own special breed of Wasp—elegant but eclectic, cultured and cultural, upstanding and up with the times. We were well-bred bohemians, an identity, once I thought about it, that suited me just fine.

Therefore it didn't matter that I wasn't invited senior year by the local cotillion committee to be a debutante along with some of the girls from my crowd. My mother claimed that she and my father could fix it for me to be included if that's what I wanted, but then she told me about the time she was hired to teach the debutantes to waltz, and how at the balls, they spent the entire evening in the bathroom where they smoked cigarettes and complained about the snugness of their dresses. Neither did it hurt me that I also wasn't invited to some of the holiday balls where my schoolmates slow danced with the boarding-school boys home on Christmas break from Choate, Taft, and St. Paul's. These blue-blood traditions were outdated and corny. In the end, it was my mother and I who rejected *them*.

It didn't matter, finally, because my father was famous, at least among the people I knew, not only for being a public intellectual with a regular byline in the paper of record but for being successful at life. At parties at our house, I'd watch the way he moved through people, laying his hand on a shoulder, firmly gripping someone's arm, and how they turned to him, their faces lit and expectant, as if he held a fistful of fairy dust over their heads, and he'd offer a word or two, nothing much, but with a subtext that declared, *Aren't we fantastic, you and me? Isn't this world great?* And because he was smart and observant, they believed him, and they answered back with a line that was extra funny and sharp, and he'd laugh and move on, and they'd turn around again and dig their heels a little deeper into themselves and think, yes, life is all right. It sure is.

That was my dad, at least the way I saw him. And this man loved me with the conviction of someone who, after being often disappointed by love, had finally found one that lived up to its billing. Loving your kids can be sweet and easy.

When I was growing up, my father and his success were my ace in the hole, my divining rod, my saving grace. If I ever wondered about my place in the world, I'd always have that on everybody else.

In order to be hired by Scudder, Stevens & Clark, the mutual funds company where I was working when my father died, I had to take a personality test. I didn't particularly want to work answering shareholders' letters, but I'd just moved to Cambridge and was living with my mom and dad until I found a job and could afford my own apartment. The only way I knew of getting a job was to appeal to my parents' circle of friends. Someone knew a director at the mutual funds company; he was a Saltonstall, from one of Boston's oldest and most prominent families. This friend called up the director, and then, after a five-minute chat with me in his office high above Boston Harbor, the director called down to human resources and told them, in so many words, to hire me. The personality test was a formality, given that I came so highly recommended, or rather that I had been recommended by someone so highly placed in the firm.

I stayed at this company for five years, moving up through the ranks until I eventually had my own (much smaller) office overlooking Boston Harbor. Each time I applied for a new position, I had to take the personality test again. It involved picking from a list of adjectives those that you thought other people would use to describe you, and then picking from the same list the words that you would use to describe yourself. According to your selections and the discrepancies between the two lists, you were fit into a personality model—leader, team player, rule breaker, and so on. Normally your results were not revealed to you, and I never gave the whole business much thought.

When I met with the human resources administrator after taking the personality test for a third time, she told me that I had gotten the job despite my results—my new boss was willing to overlook them. She went on to explain that, in fact, each time I'd taken the test, the results had raised a red flag, so much so that if I had walked in off the street, the company never would have hired me in the first place.

I sat in the chair across from her. She had my personnel folder open on her desk and the diagrammed results of the three tests spread out before her. She kept looking down at the papers and shaking her head. The administrator was the practical, exacting type that ends up in human resources, and I could see that I had truly stumped her. After all, I had done well at Scudder, moving up from a customer service representative to an assistant supervisor—in record time, I was told—and now I'd gotten another promotion.

"What do the tests say?" I asked, trying to keep the apprehension from my voice.

"Every time it has matched up with the model for 'impostor.' According to this"—she ran her finger along a zigzagging diagram—"you're not living in a way that's true to who you are."

My face reddened, because this diagnosis felt so conspicuously correct: I wanted to write stories and novels, not letters to shareholders. But who among my coworkers, other twenty-somethings with degrees from good colleges and dreams of "not selling out," had found their calling among the customer complaints? Couldn't the same be said of all of them?

Apparently not. "The only thing I can think of is, sometimes if the test is completed too quickly, the outcome gets skewed."

"That must be it. I always rush through tests. In high school I would finish the SAT practice test way before anyone else."

We decided that I would take it again. She gave me a fresh booklet and sent me into the conference room next door, telling me to take my time.

Slowly I made my selections, turning each adjective over carefully in my mind to see if it felt true, if it fit with my sense of who I was. *Yes* to self-assured, sensitive, observant, cranky; *no* to gentle, patient, detail-oriented, deceptive. I suspected that in the previous tests the discrepancy between my self-image and my conception of how others saw me was too great, so I made sure this time that there was only a slight variation in the two lists. All the while, an indignant sound track repeated in my head: I am not an impostor, I am not an impostor. But when she scored my test, I *was,* for a fourth time.

In the end the administrator decided that she had stumbled on a new paradigm for a leadership model. She presented the results of my four tests at the annual employee personality test conference that year, where, she told me upon her return, she was met with little fanfare.

During the months following my father's death, after I got off from work I would take the subway from Scudder to the Boston Public Library on the nights it was open late. The library was usually bustling: professionals browsed through the career section, high school students giggled behind piles of textbooks, and lonely office workers read magazines before heading home.

In 1990 the card catalog was not yet computerized, and the massive wooden filing cabinet that housed the thousands and thousands of alphabetized index cards itemizing the book collection stood in the center of the main room. When I extended the *P* drawer, it jutted three feet out from the cabinet, and as I hunched over it, searching through the cards for an entry about "passing," I was acutely aware of all the other patrons having to move around me to cross the room. If someone approached to use a neighboring drawer, I would become as nervous as if I were searching for a title on masturbation.

I was looking for a way to understand my father. As the months passed after his death and I became able to think about him without grief swamping all other emotions, I began to wonder if he had been living in a way that was true to who he was, whether the aspects of his personality that had seemed so inimitably *him* were actually facets of his camouflage. He was unrepentant boast—in his weekly volleyball game, he bragged, he was always among the first picked when choosing sides—and incredibly vain—he never had to worry about developing a receding hairline, he told me, since the thickness of hair on the back of his head made him "a very good candidate for a transplant." His hyperbole also fell on those around him. His friend Morgan held the record for the longest Frisbee throw in the state of Connecticut. My brother, Todd, had the longest eyelashes on a newborn ever recorded at Greenwich Hospital. Were these moments that I'd once seen as mostly harmless and charming actually efforts to elevate himself, and the flattery meant to seduce everyone else into collusion? I'd lost my father once, and now I was losing him all over again.

When I tried to picture my dad, the image of him prostrate in the hospital bed appeared. When I tried to think back to when he was well, a shade drew down between us. I couldn't remember, for example, if he kept the door open or closed when he worked in his study. I couldn't remember what we would talk about when he came to kiss me goodnight—a ritual he continued well into my teens. I leafed through our family albums and looked at the pictures of the softball games, the birthday parties, my dad and me playing paddleball on the beach, but these scenes refused to reanimate in my head. Only the quality of his voice, both growling and melodious, stayed with me with lasting specificity. Of course many people, when trying to conjure someone who has died, feel this same frustration and loss, but it doesn't necessarily make them question how well they'd known their loved one at all.

All I could find under the entry for "passing" were books about football and college study guides. I tried looking up "mulatto" (which I learned came from the word "mule") and was directed to "miscegenation," a term that I'd never come across during my schooling. It sounded like something illegal, and, of course, it was. In a book on the subject, I discovered that in many states until the late 1960s, and in Louisiana until 1972, marriage between members of different races was against the law. I wondered briefly if my parents' marriage in New York State in 1960 had been unlawful, making me illegitimate on top of everything else. Then I read on and discovered that it was mostly southern states that outlawed intermarriage.

I read about the many definitions of Creole, which was the term my mother had used to describe the kind of black person my father was. Creole originates from *crioulo*, a Portuguese word meaning "a slave of African descent born in the New World." Did that mean that my ancestors had been slaves? My keen interest in this question felt prurient and embarrassing; at the same time, it seemed incongruous that I should not know the answer. I imagined that had I been raised as black, this knowledge would have been as basic to my history as Viking ships were to my mother's Norwegian ancestry.

In the old *American Heritage Dictionary* at my parents' house, other definitions of Creole included "any person of European descent born in the West Indies or Spanish America," or "any person descended from or culturally related to the original French settlers of the southern United States, especially Louisiana," or "any person of Negro descent born in the Western Hemisphere, as distinguished from a Negro brought from Africa," or "any person of mixed European and Negro ancestry who speaks with a Creole dialect." Which one applied to me? I wondered. And what was the difference between Creole and African American?

I came across terms that described just how mixed someone was: a griffe was three-quarters, or the offspring of a black person and a mulatto. A quadroon was one-quarter, or the child of a mulatto and a white; an octoroon described someone who had one-eighth African heritage; and a 'steenth was one-sixteenth. In F. James Davis's book

Who Is Black? One Nation's Definition, I read about the "one-drop rule," which classified as black any Americans with the tiniest fraction — just one drop — of "black blood." It had grown out of a practice dating back to slavery known as hypodescent, which assigned someone of mixed parentage to the lower-status race, and had become the legal and social custom in the country during the era of legalized "Jim Crow" segregation. The rule, however, wasn't applied to any other minority group, nor was it used to define blackness anywhere else in the world.

Overnight my father's secret turned my normal young adult existential musing of *Who am I?* into a concrete question, *What am I?* I hoped that I'd find in a book somewhere an equation, an algorithm, or a decision tree into which I could plug the circumstances of my life and come up with the verdict.

When someone asked, I used to say that I was French and Norwegian, a combination that felt right, based on my looks. But beyond providing an explanation for my olive skin and the angularity of my face, my heritage had never been of much consequence, probably because neither ethnicity is a favored target for teasing. Where I was raised, lots of people were French and Norwegian.

My old identification no longer worked. I was determined that unlike my father I wouldn't keep my African ancestry hidden. My mother had said that his secret caused him more pain than the cancer in his bones. I didn't want any shame clouding up my life. Besides, I wasn't any good at keeping secrets. When people asked me what I was, I would tell them. But the question was, What exactly would I say?

From the start my mother's phrase "mixed blood" sounded old-fashioned and too elemental for my tastes. It brought to mind images of science experiments and large fluid-filled beakers. How were black and white blood different anyway? I wasn't satisfied with the shortened version "mixed" either: too much like an admission of being mixed-up or confused, which I was, but no need to advertise that fact. Also, "mixed" was vague.

But being too specific presented its own set of problems. Declaring myself as Norwegian and black lacked symmetry: one refers to a location, the other is a color. Calling myself a black Norwegian wasn't right either. Norwegian and African? Nordic African? They all sounded absurd. Also, how to fit in the French, the identity which for the first twenty-four years of my life seemed like the best fit? I had begun noticing, though, that African Americans, even those who were definitely part Caucasian, didn't generally acknowledge being anything other than black.

I settled, grudgingly, on the term "biracial," which sounded to me more like a phenomenon than an identity. Then one night in the fall of 1993, I was looking over some applications to graduate school. I'd just had a short story accepted by a literary magazine, which gave me the idea to apply to an MFA program where I could study writing full-time. Under the general information section, after the space for sex and birth date, there was an optional question about race. A footnote explained that the responses were used in aggregate to track the university's demographics and your answer made no difference in your chances. The usual choices appeared: White, Black, American Indian and Alaskan Native, Asian and Pacific Islander, or Other. What caught my eye was the instruction: "Check only one box."

I was at my desk in the basement apartment of my mother's house, where I was living, and I remember looking up, out the high casement window, where through the shrubbery I could spot cars going by. I was stunned by the revelation that a person could be either black or white but not both. Of course I knew that plenty of people had a parent of each race, but I realized for the first time that when it came to identifying themselves, the de facto method of racial identification required that you choose only one label. And if you chose white over black, then—no matter what you looked like or how you were raised—you were passing or ashamed of the stigma of being black or denying your true self. So the "one-drop rule" still existed.

I'd finally cracked the code: since my father was "really" black, then I must "really" be black too. Yet I still felt unsettled: I'd already experimented with describing myself as black on a few occasions, and it hadn't gone over well.

Not long after my father died, I was in New York for the weekend with my old gang from college at a bar on the Upper West Side. I was chatting with a white guy named Sven, with whom I'd had an on-again, off-again fling at school. He'd lost both his parents by the time I knew him, and I'd been particularly moved by his condolence letter after my father's death, illustrating as it did the compassion of the initiated and a rare break from his usual reserve.

It was a Saturday night and the place was packed. I'd found myself standing next to Sven by the curve of the bar, both of us waiting to refill our double vodka tonics. We were near the door, and every few minutes it would open and people would jostle us, trying to get by. I leaned in and told Sven that I'd found out some things about my father before he died.

"Oh yeah?" he said, displaying little of the gentleness he'd shown in his letter.

"Yeah," I said and blurted out with: "It turns out I'm really black."

"What?" he asked.

The music was loud and I had to raise my voice to be heard. "My dad was actually black. It came out right before he died. So"—I shrugged—"I guess that makes me black too."

Sven made a face like I was playing a trick on him and he wasn't in the mood. "How can you be black? That doesn't make any sense."

My friend Allison, who was standing nearby, chimed in. "It's true.

Her dad was really black." She was smiling a little queerly, as if we were discussing the fact that I actually had six toes.

He still looked skeptical. Sven had grown up in Manhattan, where he'd attended Bronx Science, a public high school, and met one of his best friends, Chris, who sometimes hung around with us and was most definitely black. Sven knew a black person when he saw one, and the white girl from Connecticut he used to tease for her Waspy ways wasn't it.

A couple of years earlier, before I'd learned about my father's secret, my friends and I had started out at this same bar one night, gotten drunk, and then headed down to a club in Greenwich Village to go dancing. There was a guy with us that Sven or someone knew—a handsome, dark-skinned black guy in a blue oxford shirt and tweed blazer. When I asked him why he was so dressed up, he explained that he'd been out to dinner with his parents. He'd already told me that he'd attended Dalton, an elite prep school in Manhattan, which pegged him in my mind as even wealthier and more sophisticated than the kids I'd known growing up.

The club was decorated like a harem, and this guy and I danced in the middle of other drunk young couples in a round dark room, surrounded by curtains of red-and-gold tapestry. When the music turned slow, I leaned into him a little, and he put his arms around my shoulders, pulled me close, and after swaying back and forth awhile, he lowered his mouth to mine and kissed me.

I had never been kissed by anyone black before, and I can remember catching sight of the deep pink of the inside of his mouth despite the darkness of the room and being surprised by it. He tried to get me to leave the bar with him, but I declined. I didn't go home with men—white or black—that I'd just met. He took my number and said that he would call, but I never heard from him. I wasn't too hurt, since he hardly knew me. Also, as a budding writer, I was in the business of collecting experiences, and now I had another one to cross off the list: kissed black guy.

Here was the problem: I could check off "black" on that graduate school application, but I would be an impostor. How could that same young woman who imagined the foreignness of a black man's kiss now be a member of the tribe herself? I could scratch out the "white" next to the race of my father on my birth certificate and write in "Negro," the term used in 1966, the year I was born, but I would still be the same person.

From my reading I'd learned that it was culture as much as a color that made a person black, and besides not looking the part, I wasn't raised knowing about that side of my heritage. But then I considered the clues during my childhood—however superficial or stereotypical—that my dad wasn't exactly white. There was the music—James Brown, the Commodores, Machito, Miguelito Valdés and the rest of the Afro-Cuban players—and the central role that dancing played in my family. I'd remember the stories my father told about the nightclubs in Harlem where he used to hang out and the black company he commanded during World War II (to which he'd been assigned, ironically, as a white officer), and his foregone conclusion that black athletes and black performers were superior to their white counterparts. I'd compare my father's style to that of other fathers: his natty dress code of slim pants and colorful sweaters, his belted jackets and carefully combed hair; and the rhythmic, graceful way he moved and talked. And I'd remember the nights my family crowded around the TV set to watch Ali and Foreman fight, the special on the Jackson Five, and, later, *The Cosby Show*, during which my father admired the sweaters worn by Dr. Huxtable—he owned similar sweaters himself. I'd consider my own kinship with black culture, which made me choose South African literature as my focus in a world lit class and jazz as my one elective during my college freshman year, and led me to work during my semester abroad in England at an arts foundation in Dalston Junction, London's equivalent of the South Bronx, where I was the only white person on staff besides my boss. When I'd weigh these factors in my mind, I'd wonder if calling myself white would make me an impostor too.

These recollections represented means by which I felt connected to my father's hidden ancestry, and I wasn't willing to deny them. I wanted to take his secret history and make it my own, to cultivate these bits of heritage and celebrate them. Most of all, I wanted to convince myself that I'd understood all along everything that mattered about my father, and that this legacy had always marked me, whether I realized it or not.

When I was still living with my parents in Cambridge, before my father died, I used to go dancing at a place called the Cantab Lounge in Inman Square. The house band that played every weekend featured an older black man who was so short that he had to stand on a chair while he performed. He was famous for a song called "Mr. Peanut," which he crooned in a falsetto, swaying back and forth on his perch. Every time I went there, he sang the same two sets, repeating the first one again at the end of the night. The Cantab attracted a mixed crowd of graduate students from the local universities, yuppies and hippies, and some regulars from the neighborhood, which was mostly African American.

I usually danced with my girlfriends, but sometimes when the song ended and we began to move off the floor, one of the regulars would intercept me. Generally I preferred women as dance partners because they tended to be better at it — we'd mirror each other, one taking the lead, then the other, and test out our moves. But black men were different. I didn't feel like I had to hold back, as I often did with white guys.

We'd start up, syncing into each other's movements, and my partner would grin a little and say something to encourage me. I'd show off my fanciest steps, and he'd make them his own and hand them back. Sometimes the crowd would part a little to give us room.

He'd take me in his arms, stick a knee between my legs, and pull me forward and back, pantomiming a grind. I didn't worry, because I believed that black men understood, as I did, that dancing is all about sex; therefore it was fine to bring it onto the floor, since that's where it would stay. (If I ever danced with a white guy like that, he'd be following me around for the rest of the night, sure that he'd get lucky.)

When the song finished and I was panting a little, my partner would nod appreciatively. More than once I was told that I danced like a black girl. And once one of my partners asked me if I was black.

The next morning over breakfast, I would tell my dad about my night. "All the black guys ask me to dance," I'd say, shrugging modestly. "They think I dance like a black girl." This was a brag in our household. I once had a boyfriend named Peter who my father declared was the best white dancer he'd ever seen. Whenever Peter came over, my dad would take him into the living room, where the record player was kept, put on some funk, and entreat him to demonstrate his moves. But always Peter's skill was noted with the disclaimer "for a white guy."

I told my father, laughing, incredulous: "One guy even asked me if I was black." He raised his eyebrows. *You don't say.*

What could he have been thinking in those moments? Did he ever contemplate telling me? Was he looking at me and considering just how black I seemed? Was he thanking his lucky stars once again that my hair was curly, not kinky, that my skin was olive, not dusky, that my lips were thin, my nose only slightly wide, and that my ass was small? Did he worry that someday one of us might be found out?

Later that spring I invited my friend Chinita and her boyfriend, Mike, to come visit my family on Martha's Vineyard for Memorial Day weekend. Chinita was renting an apartment next door to my parents, and she'd been dating Mike for a few months by this time. Through conversations in the shared driveway and over dinners, the couple had become family friends.

Before the weekend arrived, Mike was chatting on the telephone with his grandmother who lived in Greenwich, also in Fairfield County, near where I'd grown up. He mentioned that he was going to Anatole Broyard's house on Martha's Vineyard. He trusted that his grandmother would know the name — she was literary and she socialized with the handful of *Times* higher-ups who had also made Greenwich their home.

"Oh," she said. "The black Haitian who writes for the *New York Times.*"

"He's not black," Mike said, amused. "I've met him. He's as white as you or me."

Mike relayed this story to me after he arrived on Martha's Vineyard and then again at my insistence one evening during a dinner party thrown by my parents. I remember now how everyone, including my father, laughed and shook their heads. *What a strange thing for his grandmother to think.* If there was any pregnant pause, a holding of breath or darting of eyes, it escaped my attention. The moment was of so little consequence to my mother—who had known about my father's ancestry since before they were married and had been beseeching him to tell Todd and me for years—that she barely recalled it when I reminded her. Most startled perhaps were any guests who knew the truth and realized that my brother and I were completely unaware.

I didn't spend one minute wondering why someone would confuse my father with a black Haitian. Even the next day on a stroll down the beach, when I was walking behind my dad and noticed his long, rhythmic, loping stride, and blurted out, "Look, he even walks like a black guy," and Mike and Chinita agreed, and my dad kicked out his legs and swiveled his hips a little more to make us laugh—even then, I still didn't pause and wonder.

If you asked me why not, I might have told you that people never knew what to make of my father's name — who ever heard of someone called Anatole? — or that growing up in the city, he'd developed an urban, hipster style of writing and being in the world that might mislead the unsophisticated. Probably, though, I would simply shrug. I was aware that my father had his secrets, mostly — I suspected — about women and his long career of seducing them, but I thought that essentially I knew him. In fact I knew much more about him than most daughters know about their fathers, such as all the girls he'd impregnated during his bachelor years and the difficulties back then in obtaining abortions (which he told me about as a kind of cautionary tale). But he was my dad, and we loved each other. I couldn't imagine him deceiving me.

After he died I recalled a conversation we had when I was in my early teens. "What are you again?" I asked him out of the blue one day.

"French," he said. "You know that."

"Isn't there something else too?"

"Why are you asking this?"

"I just thought there was something else. Are you sure there isn't something else?"

After a moment he said: "Maybe a little Portuguese."

I have no idea what made me press my father this way. To my knowledge this is the only time my father ever specifically lied to someone about his background. He would mark his race as white on official forms, as many light-skinned black people did, but when the subject came up in conversation, he would either reveal his ancestry, avoid answering the question, or, if cornered, occasionally grow angry and walk away. I haven't found anyone else, though, to whom he unequivocally, directly lied.

In the years right after my father's death, however, I clung to a theory that he was not deceptive but confused. I imagined him growing up ignorant of his own ethnicity — that his parents had managed to keep it from him somehow; that he'd lived among others like himself, all caught in a racial limbo; that when checking white on those forms, he was actually making his best guess.

I know from journal entries I made around the time of my father's death that my mother had said that both of his parents were black, but somehow I began to misremember it as being only his mother. And she was so light-skinned! There she was in our family photo album at my parents' wedding. Wasn't it slightly absurd to expect my father to identify as black? Hadn't I discovered myself how inscrutable the logic to racial identity could be? Couldn't my father's rejection of the racist, antiquated one-drop rule be considered courageous even?

If these things were true, then also true was the sense my father gave me of my rightness in the world. If he was authentic, then so was I. If he was honest, then I could believe that he really loved me. The only problem was his family.

The winter after the memorial service, I made a trip to New York to see my aunts and cousin. Shirley had me over for dinner, along with her son Frank and his wife and their two kids. My other aunt, Lorraine, was there too.

Shirley was petite, lively, expressive. When she told a story, she splayed large hands that reminded me of my own and widened round hooded eyes that looked like my father's. Shirley lived in the large

parlor-floor duplex of a five-story brownstone that she owned on the Upper West Side. The living room was elegant, with brick walls, a fireplace, and floor-to-ceiling windows edged in wrought iron that looked down on a back garden. I sat on the sofa and looked around at the African art collected by Shirley and her late husband when they lived abroad—masks, shields, and an array of antique metal crosses displayed under the glass-topped coffee table. I noticed the elegant traditional furniture and the attractive oriental rugs on the floor, and felt quietly relieved to see that my father's family, like my own, had good taste and appreciated nice things (as if it would be easier to feel comfortable with my newfound family amid such comfortable surroundings!).

We talked about living in New York, movies, current events. Although it was my dad who connected us, I felt shy about bringing him up. Frank surprised me by referring to my father as Uncle Bud, which was the first I heard of his childhood nickname.

Frank had lost his own father a few months before I'd lost mine. His dad, as an ambassador and civil rights activist, had also been well known in his field. I was curious to know more about their relationship—Frank mentioned the many demands on his father's time and then quickly asserted that he was proud of his dad's accomplishments—but I didn't feel I had the right to ask such intimate questions. I wondered if Frank and I, had we grown up together, would have become friends. He struck me as a soft-spoken, thoughtful, gentle man. Perhaps, despite his being almost twenty years my senior, we'd have found some common ground. We might have turned to each other during this time, each looking for some solace.

Frank's wife, Denise, who was originally from Belize, was pretty with closely cropped hair and large alert eyes. She reminded me slightly of her mother-in-law: capable, confident, and strong-willed. And their kids, then about six and eight, were cutely nonflummoxed on meeting their long-lost cousin, the white girl. Throughout the evening, though, I noticed an edge to Denise's voice. It was softened slightly by her rather dutiful inquiries (where did I go to school? what did I do for work?), but I wondered if a few hours earlier her voice had been raised in argument with her husband: *Why should we have to make nice and have dinner with her when her family would never share a meal with us?*

Unmistakably, I was the outsider at this gathering. I sat among my relatives and noticed the easy rhythm they fell into, the apparent closeness between Frank's kids and their great-aunt Lorraine. I sensed the shared history they had—the many other dinners, trips, and holidays spent in each other's company. Also the culture they shared, black culture, was subtly evident throughout the evening—in the Caribbean meal of chicken cider stew Shirley prepared; in the art from Africa, Haiti, and by African Americans on the walls; in the woodcut print of James Baldwin propped up next to the fireplace; and in the conversation, which included a different set of references than those I was used to: Jesse Jackson, Jackie Robinson, Harlem, and apartheid.

Yet, although we were strangers to one another, I realized that my father had been a character in these peoples' lives, albeit an infrequent and disconcerting one. From the few stories they shared about him, I recognized the man I knew as my dad.

That evening the same progression of thoughts that I'd had at the memorial service kept repeating in my head: This is my father's family, and they are black. The thoughts lingered with the persistence of a riddle that you can't solve: *This is my father's family, and they are black.*

Therefore I'm black too?

Had I announced this over dinner, I don't doubt that I would have been met with some confused and affronted faces. What did I know about being black? About Jackie Robinson or Nelson Mandela? Had I ever had trouble getting a cab or service in a store or the respect of my colleagues because of the color of my skin? Was I ever judged not as an individual but as a credit or an embarrassment to my race? Had anyone ever assumed I was stupid, lazy, or dishonest because of the way I looked? No to all of it, yet I remained caught in that loop of logic: This is my father's family, and they're black, therefore I must be black too.

After dinner, I noticed a photo album on the coffee table, and I asked if I could look through it. The album contained pictures of my father and his sisters in Brooklyn in the late 1920s and early 1930s,

after the family had left New Orleans. There were also group shots of
kids, sometimes including Lorraine and Shirley, taken during a trip
the two sisters made back to Louisiana in 1935. I paused, intrigued
by the range of phenotypes pictured—from light eyes and loose curls
to brown skin and kinky hair.

"And all these people are Broyards?" I asked Shirley, who was looking at the album over my shoulder.

"Yes," she said.

"But how could they all be related to each other?"

"Why shouldn't they be? They're cousins."

My question seemed to irritate Shirley: Did I expect her to explain
the vagaries of genetics? And why was I asking anyway?

Some of those cousins looked no more black than I did.

Lorraine is the most shadowy figure in my memory of that evening.
Whereas Shirley, who is quite cosmopolitan in her conversation, was
hard to keep up with at times, Lorraine was a more relaxing presence.
I remember her as seeming very auntlike, touching my shoulders, taking my coat, making sure I had enough food. She'd maintained a relationship with my father over the years, and so, by extension, we had a
measure of comfort with each other.

Before I got a chance to see her again, she died from breast cancer.
I'd known that she was sick: during that visit she'd worn a head scarf
to hide her hair loss from chemotherapy. But my mother, who spoke
to Lorraine on the telephone sometimes, told me that the cancer was
in remission. I expected to have plenty of time to get to know her, to
hear her recollections about her brother as a young man, to enjoy the
relationship of aunt and niece that we'd been robbed of, and to talk
about my father's choice to live as white so perhaps I could begin to
understand it. Then suddenly her cancer returned, sending her back
into the hospital for what quickly appeared to be the final trip. I considered going to New York to see her, but I didn't feel right about

encroaching upon her remaining time with her sister and nephew, who, after all, had been her family in both name and deed. And then Lorraine was dead, and we'd never gotten past the niceties.

A few impressions—her melodious voice; her round, smiling face; the kindness and gentleness that seemed to emanate from her—were all I had to remember her by. A couple of months later, I came home from work to a fat envelope in my mailbox from somebody Esquire: it was a copy of her will. I opened the package and read that since Lorraine had never married nor had children of her own, she left her weekend house in Long Island and all of her possessions to her sister, Shirley, and her nephew Frank. The will stated explicitly that her brother, Anatole, was to inherit nothing "for reasons known to both of them," but that she left to his children, Todd and Bliss, one piece

of jewelry each, to be chosen by them as a remembrance of their aunt and grandparents.

In soap operas the reading of the will is always a suspenseful moment. It gives the departed one the power to reach back from beyond the grave to bestow or retract her favor, and there's no opportunity to plead your case. In a sense it's the dead person's true last words. I hadn't anticipated, though, that in real life the moment could pack

the same potential for surprise. Yet I was surprised. Lorraine's will, more than anything I had felt in her presence or heard from my mother, made me realize that her brother's rejection hurt her. My father had cut off his family, and here she was, doing the same thing back to him. Even through the document's legalese, her anger was palpable, and any notion I held that the siblings' estrangement might have been inadvertent or benign was dispelled. I leafed through the rest of the will and tried to piece together a portrait of my aunt from the belongings she'd bequeathed to others. A heavy exhausting sadness descended: my father had left behind so much unfinished business.

The next visit I made to Shirley's was to choose the piece of Lorraine's jewelry. My brother had deputized me to make his selection, and Shirley urged me to pick through the assortment spread across the dining room table and to try on some things. She pointed out a long strand of pearls and some particularly nice earrings. I was hesitant to rummage through everything, but Shirley, as Lorraine's executor, insisted on following her instructions. "She wanted you to choose," she said.

As I carried out this awkward duty, it occured to me that Lorraine must have realized when she drew up her will that to satisfy its conditions, Todd and I would have to meet our aunt Shirley at last, and my father's secret, if we didn't know it already, would finally be revealed. Perhaps she hoped to bring about some reconciliation, that the rift could stop here.

I settled on a ring of my grandmother's for Todd to give to the next Mrs. Broyard: a mother ring with three small stones — two diamonds and an emerald — one for each of her children. For myself I picked a diamond pendant on a gold chain that Lorraine had made from a divorced friend's engagement ring. It didn't have any sentimental value, but my aunt had liked it, and it looked good on me. I was quietly thrilled to have a piece of jewelry that was much nicer than anything I'd ever owned, and the irony that it had come from the secret black family my father had left behind, presumably in order to better himself, was not lost on me.

Afterward Shirley and I headed to dinner at a café a few blocks from her house. We sat at a small table squeezed in between other small tables in a glassed-in porch that fronted the street. Our conversation ranged from Broadway musicals to women's rights in the 1990s. Finally I said something about family secrets, and by the time our entrées arrived, we had dived into the subject at last.

I asked Shirley how she understood the fact that my family never saw hers when I was growing up. My mother had intimated that my father's estrangement from his younger sister was more complicated than just race.

"I never understood it," she said. "Sometimes Frank would threaten to put the kids in the car and drive up to Connecticut and present ourselves on your doorstep." She laughed heartily. "Can you imagine if you had opened the door and found all of us standing there? That would have been some surprise! But Lorraine always insisted that we had to respect Anatole's decision."

Shirley explained that since neither Lorraine nor Frank's two siblings had had children, my brother and I were her kids' only cousins. "They would ask me why it was that we never saw you." She paused for a moment, and the painful response to the question hung between us. "But we were in California and then out of the country. We had our own lives that we were happy with."

I asked Shirley about her upbringing and whether she thought there was any way that my father could have been confused about what race he was, as my mother had suggested.

"There was no question when we were growing up that we were black," she said firmly. "My parents passed sometimes for work. A lot of black people did if it could bring some advantage. My father couldn't be in the carpenter's union if he wasn't white! But at home we knew what we were. All our friends were black."

Shirley talked about her trip with Lorraine back to New Orleans in the 1930s during Jim Crow—how they would go to the white movie theater with one set of cousins and go to the colored one with another. "I hated it," she said. "It was so backward and provincial."

We had eaten our entrées, ordered coffee and dessert, and finished those too, and now the waiter was hovering with the check. Still we kept talking.

"How did my dad's decision make you feel?" I asked.

"As I said, we were far away, in California in the early sixties, and then Frank got the post in Ghana. By the time we got back to New York, my kids were grown. We had a busy, full life."

Besides, Shirley did see her brother occasionally after she moved back—particularly around the time their mother died. "Once he took all of us out to dinner to talk about our mother's care. It was a little French place, very nice, in Midtown, way over on the West Side"—she smiled a little bitterly and shook her head—"where he wouldn't run into anyone he knew." She went on to say that her husband and my dad had always enjoyed each other whenever they'd gotten together. "Frank used to give these radio addresses in the eighties," she explained. "And sometimes he would call up my brother to get his help, and Anatole would go over to Frank's office and work on it with him. He was very friendly and accommodating."

I was surprised to learn that my father did see Shirley and her family on occasion. Unlike his lunches with Lorraine or his trips to his mother's nursing home, these visits were never mentioned by my dad, not even to my mother.

The waiter finally deposited our check on the corner of the table. The restaurant was still crowded. A new rotation of couples had appeared on either side of us. I was afraid that the dinner might end before I got a chance to ask a question I'd been wondering about since I learned of my father's secret. I could feel myself grow nervous, and I learned forward so I wouldn't be overheard by our neighbors. It felt like such a weird thing to want to know, for a person not to know. "Do you think it's possible that some of our ancestors were slaves?" I asked.

Shirley sat back in her chair and eyed me with a mix of pity and condescension. "Well," she said, "not too many black people emigrated to America in the nineteenth century, so, yes, I expect they were." I let this news soak in. If some of my ancestors had been slaves, then the history of blacks in this country was my history too. Here was the conclusive evidence that could make my father's identity as a black man real to me. I felt perversely pleased, the way that someone does upon receiving a bad diagnosis—I knew it! It's true!—and then abruptly sad. There were still so many unanswered questions, and my sense of my father felt more distant than ever. The immense sadness and tragedy of slavery itself, however, I couldn't yet feel.

Shirley began to gather her things to go.

"But I don't know how to think of myself anymore," I persisted. "I don't know who I'm supposed to be."

"You're Bliss, that's who you are," she said, tugging on her jacket impatiently. "And the best thing you can do is to figure out what that means." She tapped her finger on the tabletop. "The minute you let other people label you, you let them take away your power."

Yes, yes, I agreed, I told her, but I felt as if my identity had been staked on false information.

She pushed her chair away from the table and offered her final word: "You're not going to be able to understand what it means to you until you understand what it meant to your father. That's the question you should be trying to answer."

In December of 1993, six months after my dinner with Shirley, I went looking for my father's birthplace in the French Quarter in New Orleans. Although he was only six when his family left for Brooklyn, in his stories and writings my dad was always offering the French Quarter as a way to explain his upbringing and the kind of man his father had been — a *bel homme* (beautiful man) and raconteur. It was there that my father's secret history began.

My boyfriend at the time, a television reporter named Bill, came with me, offering up his skills to help me get the story on my dad. I don't remember specifically discussing it, but it was understood that Bill and I were trying to find an answer to that first question I'd had on learning my father's secret: How black was he?

Before we left town, I discovered a copy of my dad's birth certificate that I'd somehow missed during my childhood snooping. It stated that before the recorder of births, deaths, and marriages for the city of New Orleans had personally appeared

Paul Broyard, native of this city, residing at No. 2444 Lapeyrouse Street who hereby declares that on the sixteenth of this month, (July 16th 1920) at no. 2524 St. Ann Street was born a male child, named Anatole Paul Broyard, Jr. (col), lawful issue of Anatole P. Broyard a native of this city aged 33 years,

occupation carpenter and Edna Miller a native of this city
aged 25 years.*

I knew from Shirley that Paul Broyard was her and my father's
grandfather. This fact and the addresses on the document were all the
information I had to go on.

On a Friday evening, Bill and I checked into a guesthouse on one
of the Quarter's side streets and then headed out to walk around. Tall
stucco townhouses painted in pale shades of pink, green, and blue sat
flush along the narrow sidewalk. Ornate iron balustrades outlined
second-floor balconies and heavy black slatted shutters folded back
from windows. We wandered down the roughly laid brick sidewalks
and peered behind gates and doors at tucked-away courtyards with
small fountains at their centers and bare trellises set against their
walls. The scene fit the image of my father's childhood home that I'd
developed from his stories and from what he'd written about the
place. Explaining his father's habit of walking down Broadway every
Saturday after the family moved to New York, my father wrote that
"every man in the French Quarter was a boulevardier, and life was a
musical comedy." I could imagine his father, who "had a blues song in
his blood, a wistful jauntiness he brought with him from New Orleans," strolling here.

Bill and I made the compulsory trip down Bourbon Street. We
passed a jazz band — with a few horns and a drum kit — set up on a
street corner and a mime with his face covered in white greasepaint
posed motionless on a stepladder under a streetlamp. The shops, still
open, displayed rows and rows of Mardi Gras beads, beer mugs with
crawfish etched into their glass, and T-shirts that said things like "I'll
show you mine if you show me yours" and "New Orleans / Home of

---

* My grandfather's given name on his own birth certificate was Paul Anatole Broyard.
But for most of his life, in both casual and official circumstances, he seems to have used
the name Anatole Paul Broyard, as he did here on my father's birth certificate. I have
called him Paul Anatole or by his nickname, Nat, throughout this narrative.

the Big Party." All the bars had their doors propped open despite the cool December evening, and music bled onto the street: drunken college boys singing off-key karaoke versions of Van Morrison and the steady throb of a disco beat. Every once in a while, we passed standing in a doorway a buxom woman clad in a sequined halter top or a metallic-colored minidress, wrapped in a fake fur stole, and perched on stiletto lace-up boots. She'd be leaning against the doorframe, chatting with the bouncer, his jacket zipped up against the cold, and when we walked by, they'd both pause, and she'd straighten up, switch her weight from foot to foot, throwing a hip out and her chest forward, wondering if the young, adventuresome-looking couple cared to come on inside.

As we walked up to Decatur Street, near the Mississippi River, passing more T-shirt shops and rowdy bars, my mood turned dark. Outside of that one charming street, the musical comedy of my father's French Quarter with its jaunty walkers and raconteurs had been usurped by this tacky burlesque. I knew that it was unreasonable to expect a neighborhood to remain unchanged after almost seventy years—and of course the city would change more drastically still after Hurricane Katrina—but I'd hoped to feel more kinship to the place, that it would call up the hidden blues song in my own blood rather than a feeling of slight disgust. We paused at Jackson Square, a small, pristine gated park with a statue of Andrew Jackson rearing up on his horse at its center. The park gate was locked, but a few homeless people had spread out their bedding and tucked in for the night. Behind the park loomed St. Louis Cathedral, built in colonial days, a tall and regal remnant of more refined times.

We headed back to our room, walking along one side of the cathedral. When we reached the next cross street, Bill paused and pointed up to the sign. We were on St. Ann, the street where my father was born. We strolled along it for a few blocks, and I noticed some of the same aspects of the town houses that had charmed me earlier. Neither Bill nor I could recall the street number from my dad's birth certificate, so we decided we'd come back the next afternoon after visiting the library. I could have already passed the house, I thought, imagining my infant father in the arms of his grandfather as he stood in the courtyard and admired his newest descendant, before setting off for the Board of Health to declare the birth.

I was also relieved to note that there *was* a street named St. Ann in the French Quarter, that at least this detail shared by father about his origins was true.

The most frequent visitors to the Louisiana Division of the New Orleans Public Library are amateur genealogists. You can spot them hunched in front of microfilm readers, searching through reels and reels of census data, city directories, old newspapers, wills, and successions; or lugging armfuls of volumes of church records or reference books back to large wooden tables; or crouched in front of filing cabinets housing index cards listing obituary notices or marriage licenses. Many of them are older retirees, but they speak about their genealogical searches as though they were work: *I'm so busy lately—too many meetings, and I still haven't gotten up to the state archives.*

Many plan on publishing the results of their research when it is complete, which is often defined as having traced their family name or group of names back to their countries of origin, with the birth date and place of the first emigrants to America. The stacks of many regional libraries are full of such volumes. The authors sometimes sell them to the general public through genealogical Web sites and newsletters, but most are content to produce a book for their relatives and colleagues, perhaps especially their colleagues.

The researchers lean over the documents for hours, occasionally taking a break to stretch their backs and rest their eyes, and then they are at it again. It is exhausting, tedious work. The historian Gwendolyn Midlo Hall spent fifteen years studying microfilmed records throughout Louisiana and in Spain, France, and Texas to create a database containing the largest collection of individual slave records ever assembled. An article about her achievement that appeared on the front page of the *New York Times* noted that Hall nearly lost her sight in the process.

Now and then you can overhear someone talking to herself: *There you are!* or *Well, lookie here.*

Always they are searching for a name—their surname, or their mother's, or their grandmother's, or the maiden name of the mother of their great-grandfather. When they find these names, they can begin to lay claim to history. They tell themselves a story: My family has been in this city for over two hundred years. We lived in this neighborhood and on those streets. We were farmers or lawyers. We fixed shoes. We fought in wars. We had money. We knew people who were important. We were important. You'll find our name in history books. We took part in shaping this time, this place, this world. We mattered. We will not be forgotten.

I envied these people. Whereas they were unraveling a ball of thread that started with family stories and yellowing photos displayed in the hall, my lead was a dusty, tangled thing that had been kicked under the bed years before. Unknotting it wasn't going to be easy.

After Bill and I spent a few hours before the microfilm readers ourselves, all we had was a handful of seemingly unrelated facts. I'd tackled the obituaries while he looked up census records. In the 1830 New Orleans census appeared a Gilbert Broyard, between the ages of thirty and forty, listed as white, living with two free colored girls and two free colored boys, all under ten years old, and one free colored female between the ages of twenty-four and thirty-five. Until 1860 only the heads of households were named in the census, so there is no way of knowing who these other people were. Did this family represent the beginning of the race-mixing in my father's tree? That would make his—and my—ancestors black for more than 160 years, more than three times as long as the 50 or so years that my dad had lived as white, and six times as long as the 24 years that I had.

Bill brought over the current New Orleans phone book to show me the dozens of Broyards listed. My family had always been the only ones I knew of, and it was strange to see the name over which I'd felt so proprietary repeated again and again.

"I'll get a copy of this page so we can start calling people," he said.

I told him not to bother, that we wouldn't have time this trip to see anyone. I didn't tell Bill that I had already run across some Broyards myself in an index of articles appearing in New Orleans newspapers between the eighteenth century and the mid-1960s. I had been thrilled to find numerous entries, until I looked them up and saw that two were references to Broyards who had been arrested — one for immoral behavior with a fourteen-year-old and the other for being caught with $20,000 worth of narcotics — and a third was a guy who'd witnessed a murder. Their names had appeared in the police logs of the paper, which made me hesitant about getting in touch with the rest of my relatives.

Anyway, we had to get going if we wanted to hunt down the house where my father was born. We left the library and, after a quick sandwich, made our way to St. Ann Street and looked for 2524. The block that ran along St. Louis Cathedral was numbered in the 600s; we started walking away from the river, figuring that it couldn't be too far. The route led us through Louis Armstrong Park, which runs along the edge of the French Quarter proper, and when we got to other side, the street numbered only in the 1500s — and the neighborhood had suddenly, dramatically, declined.

Here and there a few brightly painted wooden cottages remained with their lacy Victorian ornamentations, but most were in need of a paint job and had fallen into disrepair. Tall onion grass grew up around the foundations. Rooflines were pocked with gaps in the slate shingles. A surprising number of lots were empty, with just a square of scorched earth marking where houses had once stood.

Everyone we saw was black and looked poor. A young woman stood in an open doorway and watched us as we walked by. With loose jeans that snagged on her hip bones, she was rail thin. A little girl with holes in the knees of her pants was by her side. When she saw us, she reached for her mother's hand. On the next block, some teenaged boys stood around a car with the doors opened and the radio blaring. They also turned to stare. We hit the 2000 block; another five to go. I felt as though we had been walking for hours.

For his job Bill sometimes had to travel to Boston's inner city, knock on strangers' doors, and ask if they had a photo of the son or daughter who had just been killed or arrested, and if a parent, uncle, or sister would be willing to talk to him for a minute. As we walked down St. Ann Street, he seemed perfectly at ease. He kept commenting on our surroundings, noting an interstate that we had passed under and wondering when it had been erected and about the effect on the neighborhood. He pointed out nice details on houses and speculated about urban renewal programs.

I remember wanting to ask Bill to lower his voice, to stop gesturing at people's homes, to stop calling so much attention to us, but I was grateful for his company and his interest in my search, and I didn't want to do anything that might discourage him. I was also hesitant to show my own discomfort, lest I appear cowardly, or worse, racist or elitist in his eyes. But the truth was, I was shocked by the poverty around us.

I'd known that my father's parents weren't well-off or educated — neither had gone to high school — but if I'd thought of them as poor, my vision of that was more rural and innocent: closely set houses with sparse furnishings in well-swept rooms, a small yard with some chickens perhaps, a tight square of a vegetable garden, some washing on the line. I'd expected to see in the windows simple white curtains, slightly frayed from constant laundering, rather than the old sheets tacked over the windows that were not already boarded up.

This was gritty ghetto poor, like the neighborhoods on the outskirts of Manhattan that, as a child, I'd peered down at from my family's car. Again I wasn't allowing for the fact that seventy years had passed. Bill was right about the construction of I-10 in the 1960s, bi-secting the French Quarter and the Tremé neighborhood where my fa-ther was raised: the impact was devastating. Also, in 1993, the year of this visit, New Orleans was in the midst of a crack epidemic that con-tinues today, and the area where we walked was among the hardest hit. But all I kept thinking was that no neighborhood that I had ever lived in would have declined so much.

Bill asked me for the house number as we crossed onto another block. Suddenly we were standing in front of a faded blue one-story

cottage that appeared aban-doned: the paint was peeling and there was no evidence of anyone living inside. We knocked for a while with no response.

"It's small," I said.

"It's deep," Bill said, peer-ing down the alley alongside the house. "Look how far back it goes. And it looks like there used to be a nice yard."

He suggested that we knock on the door of the neighboring house. I told the middle-aged woman who answered that my father had lived next door. "Anatole Broyard? People called him Buddy?"

She shook her head no. I went on to explain that his family moved out in the 1920s.

"Is there anyone older on the block who has lived here for a long time?" Bill asked. The woman's son came to the door and said that we should talk to Miss Barbara down the street. "She's lived here forever." He offered to take us to her house.

As we followed him, I mouthed to Bill, "Miss Barbara," slightly buoyed by the stately sound of the name.

We entered the house, and the smell of urine hit me. Towels covered these windows, and it took me a moment before I spotted in the darkness an old woman in a plaid housedress propped up on a mattress on top of a box spring in a corner. Piles of clothes surrounded her, and a small child wearing a diaper and a T-shirt lay sleeping beside her.

"This girl is trying to find out about her daddy. He lived here seventy years ago," the neighbor explained. Miss Barbara pushed the sleeping child closer to the wall and told me to sit beside her.

"She can't see so well," said the neighbor, prodding me forward. I perched on the edge of the mattress and discovered that Miss Barbara was the source of the urine smell. She laid a hand on my arm and asked again who my father was. We quickly established that she had only been two when my dad's family left town, and she didn't remember any Broyards on the block when she was growing up. The little girl woke and started to fuss. She stood and tottered out of the room, one hand on her hip to keep her diaper from slipping down, looking, it seemed, for an adult who might change her.

After Miss Barbara talked for a while about the people she did recall from her childhood, prompted by Bill, who asked question after question in hopes of uncovering someone who might remember my father, I interrupted, saying that we'd taken up enough of her time. The diapered girl circled back into the room and started to cry. I got up, said again that we should go, thanked Miss Barbara, and headed past Bill out the door.

The walk back to the French Quarter went much faster than the way there. It was starting to get dark, and Bill suggested that we take Canal Street, which, as a well-traveled business thoroughfare, seemed safer. I was quiet while he read from the notes he'd made during the conversation. He was walking fast as he talked, making plans for the next day, trying to figure out when we could return to St. Ann Street to look for some of the people Miss Barbara mentioned. "We should go to the library first and check out the phone books, because they might have moved," he said. "Oh shoot. I wonder if it's open on Sunday. I forgot to look."

I grabbed his arm. I was crying. "Just stop, all right?" He looked confused and stopped walking, but that wasn't what I meant.

"Stop with the reporter bit," I said, my voice rising. "This isn't some story you're doing. Okay? This is my family. My fucking father. Enough. All right." I started walking again, a few steps ahead of him, crying noisily. We didn't speak the rest of the way back.

I couldn't explain what was upsetting me, because I was embarrassed and ashamed—that my father's family had been poor, that I hadn't realized how poor, that I cared so much. Bill's ancestors had come over on the Mayflower, or close to it. His grandfather had been the dean of a prestigious medical school in New York City. Another ancestor, a great-great-great-grandmother or somebody, had been the first white woman born in Bronx County in New York. Bill had shared these details of his family scornfully, eschewing the Waspiness of his upbringing. He had told me more than once that he would gladly trade his own illustrious ancestry for my more exotic past, placing me as it did closer to the salt-of-the-earth folks who figured so heroically in the left-wing newspapers that he liked to read.

His glorification of my past I also found shameful and embarrassing, and on another level, perhaps the more honest one that made me yell at him, I recognized it as a fiction, one that was as convenient as the romantic image I'd held of my father's youthful poverty.

When we got back to Cambridge, I made a folder, labeled it GENE-ALOGY, tucked all the notes we'd taken inside, and filed it away. Over the next three years, I would pull the folder out occasionally, spend half an hour trying to connect the dots, and then put it back. I didn't return to New Orleans, nor did I try to call any of the people there who shared my last name.

*   *   *

In the fall of 1994 I moved to Charlottesville, Virginia, to attend graduate school. I got an apartment a mile outside of town in an old mansion that had once belonged to the owners of a woolen mill. From my front porch, I could see the mountain on which Monticello was located, home to Thomas Jefferson and his slave mistress Sally Hemings.

My first morning in my new place, I didn't have any food, nor had I unpacked my dishes, so I headed out to a little breakfast joint I'd noticed up the road. It was a small building, not much bigger than a shack, set in between a couple of houses. I sat down at the counter, and a few moments later, a cop walked in. He went to a back hallway and returned with an apron, which he put on over his uniform before sitting down. I asked the cook, a heavy-set red-faced man with the slightly bulbous nose of a drinker, if he had a whole wheat bagel and some herb tea. He and the cop grinned.

"You'll be wanting the biscuits and sausage gravy, ma'am," the cop said.

"Okay," I said, feeling my face redden slightly.

The cook added: "And there's no tea. Just coffee."

"That'll be fine, then."

I dug into my breakfast, listening to the cop and the cook chat with their y'alls and heavy drawls, and I realized that while I was only two hours from Washington, DC (and six and a half from New York), I was in the South.

The cook asked me if I was new in town.

"I just arrived," I told him. "I'm starting school up at the university to study creative writing."

They seemed impressed. The cook asked what I wrote.

Stories, I told him.

"True ones?" the cop wondered.

"No, mostly made-up, but I hope that they'll feel true to people."

"We'll have to keep an eye out for your name," said the cook. "What'd you say it was?"

Bliss, I told him. Bliss Broyard.

"Bliss?" he repeated, making sure he got it right. "That sure is a funny name. Sounds like one of them names the colored girls give their babies. They come up with the strangest-sounding names — Keisha, Shawanna — just make 'em up." He and the cop laughed.

I remember that I raised my eyebrows — *Is that so?* — and how my face felt frozen in that expression, as if by relaxing it, I would give something away about myself.

He extended his hand. "My name's Frank, and this here's Fred." He gestured to the cop's apron: "He comes every morning."

I shook their hands and told them that I'd be seeing them, but as I left, letting the screen door slam behind me, I doubted that I would be going back to that place again.

Charlottesville was where I began to learn about race in earnest. For the first time in my life, my world was somewhat integrated. Unlike most people's, my sheltered existence hadn't been challenged much in college. The University of Vermont, where I'd done my undergraduate work, was overwhelmingly white. In 1988, the year I graduated, there were only forty African American students out of more than eight thousand undergraduates. The one black student with whom I was friendly was a wealthy Nigerian guy who everyone said was a prince back in his country. While some of my course work brought me into contact with the music and literature of Africa and African Americans, my interest in "black subjects" didn't extend to political issues. When some of the "hippie crowd" set up a shantytown in the quad to try to force the university to divest its South African holdings, my friends and I joked that demonstrators would be driven out by their own pungency from lack of showers. And my years in Boston working at the blue-blood investment firm weren't much better. Since learning about my dad's ancestry I'd been reading extensively about race and African American history, but I'd barely had a conversation about the subjects with anyone who knew them firsthand.

Hank, a recent graduate of the writing program, was the first African American with whom I shared my father's secret. Over beers late into the night at a local bar, the stories came tumbling out of me: about my father being ostracized by both the white and black kids in his neighborhood, about his father having to pass to be in the carpenter's union, and my dad's fear of being pigeonholed as a black writer. Hank offered stories about his own light-skinned relatives. He'd also known of people who'd crossed over. Every black person did, he said. He went on to explain how racism could drive a man to deny his identity. He described how helpless and angry it made him feel when he saw a white woman cross the street to avoid him, and how difficult it was not to turn that anger inward at himself.

Up until then, I had seen my father mostly as an anomaly, a lone dropout from the struggle for civil rights, but the conversation that night made me reconsider: apparently lots of people had opted out. Much later I'd recognize how magnanimous it was of Hank to respond to my father with compassion, given that he didn't have the same choice to control how he was perceived by the world.

With other African American graduate students, these conversations continued — about the subtle racist attitudes that persisted into the late twentieth century, but also about matters particular to being raised African American. Erica, another short-story writer, told me about the times she had to prove that she was "black enough." She'd grown up in an inner-city Philadelphia neighborhood, and her family's insistence that she speak "proper" English had made her a target on the street. On the other hand, she'd recently decided to lock her hair because she liked the look and was tired of the hassle and expense of chemical relaxants, and suddenly she was seen differently — more politicized and militant — especially by black men. Walton, a first-generation American whose parents were from Zaire, taught me about poetry, American jazz, and African high-life music, and explained the special meaning that the hyphenated identity of African American had for him.

I talked the most with Anjana, a cultural anthropologist who was writing her dissertation on multiracial identity. In her late thirties, Anjana was older than many of the other graduate students, having returned to school after a child and a divorce. A curvy woman with dreadlocks and a wide, open face, she was forceful, funny, and intensely fair-minded. We talked usually on the phone and often about the question of what one calls onself. Anjana had European, African, Hispanic, and Native American ancestors all in the first and second generations preceding her. For political reasons she identified as African American in any official capacity, but otherwise she resisted labels. A professor in a class she was taking once had the students go around the room and describe how they thought of themselves. People answered Hispanic, African American, Jewish, et cetera. When it came to Anjana's turn, she wryly offered, "Empress of the Universe."

Time and again I asked her what she would call herself if she were me, and she always gave some variation of the same response: What's wrong with Bliss? It's a fine name.

Some things that changed during that time: I stopped pussyfooting around race. I didn't lower my voice anymore when I said the word "black." I didn't shy away from asking a question because I worried that it might make me sound ignorant or unwittingly racist. I began to stare, looking closely into the faces of my black friends, trying to see them rather than, as Ralph Ellison described, their surroundings, myself, or some figment of my imagination. I avoided that exchange of glances among white people — in a store, on the street, in a bus — when a black person has done something they disapprove of: that quick network built from strangers rolling their eyes and raising their eyebrows to remind themselves of their united front. And I started to notice the dozens of thoughts that zoomed through my brain every day carrying racially coded messages. I didn't make a conscious decision to do this, but as I learned and talked about race, these thoughts that had once been background noise suddenly captured my attention.

I remember the first time that it happened. I was driving through the parking lot of my local supermarket and I spotted an old sedan that was speeding too fast down a neighboring row. I crossed the car's path, and I noted with satisfaction that the driver was a black man — *It figures* — and in that split second, the belief that black men were reckless and inconsiderate, one that I wasn't even aware of holding, had been confirmed, and I was pleased about it because I'd been proven right!

I parked my own car and sat there, trembling slightly. The thought lay in my brain like a mess on the carpet. I wanted nothing to do with it, but there it was, as plain as could be. Was that really me who just thought that? Or had the cook from the restaurant up the street possessed me for a moment? Given all the conversations that I'd had, all the friendships that I'd developed, what I'd learned about my father, how could I possibly be growing even more racist?

This experience repeated itself in the creative writing class I was teaching. I became conscious of slightly lowering my expectations of a black student by pandering to her hackneyed treatment of her story's theme of discrimination. In the drugstore I watched as my annoyance with a slow cashier, who was black, widened into a general condemnation of certain types of young African American women as lazy. In the past these thoughts had passed stealthily through my brain the way the fact that you are reading subtitles during a foreign film fades from your awareness, yet their message still dictates how you see what's happening before you. Now I began to try to intercept them.

I developed a method by which I hoped to deprogram myself. First I would forgive myself, because the only other choice, self-censure, didn't leave any room to correct the problem. I reasoned that given the pervasiveness of racism in America, it's impossible for a person to escape its effect. Of course I was racist, meaning I made judgments, valuations, and assumptions about people based on what I perceived their ethnicity to be. After all, fitting information into categories is how we make sense of the world. Perhaps if people felt less apprehensive about acknowledging their racist thoughts, then they could move on to addressing them.

Next I would try to identify which particular stereotype of African Americans had fueled the belief in question: that black men are dangerous, or black students aren't as smart as white ones, or black girls have no ambition. And then, in a logical fashion, I would attempt to debunk it: What proof did I have that black men were more dangerous? Well, they are incarcerated at a higher rate than white men — but isn't that also due in part to the bias of the justice system, issues of class, and a historical deprivation of opportunity? If all other things were equal, was there any evidence that black men would be constitutionally more prone to reckless behavior than white men? Hadn't I in fact known white men who were reckless and black men who were not? Couldn't that encounter in the parking lot have been a singular incident? And why should the driver be made to stand in for all other black men and not, say, all other people who drive old sedans? Couldn't I have just as easily judged him as yet another inconsiderate old-sedan driver? Once I was satisfied that my belief was unfounded, I would make a pledge to myself to try to do better the next time.

It was strange to take such a systematic approach to changing the way I thought and behaved, as if I were making myself the subject of a psychological experiment. And it was hard work. Trying to be constantly vigilant wasn't fun or easy. Sometimes it was difficult to resist the desire to feel superior over another person. Sometimes I got a thrill from thinking something that was ugly and extreme, the way that smelling a terrible smell can be perversely exhilarating. But mostly I didn't feel I had much choice in challenging these thoughts. Along the way my loyalties had shifted without my even realizing it.

When I arrived at Southern Culture, the restaurant where I worked as a waitress, on the day that the O. J. Simpson trial was decided, the television in the bar was tuned to CNN and my coworkers were gathered around. Many of them were also graduate students or alumni of the University of Virginia, well educated and liberal in their politics. Everyone was white except for one dishwasher, a black man in his midfifties whom the owners had taken under their wing. He had once been in prison for failure to make payments on his child support and was constantly struggling to stay on the wagon. So long as he was sober, he'd be given work; when he wasn't sober, he'd sometimes show up in the middle of service to ask for a drink or some money, and then the owners would turn him away.

The verdict had been announced a few hours earlier, but many people hadn't yet seen the televised decision. The case had been the topic of discussion over beers at the end of many shifts. I stayed out of it for the most part. I'd missed seeing the live footage of the flight of the white Bronco, which was the initial hook for so many people. Also, the debates often unwittingly exposed peoples' attitudes about race in a way that was uncomfortable to hear.

O.J. rose along with his lawyers, and we stood there too, silently, as the charges were read. Then came the verdict: not guilty. I watched the relief pass through O.J.'s body, as his mouth rose slowly into a smile. Johnnie Cochran thumped his back in congratulations. I smiled too and turned around to begin setting up for dinner. My coworkers remained staring at the television in disbelief. "It's outrageous!" someone said, shaking his head. "He's guilty as sin!" By the kitchen door stood the dishwasher, who wore a shit-eating, I-can't-believe-it grin. I imagined what he was thinking: *Finally, a brother catching a break, a black man buying himself some justice.* He shook his head and went back into the kitchen.

I didn't actually believe that O.J. was innocent, and I appreciated the seriousness of the crime he was accused of. I would also come to realize the complex emotions provoked by the decision for many of my African American friends. But in that lightning moment that exposed the country's deep racial divide, there was something about O.J.'s going free that, to my surprise, made me inexplicably happy.

During my twenties I went through a phase of giving away my father's clothes to various boyfriends. One of these men, Jack, happened to share my dad's shoe size. At the time, I was living in my mother's house in Cambridge. One Saturday night when Jack was over, we went through the jumble of shoes that my mom had gotten as far as moving out of her bedroom and into the closet in my dad's study.

My father liked fashion and high-quality brands. Among the pairs Jack chose were some Paul Stuart loafers, some low-top city boots from Barneys, and a pair of hardly worn Timberland hiking shoes. Jack was a writer and lived frugally. He was more than happy to put these shoes to use.

We packed them up in a duffel bag. Since Jack had to get up early the next morning for an extra job he'd taken overseeing the delivery of the Sunday papers, I placed the bag by the front door where he wouldn't forget it. He left out some beat-up Buster Brown–type boots—good for work, he'd said—to wear the next day, and we went to bed.

At 4:30 a.m. Jack slipped out without waking me—until he opened the front door, tripping the burglar alarm. I bolted upright in bed, *Shit! Shit! Shit!*—I'd forgotten to tell my mother not to arm the alarm—and went racing downstairs to turn it off. But my mom was already at the panel, punching in the code, and then the phone rang with the call from the alarm company, and she beat me again. I stood in the kitchen, naked except for the towel I'd grabbed, and smiled sheepishly while my mother relayed the password to the caller that indicated everything was all right. She hung up, shot me an annoyed glance, and disappeared back up the stairs without a word. This wasn't the first time I'd caused a false alarm.

On the phone that night, Jack described his version of the events—the earsplitting wail pulsing from the house and the flashing lights that illuminated the sidewalk as he scurried down the street to his truck, his feet clad in his girlfriend's dead father's shoes and a bag full of half a dozen more banging at his side. The incident became a funny story he'd tell to friends. Everyone would laugh and roll their eyes at the obviousness of the metaphors—trying to fill my father's shoes; stealing away, a thief in the night, from his house. I would laugh too, but the story exposed the conflicted place my father occupied for me a little too baldly for comfort. That Jack was fifteen years older, a nurturing fatherly type, and also a writer didn't help matters.

Yet I persisted in my strange practice. The next boyfriend, a musician named Al, got some of my dad's colorful sweaters and a jacket or two. Al was good-looking and a little cocky. He'd put on these jazzy sweaters and strut around. But the boyfriend after that, Bill, who accompanied me to New Orleans, was taller and broader than my father. He also flatly refused to be dressed up in his clothes (although he did end up with my mother's dead brother's tuxedo), and the habit was finally broken.

The obvious explanation is that I was looking for a man like my father, but the more I learned about my dad, the more I became determined to avoid men like him. Rather, I didn't know how to rid myself of him, nor did I exactly want to. I missed my father even as my vision of him became more and more obscured, perhaps particularly as it became obscured. It felt like missing a ghost. If I placed his clothes on some form, maybe he'd reappear, the way the invisible man does at the end of the movie—slowly materializing to fill the empty suit.

At graduate school, in the stories that I was trying to write, fathers were appearing: charming, slightly bullying, sexy, artistic types not unlike my own dad. My classmates generally applauded them for their swaggering ways. I didn't think of them as my father exactly, but I would borrow aspects of his character and then exaggerate them to explore some dynamic between fathers and daughters that I'd become fixated on.

After I'd been in Charlottesville for a few months, I received a letter from an editor at a New York publishing house. She'd come across the one story I had published so far, which described a daughter attending her dying father, and she wondered if I had more stories to show her. I didn't, but I wrote back suggesting that after I finished graduate school maybe we could get in touch again.

A few months earlier, I'd heard from an editor at another New York publishing house, who invited me to lunch. When we got together, I learned that this woman wasn't particularly interested in my fiction. She'd heard about my father's racial identity from a mutual friend. The story had never been told publicly, and she thought that I was the person to do it.

I'd always imagined that I would eventually write about my father's secret. A book would give me the courage and impetus to forge ahead in the rocky terrain of race and family rifts. Also, since this information about my identity had not been made public to me as I was growing up, the act of my making it public always felt like my right. Yet although I was becoming more comfortable and familiar with questions of race, I wasn't ready to embark on this project. I put the editor off by explaining that I wanted to first work on a book of fiction so that I could try to find an audience on my own merit.

When classes ended in June 1995, I headed to Martha's Vineyard for the summer to wait tables and clean houses to earn money for the following school year. One day I got a phone call at home from Rick Grand-Jean, a neighbor of ours and a close family friend. My mother and I often had dinner with Rick and his wife, Christine, during which we would sometimes talk about my father's racial identity and my plans to write about it.

Rick was calling to report that at a cocktail party the night before, he'd met Henry Louis Gates Jr. "He's the head of the Afro-American department at Harvard," he said.

"I know who he is," I said, slightly annoyed. Even if I weren't reading and thinking about race all the time, it would be hard not to be familiar with Gates's name. He was everywhere: on political talk shows, in the table of contents of the *New Yorker*, listed in some capacity (author, editor, foreword by, writer of a blurb) on the cover of almost every book on the black history table in my local Barnes & Noble.

Rick explained that my family's name had come up in conversation, and Skip, as most people called him, had expressed interest in my father's story. He'd known about my dad's black ancestry from Shirley Broyard's husband, Frank Williams, whom he'd met while at Yale. When Rick mentioned that I intended to write a book about my dad, Skip passed along his number to give to me.

I wondered out loud why the top African American academic in the country would want to talk to a twenty-eight-year-old short-story writer with one publication to her name.

"Maybe he wants to help you," Rick suggested. "He seems like a nice guy."

Five minutes later I was talking to the man himself. I'd called from the phone in the kitchen, an old-fashioned wall model with a rotary dial and a stretched-out cord that was always getting tangled. I started out the conversation pacing back and forth in front of the counter—I was anxious about sounding stupid or ill-informed—but his easygoing manner and a conversational style peppered with words like "dig," "brother," and "crazy motherfucker" soon relaxed me, and before long I was perched on the kitchen stool, my elbows propped on the counter, relaying my story with my own saucy language: *So then my mother says, Your father is part black, and I'm like, That's the secret? Big fucking deal!*

Skip asked me question after question: about my father's family and whether we ever saw them when I was growing up, about the manner in which I'd learned the secret, about my dad's attitudes toward African Americans.

"He was totally prejudiced," I said bitterly, feeling a small prick of betrayal. "You should have heard the things he said."

Skip didn't sound surprised. "That was probably the blackest thing about him," he said.

I confided my confusion about what to call myself, and Skip told me a story about a student of his who'd discovered her black ancestry over one summer and returned to college with her hair in dreadlocks. I waited for him to add a coda: *As if being black were as simple as changing one's hairstyle.* But he didn't, which prompted me to wonder if I was making my identity quest too complicated.

Skip explained that his interest in my father's story began back in the midseventies, while he was teaching at Yale. In 1971 my dad had gotten the job as the new daily book critic for the *New York Times.* No major daily newspaper in the United States, aside from Negro newspapers (as they were then called), had ever had a black critic on staff, and African American intellectuals around the country had been buzzing with the news ever since. Skip was occasionally contributing book reviews to the *Times* himself. One day he took the train down from New Haven to have lunch with a senior editor there. As he and the editor were chatting, Skip made a comment—a mischievous one—about being pleased to see a black critic on staff. The editor looked confused and asked him who he was talking about. "Why, Anatole Broyard," Skip said. The older man pushed back his chair from the table and said—Skip put on a scolding patrician voice here—*That sort of scandalous talk will not be tolerated if you hope to keep writing for the* New York Times. Because he did want to keep writing for the paper, Skip muttered something about how he must have been mistaken. The conversation resumed, but a few minutes later the editor circled back to the topic: *Well, he might be one thirty-second black — a great-grandmother or something somewhere — but no more than that.*

"No more than that," I repeated sarcastically. "Thank God."

After talking for almost an hour, Skip promised to put together a reading list for me and get back in touch. I stood in the kitchen for a minute after we hung up, staring out the big picture window onto the jungle of my mother's garden. The head of Harvard's Afro-American department had told me emphatically that I had to write about my father's racial identity, that it would make a wonderful and important story. The notion of my life having a grand purpose swelled my chest, and for the next few days, as I cleaned the houses of the Vineyard elite, I imagined them saying, years from now, *To think that the author of that book used to mop our floors!*

The next time I heard from Skip, I was back in Charlottesville. He called to say that he was going to be in town for a memorial service for the director of the university's black studies institute, and he wondered if I was available to have lunch.

"Uh, sure," I said, a little hesitantly. I couldn't imagine why he was being so generous with his time. "You can give me the titles of those books that you mentioned I should read."

"Oh, right," he said. "I've got to put that together."

I wondered briefly if his interest was romantic. I'd run across such men before: older intellectual types who fancied themselves Don Juans. They'd develop a fascination with my father, and in his absence, settle on having me as the next best thing.

A day or two before our lunch date, Skip called again to say that he had to cancel. "I was really looking forward to meeting you," he said. "But I've got to go to Washington because they're giving me this award." He hoped that I understood.

"Well, of course," I said, more confused than ever. "Wow, congratulations."

"Yeah," he answered modestly. "But listen, I've got some good news. You know that I'm under contract to write these profiles for the *New Yorker*. Well, I talked to the editor, Tina Brown, and she's interested in a piece about Anatole."

I hadn't known about the contract. I swelled up again, this time with my own naïveté, which threatened to rise in my throat and choke me. Besides being an academic, Skip was a writer too. Of course his interest in my father's story would involve telling it.

"Isn't that great?" Skip asked.

No, I told him. It wasn't great. Not at all. *I* was planning on writing about my father. "As you know," I added pointedly.

"Well, why haven't you, then?" he asked, a new sharp tone in his voice. "You've known for over five years now."

I couldn't believe this. "I'm not going to fight with you over my own father like he's some sort of commodity," I said.

"I'm not trying to scoop you, Bliss," Skip said, sounding insulted.

My voice rose. I didn't care who the hell he was. But I couldn't make the Harvard professor understand how important it was to me to be the one to publicly identify my father as black for the first time.

"You're worried about the stigma. That's it. Isn't it?" he said. "You're afraid of being identified as black."

Now it was my turn to sound insulted. I told Gates that I felt I'd been done an injustice by having my father's ancestry kept from me, and that it was unfair for him to wrest away control over my identity once again. But of course my personal battle was not his concern. My dad was the most well known defector from the black race in the latter half of the twentieth century, and Gates was determined to tell his story.

We hung up at a crossroads. As he continued to call throughout the fall, trying to win my cooperation — and by extension, my family's — my trash-talking buddy Skip rapidly disappeared. Messages from Henry Louis Gates, Professor Gates, Dr. Gates, and then finally Dr. Henry Louis Gates Jr. piled up on my answering machine.

We argued back and forth. He later told my mother that except for Louis Farrakhan, nobody had ever been as angry with him. He kept insisting that his article wouldn't get in the way of my own writing project; in fact it might generate more interest. He even offered to ask Tina Brown if she'd run a thousand-word essay from me about my dad in an upcoming "black issue" of the magazine.

"I told you, I'm not ready yet," I said petulantly.

Eventually Skip realized that he was barking up the wrong tree. Someone introduced him to my mother, whom he managed to persuade to participate with the argument that of all the black writers who were lining up to take on the subject of Anatole Broyard, he would be the most sympathetic.

The article appeared the following June; I flew up to Boston the day the issue was released. A row of *New Yorker*s lined the glass window of a Logan Airport newsstand. The white wrapper advertising highlights from the magazine read in big black letters: WHITE LIKE ME. THE PASSING OF ANATOLE BROYARD. I had a wild impulse to charge inside the store and rip all the magazines down. *I wasn't ready yet.*

I headed to the house of my dad's old pal Mike Miller, where family friends were gathering. The party had been planned the way politicians plan events for election night, allowing room for positive and negative contingencies, with lots of booze and food on hand. I'd managed to get an advance copy of the issue, and I'd spent the last twenty-four hours poring over the twenty pages recounting my father's life, and my own, underlining passages and taking notes.

I read about my grandparents Nat and Edna, and my father's childhood. I read about what people had thought and said about my dad—his racial identity and romantic career—behind his back. I read about my father's desire to write fiction and the theory that he was unable to do so because he was living a lie. I read about that day at the hospital when I was told the secret, and how my aunt Shirley thought that I was handling the news rather well. I read about this man, my dad, who was a "virtuoso of ambiguity and equivocation" and "a connoisseur of the liminal—of crossing over and…getting over." And I read about my own need to now reformulate who it was that I understood my father—and myself—to be.

Years later I'd realize that my biggest fear was that Gates, a stranger who had never even met my father, would understand him better than I could, who had known and lived with him for most of twenty-four years; that I'd be shut out of the conversation by their shared language of blackness. And so, most of all, I read for the ways that Gates had gotten my father wrong.

"It's not so bad," people at the party said. "It could have been worse."

And they were right: the piece was not unsympathetic, despite its summation of my father's life as a kind of Faustian bargain. But my family and I stood stiff with anger, blinded under the glare of this sudden spotlight. The characterization of my father as an obsessive seducer of women particularly upset my mother. My brother, who was sensitive to any slight of our dad, talked about wanting to punch the professor's lights out. I took issue with Gates's claim that my father wanted to be someone other than Anatole Broyard. "The exact opposite is true," I said to anyone who would listen. "He just wanted to be himself, without all the restrictions and stereotypes of being black."

For their part, my father's friends disputed the extent to which my father's racial identity was described as a secret—most everyone in his life knew. And they especially took objection to Gates's portrayal of my dad as evasive or a trickster. My father's charm, unlike that of some charismatic people, didn't rest in his mysteriousness but in how genuinely he connected to others. My father's friends were smart, observant, sensitive people; they couldn't have been fooled so easily.

But, someone pointed out, there was no denying that earning a long profile in the favored magazine of the country's intelligentsia represented a certain level of achievement in a person's life. Then the conversation moved on. Anatole had been dead for nearly six years now, and these various friends from the different walks of his life welcomed the chance to catch up.

The next day I returned to Charlottesville, where I had decided to spend the summer. I'd just graduated from the writing program, and I busied myself trying to figure out how to assemble the life of a writer. One morning I received a thick envelope in the mailbox. It was from Gates's research assistant, and it contained all the genealogy that had been collected to prove my father's race. I could barely make out the various names on the census records, obituaries, and marriage licenses, which appeared to have been photocopied many times. But there was a copy of my father's birth certificate, which I hadn't looked at since my trip to New Orleans three years earlier. Someone had penned the word "colored" in the margin in case the "(col)" following my father's name wasn't clear. On my own birth certificate, my father's race was listed as white.

Gates had advised my mother when they were discussing my objections to his article that the best thing she could do was to help me accept my blackness. He suggested that I could even petition the court in Connecticut to change my father's race to "black" on the record of my own birth. As I filed away these papers with the rest of my genealogical data, I wondered how a man whose lifework was dedicated to the notion that a person's race was the most signifying element about him could propose that switching sides was as easy as changing a word on a piece of paper, as simple as restyling one's hair.

In September a friend from high school called to let me know that another friend of ours, Eric, had died. He'd been sick with a brain tumor for a few months, and I'd missed my chance to visit him in the hospital when his wife, Amy, who also went to our high school and had been a good friend of mine, was still allowing people to come.

Everyone from our class and the class above us was flying in from around the country for the memorial service, and I promised that I'd be there too.

I'd lost touch with many of these people since my parents had left Connecticut seven years earlier, but I was reminded over the course of the visit how intimately these friends had known me and my family and how they were among the shrinking population in my life who had known my dad. Yet the specter of the *New Yorker* profile, which described my father's acceptance by the Connecticut gentry as the ultimate test of his reinvented self, made me feel awkward and self-conscious. Over the years I'd told a few of my closer friends about my dad's secret, and since I'd arrived, one or two people had mentioned quietly that they'd seen the article, but for the most part the subject wasn't openly addressed.

On Sunday morning before the service, we were hanging out at the home of two other high school friends who'd ended up marrying each other. They lived in the kind of eighteenth-century farmhouse that my own parents would have coveted: low-beamed ceilings, oversized fireplace, and wide pine floorboards. A group of people were gathered on the couch, leafing through old photo albums, when my friend Nick, on seeing a picture of one of the two black guys in our upper school, made a joke about never being able to tell the men apart. A few people laughed, and I noticed Chris, the same guy who'd gone after Bob that day in the lunchroom, glance at me. Now I was the one unseen at the far end of the table. I got up and left the room.

Compared to the jokes that I'd made in the lunchroom, Nick's was pretty benign. Part of what made everyone laugh was the fact that Nick had been particularly close with Ed, the other black guy at our school. Of course he would recognize him. But as I walked down the hallway toward the bathroom, I was shaking. A little while later, I pulled Nick aside and told him about my father's ancestry. He grinned and said, "So you're telling me you're a sister?" And then I told him how his comment had made me feel.

"But you know me, Bliss," he said. "You know I'm not a racist. That's just my obnoxious sense of humor."

The problem was, I had lost my sense of humor, at least on this score. I could no longer locate myself in the world I was raised in. I didn't have a perspective on the landscape anymore; I couldn't gauge how big anything was, or how small. It was as if my own life in Connecticut had existed only in my father's fantasies, and now that they'd been laid bare, I'd ceased to exist there at all. One night over the weekend, I kept my friend Holly awake for hours, questioning her about who I'd been back then and what role I'd played among our gang. I honestly couldn't remember.

I knew that these old friends looked to me to set the tone about my father's blackness. If I didn't make a big deal out of it, then neither would they. They'd look past it, just as we had looked past that time when we'd seen another friend's mother run screaming across their front lawn as her husband chased her and the friend's little brother hopped up on his father's back, crying and yelling for him to stop. It was clear that we'd seen something we shouldn't have, and so we gathered our things together and stood to go.

But I wasn't sure I wanted to pretend that everything was still the same, even if I could. The world and manner in which we'd been brought up were implicated by the revelation about my father. I was coming to realize that, like the old Groucho Marx joke, one of the attractions this particular club held for my dad was the fact that it wouldn't have accepted him as a member.

My friends had liked, or even loved, my father, especially the boys, whom my dad had talked to like men, over beers and cheese and crackers (which I was dispatched to the kitchen to fetch for them) after games of touch football or swims in our pool. He showed these young men that literature and the emotions it invoked could be sexy and cool. He told them stories about women and war and running a bookstore in Greenwich Village. But mostly he asked them about themselves, and as they formulated their answers, he taught them that they actually had something to say.

Nevertheless, over the weekend, I'd heard that in Eric's hospital room, back in June when the *New Yorker* article came out, the word "nigger" had been tossed around in conversation. I wasn't told whether the term was used in connection with my dad or not, and I didn't ask. But I decided then and there that I would no longer put myself in the position of finding out what these people thought about my father—and me. I would never give them the opportunity to shut me out.

I left town shortly after the memorial service and didn't return for years. When people asked me where I was from, I started to answer that although I'd been raised in Connecticut, that fact didn't say anything about me. I began to joke that I didn't even like driving through the state.

Before I left, though, at the church that Sunday afternoon, as I was waiting for Eric's service to start, I felt a hand touch my shoulder. I turned around and saw Dawn, the girl who'd made the comment about being one of the few chips in the cookie.

"Is that Bliss Broyard?" she said. We hadn't seen each other in ten years.

I nodded and said hello.

"Well, bless you," she said, smiling broadly.

Perhaps Dawn was just happy to see me, but I imagined as I watched her walk away down the aisle that actually she'd seen the article about my dad, and her blessing was a welcoming home of a different sort.

I took advantage of being up north to visit my mother on Martha's Vineyard, where she was in the process of taking up residence full-time. I'd been there for a few days when I answered a phone call from someone asking for Sandy Broyard.

"Anatole's wife," the woman said in an accent that I couldn't place.

"Can I tell her who's calling?" I asked.

"Bliss?" the woman said. "Is that her daughter?"

"Yes."

"Well, hello," the woman said, her voice suddenly excited. "This is Vivian Carter, your cousin from California." She went on to explain that she and my father were second cousins, which made Vivian and me second cousins once removed. She said something about six brothers and started rattling off a list of names: Emile, Octave, Anthony, Henry, Gilbert, and Paul, my great-grandfather, whom she had known when she was a child in New Orleans.

"I read about your dad in that magazine," she said. "And I've been wanting to get in touch with you ever since. The article was full of lies. Your father was white."

I sat down on my mother's bed. "What do you mean?"

"There was this woman at the Board of Health in New Orleans who used to change people's birth certificates," Vivian said. "It was written up in all the newspapers." She told me that the Broyards were French, that they'd always been French, that she'd been researching the family for years.

I fantasized briefly about proving Gates wrong, forcing the *New Yorker* to print a retraction explaining that all of this had turned out to be a colossal mistake.

"Why would this woman want to change someone's birth certificate?" I asked.

"Because she was trying to pin something on them."

"But I've also seen Broyards listed as mulatto in the census."

"They could have had Indian blood. The Indians were listed as mulattoes too."

"Is it a problem," I asked, "if we are part black?"

"Well, it doesn't matter, because we're not," Vivian said breezily. "We're all white. And there are other Broyards out here in LA, and they're white too."

She urged me to come out to California and see for myself. I said that I would try. In the meantime I offered to send her the genealogy I'd collected so far. I hung up the phone, unsure what to make of this news.

That night I called up Todd, and we joked that next we'd learn that we were really Jewish or that we were descended from English royalty. For my mother's part, she felt vindicated by the phone call. After living with my father for thirty years, she didn't think of him as black, insofar as she thought of him as any race at all. I understood her reasoning: My father had never played by the rules; why should we have expected him to follow the one-drop definition of blackness? Such arbitrary boundaries were no match for his outsized personality, and it was incomprehensible to imagine anyone but him arbitrating over his identity. But it had never occurred to me that other branches of the family had followed the same course.

A few weeks later, I received a card from Vivian saying how glad she was that we had connected. She wrote that the article had really done a number on her. She included a picture of herself and her husband, Anthony, posed on a balcony outside of what looked to be a condominium complex. The month and year, September 1996, were recorded on the back. Vivian had told me on the phone that her husband was a photographer, and I imagined her waking up one morning to the bright blue sky in the photo's background and asking him to set up his tripod outside to take a picture for her newfound cousin back east. I imagined Vivian thinking to herself, and perhaps even saying to her husband too, *I want to show her how white we are.*

The couple looked much younger than their age of midsixties. Her husband was tall with thick gray hair, brown eyes, and square, handsome features. She wore her straight dark hair in a side part and had black eyes and thin lips, which were accented with bright pink lipstick. They looked happy, and they looked almost entirely white except for their skin, which glowed with a warm yellow undertone, as if it had absorbed some of the sun's light and was now reflecting it back.

I believed that most white people accepted the couple as white. Black people, on the other hand, would recognize their roots in an instant.

I began to look for other Broyards in Los Angeles to see on what side of the color line they fell. I came across a review in an LA paper of a play called *Inside the Creole Mafia*, coauthored by someone named Mark Broyard. The review, titled "Skin Test," described the play's spoofing of the Creole community's obsession with color: the intrigue of who was passing and who was not and the tests once used to gain entry to dances — was the person lighter than a paper bag? could he pass a fine-tooth comb through his hair? I thought to myself that this guy and I had to be related.

I telephoned Mark and told him who I was.

"I think we might be cousins," I said.

"I'm sure we are," Mark said. "I'm in the middle of reading your father's memoir right now."

My dad's account of life in Greenwich Village in the 1940s, *Kafka Was the Rage*, which my mother published after his death, had just come out in paperback. Mark told me that as a musician and an artist, he related to my father's story about art and music (and women) beyond the family connection.

"Man, your dad could write!" he said.

I was so excited to find a relative who spoke the language of books and making art that I forgot for a moment about the purpose of my call.

"Oh yeah. So Mark. What's the deal? Are the LA Broyards white or black?"

"Well, I'm a Broyard," he said, sounding annoyed by the question. "And I live in Los Angeles, and I'm black. I know other Broyards out here, and they're black too."

I told him about my conversation with Vivian Carter.

Now Mark sounded sad. "Yeah, I've heard about her. I think my father talks to her once in a while. Well," he said. "I guess you're just going to have to come out here and check us out for yourself."

~9~

In September of 1997, a few months after I spoke to Mark Broyard, I flew out to Los Angeles. On the second morning of my trip, I headed in my rental car to a local Creole restaurant called Harold and Belle's to meet the white and black clans of the LA Broyards. Mark had picked the place and was contacting his relatives to invite them along, and I'd relayed the plans to Vivian Carter, whom I told to bring the family members that she knew.

I was staying with the older brother of a friend from college. Earlier that morning I asked his wife to help me with directions to the restaurant, and after looking up the address on the map, she said with alarm in her voice that it was located in South-Central. I had already told this couple my father's story, but I could see that this detail — I was heading to the land of the LA riots — made my black ancestry true to her in a way that it wasn't before. Although she was the metro editor of a local paper, which I imagined would make her familiar, if not comfortable, with the different parts of the city, she talked about South-Central as if it were behind enemy lines. She made me promise to ask one of my relatives to lead me out of the neighborhood when we were done.

I started to feel apprehensive when I turned onto Jefferson Boulevard, where Harold and Belle's was located, but as I passed some automart stores and a hair salon and then a gas station and a bank — all the usual features of an urban landscape — and noticed the people

on the street — mostly women pushing strollers — I couldn't see what
was supposed to be so threatening about the neighborhood.

I pulled up to the restaurant a few minutes early. I was sitting in
my car, putting on some lipstick, when suddenly a man's face appeared
outside my window. When I turned toward him, the man smiled and
held up a bouquet of yellow tulips. I opened the car door and Mark
Broyard leaned inside to hug me. "Welcome, cousin," he said.

We sat in the car for a moment, looking through the genealogy
that I'd brought, trying to figure out how we were connected. But I
didn't need old census records to tell me that this man and I shared
the same blood. His compact, narrow frame reminded me of my
father's or my brother's build, and he shared my dad's smoky good
looks — with soft brown eyes, a cleft chin, and a mustache.

Everyone else arrived at once. Thirteen of us in all gathered in the
lobby of the restaurant; from the black side, ten members of Mark's
extended family, and from the white side, only Vivian and Anthony.
Vivian explained that the other relatives she invited couldn't make it
on such short notice. I was trying to pick no side, as the intermediary
of sorts.

If I hadn't been told already who was living as white and who
was living as black, I wouldn't have known. In the pictures that were
taken outside under the midday sun after the meal, we all appear
roughly the same shade of golden brown. We also looked as if we'd
been raised in the same types of neighborhoods and shopped at the
same types of stores, with everyone dressed in comfortable stylish
clothing, wearing tasteful jewelry and chic sunglasses. My relatives did
not look like the kind of black people my host's wife might have pictured that morning on discovering that I was meeting them in South-
Central LA.

I pulled out my genealogy again, in hopes of establishing some
common ground. Nobody could make much sense of the jumble

of census records and obituaries, but Vivian, who seemed most familiar with the family tree, managed to explain how everyone was
related.

After we were seated, the waitress came to take our orders. She
looked to be a Creole, and as I watched her move around the table,
chatting easily with my relatives about the specials of the day and answering their inquiries after the owner, I wondered whether she would
see me as one of them. Suddenly it was my turn. I hadn't had a chance
to look at the menu and blurted out that I would have a club sandwich. Mark's father, Emile, who was seated across from me, looked
down and shook his head. He told the waitress to bring me some
gumbo too.

"She just found out she's Creole," he explained. "She's still learning." He turned to me and said, "Gumbo, that's what we are."

Heads nodded around the table. "That's right," a voice chimed in.

"A little bit of everything," Emile continued. "Black, white, French,
Indian. A delicious stew." With his big belly and knowing smile, Emile
was the elder statesman at the table. A lifelong smoker, he'd been af-
flicted with emphysema in recent years, which turned his voice husky

and thin. Everyone quieted to better hear him. "I'm curious," he said, nodding at me. "What did you and your brother think when you heard that your father was black?"

"It must have been quite a shock," one of the younger cousins offered.

"It wasn't, actually," I said. "Suddenly a lot of things made sense—like why we never saw my father's family when we were growing up." I explained that we'd learned about the presence of a secret a few weeks earlier, and we were relieved that it wasn't something more troubling. I told them Todd's joke about always knowing that he wasn't built like the average white guy, which made everyone laugh.

Emile took an envelope out of his jacket and handed it to me across the table. Inside were photos of my dad, fifty years earlier, on a street corner wearing his army uniform; his sisters as young women; and my grandparents Nat and Edna.

"You knew my father's family?" I asked, looking up at Emile.

He shook his head. "These were taken by some mutual friends," he said. "But we always knew about your dad, and your family too, out in Connecticut. You just didn't know about us."

I imagined my family as a subject over dinner—someone mentioning that she'd spotted my father's name in the newspaper or a magazine, a debate ensuing about the choices he'd made, difficult questions from children about why a person wouldn't want to be black. I pictured myself at dinner with my own family, asking my father why we never saw his mother or his sisters, scolding him for his old-fashioned ideas and bigoted ways.

Vivian had some photos too. Hers were organized in a series of albums that she'd brought in a big plastic bag along with her folders of genealogy. She had the most documentation about the family of anyone there, although she had the least contact with the members themselves. She was sitting next to Emile, and as she went through her pictures, naming this person and that person, she kept mentioning how all of them went for white.

Emile looked over her shoulder and asked, "So he doesn't own up to his color?" And then he'd pick out someone else, "She doesn't either?"

Vivian's photo album made its way around the table. As Mark passed it to me, he chucked me in the ribs and whispered: "Check out all these white Broyards."

We both laughed under our breath. Most of the people in the photos looked phenotypically black. Later I wondered whether the pictures we'd taken after the meal would eventually end up in Vivian's album, where we'd all be reclaimed as white one day too.

For the next three days, I shuttled between the different camps of the LA Broyards, learning about the various paths my relatives had taken as they negotiated the color line. First I visited Vivian.

She opened the door, hugged me hello, and immediately began complaining about the conversation during brunch.

"Black this, black that," she said. "It was too much, didn't you think?"

Before I had a chance to answer, she took off into the apartment to give me a tour. I followed her through the living room, past the dining alcove and galley kitchen, into one crowded bedroom, then a second that had been turned into an office, and then out onto a balcony, where we stopped. I recognized the setting from the picture Vivian had sent.

"It's nice," I said.

"It's private," she said.

Then we headed back inside, down the hallway, past a row of photographs. I paused at one of a young woman with big brown eyes and olive skin. "Who's this?" I asked, turning to Vivian and Anthony.

"My grandmother," Anthony said.

"She's beautiful," I said, surprised to see the picture of a relative who looked recognizably black hung in such a prominent location.

We sat down at the dining room table. Birth certificates belonging to various relatives covered the tabletop—some carrying the racial designation white and others with a "col" appearing after the name. Vivian invited me to inspect them more closely.

"See how the *c-o-l* is sometimes written faintly, the letters made up by a series of dots?" she asked. "That means that the people at the Board of Health weren't sure what race the person was." She told me that she'd taken my father's own birth certificate (which I'd sent to her along with my package of genealogy) to a handwriting expert, who determined that the notation "colored" in the margin had been penned by a different hand from the rest. That was proof, Vivian said, that the record had been doctored.

I looked at Anthony for some recognition of the paranoia in his wife's appraisal, but he was smiling and nodding along, as if he were proud of her ingenious sleuthing.

"But I got this copy from Henry Louis Gates," I said. "I imagine that the note in the margin was made by the person who collected the genealogy for him."

"Exactly!" Vivian said, pounding her finger on the tabletop. "That writer was trying to pin something on your dad. What right does he have to decide what your father was?"

Actually, I'd been wondering the very same thing. "But you'll admit, won't you, that somewhere, way back, there were some black ancestors?"

No, Vivian wouldn't admit that. She preferred to attack the system instead. Why should she let some outdated one-drop rule held over from slavery times tell her who she could be? Besides, she didn't feel black, she said.

"That's right," Anthony agreed. "It's all about the attitude, and we don't have the black attitude."

"Which is what?" I asked.

"Inferior," Anthony explained. "Lower class."

*   *   *

Vivian and Anthony wanted to know what I would tell people when they asked me what I was. Before I could answer, Vivian volunteered, "When people ask me, I turn the question around and ask them why they want to know. I tell them"—her voice went coy and she smiled seductively—"'I'll be whoever you want me to be.'" She leaned back in her chair, looking satisfied. Other times, Vivian said, she might tell them that she was from Louisiana, and they'd say, "Oh, so you're one of those crazy Cajuns." Now her smile turned cockeyed. "And I tell them, 'That's right!'"

"Well, I think I'll just tell the truth," I said, when Vivian was finished.

"The truth," she repeated with a dismissive wave of her hand.

"That I'm mixed," I continued. "That I'm Norwegian and Creole." I hesitated for a moment. Why wasn't I saying that I would tell people that I was black? Wasn't that what I expected of Vivian and Anthony? "And I'll explain what Creole means," I said more firmly, "in case they don't know. That it means French and African."

Vivian jabbed her finger at me. "The minute you say that, people will try to pin it on you. They'll start thinking differently about you." She crossed her arms over her chest, scrutinizing me. "You don't look black and you weren't raised with the black attitude. Why say anything at all?"

I knew that no matter what else lay behind Vivian and Anthony's pitch for whiteness, they truly believed that they had my best interests at heart. I tried to explain that it seemed easier to be honest, that I didn't feel ashamed of my black ancestry, that times were different now.

"Oh no," Anthony said, shaking his head. "There's still a stigma attached to being black. There are still plenty of people who are prejudiced."

I said that I didn't want to hide anything. That I was afraid of being caught in a lie. "What if I have a child and it comes out dark?"

"But that won't happen so long as you don't marry beneath you," Vivian said.

"Beneath me?" I repeated. "What does that mean?"

"She means education level," Anthony said. "Stuff like that."

I was tempted to tell them that I didn't want to end up like them: lost inside the maze of my own arguments, trampling on some part of myself in the process of trying to flee it. But no matter what, they were my family, and I didn't want to hurt them, so I told them that I'd never had any Broyard relatives growing up, and now that I was finally meeting them, I didn't want to do anything that might estrange us again.

Vivian grabbed my hand and squeezed it. "No, you should never lose touch with your family." She told me about a cousin who lived on the outskirts of LA who didn't see the rest of the family. She tried to get him to come to the brunch and meet some of the relatives, but he was living as white, and he worried that if he was seen associating with blacks, it would raise suspicions.

I pointed out the unlikehood of his bumping into any white people he knew in South-Central, but Vivian just shrugged and kept talking. "It was his mother's doing," she explained. "She was illiterate, and she desperately wanted her children to learn to read and write. So back in New Orleans in the 1930s, she changed the family's last name to something slightly different so she could send her kids to the white school, which, of course, was much better than the colored one."

I nodded. I could understand this reasoning.

"I'm the only one he talks to," Vivian went on, "and he's petrified that I'm going to die and he won't have any connection to the family at all."

I wondered what he'd gained for all that he'd lost; whether it was worth it.

"He's obsessed with genealogy," Vivian continued, "but he's afraid to request the records from the state archives himself because someone might connect his last name with the Broyard name. So he has me write away for them instead." She scooped up the pile of certificates still scattered across the table. "That's how I ended up with these."

A sudden urgency entered Vivian's voice: "But I never cut off ties with my family. I see everyone when I go back to New Orleans, no matter how they live. My cousin, though"—she tossed the pile of records back onto the table—"this is all he's got."

The next morning I met Erin, Mark's sister, at her mother-in-law's house, where she and her husband, Michael, were living, so we could ride together over to her dad's place. The house was in Hancock Park, an upscale Los Angeles enclave. As Erin showed me around the Tudor-style mansion—the gardens, pool, and guesthouse out back—she told me stories about the previous owner, Nat King Cole.

Cole bought the house in 1949. He was the first black person to move into the neighborhood, and he was at the height of his fame. But the white residents didn't want him there and even formed an association to keep him out. One day, Erin told me, Cole was invited to a local party, and he thought that he'd been accepted at last, but when he arrived at the door, he was told to go around to the back. A maid showed him to the piano. He'd been invited to play. "They could never get him to leave here, though." Erin shook her head. "He stayed until he died, and then Michael's parents bought it from his widow." Tourists still stopped their cars out front from time to time to take pictures.

She explained that her husband's family owned a chain of fried chicken restaurants called the Golden Bird that was mostly concentrated in South-Central. At one time it had been the biggest black-owned business in LA, but during the riots in 1992, seven of the ten stores were looted and vandalized, and two others were burned to the ground. Michael, the president of the Golden Bird, had appeared on Oprah and ABC News and in newspapers across the country, vowing that he'd stay in the neighborhood and rebuild. Governor Pete Wilson even honored him that year in his State of the State address, calling

Michael a hero for his commitment to his community. But, Erin said, five years later, insurance and business improvement loans hadn't covered even half of all the losses, and the majority of the population in South-Central had shifted from African Americans to Latinos, who didn't like southern fried chicken. The family started selling off the stores one by one, and Erin and Michael had moved in with his mother until they could figure out their next step.

We were driving now in Erin's massive SUV over to her parents' condo. We'd quickly fallen into a comfortable rhythm with each other, which made these personal revelations come easily. I sensed that Erin was proud of her husband and his family, but I also thought that she was trying to tell me something about black success and black struggles.

"Michael seems like an impressive guy," I said. "I couldn't help but notice, he's pretty cute too."

Erin grinned. "I'm telling you, girl. There were a lot of unhappy women the day that we got married."

I imagined that there were a lot of unhappy men too. Erin had beauty pageant good looks: everything in place and perfect—flawless skin, sweeping cheekbones, big toothy smile—with a friendly and wholesome sheen. Michael, appropriately, was all-American hand-some: square jaw, sparkling eyes, and wide shoulders that whittled down to a narrow waist. At the brunch, though, I'd noticed that he was much darker than Erin was. In fact, he'd been the darkest person there by far.

"Did his color make a difference to anyone?" I asked.

"Are you kidding?" she said, glancing toward me. "It definitely raised some eyebrows."

"Even though he came from such an accomplished family?"

She shook her head. "Didn't matter." We were quiet for a moment, and then she spoke again. "It's funny, though. I never saw him as being different. I really didn't."

Erin explained that her parents, particularly her mother, had made a point when they moved to LA to give Erin and her brothers a grounding in an African American identity, in addition to their Creole roots. In places like Jack and Jill, the nationwide organization for African American children, Erin had a chance to meet a kind of black people she hadn't known in New Orleans: kids who went to different churches, ate different foods, and often looked different—darker, more African—than she did.

"And that was fine with me," she said. "My mom would always say, 'We come in all colors of the rainbow.'"

So Erin was unprepared when she traveled with Michael to New Orleans soon after they got engaged, and some of her relatives had taken her aside and said, "Oh, he's a dark boy, but he's nice."

Emile told me the story behind the family's decision to leave Louisiana. We were sitting with Mark and Erin around a patio table under a big umbrella by his condominium complex's pool. "In 1960 integration was finally getting started in New Orleans," Emile explained. "One day, Kippy—he's our oldest, although he was just in kindergarten at the time—anyway, Kippy was walking to school with some other kids from the neighborhood, and these white boys drove by in a truck and threw rotten fruit and a brick at them. That was it." He sat back in his chair and rested his hand on the oxygen tank that his wife, Beverly, had insisted he bring outside.

"We all decided to leave at once, me, Beverly, my two sisters, and their husbands," Emile said. They sent the women and the kids ahead on the train, and then the men drove the cars loaded up with their stuff in a convoy across the country.

Erin chimed in: "It wasn't safe back then to drive through certain parts of the country if you were black."

"It's still not," Mark added.

"Lots of people were heading out to California then," Emile said.

"Many of them became a part of the Creole community here that was growing up along Jefferson Boulevard, and others...well, they disappeared."

"Disappeared how?" I asked.

He shrugged. "They started living as white."

I asked Emile if Vivian and Anthony were among the people who had disappeared into whiteness.

"Not entirely," he said. "Vivian will call when they're in the area, and they'll ask if they can stop by. But we're never invited back to their house."

Erin said it was hard for her to understand Vivian's choice when she'd also heard stories from her parents about relatives who could have passed and didn't. "They sat in the back of the bus in New Orleans because they were proud of being black," she said. "I respect that."

"You have to understand Vivian's choice and respect it too," Emile said. He turned to me. "Just like we understood why your father kept his identity a secret. He was trying to make a better life for himself and your brother and you. But I do get tired of Vivian and Anthony dipping into our lives whenever they feel like it and we can't be a part of theirs."

Mark said that he felt sad for people who didn't see the beauty of what it meant to be black in America, and the unique beauty of what it meant to be a Creole. "Why just want to be bland and boring and white? We weren't raised to see that as any great advantage," he said. "Our parents were successful. We were fed, clothed, had a roof over our heads, and we were happy. It didn't seem like we were missing out on anything so wonderful by not being white."

That night I had drinks with another set of cousins, Robert and his sister Marchele, at a trendy bar in West Hollywood. We sat perched on stools around a high table in a quiet corner. Robert's friend Steve from grade school had joined us too. Steve was a black guy who actually looked black compared to Marchele and Robert, whose honey coloring and loose curls made them look as if they might be anything from Italian to Puerto Rican to Jewish.

"Steve," Robert said, turning to his friend, "tell Bliss how the white kids used to come up to me in school and say, 'Tell them, Robbie, tell them how you're really black!'"

"That was tripping," Steve said, shaking his head. "But, hey, at least they weren't patting your hair all the time."

We all cracked up, and I let that wave of laughter ride me into a secret world where I could talk about white people as if I had not been raised as one myself.

"Sometimes they think I'm trying to trick them or I'm making a joke when I tell them my father was black," I said.

Robert and Marchele knew what I was talking about.

"Or if they do believe me, they expect me to start acting different, more black or something, which, you know, I'm still learning." I did a mock imitation of a girl from the 'hood, rolling my head and snapping my fingers, which broke everyone up again. "But when I'm dating someone new, especially a white guy, I make it a point to tell them about my dad's ancestry."

"Right away?" Marchele asked.

I nodded. "Before they can say anything that might offend me. Of course they usually get offended that I think they might make some comment. But I know what white people are like, after all."

Robert shook his head. "They don't even realize when they're doing it," he said. "I have some friends, close friends, who are white, who have said stuff in front of me. It's this very subtle attitude of superiority. But because I don't look black, they don't think of me that way. It's like, 'Oh, Robert, you're different.'"

Marchele told me that she had gone through a period of being very militant, announcing her blackness everywhere she went. But it got exhausting after a while. "And people end up thinking that you're the one who's hung up about your racial identity," I said, "because you keep bringing it up all the time."

"Right," Marchele said. "Exactly."

I took a sip of my drink. The conversation had winded me. I'd never talked about this stuff before, never known other people who'd been in these same situations that I viewed as so odd and singular.

Marchele said that she worked as an agent in Hollywood now, which led people to assume that she was Jewish. "I don't really mind," she said, shrugging. "If it makes people feel more comfortable with me than…" But her looks and racial identity made it hard to date. She never knew when to tell men. "Some people my age still have strong feelings about interracial dating," she said. "They're old enough to remember when the schools were being integrated."

Robert and Marchele described the moment when they realized that some love interest might care about their black ancestry—a joke the person made, or even a look given to somebody of color on the street, and how it was sometimes easier and less painful to just end the relationship rather than confront that person's belief. I wondered if this worry was part of the reason that neither of the siblings had married, although they were both in their midforties.

Robert explained that when they were growing up, their father had counseled them to not tell people about their ancestry if they didn't have to. Although their father came from an illustrious Creole family—an elementary school in New Orleans was named in honor of his father, who had been a civil rights activist and a community doctor—he couldn't pass the "paper bag test." When they were kids growing up in the South, Robert remembered, his father would send his mother into certain stores because he wasn't allowed to go inside himself. And if they were with their dad, the family couldn't sit in the nicer "whites only" section of the beach or the movie theater with their lighter-skinned relatives.

"He doesn't really talk about it," Robert said. "But obviously it affected him. He wanted to protect us from all of that, and so he reasoned that if someone didn't need to know, then why bring it up."

I wondered to myself whether their father's tact had made things more or less confusing for them. I believe that my father had wanted to protect us too, but we were never given the choice about how to handle our ancestry.

Steve and Marchele went home, and Robert and I moved to the bar. The bartender brought over another round of martinis. Robert and I both reached for our wallets, but he insisted on buying the drinks. "You're my cousin," he said. "I want to treat you."

Robert told me about the first time he realized that he was black. A few years after arriving in Los Angeles, his family moved to Altadena, up in the hills, where they were the second African American family in the neighborhood. Their new neighbors seemed to view them more as a curiosity than anything else — some in his family had light skin and blue eyes, and they all looked so different from one another. Even their dad didn't appear typically black, with his straight hair and American Indian features.

Before long, Robert became close friends with a white boy down the street who wanted Robert to join his Boy Scout troop. "A few days later, though, he came back and told me, 'They won't let you join because your father's a Negro.'" Robert paused, recalling the moment. "I remember my ears roaring at that word. It was the first time anybody had ever said that to me, and I was just shocked. What was the big deal? Why would that matter? And then it hit me that instead of me just being me, I was a Negro now too."

Robert looked down at his drink and said, "I've never really felt accepted by either side. There's a lot of prejudice on the black side too." He glanced at me. "It's like, 'Yeah, maybe you're a brother, but you've got the good skin, the good hair, you didn't go through what we went through.' I get that from my own family even," he said, widening his eyes.

He shrugged and continued, "But this life has its benefits, I guess.

Since I'm not on one side or the other, I can see all sides. I can see things from both the black and the white perspective." He raised his glass. "Not that many people can say that, can they?"

I touched my glass against his. "They certainly can't."

And then I was flying home. On the approach to LaGuardia Airport, the stewardess came over the intercom to remind us to set our watches ahead three hours to the local time. As I adjusted my watch, that device in old movies to show the passage of time leaped to mind: the hands of the clock spinning wildly forward or the pages of a calendar falling away like leaves. I half expected my own watch to start spinning out of control. I'd changed and learned much more than seemed possible over the course of five short days.

Before I parted ways with the different sets of LA Broyards, they each offered a piece of advice about what they imagined my dad would have wanted me to do.

Vivian said: "The way I look at it, your father gave you the gift of whiteness, and out of respect for his memory, you should follow his example."

Robert said: "I'm sure if your father had lived longer, he would have told you about his ancestry eventually. He probably just wanted you to have the choice to decide who you wanted to be."

And Erin said: "I feel like your dad left this subject of race for you to tackle. In his time he couldn't address it and still do what he wanted in his life. But you can. And that's what you need to keep doing."

I gazed out the airplane window, down onto the city, all lit up and twinkling, as bright and promising as a new star. I wondered about my ancestral city, New Orleans, and how one place and one family could give rise to three such different approaches to being black — or not — in the world. And I knew that before I could understand what my father's blackness meant to him, and means to me, I would have to go back to the place where his secret history began.

II.

Infinity of Traces

~10~

In Washington, DC, across Louisiana, and especially in New Orleans, I searched for the story of my father's history... In the windowless basements of courthouses that sit at the bottom of long metal stairs; in glass-partitioned special collection areas at state and university libraries; among row upon row of microfilm readers at the National Archives; in the brightly lit Notarial Archives, wearing cotton gloves to protect 250-year-old documents from the oils in my skin; in one-room country museums staffed by terse old lady volunteers; in the aisles of the cemetery; in the Conveyance Office up some metal stairs (*Careful, now, watch your head on that pipe*); in the office of the church in heavy fragile ledgers that record the births, deaths, and marriages in New Orleans dating back to 1718; in question after question asked from the backseat of an old man's taxicab; in a rental car with a different old man driving slowly down a country lane; in telephone calls made nervously to people whose names I found in the phone book; in carefully composed letters written to people from whom I never received any reply; among the millions of names posted to the hundreds of genealogical websites that, after pornography, are the most frequently searched destinations on the Web; in the index of *Old Families of Louisiana*; in the index of *The African American Experience in Louisiana*; in the footnotes of history books; in the pages of dissertations written forty or sixty years ago that I ordered on the Internet and were delivered to my door; in the middle of the woods at a Civil

War battleground site; and at the kitchen tables of people for whom the name Broyard held meaning.

At the end of these travels, I had an assortment of facts: What my ancestors did for work, where they lived and with whom. I knew who could read and write and who could speak English. I learned where their parents were born and what property they passed along when they died. I found records of their military service — enlistment dates and pay stubs — that did little to illuminate their experience of fighting in a war. I came across their names in the local newspapers when they had done something particularly good or bad. In those same pages I found their obituaries, in which their lives were summed up by the names of the people they'd left behind.

Besides these facts and a few stories told by the survivors, I had little else to go on. None of my ancestors made enough of an impression on the chroniclers of their time to earn mention. No diaries or packets of letters turned up in an attic somewhere that described their feelings about themselves and the world around them. A single correspondence carrying the signature of my great-grandfather Paul Broyard appears in an 1894 New Orleans newspaper, but it is coauthored by a gentleman who was a frequent contributor to the publication and likely composed the letter mostly on his own. I had even less insight into the personal lives of my father's female ancestors, whose domestic roles left little imprint on the official records.

Yet as my facts accumulated, distinct people started to take shape with personalities and opinions, particularly when set against the backdrop of New Orleans, an image of which was also materializing in my mind.

During the three years, from 2000 to 2002, that I regularly visited the city, I often ran in the mornings along the Mississippi River, the aspect of New Orleans's landscape that perhaps best accounts for its unique personality. For hundreds of years, these waters delivered Americans from the rest of the country and foreigners from all over the world to the city's shoreline, where they introduced their own customs and beliefs into the cultural mix. Shipping remains the most important commercial activity for this self-described "port at the center of the world's busiest port complex." New Orleans also owed its physical existence—the land on which it sits—to the river and its centuries-old habit of regularly overflowing its banks. More recently, Hurricane Katrina demonstrated how the Mississippi and other waters surrounding New Orleans could also, catastrophically, snatch that land away.

I usually ran along the mile-long brick promenade that sits on top of the French Quarter's levee—the mound of earth built up along the riverbank that is supposed to protect the surrounding areas from flooding. In the early morning hours, the benches along the promenade were often filled with homeless people, sleeping or organizing their possessions for the daily shuffle. On the other side of the walkway, a rocky slope led down to the river, which, depending on the time of year and the amount of recent rainfall, could range from five feet to twenty-five feet below the top of the levee. The Mississippi's surface was brown, rolling, impenetrable, but the caps of waves or some debris—a bright plastic jug spinning and jerking along, or a thick branch jutting oddly out of the water as if fighting to keep its head up—called my attention to its fast-moving current.

New Orleans hugs a sharp bend in the Mississippi, earning it the nickname Crescent City, and from the promenade, the ends of the river curved out of my sight, making it difficult to recall its great length—the fourth longest in the world if you measure it from the beginning of its tributary the Missouri, and, according to Mark Twain, the most crooked. The Mississippi didn't evoke any of my usual associations with water: the expansiveness dissolving to melancholy when standing on the edge of the ocean, or the clean deep breath of a clear flat lake. Yet as I got to know it better, I came to like it and even feel a particular kinship with it.

Algonquin Indians named the river Father of Waters, which translates literally as *misi*, big, and *sipi*, water. T. S. Eliot called it "the strong brown God." In *Life on the Mississippi*, Twain called it "a wonderful book…that was a dead language to the uneducated passenger, but which told its mind to me without reserve, delivering its most cherished secrets as clearly as if it uttered them with a voice."

On a map the Mississippi River system looks like a tree with the trunk planted in New Orleans and the branches reaching up across the United States. Sometimes, when I was running, I would picture this river tree and all the traces of earth collected from all over the country that had floated down it to make up the land beneath my feet. And then I'd think of my family tree, and the traces of my ancestors' lives that had floated down to me, and I'd try to fit together those bits and pieces into something solid, with substance and a form. And suddenly my great-great-grandfather Henry might appear in my mind's eye, blurry and fleeting, as if he were floating by on the river beside me. I would try to imagine how he'd felt when marrying my great-great-grandmother or setting off to fight in the Civil War. I'd see him as romantic and courageous, someone who took stands at important moments in American history, someone who had a hand in making history himself. Yet how accidental my picture was, made up from this flotsam of the past that happened to dislodge and remain intact during the trip down through time. I was always waiting for some fact to appear — a criminal charge, say — that would spoil the image I had conjured.

The first piece of advice that experienced genealogists offer to beginners is to rid themselves of the expectation that they will discover a famous forebear. Most everyone, whether they admit it or not, starts out with the hope of finding in their past an accomplished artist or a military hero or at least someone who was really rich. Such secondhand glory can soften the blow of one's own failures: *I may not have amounted to much, but at least my ancestors did.* People are also looking for an affirmation of the person they feel in their hearts capable of becoming. To serve your country in a war is an honorable act, but to have come from a line of men who served in wars transforms this act into an identity that a person can live by.

In the end the process of re-creating my family story was as constructed and provisional as the physical landscape of New Orleans. History, as the Italian political theorist Antonio Gramsci put it, "had deposited in me an infinity of traces without leaving an inventory." As I sifted those traces, looking for the shape of my past, I was always sifting them through a screen fashioned in my likeness, so that my origins came to resemble nothing so much as my own wishful thinking about myself.

When I arrived in New Orleans in the winter of 2000, I already knew from Internet research that the first Broyard to set foot on these shores was a white man from France named Etienne, and that he had arrived sometime in the early 1750s, thirty-odd years after the French explorer Jean-Baptiste Le Moyne, sieur de Bienville, founded the city on behalf of the French crown.

I'd also learned that a hundred years later, in the 1850s, when my great-grandfather Paul was born, the Broyards had begun to be identified in public records as mulatto or free people of color. What I didn't know was which man, or men, in the intervening generations was responsible for the change in the family's racial identity. Nor did I know what the moment of mixing was like: Was it a rape in a slave cabin or the conclusion of a business deal between a white "protector" and his quadroon mistress? Did the couple feel tenderness for each other? Or love?

My father's explanation of his origins, told to my mother and a few friends, played like a scene from a 1930s Hollywood romance, an inverted *Tarzan and His Mate*, one of his favorite movies: *My father's grandfather was walking along one day when he saw a pretty girl sitting in a coconut tree. He coaxed her down and made her his wife.* The tree was my dad's way—ironically, offensively—of acknowledging his great-grandmother's Caribbean roots, her blackness. The story also paid homage to the long line of sweet-talking Broyard men and their helplessness before a lovely face. In his memoir about Greenwich Village, my dad described how he, when walking down the street, would ditch a friend in mid-sentence to chase after an attractive girl "whose smile held the very incandescence of meaning." Ultimately, though, my father's creation myth allowed him to dismiss his bit of blackness as just another accident of lust—as inconvenient as an unwanted pregnancy and as inconsequential too, if you could harden your heart enough to cut it out.

How much my father knew about the actual truth of his family tree is anyone's guess. The preposterousness of his story tended to discourage further inquiries, as I imagine was his intention. But even among the relatives who had always known about their African ancestry, mystery or mythology seemed to surround the origins of the Broyards' mixed-race identity. The version passed down to Emile Broyard out in California had the six brothers of my great-grandfather's generation as originally hailing from Morocco—an account that explained away their looks without the taint of sub-Saharan Africa, slavery, or rape.

During my first full-scale research trip to New Orleans, I was lucky to team up with another newfound cousin from the black side, Sheila Prevost, a native of the city, who wondered the same thing I did: how mixed we were and how we got that way. Sheila and I had first bumped into each other a few months earlier on a genealogy Web site. She'd been corresponding on a "Broyard" message board, and I stumbled across a chat in progress about the *New Yorker* article on my father. After lurking for a while, I mustered up the courage to join in with the announcement that I was the daughter of the man under discussion.

Sheila, like many Broyards who stayed in the black community, viewed the outing of one of her "white" kin as both a hilarious comeuppance and a disturbing abrogation. When we finally met, she exclaimed, hooting with laughter: "Ooh, your father got caught," and then turned serious. "But nobody can tell him who he has to be."

We soon figured out that Sheila's grandmother Rose, who was still alive, was my father's first cousin. Rose didn't remember my dad—she was four when his family moved to Brooklyn—but she'd met his sisters, Shirley and Lorraine, during the visit in 1935 of which I'd seen photographs in Shirley's album. And Rose had known her grandfather Paul Broyard, who lived with her family for the first eighteen years of her life, until he died in 1940, at the age of eighty-four.

My father had also known his grandfather Paul, although he never saw him again after his family moved north, when my father was six. But his father would tell him stories, which my dad passed down to my brother and me and included in his writing. My father clearly identified with his grandfather: in his fiction, which was mostly autobiographical, he always chose the name Paul for his narrator.

According to my dad, Paul Broyard had been famous in New Orleans for his skills as a builder and his talent with the ladies. His nickname was Belhomme, beautiful man, and he was supposed to have sired "half the bastards in New Orleans," many of whom took the Broyard name. But Paul, I'd eventually discover, was also the reason that my father's family left town.

My great-grandfather was an overlap between my life and the lives of my New Orleans cousins. He made me feel as if the distance between us would be less than I'd imagined. As I planned my trip to New Orleans, I began to wonder what else Sheila and I would find in common. There was a directness in her conversation and a playfulness that was familiar to me. I started to fantasize that despite Sheila's upbringing in a black community in the South and my childhood as a white girl raised in Connecticut, we'd find that there was hardly any difference between us at all.

My first afternoon in New Orleans, Sheila picked me up at the guesthouse where I was staying for a quick tour around town. I jumped into her car, we shared a brief hug across the gear shift, and then we sped off. We were shy with each other. As Sheila pointed out the locations of various archives and historical sites of interest, she kept stealing glances at me and saying, "This is so weird." I wondered if what she meant was that my white appearance was weird. Like many of my Broyard cousins, Sheila had always known that she had kin "living on the other side," but I was the first one that she'd actually met.

With her caramel-colored skin, wavy brown hair, little button nose, and full round cheeks, Sheila looked to me as though she could be any number of things: South American, Indian or Pakistani, Puerto Rican, or light-skinned African American. People in New Orleans, however, were accustomed to her Creole looks and seemed to generally recognize her for what she was. It helped that she spoke with the Yat accent—a kind of Brooklyn drawl adopted by locals—and greeted people with the popular expression "Where y'at, girl?" and called them "bay" for "baby."

Sheila had always known about her Creole roots, but by the time she was born, in 1964, Creole identity in New Orleans had been folded into a larger black identity in the fight for civil rights. (Only in recent years have some Creoles of color started to reclaim their mixed-race ancestry.) After we had known each other for a while, Sheila confided that my interest in my black roots made her feel less self-conscious about searching out her white ones. Although many African Americans have European forebears, curiosity about this branch of the family tree is often viewed with suspicion by other blacks. But research into the black branch can often be a disappointing dead end.

Some African Americans have a precious handful of photos or letters or a Bible inscribed with their lineage that has been passed down from one generation to the next; others have stories—about the trials endured by a great-grandmother born into slavery or the whispered name of some prominent white man who makes a cameo on the family tree. Most black people who are descended from slaves, however, have missed out on accumulating family artifacts, since their ancestors were legally forbidden to learn to read or write, nor did they have the income to hire a photographer or the urge to capture for posterity the meagerness of their existence.

Census slave schedules list individuals only by age, skin color, and gender. Newspapers didn't include details about blacks' lives or were too prejudiced to be reliable as sources. African American publications were rare and more rarely preserved. Personal records such as receipts for slave sales, if they exist at all, often remain in the private hands of the descendants of slaveholders. Louisiana is an exception: unlike the British-derived common law used in the rest of the United States, the legal system bequeathed by its French colonial history was based on civil law, which required the execution of all financial transactions before a notary public. As a result the Notarial Archives in New Orleans contain records of slave sales and purchases, as well as wills, successions, and marriage contracts that often include details about slaves in the property inventory. Even with these abundant sources, however, it can be very difficult to locate an enslaved ancestor without the name of the owner. And documenting the trip across the Middle Passage can be impossible without the serendipitous mention somewhere of the ancestor's African origins.

In the absence of a specific personal history, many African Americans have only the general narrative of black American history, much of which is tragic, in which to insert themselves. The other choice has often been to either mythologize the past with stories of African kings and queens or to ignore it completely.

On my second day in New Orleans, Sheila and I got down to work. We headed over to the Historic New Orleans Collection, where we spread our research across one of their large oak tables. After a couple of hours comparing notes, Sheila set down her best guess of the line of our male ancestors from Paul Broyard back through four generations to the first settler, the white Frenchman Etienne.

Sheila's records were organized into separate binders for each branch of the family. She knew all the names, dates, and places off the top of her head. I tried to follow along with her reasoning, but I kept confusing this person with that person as I shuffled through my own heap of papers, on the verge of throwing my hands up in despair. However, a part of me was also relieved to find myself in the role of her apprentice, self-conscious as I was about the advantage my father had already secured me. But Sheila had no better idea than I did which of our white male ancestors was responsible for the origins of the family's mixed-race identity. We started searching through the archdiocesan volumes recording all the Catholic sacraments performed in the city, looking for more clues.

As we worked, another researcher—a white woman—was scrolling through microfilm at a nearby reader. She called over to one of the archive's assistants.

"It says here that the mother of my great-great-grandmother was born in St. Domingue. Where's that?" she asked.

"Present-day Haiti," the assistant explained. "It used to be a French colony."

"Haiti?" the woman repeated in a surprised voice.

The assistant seemed accustomed to this response. She gave a little speech about how the island had once been populated by blacks *and* whites, many of whom emigrated to New Orleans in the wake of a slave revolt at the end of the eighteenth century.

"So it doesn't mean that she was black," the woman said.

Sheila and I, catching each other's glance, had to fight back laughter.

"Not necessarily," the assistant said. But the woman had learned all she wanted for one day. She packed up her things and stood to go.

On January 13, 1753, Etienne Broyard arrived in New Orleans from La Rochelle, a port city on the Atlantic coast of France. He was about twenty-four years old, a soldier in the French Royal Army. More than likely he'd been assigned to the Louisiana colony against his will.

In fortresses around France, soldiers attempted to mutiny when they heard they were being sent to the "wet grave" of the New World, so called because its location placed inhabitants in the path of floods and hurricanes and exposed them to a damp climate that brought on sickness and famine. The discontent of the soldiers made the trip across the ocean tense, with the officers barely able to control the men. On landing in New Orleans, the soldiers were sometimes assembled in the town square and made to watch as the most defiant among them were hanged, to discourage further disobedience.

Etienne had indeed found himself in a new world. La Rochelle had a population of close to twenty thousand people and boasted a grand theater, numerous hotels and churches, taverns and shops. New Orleans was a small grid of dirt streets, nestled up against the riverbank, surrounded by swampland. Most of the buildings were simple one-story wooden houses. About three thousand people lived there—almost half of them were slaves. Etienne had probably never seen sub-Saharan Africans before. Despite La Rochelle's position as a midway point in the triangular Atlantic trade route, slave ship holds were empty when stopping off to sell their goods on their way back to Africa.

Few people in Louisiana had come there voluntarily. Beyond a handful of Canadian fur trappers and holders of land concessions, the white colonists were mostly rejects from French society: convicts who'd been condemned to the gallows, vagabonds, and prostitutes, all deported to help populate the inhospitable outpost. To make matters worse, the Natchez and Chickasaw Indians, upset over French encroachment onto their lands, kept raiding the settlements, killing the men and taking the women and children as prisoners.

Back in 1731 the Company of the Indies, hired by the crown to colonize Louisiana, had gone bankrupt and pulled out. With their departure the slave trade into the colony temporarily dried up. The Africans who were already there were overworked and underfed and often ran away, sometimes taking their masters' guns with them and teaming up with the local Indian tribes. In 1754 the outbreak of the French and Indian War between France and England over control of North America brought British blockades of French ships carrying desperately needed supplies.

As a soldier, Etienne fared no better than anyone else. Corrupt officials sold the food intended for the troops, leaving them with little to eat besides Indian corn, which the French considered animal feed. A French official complained to powers back home that the fighting force was often left hungry and naked. The soldiers who dared to desert risked capture by hostile Indians, who might burn them alive or scalp them. If the soldiers were caught and returned to the colony, the deserters would also almost certainly face execution.

With such desperate conditions, nobody paid much attention to segregating the races. From the very beginning, white men, confronted with a shortage of white women, had taken up with Indian women or slaves. Initially French authorities followed a policy established in Canada of encouraging mixing with native women to increase the colony's population. Louisiana's first priest went so far as to publicly declare that "the blood of the savages does no harm to the blood of the French," and went around trying to get these couples to come to the church so he could marry them.

A few white men even managed to legally marry black women before the French Code Noir, or Black Code, introduced in 1724 to regulate the control of slaves and the few free blacks, put an end to the practice. It became a crime for white men to even have sexual relationships with slaves or women of color, although the many mixed-blood children whose baptismal records described them as having a "father unknown" suggest that this particular law wasn't regularly enforced. Some of these unknown fathers eventually paid a visit to the notary public, where they acknowledged the children as their own and occasionally granted them their freedom too. Less frequently, the men emancipated the children's mothers. Before long a new population of people began to emerge in New Orleans: blacks who had been born into freedom, who became known as *les gens de couleur libre*, or the free people of color.

A slave could also gain his freedom on the battlefield or for faithful service to a master or mistress. One African native, named Louis Congo, was emancipated in exchange for agreeing to serve as the colony's official executioner. Nobody else wanted the job: it was brutal work, and Louis was always in danger of being assassinated by the friends and family of those he'd punished. Now that he was free, though, Louis could buy and sell property, marry whomever he wanted, and testify against another free person in court, just like white people. Marriage to a white person, however, was still off-limits. And he was no longer subject to the punishments outlined in the Code Noir that he was occasionally obliged to carry out—branding for first-time runaways, severing the hamstrings of those who made a second break for freedom. If a slave struck his master "so as to produce a bruise or shedding of blood in the face," Louis was charged with executing him.

While many of Etienne's fellow soldiers defied the Code Noir and slept with (or raped) black women, Etienne appears to have been an exception. He had barely arrived when he impregnated a young white New Orleans native named Louisa Buquoy. Louisa's mother's family was originally from La Rochelle, which may explain this speedy conquest.

The couple married before the baby came, and went on to have ten more children over the next twenty-five years—each one promptly baptized, sometimes at all of a day old. In a city fraught with famine, flood, and frequent outbreaks of smallpox and yellow fever, Etienne and Louisa apparently were unwilling to take any chances of a dead child ending up in purgatory. Despite the difficulty of life in the territory, nine of the eleven children survived to reach adulthood and have families themselves.

In 1763 New Orleans was handed over to Spain, as part of a peace treaty brokered at the end of the French and Indian War. The French settlers, resentful of Spain's attempts to curtail their commerce, organized a revolt and kicked out the first Spanish governor in a coup that left the colony unstable for a few years. Though Etienne was educated and had a useful trade—master carpentry, which every Broyard male in my line practiced until my father—the few notarial records I could find suggest his fortunes rose and fell through the rocky transition. At one point he had enough money to lend 10,000 livres—about $500 at the time, or $12,000 today—to an associate; at another, a surgeon to whom he owed money got a court order allowing him to intercept Etienne's wages and collect his debt.

But Spanish rule eventually brought an influx of cash and people to Louisiana—the Acadians came down from Canada (and became Cajuns), and emigrants arrived from the Canary Islands off the coast of Africa, which were also under the Spanish crown. And Spain began importing again the slaves that settlers viewed as crucial to their economic success. By the time Etienne died, in 1791, he'd become the owner of several houses on the corner of Bourbon and Orleans streets in the French Quarter and a Negro woman named Mariana.

That the Broyards owned a slave didn't necessarily place them among the elite of New Orleans. Mariana likely worked together with Louisa—cooking, cleaning, and caring for the children. Nevertheless, Etienne could afford to educate his children, probably at one of the local private libraries that served as schools, and they went on to marry well and become property and slave owners themselves.

The couple's ninth child was my great-great-great-great-grandfather Henry, a name that would reappear in almost every generation of Broyards to come. He was born around 1770, which made him twenty-one when he lost his father. His mother had died a year earlier. In the eyes of the law, he and his younger sister, Emilie, were still minors, and their share of the inheritance was entrusted to custodians, who probably auctioned off the houses and Mariana. Slaves weren't fetching very high prices at the time. The agricultural market was soft, and there were stirrings of rebellion on the neighboring French colony of St. Domingue, which was making people wary of buying unknown hands lest they carry the "infection" of revolutionary ideas.

A few years before Etienne died, a crisis in the royal finances of France sparked a general rebellion in the country against the aristocracy. In August of 1789, the revolution led to the convening of a new government body, the National Constituent Assembly, made up solely of "the People" (rather than the clergy and nobility who had been ruling). Inspired in part by the U.S. Declaration of Independence, the assembly outlined a set of principles for writing a constitution, entitled the Declaration of the Rights of Man. The document established as its guiding principles *liberté, égalité,* and *fraternité* and, more to the point, declared that "men are born and remain free and equal in rights." As soon as the free black population in St. Domingue heard the news, they rushed representatives to Paris to demand equal citizenship. Many of them owned sugar and coffee plantations on the island, on which they paid taxes, earning them the right to vote too.

At the time about twenty-eight thousand people of color on St. Domingue had managed to gain their freedom through means similar to those used in Louisiana: by serving in the military, being freed by their master, or, most frequently, having the good or bad luck to be the mistress or child of a white man. The revolution-era French government didn't immediately capitulate to the free blacks' demands, but in 1792, after two slave uprisings, the government granted the freemen their request, in hopes they'd help to keep the slaves in line. Since many of the free blacks were also planters, they counted on slave labor to work the fields too. But the slave revolt was too far along to stop, and finally, on February 4, 1794, the French government voted on the question of abolishing slavery altogether.

By this time the French legislature had become even more radicalized. When a deputy announced to a packed hall that "a black man, a yellow man, are about to join this Convention in the name of the free citizens of San Domingo," the new members entered amid cheers and applause. The black man, an ex-slave named Bellay, took to the podium to call upon the French legislators to free his brothers. When Bellay finished, a white member stood up and made this motion: "When drawing up the constitution of the French people we paid no attention to the unhappy Negroes.... Let us repair the wrong — let us proclaim the liberty of the Negroes." Every last member rose to make known his acclamation.

Back in Louisiana the Spanish governor, Esteban Rodríguez Miró, heard news of these developments and grew increasingly worried.

Under Spain's watch the colony's population of free people of color—believed to be the principal instigators in St. Domingue—had swelled to more than eight hundred people by the early 1790s. That made them 15 percent of New Orleans's residents, which, combined with the slaves' 36 percent, put whites in the minority. Indeed it was Spain's very policies that caused the great increase in the free blacks' numbers. Bondsmen and women could purchase their own liberty through wages they'd earned by doing extra work for their masters or from hiring themselves out during the little spare time they had.

The colonial society not only tolerated the newly freed Africans but had come to depend on them so much that Louisiana would be hard-pressed to function without them. The free blacks provided much of the skilled labor—the men became carpenters and shoe-makers, and the women worked as seamstresses or laundresses. Spain also relied on the free blacks for help in defending the territory and controlling the slave population. Organized into light-skinned and dark-skinned militias, these soldiers served as a wedge between the free and enslaved black populations. For the most part, though, every-body—whites, free people of color, and slaves—had been coexisting peacefully for years.

Governor Miró began introducing measures aimed at reminding the free blacks about their proper place—beneath whites. He banned them from gathering in groups, which had little effect on the men's card games and cockfights. And he forbade the women to wear any-thing ornamental—no more feathers, jewels, or silks—while also requiring them to cover their hair with kerchiefs to signify their lower status. They obliged by wrapping their heads in colorful scarves, called *tignons,* in a style made popular among the fashionable women of Paris by Empress Josephine.

When refugees from St. Domingue started trickling into port, bringing stories about former slaves slaughtering their masters and raping their white mistresses, Miró started to clamp down on the slaves. The Africans' tradition of gathering on Sundays in Congo

Square on the edge of town to trade their wares, play their drums, and perform the dances they had danced back home now came under attack. No matter how well everyone had gotten along in the past, the revolution in St. Domingue pointed out blacks' and whites' inherent status as enemies.

Within months of his father's death in 1791, my great-great-great-great-grandfather Henry became a father himself, to a little girl named Felicity. The mother was twenty-one-year-old white New Orleans native Adelaide Hardy. Although the couple went on to have four more children, they never married. At the time, lots of couples didn't bother to get married—weddings were expensive and unnecessary to establish legitimate heirs.

After their second child, my great-great-great-grandfather Gilbert, was born, on October 11, 1795, Henry paid a visit to the notary public in town. There he recorded an official declaration that read "for the great love and affection that he professes for his natural children," Henry Broyard donated a house to Gilbert and his sister "to have and to hold from now and always." This act ensured that the children could inherit their father's property even though they were illegitimate.

The ongoing political and racial tension in Louisiana gave Henry reason to put his affairs in order. In 1795 Governor Miró's fears proved to be founded. An elaborate plot for a slave insurrection, hatched over months of secret meetings between free people of color, slaves, and white radicals, was discovered in Pointe Coupée, the outpost a hundred miles upriver where Henry's older brother Etienne lived. Before the date set to begin the revolt arrived, some Indian women revealed the plan. Fifty-seven slaves and three local white people were found guilty of the crime of plotting revolution. The prisoners were sent to New Orleans for sentencing, bringing the threat of racial unrest closer to home for Henry.

While the condemned men waited in prison, their family and

friends among the local slaves set a series of fires throughout the city. Six months earlier a massive fire, started from a prayer candle tipping over in a breeze, had torn through the streets, burning up entire blocks. The slaves hoped to create a similar state of chaos, during which the prisoners could escape. But the militia—including free black members—managed to contain the fires, and the sentences were carried out without further disruption. Twenty-three of the slaves were hanged in the town square. Their severed heads were displayed on poles along the banks of the Mississippi, all the way from Pointe Coupée to New Orleans.

In 1800 Spain, under pressure from Napoleon, with whom the country had formed an alliance, ceded Louisiana back to France in a secret treaty. Before the transfer of government took place, Napoleon turned around and sold the colony to the United States to help cover France's debts from the war in St. Domingue. Throughout these changes in power, the intermingling between the races in the city went on as it always had, and during the American regime it even increased.

The Broyard family suffered a personal tragedy as the century drew to a close. Henry's wife, Adelaide, gave birth to their fifth child on Christmas Day in 1799, which also happened to be Adelaide's thirtieth birthday. She developed complications from the labor and died the following day. The Broyard children disappear from the public records for the next fifteen years. Most likely they remained with their father, who soon got married to a woman who also happened to be named Adelaide. Gilbert was only four when his real mother passed away. She had belonged to a world that was quickly disappearing.

-13-

After a few months in New Orleans, I'd gone from having no past at all on my father's side of the family tree to uncovering 250 years of history. Where before I only thought of myself as an "American" during a college semester in Europe—and then with some reluctance because of the negative associations it invoked: loud, crass, materialistic—now the term began to actually mean something to me. I came from a line of people who had helped to settle the country, who'd arrived here under difficult circumstances and made the best of it, who had sometimes even flourished. It amazed me to realize that my family's story paralleled much of the country's larger narrative; to discover that we, the Broyards, were at once ordinary and emblematic.

Walking through the French Quarter, I thought of my ancestors traveling these same streets more than two centuries earlier—heading to a job with a wooden box of tools propped on one shoulder or going off to church with a gang of kids in tow. I imagined them walking along the *banquettes*, the plank walkways that served as sidewalks, and wading through the rivers of mud that filled the streets when it rained. I pictured my ancestors' shoes: leather clogs or boots caked in mud or covered in dust; Etienne or Henry cleaning them the first thing when they got home, perhaps the father and son performing this chore together. And then I remembered something that I hadn't thought of in years: my father's own ritual of cleaning and polishing my brother's and my shoes—his wicker basket full of brushes and tins of polish; the rags he made from lone socks and ripped T-shirts; his caution against gumming up the brush's bristles with too much wax; the last step, when he'd have us put on our shoes and prop up each foot on a stool while he knelt on the floor. *Put your hand on my shoulder,* he'd say, and we'd balance ourselves as he shimmied a cloth hard and fast across the leather, teasing out a high and glossy shine.

It was strange to stumble onto this memory of my father as I strolled down the streets of New Orleans, to suddenly feel this connection from his ancestors to him to me. I began to notice other traits that had traveled down the family tree, many landing on my brother despite his scant knowledge of our father's past. I had always thought of myself as the child that most took after my father, but Todd turned out to be the classic Broyard of the family.

We didn't grow up attending church, nor were we even baptized, but Todd had become a Catholic when he was twenty-one. Although we'd been surrounded during childhood by artists, intellectuals, and professionals, my brother worked first as a carpenter after graduating from college and then started a business installing security systems, a career, as he proudly declared, that placed him squarely "in the trades." In high school he began playing the harmonica; his favorite numbers were the blues. The more I learned about our history, the more it seemed as if heredity was a force as inescapable as the gravity that had pulled Newton's apple to the ground.

The Broyards officially became Americans on the twentieth of December in 1803, but they were still thinking of themselves as French in 1920, when my father was born. On the day of the ceremony transferring Louisiana to the United States, crowds of Frenchmen gathered in New Orleans's town square to watch their beloved tricolor flag lowered for a final time. Men and women dressed in their finest clothes packed the balconies surrounding the square, with a se-

lect few invited to join the civic leaders in the inner chambers of City
Hall.

A roll of drums accompanied the American troops as they marched
into New Orleans along the riverfront. They turned into the square
and came to a stop in front of the French militia—including the two
black units—assembled in battle formation. The Americans were
shocked by the great num-
ber of brown and black
soldiers staring back at
them, all with muskets in
hand. The territorial commissioners, William Clai-
borne and General James
Wilkinson, later confided
that they were barely able
to get through the cere-
mony without registering
their alarm.

My great-great-great-
grandfather Gilbert Bro-
yard was seven at the time.
His uncle Louis was a mem-
ber of the French militia, which might have drawn his family out to
watch. Also, as members of the *ancienne population*—the settlers who'd
arrived during the first French rule—the Broyards would be stirred
by the brief reappearance of their flag. The scene would have made a
lasting impression on a young boy, even if the new rule didn't have
much effect on Gilbert and his family. For all of his young life, the
flag of Spain had flown over New Orleans, yet everyone around him
still spoke French, drank café au lait, and scanned the French paper
for the latest news about the upstart general Napoleon Bonaparte
overseas. It would take more than a change of colors on a flagpole to

make the French of New Orleans think of themselves as anything but French.

And so while the tears may have fallen freely on some faces in the crowd that day, the champagne flowed just as copiously at the ball that night. Glasses were raised to Spain, France, and the United States, and partygoers of all three nations danced, drank, and played cards together well past dawn. They weren't stupid, after all: since the river had reopened to trade with the United States, Louisiana had more than doubled its exports in just three years. Membership in the Union could only bring greater financial gain to the aspiring merchant class.

New Orleans could stand some progress. The city hadn't grown much in the fifty years since Etienne, the first Broyard settler, arrived. A little more than eight thousand residents were now living in New Orleans. Charleston, South Carolina, by comparison, had almost four times as many residents, according to the 1800 census. While the Spanish-style brick-and-stucco Creole town houses that replaced the old wooden one-story buildings destroyed in the fires were much more substantial, open sewers still ran down the center of many streets, and they were often clogged with garbage and the carcasses of animals. New Orleans was world famous mainly for its stench.

Watchmen went around in the evenings, lighting rows of lanterns that hung from ropes strung across the street intersections, but the blocks themselves remained in darkness, offering cover for the robbers and vagabonds who roamed about freely. At nine o'clock, the guards shut the city gates, closing in the residents for the night behind a crumbling earthen rampart that had never been effective in the first place. Most would agree that the city could tolerate some internal improvements.

The morning after the ceremony transferring Louisiana to the United States, General Wilkinson shot off a dispatch to the secretary of war calling for more troops and ammunition with the explanation that the "formidable aspect of the armed Blacks & Malattoes [*sic*], officered and organized, is painful and perplexing." Claiborne sent off his own letter to James Madison at the State Department, asking for advice with his problem. He needed to commission the French militia into the American army, but if he included the colored troops, he feared objection from whites; yet if he didn't muster them in, he feared creating "an armed enemy in the heart of the country." Both commissioners resolved to do nothing until they heard back from Washington.

The black and mixed-race soldiers, though, were impatient for recognition. A few weeks after the change of rule, fifty of them signed a petition stating that they expected full rights of citizenship. During the transfer ceremony, they'd listened closely as Louisiana's cession treaty was read aloud, in English and in French, and they'd heard how every inhabitant of the colony had been granted "the enjoyment of all rights, advantages, and immunities of citizens of the United States," with no qualification about race or color. Furthermore, the soldiers reasoned, they'd fought on the American side during the American Revolution. Didn't that count for something?

Claiborne stalled the men with the assurance that the United States wouldn't try to take away their freedom or property. But he and the administration in Washington—who answered back with little practical advice—were both caught off guard: nowhere else in the United States had free blacks demonstrated such a sense of entitlement.

For the Louisiana planters, the unfolding drama, with free blacks agitating for equal rights, resembled events in St. Domingue too closely for comfort. The sugar crops in Louisiana were finally bringing in some profit, and the planters weren't about to risk losing their precious slave labor, especially with all these Americans pouring into the territory, eager to grab up power and patronage for themselves. As it was, the new government was interfering with the planters' efforts to expand their plantations. Claiborne had continued the Spanish ban on importing Africans from the French Caribbean, and the U.S. Constitution, to whose laws they were now bound, seemed to suggest that the import of foreign slaves might be outlawed altogether as early as 1808.

While Commissioner Claiborne (soon to become territorial governor) fretted over a response to the free blacks' demands, boatloads of refugees from St. Domingue were arriving daily on Louisiana shores, keeping the specter of a slave revolt on everyone's minds. A few weeks before the transfer ceremony, the insurgents had succeeded in overthrowing the French local government. Then on January 1, 1804, the victorious blacks in St. Domingue declared their independence. Their new nation—the first black republic in the Western Hemisphere—was called Haiti after the name given to it by its original inhabitants, the Indian natives, before the colonizers wiped them out.

A few weeks later, twelve black Haitians were spied on a boat heading up Bayou Lafourche, just west of New Orleans. In a letter to Claiborne, a white informant described the blacks' taunting of whites on shore with stories about "eating human flesh" and "what they had been and done in the horrors of St. Domingo." Word spread throughout the territory that the principles of liberty and equality would soon be delivered to Louisiana in an equally bloody fashion. Up in Pointe Coupée, where the blacks greatly outnumbered the whites, Henry's brother Etienne, along with ninety-seven other men, added his name to a petition asking for more troops, saying that the slaves were showing a "spirit of Revolt and mutyny [*sic*]."

Troops, however, were in short supply. Claiborne resolved to ask the territorial legislature to enlist the black and colored militia's help in controlling the slaves. After all, as in St. Domingue, many of the free men of color were slave owners themselves, and they hadn't been asking for the emancipation of their bonded brothers, only that their own political rights be recognized. Claiborne reasoned that by treating the colored men as if they had the same concerns as whites, the state could win their loyalty. But the legislators wouldn't stomach any action that further emboldened the free people of color. As it was, some colored planters were beginning to outstrip their white counterparts in amassing money and land. And so over the next few years, the lawmakers repeatedly ruled against the inclusion of the black and mixed-race corps in the militia and tightened the codes governing the rights of slaves and free people of color too.

Now blacks were expressly forbidden to even *conceive* themselves equal to whites. If they struck or insulted a white person, they faced fines or imprisonment. Free black men were restricted from emigrating to Louisiana, whether from Haiti or anywhere else. Many managed to enter the state anyway, particularly during the second migration of St. Domingue refugees at the end of 1809 and the beginning of 1810. They came from Cuba, where they'd settled after fleeing the slave revolt, but with France and Spain back at war in 1808, they'd been kicked out. These ten thousand new residents, about evenly split between whites, free people of color, and slaves, made even more difficult the execution of another new law designed to prevent free blacks from trying to pass into white society. All public records had to include an indication of racial status—with FMC for free man of color and FWC for free woman.

In 1811 the planters' fears came to pass, with the biggest slave revolt in the history of the United States. Fifty miles upriver from New Orleans, three hundred slaves rose up, led by a free man of color from St. Domingue. The city's free blacks saw their chance to demonstrate their solidarity with whites and rushed to volunteer their assistance to Governor Claiborne. The slaves were poorly armed and quickly put down. After the danger passed, Claiborne wrote testimonials lauding the free blacks' patriotic conduct and again pressed for their enlistment into the militia, but the planter-legislators refused to be persuaded.

Soon, however, the United States was at war with England, and the lawmakers had no choice but to accept the colored militia's offer of aid. At Claiborne's urging, General Andrew Jackson, who was charged with defending New Orleans, wrote an appeal that was posted throughout town, in which he formally requested the service of free men of color in this "Glorious Struggle for National Rights." He referred to them as "sons of freedom" and the country's "adopted children." He also promised the colored soldiers that they would receive the same pay, $124 in cash and 160 acres of land, as the white troops.

The speech infuriated many white Louisianans, who resented its suggestions of equality between the races. They predicted—accurately—that such treatment would encourage the free men of color to keep pressing their case for recognition. But the headstrong general had no patience for racial disputes. Over the summer, British troops had marched into Washington and torched the White House and the capitol building. Jackson couldn't let America's newly acquired southern port fall too.

After arriving in New Orleans in December of 1814, General Jackson immediately mustered the existing battalion of 350 men of color into the U.S. Army, and directed Colonel Joseph Savary, a free man of color who'd served in the French Republic Army in St. Domingue, to raise another unit among his countrymen. Jackson also enlisted a ragtag crew of white and black St. Domingue revolutionary insurgents led by pirate Jean Lafitte, who agreed to lend desperately needed flints and muskets to the cause. Whites also rallied to the general after witnessing his forceful speech in the town square, where Jackson had sworn to "drive their enemies into the sea, or perish in the effort." Henry Broyard and his son Gilbert were among those who signed up.

In the early morning hours of January 8, 1815, British general Sir Edward Pakenham led an army of 8,700 veteran soldiers in a two-pronged attack that straddled the Mississippi at a point nine miles below New Orleans. Pakenham was so sure of victory that he carried on him papers appointing him as the British governor of Louisiana. But Jackson anticipated the assault and had 4,000 troops—including

Lafitte's followers and two battalions of free men of color—waiting behind some hastily erected fortifications.

The British troops advanced across the plains of Chalmette hidden in a swirl of morning fog. The wind shifted and the mist was gone, leaving the winter sun to light up the Brits' red coats. Jackson's forces let loose a torrent of cannon shot and rifle fire, and in less than thirty minutes the field was empty except for the masses of dead and wounded British soldiers. The day scored a decisive victory for the Americans: the British retreated and soon left Louisiana altogether. In fact a peace treaty between the two countries had  already been signed in Belgium, but the news hadn't yet made it to American shores.

The Louisiana legislators recognized the bravery of Lafitte's men and the free men of color, noting in particular Joseph Savary's brother, who was credited with sacrificing his own life in order to kill the British general. But the sight of so many black men walking in the streets carrying guns roused the old fears of insurrection. Perhaps bending to local pressure, Jackson gave orders for the two colored battalions to repair some fortifications outside the city. Colonel Savary answered back that his men "would always be willing to sacrifice their lives in combat in defense of their country as had been demonstrated but preferred death to the performance of work of laborers."

Henry and Gilbert were already out at the fort, hired on as carpenters to assist with the repairs. Savary's defiance of Jackson's order made the Broyards' lives difficult: they were shorthanded on laborers, and the rest of the colored soldiers began grumbling about the insult

of doing this menial work. The troops began deserting the post en masse. Henry and Gilbert soon walked off the job too, in solidarity perhaps, or because they were the last ones left.

The colored veterans were granted small pensions, but they didn't receive the land they were promised, nor the recognition that Jackson had led them to believe was their due. Every year in the parade commemorating the battle, they marched with the whites — and were even in later years granted the honor of leading the procession — but their war efforts never brought them the equal political footing they'd hoped for. Anyway, with the war over and the threat of foreign invasion gone, the pace of migration to the port city was picking up, which gave rise to a different kind of ethnic tension.

In 1817 Captain Henry M. Shreve's new steamboat, *Washington,* made the round-trip journey from New Orleans to Louisville, Kentucky, in an astonishing forty-one days. A trip that once took many months of hard rowing could now be completed in relative comfort in just six weeks. More and more Americans started the journey south. Goods from across the United States followed close behind.

Parades of pine rafts, each stacked with an acre's worth of freshly cut boards from the forests of western Pennsylvania and upper New York State, began arriving regularly at the levee. From there the wood was carted away to the various building sites springing up all over town. From Pittsburgh came more barges, these piled high with coal to heat the blast furnaces in which ironworkers fashioned the ornate balcony railings and balustrades that began appearing in New Orleans architecture in the early nineteenth century. Other flatboats, from the Midwest, arrived jammed with cattle, hogs, and horses, or barrels of flour and whiskey and sacks of corn.

Captains and merchants shouted back and forth from ship to shore, striking deals. Sailors, roustabouts, draymen, and laborers unloaded and reloaded cargo, barking orders and trading curses in half a dozen languages. Negro women wove through the crowds, selling

cakes, apples, oranges, and figs from trays they balanced on their heads. Groups of slaves worked the levee too, many of whom had first come to New Orleans as yet another type of goods to be unloaded and sold.

In 1808 the United States carried through on its promise to abolish the import of slaves from foreign countries; however, a domestic slave trade developed in its place that would thrive until the Civil War. By the 1840s slave markets populated many southern cities, with the largest one in New Orleans. The traders initially concentrated their slave pens in the far end of the French Quarter, with the Americans opening a second, larger slave market in New Orleans's central business district after the 1840s.

During the day the enslaved men might be dressed up in blue suits and top hats, and the women in long-sleeved blouses and ankle-length skirts, and made to walk back and forth on the street outside the firm's office. Sometimes a fiddler was produced, and the slaves were commanded to dance to show off their vitality. The markets became a popular destination for tourists visiting from across the United States and from Europe.

Buyers from Louisiana, Texas, Arkansas, and Mississippi purchased their field hands or house servants, blacksmiths or "fancy girls." In the decades before the Civil War, a healthy good-sized

seventeen-year-old boy cost around $1,200 (about $28,000 today), while a wealthy New Orleans man might pay as much as $5,000 ($116,000 today) for a light-skinned beauty whom he "fancied" for his own.

The increasingly profitable cotton and sugar plantations fueled the need for slave labor and provided the fortunes to buy it. During February and March, when the cotton crop was brought into town, hundreds of thousands of bales piled up on the levee and barricaded the streets until they were sold and reloaded on ships, bound for France or England or New York. All this activity meant more duties and taxes for the city and more business for nearly everyone: commission merchants, exporters, importers, banks, insurance companies, lawyers, hotelkeepers, tavern owners, shoemakers, tailors, and carpenters too, all stood to gain.

In the decade following the transfer of Louisiana to the United States, my great-great-great-great-grandfather Henry started to acquire slaves. There were two male African natives in their early twenties, who probably assisted on carpentry jobs, and a thirty-year-old black woman, who likely helped Henry's wife with the cooking, cleaning, and care of Gilbert and his siblings. No details of these peoples' lives exist beyond the records of their purchase and sale, so I don't know whether Henry was kind or cruel to his human property.

While New Orleans natives such as Henry welcomed the increased opportunity brought by American rule, the newcomers' attempts to impose their own lifestyle and values set off a culture war that would eventually divide the city. Part of the problem was that the two populations shared so little common ground. New Orleans natives spoke French, worshipped in the Catholic Church, bet on cockfights and cards (even on Sundays), and favored a spicy cuisine full of Spanish and Indian influences and cooked with methods that the slaves brought over from Africa. The Americans, on the other hand, had Anglo-Saxon roots, spoke the Queen's English, were Protestants, frowned on gambling—especially on the Sabbath—and liked their food boiled and bland. Also, New Orleanians were far more casual than the Americans with their slaves and the local free people of color—appearing in town with their colored mistresses and illegitimate colored children, which the Yankees pointed to as ultimate proof of the moral bankruptcy of the Latin race.

For their part, New Orleans natives bristled at the hypocrisy of the Protestant ministers' sermons railing against their pastimes when half the churchs' parishioners had been enjoying those same pleasures twelve hours before. They referred to the northerners as "Yankee Buzzards" and griped that they were only drawn to the port city by their get-rich-quick schemes. More practically, the natives also recognized that in the contest for city rule, the Americans, with their experience in democratic government, held the upper hand.

In trying to distinguish themselves from the arrivistes, the New Orleans natives began referring to themselves as Creoles. Previously the term had been mostly used as an adjective to differentiate between native and nonnative born, but now it became a catch-all description for the ancienne population and St. Domingue refugees, both black and white. It wasn't until American mores, including their racial attitudes, prevailed after Reconstruction that the white Creole population began insisting that it had always applied only to themselves, lest the Yankees doubt their racial purity. The ubiquity of *plaçage* relationships (a formalized mistress or common-law relationship) between white men and women of color gave the Americans reason to wonder about the Creoles' blood.

Shortly after the Louisiana Purchase, marriage between the races had been outlawed, making such unions null and void. In 1828 the legislators changed the state's civil code so that illegitimate children could no longer inherit from their fathers—even in cases where paternity had been officially recognized before a notary. At the same time, the New Orleans city council began to ban the attendance of whites at the "quadroon balls," where many plaçage relationships were initiated. But threats of fines and imprisonment couldn't keep the white men—Yankee and Creole alike—from searching out these nightly affairs. For male visitors to New Orleans, a trip to a quadroon ball was as customary as a tour of the slave pens and a stroll along the pier.

The most elegant of the balls were held at the St. Phillips Theater, off Bourbon Street, or the Globe, just outside the French Quarter. On most evenings white balls were held too, and men would leave one, meet up in the street to swap tickets, and then go to the other. When they recounted the dances later in their diaries or in letters to friends, they often commented on the superiority of the colored events: their finer furnishings and better orchestras, the exceptional poise and propriety of the young women in attendance.

At the St. Phillips Theater, three immense cut-glass chandeliers flooded the ballroom with light. The finest liquors lined the bar at one end of the room, and on the other end, one of the best orchestras in town accompanied the lines of quadrilles and rounds of waltzes. The women wore long gowns, and masks to cover their faces. Some of them had fair hair and pale skin, while others were almost as dark as Africans. The men disguised themselves too, dressed as young Turks or Peruvian Indians. In between dances and polite conversation, the men and women sized each other up as potential companions, and outside on the balcony or in the courtyard, under the cover of shadows, the couples appraised each other more frankly.

Among the wealthiest white men and most desirable young women, courtship involved a negotiation with the girl's mother. She'd question the suitor about his net worth and business affairs to ensure that he could support her daughter adequately. They'd set an annuity amount, $2,000 perhaps, that he'd have to pay if he should ever leave her. Usually the man then bought or rented his mistress a little cottage on the edge of town. While her new home was being readied, the girl's friends would fuss around her with all the same excitement as if she were having a church wedding. Sometimes the couple even lived to-gether as man and wife; other times the man divided his time between his colored mistress and a white wife.

As the two branches of the family went on to have children them-selves, all bearing the same last name, it became increasingly difficult to remember who among the dark-eyed, dark-haired children carried the taint of Africa and who did not. Indeed the siblings often knew each other—if the colored children became orphaned, it was not un-heard of for the white wife to take them in. In my great-great-great-grandfather Gilbert's case, the opposite seems to have been true: his colored "wife" and their children took in his white son, my great-great-grandfather.

Gilbert was the first white Broyard I discovered who was romantically involved with a woman of color. In the 1820 census, at the age of twenty-five, he was living with a young free woman of color, and ten years later, his house was full of children: two girls and two boys, all free blacks. The nature of Gilbert's relationship to these people—who are not described in the records beyond their racial status and approx-imate age—isn't clear. He may have been a tenant in the house; many free women of color took in boarders. Yet if that were true, his land-lady's name should have appeared as the head of the household rather than Gilbert's. More likely he had taken a colored mistress.

Just as Gilbert entered his teenage years, the city's streets had filled with the daughters of the St. Domingue refugees. Many of these girls owed their freedom to the beauty of their mothers or grandmothers, which had caught the eye of their slave masters, and the young women carried this cursed legacy in their own faces. Men visiting New Or-leans likened the mixed-race women to sirens. One Englishman waxed on about their "lovely countenance, full dark liquid eyes, lips of coral and teeth of pearl, long raven locks of soft and glossy hair..." At the same time, white women were in short supply: in 1820 there were twenty-three white men over the age of sixteen for every ten white

women of the same age. A white man without much wealth or property would have a hard time finding a desirable mate. But while visiting a quadroon ball or strolling along the levee, even a young white carpenter like Gilbert might catch the eye of a free woman of color.

For men in Gilbert's class, the plaçage arrangements were neither as taboo nor as formalized. Gilbert couldn't afford to pay a hefty annuity nor buy a mistress her own home. Nevertheless, a young woman of color might opt to throw in her lot with a white man with a skilled trade. No matter his degree of success, his station would be higher than that of a man of color. And at the very least, he could lighten the stigma in her children's skin. Also, free women of color were legally prevented from marrying whites or slaves, and they greatly outnumbered the men of their caste, leaving them few alternatives.

If the woman living with Gilbert was in fact his mistress, she got a bad deal. Gilbert never acknowledged the offspring as his own: there are no records of their baptism under his name, nor do any Broyards of their age and hue appear in the public records over the next few decades. Some of them grew up and had children themselves, no doubt. Today their descendants, who would be my fourth cousins, can only guess about the story behind this empty branch of their family tree.

Gilbert, however, was not directly responsible for the mixing of my own blood. Sometime in the 1820s, he married a white woman named Marie Panquinet. He and Marie had one son together, another Henry, my great-great-grandfather Henry Antoine Broyard, born on July 18, 1829. On his baptismal record, the boy's status as legitimate was mentioned, establishing him as Gilbert's sole heir, and his name too — a combination of his grandfather's and his uncle's — indicated his rightful place in the family line.

The people assembled at Henry's baptism on the first of October, 1829, at St. Louis Cathedral — the various Broyards and Panquinets, along with Marie's aunt Adelle and Gilbert's brother Anthony, who served as godparents — surely were familiar to each other, if not old friends. The Panquinets were also members of the ancienne population. Marie's grandfather had been the sexton at St. Louis Cathedral: he rang the church's bells at funerals and weddings and oversaw the digging of graves at the cemetery. Marie had grown up on Bourbon Street, a few blocks away from the Broyards, on the lower end of the Quarter, where the poorer Creoles and free blacks lived. And her uncle had been in the French militia too.

Soon after Henry's birth, Marie vanished from her son's and husband's lives, according to public records. It's possible that she left over objections about her husband's colored mistress. The writer Charles Gayarré, who lived in the city during the antebellum period, described the scene in the home of a white husband who kept a mulatto mistress: "The household peace was destroyed; there were secret tears, placid resignation, or open strife and deserved reproaches." But in the small Catholic community, divorcing one's husband brought about just as much social stigma as an interracial affair. A more likely explanation for Marie's disappearance is that she simply died. Shortly after Henry was born, a cholera epidemic decimated the city's population, leaving no record of the deaths of thousands of victims.

By the time Henry was two, Gilbert had moved on to a new mate, a free woman of color named Eulalie Urquhart, with whom he had another five children. This time the kids received their father's last name and proper baptisms (although they still weren't entitled to inherit his property). Even Gilbert's white siblings seem to have accepted his colored brood, with a few of them stepping in as godparents.

*   *   *

The census only began enumerating the names of individuals beyond the heads of households in 1850, and so the details of Henry's young life are few. No pictures of him remain, but his military record describes him as having a yellow complexion, yellow eyes, and dark brown hair. And he's taller than most other Creoles of that era, reaching five feet nine inches in his adulthood. I don't know for a fact that Henry was raised in the house with his father and his common-law wife, but it appears that Gilbert and his colored family remained an important part of my great-great-grandfather's life. Henry also became a carpenter, and he grew up close to his father's colored children, so much so that he asked one of his half sisters to serve as godmother when his first child was born.

Yet as intimate as Henry may have been with his father's other family, the world was increasingly drawing distinctions between them. The slaying of more than fifty whites during an 1831 slave rebellion in Virginia led by slave Nat Turner, on top of a growing abolitionist movement up north, led to clampdowns on people of color and slaves alike. If Gilbert took his family to the opera or theater, he'd be able to sit with Henry in the first tier while Eulalie and her kids were relegated to the balcony above them. If Henry and his siblings took the new omnibus that connected the different parts of the growing city, they would have to ride in separate train cars. Eulalie's family mem-

bers couldn't legally meet with other free black friends or relatives (to prevent them from plotting a slave revolt or the overthrow of the government). And Eulalie and her children had to carry papers at all times to prove that they were free—the implication being that the natural state of blacks was enslavement. Also, as Gilbert's only legitimate child, Henry was the only one who could inherit his property, which further reinforced the irreconcilable differences between them.

During the 1830s, thinking among whites about the origin of racial differences began to shift as well. For centuries the subject had been a favorite for theologians, philosophers, and scientists. During antiquity, the variation in people's looks was generally ascribed to some force outside themselves. The ancient Greeks referred to blacks as Aethiops, or Ethiopians, which translates literally into "burnt face." To explain the population's darker skin, the philosophers pointed to the myth of Phaëthon, in which the god of the sun, Helios, lends his sun chariot to his son, Phaëthon. The boy crashes it, burning the earth and drying up all the rivers, "and that was when...the people of Africa turned black, since the blood was driven by that fierce heat to the surface of their bodies." Aristotle, considered the father of biology, credited the range in people's appearances to the varying climates where they lived (which is much like the way contemporary evolutionary anthropologists explain what we perceive as racial differences today).

Between the second and sixth centuries, a biblical explanation for the origin of blackness emerged in theological interpretations of a story in Genesis that came to be known as the Curse of Ham. In the text Noah is angry at his son Ham for looking at him while he is lying naked in his tent, sleeping off his drunkenness. It's actually one of Ham's sons, Canaan, though, whom Noah punishes. The passage reads: "And he said, Cursed be Canaan; a servant of servants shall he be unto his brethren." Future readings of the passage began to associate Noah's curse on Ham's son Canaan with blackness.

Proslavery forces seized on the phrase "servant of servants" to justify the enslavement of Africans. A sticking point, however, was the story's genealogical explanation for how the world became populated. According to the Curse of Ham, blacks and whites were descended from the same family tree, making them distant cousins to each other. Then, in the eighteenth century, the Enlightenment's movement away from religion toward science offered a resolution to this problem.

In 1774 the British historian Edward Long first advanced the "scientific" theory that blacks and whites belonged to different species, based on his observation that their offspring were generally incapable of producing children with each other. This hypothesis of "mulatto sterility"—with the very word "mulatto" invoking "mule"—gained support throughout the first half of the nineteenth century. (The large number of mixed-raced people in the country—nearly half a million by 1850, according to the federal census—many of whom were having children with each other, was conveniently ignored.) Proslavery forces in the United States began arguing that the inevitable miscegenation that would follow emancipation would lead to the extinction of mankind altogether.

For Henry, though, no matter what the world told him about the biological difference between him and his colored siblings, Eulalie's kids were among the shrinking number of people—white or black—who shared his last name. Even though the Broyards had been in New Orleans for four generations by this time, the family had mainly produced girls. The few sons who were born either died young or failed to have sons themselves. When Henry started fathering children in the 1850s, he was the only Broyard passing on the name to appear in the city's sacramental or civil records.

At the same time, New Orleans's population was more than doubling, jumping from 46,000 in 1830 to over 100,000 in 1840—mostly through foreign immigrants—which helped to throw into relief all that the white and black Creole communities had in common. The city limits exploded to handle the growth, overtaking swamps here, cypress marshes there, with city improvements close behind. Stones began to cover the streets' dirt surfaces; gas-powered lamps replaced their hanging lanterns. Luxury hotels sprang up to accommodate the many visiting businessmen, with their high domed roofs shining above the city's skyline.

The Americans tended to concentrate upriver of Canal Street in Faubourg St. Marie, while the French and Creoles of color stayed downriver, pushing inland into the Tremé neighborhood or farther south in the Faubourg Marigny. The arriving immigrants went where they could find housing, often along the riverfront and among the lower parts of the city. A single block in the Tremé might be home to natives of Ireland, Germany, France, Cuba, St. Domingue, Pennsylvania, and Louisiana; to people who were white, black, or mulatto and worked as carpenters, cigar rollers, laborers, or seamstresses. Surrounded by all these foreign tongues and traditions, a shared language and customs could make people forget about their differences in skin tone.

In 1835 a local newspaper had predicted that within twelve years New Orleans would rival New York City as the commercial capital of the United States. But squabbles between the French and American factions in the city council hampered progress. In 1836 the state legislators agreed to divvy up New Orleans along ethnic lines into three separate municipalities, with Canal Street as the dividing line. The Americans controlled the second municipality, upriver, and the French were in charge of the first and third, downriver. Each mini-government operated its own schools, promoted its own language, and oversaw business and economic development.

The Broyards lived among other French people in the first municipality—the French Quarter and the Tremé—where race relations were more relaxed. Free colored people were making money alongside the whites during this boom time: in 1836 they had over $2.5 million worth of real estate and slaves, with an average net worth among the property owners of $3,000, or more than $56,000 in today's dollars. This made them the richest population of free blacks in the United States, wealthier than the whites of some southern cities, and certainly better off than Henry Broyard and his father, Gilbert.

Gilbert had tried to cash in on the building boom too. In the early 1830s, he purchased at auction a lot out on Bayou St. John, in the neighborhood that ran along the busy commercial waterway leading out to Lake Pontchartrain. But Gilbert ran into bad luck—before he was able to build his house, a problem arose with the property title, and he was forced to sell the lot at the price he'd paid for it. He never purchased any property again.

When Gilbert died, in 1851, he left no estate to pass along to his son. Being the sole legal Broyard heir meant nothing for Henry in the end. At the same time, the Creole legacy was rapidly dying out. It didn't take long for the American sector to outpace the rest of the city, with more new buildings, better-kept streets, a superior public school system, and more wealth. In the cultural tug-of-war, the Americans had been helped along by the European immigrants. They'd come to the country for a piece of the American dream, and they soon realized that all its rules were written in English.

The Americans returned the favor, pushing for the right to vote for the German and Irish immigrants, despite the fact that most of them were illiterate. The move disgusted the free colored population—many of them had been educated in Europe or by private tutors and had fortunes a hundred times that of the unskilled laborers, and yet they weren't entitled to vote. Finally, in 1852, when the Americans felt confident that they had the upper hand, they moved to reunite New Orleans, and with that, Creole dominance—over the French sections of the city, the general culture, or anything else—was finished.

-14-

I was staying in New Orleans at a guesthouse recommended by my cousin Mark in Los Angeles. The owner, Keith Weldon Medley, was Creole and a writer too, at work on his own book about an ancestor: Homer Plessy, the plaintiff in the famous legal case that established the "separate but equal" precedent for permitting and expanding segregation. After a day at the archives, I'd often join Keith in his kitchen, where we'd drink wine and chat about our research.

One night his friend Beverly joined us. She later told me that Keith had invited her over to check out the writer from New York who was in town doing research for a book about her newfound racial identity. Bev, as I came to know her, had balked on the phone: "This chick finds out she's got a little black blood in her, and suddenly she's black. This I've got to see."

After pouring herself a glass of wine, Bev launched into news from her day. It didn't take long for the discussion to move on to the local black community. Bev let it be known that she found their obsession with skin color irritating. "In San Diego, where I'm from, people didn't go around with *inferiority complexes*"—she stretched out the phrase—"because they didn't have good hair or they were darker than a paper bag. Nobody cared if you were yellow or brown; you were the same black motherfucker."

Bev was medium brown and petite, with short dreadlocks, carefully applied deep-red lipstick, and quick emphatic gestures. If you said something she liked, she fixed her gaze on you, poked a finger at your chest, and declared, "Exactly!" making you feel as if you'd never been so right before. She worked raising money for Bishop Perry, a Catholic school for disadvantaged African American boys. It stood on the site of the Couvent School, started in 1848 by free blacks for their children, so she knew all about the history of the New Orleans free people of color.

In her spare time, Bev volunteered at WWOZ, the local public radio station. As I listened to her talk, I realized that I'd woken up a few mornings back to her silky-voiced entreaties during a recent fund drive. Suddenly she turned that silver tongue on me. "So, Keith tells me that you're down here looking for your African roots." She said "African roots" as if the words were surrounded by quotation marks.

"Actually I've been researching all of my father's family," I said. "The black and white sides."

"But you didn't know about the black side growing up."

I told her that I found out when I was twenty-four, just before my father died.

"How'd you take the news?"

Bev's voice contained a smirk I'd come to recognize from African Americans when they asked me this question. It was a dare for me to admit to my own racism. It held the sweetness of just desserts. I'd already heard stories from a research assistant at the library about white people who started to cry on hearing the explanation about what the "mu" stood for on the census record. Ironically, even if I had felt this way, my Wasp upbringing would have prevented me from making such a scene.

I told Beverly that at first I had thought that my black ancestry was cool — she smiled knowingly — until I realized that it was more complicated than that.

"What do you think now?" she asked.

"I'm here, aren't I?" I said. "I want to know more."

She looked me squarely in the eye. "Then there's something you need to understand. Most African Americans didn't have the same option as your father did. My grandmother, for example, had to *endure* prejudice. She never had a choice about where she could sit on the bus."

I nodded, hesitant to speak for fear of sounding defensive.

"But your dad just glided on through without having to deal with Jim Crow or desegregating the schools or any of that. And he didn't do anything to help the people who were stuck on the other side. That's why your father makes black people so angry."

Nobody had ever laid out the injustice of my father's decision so bluntly before me. I held Bev's gaze, seeing for a moment from her perspective the terrible unfairness and selfishness of my dad's actions. After a few moments, I said quietly, "His choice makes me angry too."

She inclined her head. "Why?"

"Because he cut me off from knowing about my history, my family," I said. "And it's hard to try to catch up now."

Bev nodded thoughtfully. After a moment she looked at Keith and then clapped her hands, signaling that she'd made some sort of decision. She was an educator at heart, and she liked to have a project. She pointed at Keith's chest. "You know what we're got to do. We've got to take this girl to Indian practice. She's got to meet the Chief."

A few nights later, at Club Renaissance on North Galvez Street in the Tremé neighborhood of New Orleans, a few blocks from the house where my father was born, I chanted a song of the Mardi Gras Indians, *Shallow waters, oh mama,* that Bev whispered was sung by Indian women washing clothes on the riverbank to let escaping slaves know where to cross; and I clapped and swayed with the rest of the crowd, most everyone besides me some shade of brown; and closed my eyes and listened to the thump and rattle of the tambourine and felt the wooden floor bounce, with the pounding feet of the men from the Yellow Pocahontas tribe and Big Chief Darryl Montana, a friend of

Bev's and Keith's. And I pictured the women washing and the slaves running, their movements hurried along on our incantatory beat; and opened my eyes again to find the Big Chief right in front of me, turning on one foot, his arms splayed above him like the wings of a bird, fingers curled into claws, and then dropping low into his knees and raising up on tiptoe, rocking back and forth like that, his eyes staring out between a fray of dreadlocks at the eyes of Trouble Nation's Big Chief, who had just entered the bar with his own tribe of men, wearing tracksuits or suit jackets, their necks and teeth flashing with gold; these men pushing us into one end of the room while this new chief pounded his chest and threw his arms skyward, declaring that *he*—not Darryl Montana—was the big chief; the chanting growing louder and the men's rocking and turning and posing getting smaller and tighter, as if they were balanced now on a trembling rope high above us; and the crowd pushing back against me—*Give 'em room; give 'em room*—and the air wet with the men's sweat that smelled nervous and sharp, and the spicy liquor breath all around me and the musky smell of the old bar and the rice and beans cooking in the back, and everyone fixed on this encounter before us, our chanting urging these men along, to where the waters will either rise and drown them or carry them safely to shore; and I closed my eyes again, as though my not seeing might turn me unseen, and flew in my mind's eye down the street to where my father was born to collect whatever remained of him in this place, and remained in me, to bring to this moment, which he may once have witnessed himself; and I forgot about the color of my skin and that I wasn't raised like the people here, and with my father in hand, I crossed those shallow waters to the other side.

Earlier Keith, who had written about the Mardi Gras Indians for the local paper, told me about their history. For over a hundred years, African American men from the Tremé neighborhood had been "masking Indian" and running through these streets on Mardi Gras day. In the weeks before Mardi Gras, the tribes would gather in their local bars to "practice" chanting their songs, dancing their dances, and staging confrontations with their rivals. In my dad's time, meetings between the tribes occasionally turned violent, but now the encounters had all the flaunting and preening of a beauty pageant. These men who worked as carpenters or plasterers by day spent their nights and thousands of their dollars sewing their world-famous Mardi Gras suits, and it was the "prettiest" Indian rather than the "baddest" one who ruled the streets today.

A typical suit might feature an apron with a flower garden, hand stitched from beads, pearls, and stones into a three-dimensional design; wings four feet wide and far too laden with feathers and glue to ever take flight; and a crown weighing near a hundred pounds, three layers high and as ornate as a wedding cake. On Fat Tuesday, these men, sweating under the burden of their pride, paraded through the streets of their neighborhood, on the lookout for rival tribes. Their friends and neighbors trailed behind them, accompanying their chanting on tambourines and cowbells; and when two chiefs met up, the crowd surrounded them while the men shook their giant wings and danced.

The tradition was rooted in the alliance between Indian tribes and escaping slaves during Louisiana's colonial period—the suits often carried depictions of Indians fighting off white settlers. And the ritualized choreography harked back to the dances the slaves would do in Congo Square, which themselves harked back to Africa. Keith also mentioned evidence that the original Mardi Gras Indians were inspired in part by the Buffalo Bill Wild West show that came to town with New Orleans's 1884 Cotton Exposition. The first tribe, begun by Chief Darryl's great-great-uncle in the 1880s, was in fact called the Creole Wild West. Whatever the source, Mardi Gras Indians had been a way of life in this neighborhood for more than a century, with traditions, rituals, and roles that fashioned members of the community into leaders as established and respected as those of any church. Given my father's own "masking" as white, being among these men who masked as Indians to honor their history seemed like the perfect place for me to imagine myself as black in order to honor mine.

But back at the guesthouse, I was reminded of my whiteness once again. We'd met up with another friend of Keith's at Club Renaissance, a guy named Barry who was African American, and he joined us afterward. Bev had never met Barry before, but they immediately hit if off. She made a joke about the gold teeth of one of the guys in Trouble Nation, and Barry laughed first and louder than the rest of us. They slapped hands, and Bev, in a friendly jibe about Keith's and my Creole backgrounds, declared, "It's a black thing."

As far as I could tell, Barry didn't know my story, and I wondered if he saw me as one of those white people who liked to dabble in African American culture. In my travels I'd come across people who "masked" as black: white guys with dreadlocks, wearing brightly colored dashikis, and calling everyone "brother" while engaging in elaborate handshakes; or white women who peppered their speech with "girl," accompanied by finger snaps and wagging head. And these people annoyed me, especially if I was one of the only other white-looking people there. I felt implicated by their pantomime of blackness and embarrassed by the presumption that a culture could be performed like the steps to the latest dance craze. Also, while black culture is most often appropriated for its "cool" factor, these masquerades looked anything but cool to me. I knew that many African Americans snickered behind these people's backs and referred to them as "wiggers." I'd try to indicate my disapproval too, rolling my eyes at my companions. Yet there was something about these white people that

I secretly admired, or even envied. For whatever reason—the neighborhood they'd been raised in, some perversion of white guilt, or because they just felt out of place around people who looked like themselves—these "wiggers" seemed to feel at home in black culture. Whether they were accepted or not, they had the consolation of their own convictions. They weren't waiting, as I was, for someone to anoint them.

Over the next few years, Bev and I became close friends. Every once in a while, I'd ask her how she thought of me, as black or as white. And she'd offer the same response as my aunt Shirley and my friend Anjana from Charlottesville: "I think of you as Bliss. That's how." And she'd tell me again that she'd always been friends with all types, and that her own nephews and nieces, born to brothers- and sisters-in-law who were black, white, and Hispanic, made her family look like "the United Goddamned Nations." Nevertheless, I had heard Bev talk about certain friends who were white, and the way that race could suddenly flare up and create a wall between them. And I wondered if that could ever happen to us.

During my next trip to New Orleans, a story about me and my research into my father's racial background appeared in the local newspaper. I'd felt comfortable with the reporter and had talked freely—and rather windily—while she took copious notes. I shared my theory about how in certain parts of the country, white people's only interactions with African Americans tended to be with the clerks at the supermarket or drugstore, which led them to forming negative stereotypes (since few young people of any race working in dead-end minimum-wage jobs seemed eager to be there). Here's what ended up in the paper: "[Broyard's] newfound racial identity...has caused her to examine her prejudices more carefully, she said, to think before labeling a black grocery clerk 'dumb' or 'lazy.'"

The first phone call I got was from Bev, who told me that she'd been riding the streetcar to work with her daughter Brandi when she'd

spied over a woman's shoulder the headline WRITER EXPLORES HID-
DEN BLACK HERITAGE. "And then the woman turns the page, and
there's your picture, and I'm up out of my seat, yelling across the aisle,
'Brandi, Brandi, Bliss is in the paper!'" Bev went on, comparing herself
to a woman from the projects, yelling from her front porch, wearing
her shower shoes. "You should have seen the look that white chick
gave me. She just folded her paper up and tucked it away."

"So you haven't read the article?"

"I just finished it."

"Bev, that reporter totally misquoted me."

"Right. I see how it is with you now." Bev put on her ghetto voice:
"You used to think dem niggers were lazy and stupid, 'til you realizes,
uh-oh, I'm a nigger too!" She laughed heartily.

"It's not funny. All my relatives are going to read this. People are
going to think I'm a racist."

"Yes, well, I expect they will. And what about this part?" Now she
used her radio announcer voice: "'Broyard is glad that her newfound
racial identity has allowed her to explore African American culture.' Is
that what you're doing here—exploring African American culture?"
She didn't add "with me," but I understood that was what she meant.

"Bev, you know that our friendship is much more than just race," I
said. "But I *am* grateful to you for bringing me places and showing me
things that I wouldn't have found on my own."

She considered this for a moment. Then she said: "Well, I do
know you. I know Bliss, and so I know that whatever way you come
off in the paper, that's not the end of the story about you. But you
better call dem cousins of yours, 'cuz you got some 'splainin' to do."

I was relieved that Bev and I had come to know each other as people, yet I still felt as if I had to align myself with one racial group or
the other. And I wasn't convinced yet that a person could cross from
white to the other side. Then I discovered a family member who had
done just that.

-15-

My great-great-grandfather was surrounded by the noise of revolution. It was the spring of 1848, and Henry Broyard was a young carpenter, just eighteen years old. Night after night, cannon fire disturbed the air of New Orleans, revelers paraded through the streets, shouting "Vive la République" and singing choruses of "La Marseillaise," ecstatic crowds cheered and applauded speaker after speaker at the St. Louis Exchange. Word had just arrived from France that a group of radical republicans and members of the working class had overthrown the monarchy that had been reinstated in 1814. Between increasingly repressive laws, a recent economic crisis, and the exploitation of the poor by the Industrial Revolution, the insurgents became fed up and forced King Louis Philippe to abdicate, restoring democracy to the country once more.

For some people in New Orleans, especially people who, like Henry, were outside the merchant class, the state of affairs at home didn't look very different from that in France. Over the previous two months, the city had been shrouded in cotton—nearly a million bales. It lined almost every inch of the levee and blocked off half their streets until it could be sold and shipped away. But the average worker would see only a tiny portion of the profits from its sale. Nor did much benefit trickle down through improved city services, especially not in the French parts of the city.

The sanitation in New Orleans was still world-famously bad.

Sometimes, when the wind shifted in the afternoon, carrying the stink into the Quarter, one house after another would start closing up its doors and windows until a whole neighborhood disappeared behind shutters. There were few public schools to speak of. And epidemics of yellow fever and cholera continued unabated. As Louisiana's planters and the businessmen who brokered their cotton grew richer, it seemed as if the man on the street just dropped lower on the socioeconomic scale.

But at the center of town, at the St. Louis Exchange, Louisiana senator Pierre Soulé took to the podium to lift up the workingmen. He singled out the laborers of France in whose "rough and bony hands" the aim of the 1789 revolution had been realized. A common workingman was invited to take the stage. "Oh how happy I am," the laborer began, "to be able to speak in the midst of a gathering so large and so capable of appreciating the significance of the questions that I touch on and the prejudices that I fight." The audience cheered in agreement.

The next speaker was Thomas J. Durant, the federal attorney for the Eastern District of Louisiana, who read out a drafted proclamation to send to the people of France from the residents of New Orleans. It opened with the city's response to the French provisional government's decree that ended slavery for good in the French territories. (In 1802, eight years after the French assembly had abolished slavery in the colonies, Napoleon had reinstated it.) "A ray of liberty has come to shed its regenerative warmth over nations long weighed down under the detested yoke of slavery," Durant read. The next resolution applauded the French government's second decree, granting voting rights to all men, including those of African descent who had just been freed, because, as Durant read on, "man possesses the natural and inalienable right of self-government." And finally the citizens of New Orleans offered their praise for this renewed appreciation of the worker. The crowd shouted their approval and raised their voices

in three cheers apiece for France, for the United States, and for freedom in an uproar that was said to have echoed throughout the city.

I like to imagine that at this moment Henry, as he hurrahed along
with the crowd, decided that his life would be different. Perhaps he
understood for the first time that his lot as a worker aligned him with
the slave to some degree—both were being economically exploited.
Or maybe he was just a young man swept up by a mood of rebellion.
Public support for abolition or equal rights was not only unpopular
in the Deep South but dangerous and illegal. Espousers of language
"having a tendency to produce discontent among the free colored
population, or insubordination among the slaves" could face imprisonment or death, at the courts' discretion.

It's possible that feelings Henry had been storing up already were
vindicated by this victory for *liberté, égalité,* and *fraternité.* All his young
life, he'd watched the law draw a "line of distinction" between him
and his colored half siblings and he'd heard science expound about
their biological differences. Yet in all likelihood, he and his father's
colored children looked alike, with the same dark hair and tawny
complexions. His relatives were probably at least as educated as he
was, or even more so. According to the 1850 census, 80 percent of
free people of color could read *and* write, while Henry had only
learned how to read.

Or maybe the course of Henry's life changed simply because he
fell in love. Whatever the explanation, in a few years' time, he would
meet and marry a free woman of color named Pauline Bonée. There
was only one problem: intermarriage had been outlawed in 1808. And
so just as hostility against free Negroes in New Orleans was reaching
a boiling point, my white great-great-grandfather started passing—as
black.

Up in Washington, southern senators won passage of the Fugitive
Slave Act as part of the Compromise of 1850, engineered to main-

tain the equilibrium in the country between free and slave states. The new act, which allowed the capture of runaways on free soil, emboldened unscrupulous slave hunters, who began with increasing frequency to seize free blacks and sell them into slavery.

Solomon Northup, a black man who had been born into freedom, had been kidnapped in Washington, DC, in 1841, even before the tightening of the fugitive slave laws, and sent by ship to the New Orleans slave market, where he was sold as a field hand. Northup described his capture and life on various plantations throughout Louisiana in his autobiography, *Twelve Years a Slave*, which was published in 1853, one year after the publication of Harriet Beecher Stowe's *Uncle Tom's Cabin*, also set partly in Louisiana.

Stowe's melodrama pitting virtuous slaves against wicked slave catchers had become an instant success. (It would eventually outsell every other book during the nineteenth century except the Bible.) *Twelve Years a Slave* didn't find as big an audience, but its "true story" aspect greatly stirred its readers. As a writer for the *New York Tribune* observed, "No one can contemplate the scenes which are here so naturally set forth, without a new conviction of the hideousness of the institution from which the subject of the narrative has happily escaped."

These books and other slave narratives made the cruelties of slavery real to many northerners for the first time. Passage of the Fugitive Slave Act also meant that residents of the free states had to witness blacks being hunted down in their own backyards and were sometimes even forced to join the search posses themselves. As popular sentiment against slavery grew up north, so did hostility against free blacks down south. In New Orleans it was vexing to the proslavery forces that no matter how many articles ran in the newspapers promoting the old argument about slavery being the natural state for people of African descent, all anyone had to do was put down his paper and look around him to see that Negroes were handling freedom just fine.

Strolling along the riverfront at night were free blacks riding in fine carriages, with their wives clad in silk dresses, velvet capes, and the occasional diamond. Nelson Fouché, a free black architect and contractor, had built himself a three-story brick house with fanlight transoms, French doors, granite lintels, and turned balusters. According to the 1850 census, the tailor Philippe Leogaster owned $150,000 worth of property (more than $3.6 million today), and the cigar maker Lucien Mansion had hundreds of workers under his hire, with white people likely among them.

In 1848 Fouché, along with some other leading free black men of the city, opened the Catholic Couvent School, where their children could study English and French composition, history, rhetoric, logic, and accounting under the directorship of another colored man, Armand Lanusse. The city's foremost intellectual of color, Lanusse was the publisher of a journal in which he and other colored writers wrote about the social issues of the day, informed by their reading of the European Romantic movement and German idealism. He had also edited a volume of poetry, *Les Cenelles*, whose publication in 1848 made it the first anthology of "Negro verse" in the country.

Starting in 1850, the Louisiana legislature began to pass even more laws to reduce the rights of these free blacks, and by the end of the decade, their lives were nearly as restricted as those of the slaves.

Henry Broyard's wife, Pauline Bonée, didn't come from the colored elite of New Orleans, but her family had prospered enough to annoy most southern slavery apologists. Pauline's parents could afford to send her and her brother Laurent to one of the private schools for free colored children where they'd learned to read and write. Her father, Pierre, a carpenter, earned enough money in 1850 to support his wife, mother-in-law, two children, and a widowed stepdaughter and her child. And the family had achieved these trappings of middle-class comfort despite having arrived in New Orleans as refugees to a cold welcome only a few decades before.

Pauline was first-generation American, born in New Orleans on

Negre & Negresse de S.ᵗ Domingue.

January 24, 1833. Both of her parents had come to Louisiana as small children, among the St. Domingue free people of color who had fled the island's slave revolt at the turn of the century. No specific details survive about either family's early days in New Orleans, but their circumstances couldn't have been easy. They'd left a homeland that had been scoured by astonishingly brutal violence — fetuses cut from living wombs and impaled on spears and people's eyeballs yanked out with corkscrews. And these atrocities — committed by whites, free colored people, and ex-slaves alike — had come on the heels of a slavery regime so cruel that the threat of sale to St. Domingue was enough to keep slaves elsewhere in line.

By 1850 Pauline's family had settled in the Tremé neighborhood in a two-story house on St. Ann Street, the very same block where Henry Broyard lived. And so, while my great-great-grandfather might not have spotted his future wife sitting in a tree — according to my father's mythology — he could have spied her sitting on the second-story porch of her parents' home.

A few years earlier, Henry had had a relationship with a different free woman of color, who gave birth to a daughter, but he hadn't legitimized that union. If the timing of his wedding to Pauline is any indication, Henry didn't reach the decision to marry her easily. The couple's first son, Pierre Gilbert, was born two days after the ceremony.

The mood regarding plaçage and "living in sin" had changed since Henry's father's day. In his publications, the colored intellectual Lanusse often included cautionary tales in which free women of color who took up with white men came to tragic ends. He also published poems that attacked the system of plaçage, accusing mothers of prostituting their daughters out of greed. One anonymous work, titled "A New Impression," scolded: "...a shameless mother / Today sells the heart of her grieving daughter; / And virtue is no more than a useless word which is cast aside."

The campaign seems to have worked. By the 1850s the majority of baptisms for babies designated as free people of color occurred within wedlock. Pauline's own parents, after living together for more than twenty years and having four children, finally consecrated their union with a wedding at St. Augustine's in 1847. The sacramental record makes careful note that the couple's two surviving children, Laurent and Pauline, now carried the status of legitimate, which entitled them to inherit their parents' property.

As Henry watched Pauline's waistline grow, the public shame awaiting her must have weighed on his mind. What did he have to lose, after all, by making the free woman of color his lawful wife? The few family members that Henry had left were mostly people of color already. The name Broyard was already tainted with blackness. He didn't have the money, property, or standing in society to entice a white woman. Why should he consider himself too good for another carpenter's daughter?

Because Henry was white. And no matter what else he lacked, to be white meant something in the 1850s in New Orleans. For some people it meant everything.

In early 1854, a few months before Henry and Pauline's first child was conceived, the city's newspapers were dominated by coverage of a trial that came to be known as the Pandelly Affair. At issue was the racial identity of a man named George Pandelly. He had recently been elected to serve on the Board of Assistant Aldermen (who were responsible for maintaining the streets and sidewalks), but a gentleman named George Wiltz had contested the election on grounds that only white men could hold public office. Pandelly, Wiltz asserted, was colored through his maternal line.

Pandelly denied the charge, maintaining that while he may have some Indian ancestors, as many white Creoles from the ancienne population did, there were no Negroes hiding in his family tree. Then Wiltz published a pamphlet to back up his claim, and Pandelly took him to court, suing for $20,000 in damages. The accusation was particularly scandalous because Pandelly's mother was a Dimitry, sister to Alexander Dimitry, a prominent educator and leading spokesperson for the white Creole community. The *New Orleans Crescent* reported that one of Pandelly's lawyers declared during opening remarks that "the [Dimitry] name would last when this trial and those concerned would be forgotten," and then, overcome by emotion, he burst into tears.

Day after day the local papers carried testimony about the women in the Dimitry family, trying to establish their racial identity. That the maternal ancestors carried some blood other than white was quickly established: Pandelly's great-grandmother and great-great-grandmother had been slaves during the latter part of the eighteenth century at a time when only Indians or Africans were enslaved. The question was, to which race did they belong?

The oldest residents in town were rounded up and brought to court, where a team of lawyers questioned them about the texture of the Dimitry women's hair (*crépu*, or crisp, suggested African blood), the height of their foreheads (a high brow indicated Indian ancestry), and the quality of their gaze (Africans were said to have dull eyes, while the Natives' eyes were piercing). The lawyers asked, Did whites or blacks call at their home? How did people address the women in the street: *Madame*—reserved for white women? Or *Man*—a familiar term used for colored? Where did the women attend school? In what part of the classroom did they sit?

If the trial revealed the depth of fear in the white Creole population about their racial purity, it also exposed the city's many contradictions around race. Readers discovered, for example, that back in the 1820s, Alexander Dimitry had been thrown out of a society ball for being colored, only to be spotted a little while later dining at a local restaurant with his very accusers. Pandelly won in the end, but the case marked the beginning of a resolve within the white Creole community to divorce the notion of color from Creole for once and for all.

For Henry Broyard, though, it was too late in many ways. If his racial identity had been put to trial, he'd have had a hard time defending his whiteness. No matter what he looked like or what his ancestry actually was, he could be considered black by association. His family had worked in a colored trade for generations, he'd been seen around town with free people of color, other Broyards were known to be of mixed race, and he'd consorted with at least two women of color. Perhaps, ultimately, he didn't care what people thought he was.

In the early winter of 1855, Henry accompanied a very pregnant Pauline to the justice of the peace, where they obtained a marriage license that described them both as "FPC," free people of color. And then on February 12, 1855, the couple went to St. Ann's Church, on the north end of Tremé—not St. Augustine's, where they normally worshipped. The priest, after inspecting their license, asked the congregation if anyone knew of a reason to object to the union. With no objections coming, he blessed the nuptials before a group of witnesses, and that is what the moment of mixing in the Broyard family was like.

Henry, Pauline, and Pierre Gilbert moved into a house on St. Ann Street with one of Pauline's half sisters and her family. The following summer, on July 21, 1856, my great-grandfather was born. (Pierre Gilbert died sometime before 1860, making my great-grandfather the oldest child in the family.) The family headed back to St. Ann's Church, where the infant was christened Paul after his godfather, Paul Trévigne. This choice of godparent suggests how immersed Henry had already become in the colored Creole community: Trévigne was one of its most prominent members.

A writer and language instructor at the new Couvent School, Paul Trévigne embodied the principles of the colored Creoles. Born in New Orleans to free people of color of Spanish descent, Trévigne was fluent in the classical and Enlightenment traditions, strongly influenced by the republican ideals in France, and an outspoken champion of racial equality. A colleague described him as a charming blend of playfulness and poise, "with a little of the pride (the good kind) of the Castilian character."

At the party back at the house that customarily followed christenings, Trévigne would have held forth on the news of the day. While none of the colored men could vote (nor could Henry, having forsaken this right along with his white identity), they followed local and national politics closely. Of particular interest would be the upcoming presidential election. A candidate from a new political party called the Republicans had recently entered the race, and the party's platform gave the colored men reason to feel hopeful.

The Republican Party had been formed by a coalition of political groups united by their opposition to extending slavery into the western territories. Already the question of whether Kansas would enter the Union as slave or free had sparked bloody unrest in the state. And recently in Washington, on the floor of the Senate, Senator Charles Sumner had been beaten almost to death in retaliation for a speech he made against slavery.

Closer to home, New Orleans's largest local paper, the *Daily Picayune,* had called for the expulsion of all free Negroes from the city, claiming that they were "a plague and a pest in our community, besides containing the elements of mischief to our slave population." The white Creole paper, the *New Orleans Bee*, had come out in favor of the free blacks' colonization to Liberia the year before. At the same time, the Louisiana legislature kept chipping away at the rights of people of color, most recently barring them from forming any new scientific, religious, charitable, or literary societies.

As Paul Trévigne and the other men stood outside smoking their cigars, they might have speculated about what would happen next. Forced emigration of free blacks to Africa was being debated in some of the other southern states, with a threat of reenslavement if people didn't comply. Any conversation along these lines must have been hard for Henry to hear. It was one thing for him to voluntarily enter this circumscribed life, but he'd also hung this fate on his children.

The Democratic presidential candidate, James Buchanan, won the November election. In his inaugural address, Buchanan came out in support of "popular sovereignty," the policy put forth by Democratic senator Stephen Douglas in the Kansas-Nebraska Act, which allowed territories to decide the slave question for themselves, thus postponing resolution of the slavery debate for the time being. But the Republicans' respectable showing in the election—winning 38 percent of the electoral college in a field of three candidates—highlighted the growing division in the country. Then, two days after Buchanan was sworn in, the Supreme Court announced its decision in the Dred Scott case, intensifying the split even more.

The court case focused on the status of a slave named Dred Scott, who had sued for his freedom on the basis of his four-year stay on free soil. Chief Justice Roger B. Taney, writing the majority opinion, held that slaves were not citizens of the United States, and therefore Scott was not entitled to sue in the federal courts. Taney also declared that blacks, free and enslaved, were "so far inferior, that they had no rights which the white man was bound to respect." Furthermore, the court determined that Congress had no authority to regulate slavery in the territories, overturning the Missouri Compromise and other legislation that had maintained the balance in the country between slave and free soil. The decision greatly alarmed antislavery forces and gave the Republican Party a key issue around which to rally support.

The more threatened the southerners felt their peculiar institution to be, the more they attacked the blacks who were already free. In 1857 Louisiana governor Robert C. Wickliffe appealed to the state legislature "that immediate steps should be taken at this time to remove all the free negroes who are now in the State, when such removal can be effected without violation of the law. Their example and associations have a most pernicious effect upon our slave population." The state lawmakers still weren't ready to take this step—some of them had relatives who were free people of color—but they did decide to put an end to all manumissions. Slaves could no longer be freed for any reason. Also they forbade free blacks from assembling without white supervision to worship (which had been previously excluded from laws restricting their congregation), as well as banning them from running coffeehouses, billiard halls, or any establishments serving liquor, a ruling that put many colored proprietors out of business.

In 1859 the Louisiana legislature went so far as to pass an act that allowed free blacks to choose masters and voluntarily enslave themselves for life. By this time Henry and Pauline had three small children: my great-grandfather Paul, his brother, Pierre, and his sister, Pauline. Surviving family photos suggest that the kids wouldn't have looked recognizably black, but their baptisms identified them as free people of color. If the government started to round up the free Negroes of New Orleans for expulsion or enslavement, their names would be on the list too.

Henry and Pauline's neighbors and friends began leaving the city in droves. In early 1860 the city's *Daily Delta* observed that "scarcely a week passes but a large number of free persons [of color] leave this port for Mexico or Haiti." The Broyards, however, stayed put. Pauline's maternal grandmother, who was living with them, was more than eighty years old, and she'd been moving all her life, from Jamaica, where she was born, to St. Domingue until the slave revolt forced her out, to Cuba until they were expelled, and finally to New Orleans. How could the family ask her to pick up and move again?

For the 1860 election, the Republicans put forward a young candidate from Illinois who had recently garnered national attention in a series of debates on the slavery question. His name was Abraham Lincoln, and his conciliatory stance — he was against slavery's extension into the western territories, but he wasn't calling for immediate emancipation — helped to gain him the party's nomination. Then infighting among the opposition propelled him into the White House. By the time Lincoln was sworn in, on March 4, 1861, seven Southern states, including Louisiana, had seceded to form the Confederate States of America.

A few weeks later, Alexander Stephens, the newly elected vice president of the Confederacy, made a speech in Savannah, outlining the Southern states' reason for secession. "Our new government is founded upon...the great truth that the negro is not equal to the white man; that slavery, subordination to the superior race, is his natural and moral condition. This, our new Government, is the first, in the history of the world, based upon this great physical, philosophical, and moral truth." Then on April 12, 1861, Louisiana native General Pierre G. T. Beauregard fired on a boat bringing provisions to federal forces at Fort Sumter in South Carolina, and the Civil War began.

Almost immediately the free men of color of New Orleans, along with the white men of the city, began organizing themselves into volunteer militia units to help defend against a Yankee invasion. Among those who signed up was Henry Broyard. The colored men later explained that they'd been threatened with death or destruction of their property unless they volunteered. One man claimed that a policeman advised him to join up if he didn't want to be hanged. But some men also volunteered with the hope of improving their position in society. Throughout Louisiana's history, men of color had taken up arms with this aim in mind (only to be disappointed time and again). Also many free men of color owned property, which they intended to defend, no matter the moral implications. In any case, more than 80 percent of the free blacks in New Orleans were of mixed race in 1860, and they'd already been emulating white social mores for years.

The Confederate government regarded the Native Guard (as the colored troops were called) as mostly for show. The men were never given arms, uniforms, or any tactical assignments. Henry and his fellow troops did little else but parade up and down the streets in the gray coats and trousers they had purchased themselves, carrying their own antiquated muskets or walking empty-handed. But the troops made a good story for the local papers, with one predicting that the colored men would "fight the Black Republicans with as much determination and gallantry" as their white brethren.

When the time came, however, with the run of Union admiral David Farragut's fleet past the Confederate forts guarding the mouth of the Mississippi, neither militia took a stand against the Yankees. The white soldiers fled when they heard the twelve tolls of the church bells, notifying citizens of the approaching federal forces, and the Native Guard troops were ordered by their commander to disband. They did as they were told, first hiding their muskets in buildings around the city, including the Couvent School, before returning home to their families.

Soon after Union general Benjamin F. Butler took control of New Orleans on May 1, 1862, he published an edict in the local papers, ordering the citizens to turn over any weapons. After some deliberation the Native Guard members dispatched a committee to visit Butler and offer their guns and service to the federal cause. But Butler had already contemplated using black troops and dismissed the idea, observing in a letter to Secretary of War Edwin M. Stanton that black men were "horrified of firearms."

In any case, President Lincoln was hesitant to employ black soldiers for fear that arming the former slaves would push some of the border states still in the Union into siding with the South. Furthermore, Butler had read the local newspaper accounts describing the colored men's enthusiastic response to the Confederate call to arms. Despite the Native Guard's explanation about the coercion accompanying their previous enlistment, the general was skeptical about their loyalty to the Union. Circumstances soon forced him to change his mind.

In early August the Confederates launched an attack on Baton Rouge and were rumored to be heading for New Orleans. Butler lacked the forces for an adequate defense. He'd already enlisted all the white Unionists in the city, and Secretary of War Stanton refused his request for reinforcements, claiming they were more badly needed elsewhere. Finally the general decided to "call on Africa to intervene." He issued a general order requesting the men of the Native Guard and the rest of the free colored population to volunteer for the Union army. Immediately the most prominent colored men of New Orleans began trying to raise companies. A fifty-three-year-old free man of color named Joseph Follin recruited men for Company C, and one of the first he signed up was Henry Broyard, age thirty-three.

Opposition to slavery played a role in motivating the enlistment of many colored men. They'd also grown up hearing romantic tales of heroism from their fathers and grandfathers who had taken up arms against the British in the War of 1812. But the men had practical considerations too — work and food were growing scarce under the war conditions. They needed the pay and rations to feed their families. Within two weeks two thousand colored men from across the city presented themselves at the Touro Building in the French Quarter to volunteer.

Still passing as black, Henry Broyard entered the regiment of the First Louisiana Native Guard as a colored corporal. When his turn came to swear in, his white appearance probably didn't even cause the federal marshal to look twice. As a reporter for the *New York Times* observed, several officers in the colored regiment "were, to all superficial appearance, white men." Butler himself claimed to Secretary of War Stanton that the darkest member of the new regiment would resemble in complexion the late senator Daniel Webster. In fact out of the ninety-five men originally enrolled in Henry's company, twenty-six were identified as "fair, bright, yellow, or light," while another thirty-four were described as "brown," with the remaining thirty-five listed as "black."

Some of those listed as black in the new regiment were runaway slaves. Despite the legal and social differences that had existed between the castes of free men and slaves, a spirit of solidarity and common cause now united them. In a letter to a new Republican newspaper, a captain in one of the regiments wrote, "In parade, you will see a thousand white bayonets gleaming in the sun, held by black, yellow, or white hands. Be informed that we have no prejudice; that we receive everyone in camp; but that the sight of human salesmen of flesh makes us sick."

On September 27, 1862, my great-great-grandfather Henry's regiment, the First Louisiana Native Guard Infantry, was mustered into service, becoming the first black regiment in the history of the U.S. Army. Following their enlistment, the thousand colored men marched to Camp Strong, four miles outside of town near the racetrack, to set up their tents and begin their training. The sight of these men in the dark blue coats and light blue pants of the Union uniform filled members of the local colored community with pride. They lined the streets to cheer them, and hiked out Gentilly Road to watch them drill and parade.

A few whites cheered the troops as well. The reporter from the

Times praised the soldiers' bearing and conduct. And a white officer privately complimented the colored men's deportment in a letter: "I find them better deposed [*sic*] to learn, and more orderly and cleanly, both in their persons and quarters, than the whites." The men of Henry's company benefited from the experience of their first lieutenant, a man named Emile Detiege, who'd been schooled in military deportment by his uncle, an old Belgian who'd fought in Napoleon's army.

But the majority of the white community, including Union soldiers, displayed their hostility for the colored troops at every turn. The Union paymaster refused to release funds for the colored troops; the supply officers neglected to fulfill requests to outfit them. The men had to scavenge their belts and knapsacks from the discards of the white units. Their commanding colonel, Spencer H. Stafford, described the regiment as "the most indifferently supplied regiment that ever went into service."

Black soldiers returning to camp at night risked being jumped by white Union soldiers, who stripped them of their uniforms, forcing them to walk the rest of the way back in their underwear. Whites lined Canal Street during parades to shout insults at the soldiers; they turned their families out of their living quarters for late rent despite explanations about the holdup in their pay. Police officers imprisoned the soldiers' wives and mothers on trumped-up charges and arrested members of the colored regiment at the slightest provocation.

Perhaps most insulting to the Native Guard was the whites' constant disparagement of their fitness for military service. Even before the regiment had been officially mustered in, the *Daily Picayune* forecast the men's imminent failure as soldiers because of the Negro's "innate inferiority, natural dullness and cowardice, indolence, awe of the white man, and lack of motivation." People on the street claimed that any three white men could send the whole regiment running with a whip and a few shouts.

For Henry Broyard, being in the Native Guard was probably the first time he experienced such prejudicial attitudes firsthand. No matter that the recent 1860 census identified him as a mulatto, he had still been walking around the world looking like and being treated as a white man. But now, as Henry marched alongside the other members of the Native Guard, the jeers of the crowd and taunts of "coward" and "damned nigger" fell on his ears too. At camp he felt the cold stares from the white soldiers. He listened to the hollow promises about the colored men's pay that was endlessly delayed, and his family suffered because of food rations that never came. Henry learned what it meant to be black in the antebellum South by making the concerns of people of color his concerns, by joining their fight.

~16~

When I wasn't researching my dead relatives, I tried to spend time with the living ones. Every person of color I asked—at the library, my taxi driver, the waiter at a restaurant—seemed to know a Broyard. (White people, on the other hand, had never heard of them, unless they happened to know of my dad through his writing.) I was eager to meet my family, but I also wanted their help in figuring out just how black or white my father might have felt himself to be.

Not everyone was excited to meet me. All my talk about race put off some; my interest in telling the Broyard story bothered others. After all, I hadn't been raised as a Creole, nor had I grown up in New Orleans. And I hadn't suffered from the discrimination in the South or the confusion of looking like one thing and being told that you must be another. At the library one day, a cousin who was also researching and writing about the family history loudly upbraided me for only hanging around with white people. Another older cousin, in hearing I wanted to meet him, commented: "So this girl finds out her daddy's black and now she's come down here and wants to be black too? That's plain foolishness."

Part of the problem was that Creoles tended to be private by nature. Years of living in an insulated community had made them cautious about sharing their personal business, as had their legacy of secrets, about who was living "on the other side" or the adultery once common among free people of color. "Live and let live" was a motto I often heard. "Ask me no questions, and I'll you no lies" was another. But Creoles were also wonderful storytellers, and a compelling history—full of heroic achievements and ironic twists—had given them some tales that were too good to keep to themselves.

Ultimately my New Orleans kin seemed as curious about me as I was about them. As in cases of identical twins separated at birth, our interactions offered an Alice in Wonderland view of how we might have turned out if we'd grown up on the other side of the color line.

On a Saturday afternoon, I headed over to visit Rose, the grandmother of Sheila, my cousin whom I had initially teamed up with to research the family. Rose lived in a two-bedroom bungalow in the Seventh Ward, an area of New Orleans known as the Creole ward for much of the twentieth century. In her late seventies, Rose had been there nearly all her life, first in the house across the street, where she'd lived with her grandfather Paul Broyard, and then, for the past fifty years, in this house that she and her late husband had built at the time of their marriage.

Up until the 1960s, the Seventh Ward was an integrated, middle-class community. Some residents owned their shotgun houses, named so because a bullet fired in the front door could pass straight out the back, or the bungalows that eventually replaced them. Along Claiborne Avenue were the fancier town houses, with cast-iron balconies or porches accented with fluted columns, in addition to the many pharmacies, barbershops, laundries, funeral homes, restaurants, bakeries, and markets that made the street a bustling African American business district. Down the center of Claiborne ran a wide grassy promenade, where the city's black population gathered under the shade of the tall live oak trees to picnic or watch the Zulu Social Club and Mardi Gras Indians parade during Carnival.

In 1966 construction of interstate highway 10 began. Designed to transport commuters from their (mostly white) suburbs into the city,

I-10 was routed directly over Claiborne Avenue. The magnificent oaks were chopped down — in the middle of the night, according to some older residents. Given the size and number of trees, that seems unlikely, but that's how it felt to people: one morning they woke up and their neighborhood was ruined. Businesses failed; people — especially whites — moved away; properties fell into disrepair and were abandoned.

A few years back, the local African American museum spearheaded a project to adorn the pillars supporting the interstate with paintings of the live oaks, but it would take more than some concrete trees to make the neighborhood inviting again. Beginning in the mid-1990s, the city began closing its housing projects. Displaced residents moved into the Seventh Ward — occupying St. Bernard, another housing development, and properties for which Section 8 rental assistance was available. Suddenly members of opposing gangs were down the block from each other, and residential streets that had been relatively peaceful became the battleground for turf wars.

In the middle of the increasing violence lived many older widows who, like Rose, refused to move despite the pleas of their children. They'd been in their homes all of their adult lives, raised their families there, and planned to die there too, even if it might kill them. (In June 2004, a few years after I first met Rose, her friend and neighbor, ninety-year-old dressmaker Durelli Watts, was fatally stabbed in her home by a robber on a Tuesday afternoon. Then Watts's daughter, Ina Gex, a sixty-seven-year-old former high school principal, bumped into the robber as he was fleeing and was shot to death on her mother's front porch before a handful of witnesses. Notices appeared in the newspaper pleading for these witnesses to come forward, but the threat of retaliation frightened many people into silence. Only after the amount offered for tips to a crime hotline was substantially increased did a call come in that led to an arrest.)

"There was a time when I was knowing everyone on the street," Rose said after letting me inside. "Now I look out my window and the faces are always changing." But it didn't bother her, she told me cheerfully, shuffling back to her seat. "I don't get out much since I can't walk so good no more." Her daughters or Sheila brought over groceries or whatever else she needed. Anyway, inside the house, with the iron bars bolted across the doors and windows, the drapes closed, and the television on, the world outside was mostly kept at bay.

Rose brought to mind my father's mother, at least as I remembered her from that one visit to Connecticut when I was seven. My grandmother hadn't been able to walk well either and spent most of the day in a lawn chair in the yard with her feet elevated. Rose spoke with the same New Orleans accent that I'd had trouble understanding as a child, pausing on the first syllables of words like "people," "handsome," and "babies," her voice trilling with an unfamiliar music from her first language, French. She also looked a bit like my grandmother, slightly stout with thinning wavy brown hair, light caramel skin, and typical "Caucasian" features.

Rose settled into her easy chair at the far end of the parlor, next to a tray table holding the television remote control, her address book, and the telephone. As I soon discovered, her phone rang constantly, often with calls from her Broyard cousins, many of them older widows like herself. Sometimes, after answering, Rose would roll her eyes, as if the caller was a nuisance, but it was clear that these frequent check-ins helped the housebound women pass their days. I had a feeling that my arrival in town had the telephone wires working overtime.

"I love company, me," Rose said, when I sat beside her. "I'm always glad when I see my people." That I counted as her people made me smile.

Rose said she figured she took after her grandfather that way. I asked Rose what else she recalled about him. "Paul was born before the Civil War," I said. "Did he ever say anything about that?"

She shook her head.

"How about Emancipation, before all the black people were free?"

I continued. "Did he ever talk about any relative being descended from a slave?"

"Oh no," Rose said, shaking her head again. Then she brightened. "But I *can* tell you, the house on Lapeyrouse Street, back when my grandmother was living, they had"—she paused—"not slaves, but servants. They lived above the horse stables in the backyard. So they could just come down and in through the kitchen and take care of the house." She nodded up and down. "Umm-hmm."

This wasn't quite the slave connection that I was looking for. "So Paul had a good bit of money there for a while?" I asked.

"That's what they always said."

I tried to steer the conversation back to the family's racial ancestry. "Do you remember when you realized that being Creole also meant being black?"

Rose put her hand to her chin and thought for a moment. "You know," she said, "it was years and years, I'd sit and try to figure it out." She pointed to my research binder. "Don't it say in your notes? A woman from the islands, Jamaica or somewhere, married one of the Broyards way back."

"So you did know growing up that you were part black?"

"Well, I always went to integrated schools," Rose said. "We always went to school with them."

It took me a minute to realize that Rose meant she'd integrated with African American students. (She'd been in school in the 1930s, long before the *Brown v. Board of Education* decision ended black and white segregation.) That she saw blacks as "them" surprised me. Given the fact that she lived in a black neighborhood and that some of her children had married African Americans, I'd expected her to identify more closely with the family's African ancestry. At the same time, she didn't seem to see herself as particularly white.

"In fact, we never passed for white," Rose said, although that's not what some people in the neighborhood thought. When I'd asked Rose if she had ever experienced discrimination, she mentioned a black woman who used to live across the street who'd accused the family of trying to be white. That—not some Jim Crow humiliation—was the only time she'd felt victimized by prejudice.

A while later, her daughters, Nancy and Jane, arrived with some freshmade gumbo and rice and beans. We sat around, eating and talking, inquiring about one another's lives, and I fancied that we all felt the ease of connection that came with being related. One of Nancy's closest girlfriends vacationed on Martha's Vineyard, and we discussed meeting up on the island sometime. Even Nancy's kids hung around the table for the better part of an hour before retreating to the couch to watch TV.

The next time I was at Rose's house, I asked her what everyone had thought of me. At first she didn't want to say. Finally she laughed sheepishly and offered, "Pure white." My face must have registered my disappointment, because Rose touched my arm and reassured me that it was mostly my "Yankee" way of talking.

Just as I had assumptions about my New Orleans kin based on their looks and upbringing, they held notions about me from the fact of my being raised as white in Connecticut. Rose's cousin Jeanne, another older widow who lived nearby, joined us during a different visit. Rose's daughters and Sheila were there too.

In her midseventies, Jeanne spoke in hiccups and gulps, as if, having been raised speaking French, she wasn't accustomed to fitting her mouth around the English language. As we talked she gestured at me intermittently to emphasize her point. Her hand trembled slightly, from age or the early stages of Parkinson's disease—I wasn't sure. Yet despite her apparent frailty, her conversation contained a surprising forcefulness. After a little chitchat, Jeanne blurted out: "So your family's rich." It was more a statement than a question.

"Jeanne!" Everyone scolded, but their tone suggested that Jeanne's bluntness was a familiar and often celebrated trait. Anyway, she was just saying out loud what people were already thinking. They'd all read the *New Yorker* article and knew about the homes in Connecticut and Martha's Vineyard. Also, Creoles tended to defend people who passed as white on the grounds that they were trying to improve their lot for their families.

In that moment, though, with my family's eyes upon me, I was too worried about their judgment or resentment to appreciate this point. I wasn't yet comfortable acknowledging that life on the other side had been easier. With their label of me as "pure white," I still felt implicated in the racial equation. And I didn't know where such an admission would lead me: I couldn't exactly give back these advantages, nor, if I were being truly honest, did I want to.

"I wouldn't call us rich exactly," I hedged, knowing full well that if Nancy ever came to my family's house on Martha's Vineyard, she wouldn't walk away thinking of us as poor. "My parents always struggled over money," I went on.

But Jeanne wasn't buying it. She pointed a shaky finger at me. "We know somebody's niece who works up there in Manhattan. She's an accountant at Random House, and she said that a check crossed her desk made out to your father, Anatole Broyard, for a *million dollars!*"

I couldn't help smiling—what an amazing coincidence!—but the claim was also startling. Random House was the parent company for my father's publisher and was indeed the payer on the advance for his book about Greenwich Village (which was more in the low five figures range), but how could Jeanne have known that? This detail made me realize that the New Orleans Broyards had, in some fashion, been keeping tabs on my dad and our family.

"Well," I said. "I sure wish he would have shared that with me." Everybody laughed, Jeanne sat back in her chair, and the moment passed.

Ironically, as I got to know my New Orleans relatives better and stopped viewing them constantly through the lens of race, I was able to see more clearly the specific ways that race had impacted our respective lives. To take just one example, American real estate practices during the mid-twentieth century benefited white families like my own by allowing them to accumulate capital through homeownership that could then be passed down to their children, while black families such as my cousins were largely excluded from participating in the post–World War II housing boom.

The sociologist Dalton Conley has suggested that the achievement gap between whites and blacks can be explained by differences in their net worth, which is largely a measure of inherited monies. My parents, for example, by buying and selling properties in Connecticut and Martha's Vineyard, were able to increase an initial investment of $110,000 to about $2.4 million over a forty-year time span, for a 2,000 percent profit. Conversely, the home purchased by my cousin Jeanne and her husband, Frank, in the Seventh Ward in 1965 for $10,000 increased in value to about $80,000 over the same time period, for a 700 percent return on their investment. (Neither example takes into account the effects of inflation nor the money spent on improvements.)

The discrepancy can be explained in part by the differences between the northern and southern economies, but it was also rooted in racism. All over the country, lenders frequently deemed black neighborhoods as too risky an investment, which made it hard for African Americans to secure mortgages. Redlining, as the practice was called, was so widespread that whites received 98 percent of the $120 billion of federally financed home loans issued between 1934 and 1962. In New Orleans, passage of the Civil Rights Act in 1964 sparked white flight from mixed neighborhoods. Then construction of I-10 two years later, to provide access to the booming white suburbs, further segregated neighborhoods and depressed property values in the increasingly black communities. Black middle-class families began to leave too, exposing the Seventh Ward to more blight. (Many moved out to New Orleans East, a low-lying area adjacent to Lake Pontchartrain that would be devastated by Hurricane Katrina forty years later.)

The neighborhoods where my parents had lived would never be similarly scapegoated by local planning policy. The substantial proceeds from their real estate investments will eventually be passed along to my brother and me, and used, most likely, to pay for our children's college educations, further perpetuating my family's legacy of privilege.

Until I thought through these specifics, the idea that race mattered in people's lives remained an abstract truism that I mostly ignored. I hung out with my New Orleans kin, feeling vaguely guilty, occasionally making awkward gestures at compensation. One time I tried to pay for the takeout from Popeye's that Rose had asked Sheila to pick up on our way over. "Grandma will get it," Sheila assured me, with a slightly annoyed tone in her voice. She didn't say anything, but I imagined her thinking, "Geez, she doesn't think we can afford a bucket of fried chicken?"

In fact most of my New Orleans relatives were earning far more than my measly freelance writer's income. I still had to occasionally call my mother for a "loan" to pay my health insurance bill or the mortgage for my studio apartment (acquired with my mother's help). Many of my cousins — working as nurses, social workers, small business owners, TV producers, radio talk show hosts, doctors, bricklayers, bar owners, firemen, carpenters, speech therapists, engineers, and technology administrators — had purchased their homes and the multiple cars parked out front, took their families on nice vacations, and sent their kids to college.

But as my candid cousin Jeanne told me a few years after we met, it was a real struggle. Along with her husband, Frank, Jeanne had been active in the civil rights movement, registering black voters and boycotting white-owned businesses. Her son, Joe, helped to integrate the

New Orleans Public Library, sitting with other demonstrators in the seats reserved for white kids; when the police came to kick them out, they moved the chairs outside to continue their protest.

"I never miss the vote," Jeanne said. "Even if I'm lying in bed. Because I fought for it." Despite failing health and bouts of pneumonia that kept sending her to the emergency room, Jeanne made it to the polls for the 2004 election.

We come from a family of fighters, Jeanne told me. "Are you a fighter too?" she asked. Before I could respond, she answered the question herself: "But you never had to fight, did you? You grew up white."

M y great-grandfather Paul turned six the summer that his father put on the blue Union uniform and moved out to Camp Strong. For a few weeks, Paul's father remained an intermittent presence in his life. Paul probably headed out to Gentilly Road with the rest of the free colored community to see his dad march and drill, and Henry might have come back for a home-cooked meal a few times. But at the end of October 1862, Henry's regiment was sent out of the city for its first assignment, and Paul wouldn't see his father again for months.

My great-grandfather was just old enough to understand that the country was at war. He might have picked up bits and pieces of news: about the holdup in his father's pay, about the terrible conditions and rampant fever out at the camp, or about President Lincoln's recent Emancipation Proclamation, which would free all the slaves in Confederate territories. And the day-to-day hardships that the War Between the States was imposing on the family's life would be impossible to miss.

Food had become scarce in New Orleans and outrageously expensive, with the price of flour shooting up to $30 a barrel (equivalent to about $540 today). Henry would serve for six months before he received his first paycheck. And then his salary was short: only $7 a month, not the $13 that was promised—and was the salary paid to the white troops. But the colored soldiers had little recourse, and there was no work to be had in New Orleans either. Most trade and businesses had slowed to a halt. The levee sat quiet and deserted. The city's streets, though, were packed with runaway slaves, all looking for work themselves.

Since the war began, slaves had been stealing away from their plantations and making a dash for Union lines. They arrived in New Orleans, sometimes as many as two hundred a day, close to starving and nearly naked. Unable to find employment or food in the city, they took to hanging around the Union camps, offering their labor in exchange for leftovers from meals.

The packs of desperate-looking Africans wandering the streets sent alarm through New Orleans's white population. After numerous complaints, General Butler began rounding up the runaways, snatching back the freedom they'd just tasted for the first time. He placed them in refugee camps on the edge of town, where conditions were so crowded and unsanitary, especially during the summer months, that many people died.

To stem the arrival of more runaways, Butler issued an order that any Negroes caught on the street without work passes were to be seized and sent to one of the abandoned plantations taken over by the federal forces. The new pass system made it dangerous for free black people to venture onto the streets as well. Paul's godfather, Paul Trévigne, who'd been free his entire life, was thrown into jail and had to bribe a marshal to avoid getting shipped out of town with the runaways.

Many blacks in New Orleans, free and enslaved, were beginning to realize that the presence of the Union army didn't necessarily mean an end to their bondage and discriminatory treatment. They began to organize themselves in order to demand what they saw as their natural rights. Leading the way was Paul Trévigne.

On September 27, 1862, the same day that Henry Broyard's regiment became the first officially sanctioned black regiment in the Union army, Trévigne put out the inaugural edition of a new French-language biweekly newspaper called *L'Union.* The paper was funded by a colored Creole doctor, Louis Charles Roudanez, who had been educated in France, where he'd witnessed firsthand the revolution of 1848. Trévigne as editor was an obvious choice for the doctor. They both thought of themselves as equal or superior to the average white man and resented being viewed as no better than the common slave.

In the first issue, Trévigne announced the basis of the paper's platform as the Declaration of Independence and its founding truth that "all men are created equal." He condemned slavery and the degradation it brought on American values, writing, "Equal rights before the law, freedom of conscience, freedom of the press, all of these things were...trampled underfoot and spat upon." About the war he predicted swift Northern victory and the end to slavery for good. And a few months after the Emancipation Proclamation took effect, Trévigne began to campaign for the black man's right to vote. Given all the Confederate loyalists remaining in the city, Trévigne was putting himself at great risk by making public such opinions.

At just six years old, Paul Broyard wouldn't be able to understand much of what his godfather wrote about in his paper. But I imagine that some of Paul Trévigne's radicalism rubbed off on young Paul, because my great-grandfather grew up to agitate for equality and universal suffrage himself. Then too there was the example of his own father's courage in battle when Henry Broyard finally got his chance to fight.

As fall stretched into winter, Henry's regiment waited for an opportunity to prove itself. At every bivouac the men of the First Louisiana were stuck with the worst of the fatigue duty—digging latrines and unloading supplies—while the white soldiers stood around and watched. The blue uniforms that the colored men had once worn so proudly had become tattered and filthy. Tempers flared and morale sank under the steady dose of hard labor. Henry's first lieutenant,

Emile Detiége, shot and killed a new recruit for not falling into line quickly enough.

When Nathaniel P. Banks replaced Butler as commander of the Gulf, conditions worsened. While Banks wasn't necessarily opposed to black soldiers, he certainly didn't support them and even began demoting some after an incident in which white enlisted men refused to obey their orders. Henry's own captain would eventually resign with the explanation that "daily events demonstrate that prejudices are so strong against colored officers, that no matter what would be their patriotism and their anxiety to fight for the flag of their native Land, they cannot do it with honor to themselves." Even the white officers associated with the Native Guard began to suffer.

The First Louisiana's immediate commander, Colonel Spencer H. Stafford, was a New Yorker by birth and a lawyer before the war. He frequently championed the intelligence and discipline of his colored charges, and he petitioned his superiors to ease the regiment's fatigue assignments so the men would have time to drill for combat. Stafford knew that his soldiers were eager to prove themselves, and he believed that "when tried, they shall not be found wanting."

Before he got the chance to lead his regiment in battle, Stafford was dismissed. After another episode of prejudice against his troops — some white sentries refused to let his men reenter the camp after collecting firewood — the colonel lost his temper and called a subordinate officer "a God damned pusillanimous, stinking white-livered Yankee." Stafford was found guilty of "conduct unbecoming of an officer and a gentleman" and removed. Four days later his regiment shipped out for Port Hudson — without its commander — where it would face off against the Confederate forces at last.

The town of Port Hudson sat on the Mississippi River about seventy miles north of Baton Rouge. Union control of it would effectively cut the Confederacy in half, but rebels had been dug into Port Hudson for months, and a Union fleet had already been badly cut up on one attempted run past the fort. By the middle of May, though, General Banks was ready to try a simultaneous naval and infantry assault on the Confederate stronghold, with the First and Third regiments of the Louisiana Native Guard assigned a place on the extreme right of the Confederate line.

With Stafford gone the command of Henry's regiment fell to a diehard abolitionist, Lieutenant Colonel Chauncey J. Bassett; but unfortunately for the Native Guard, overall command of the colored regiments had been given to one General William Dwight. Dwight was a drunk who resented having to be associated with the black soldiers. His interest in them didn't seem to extend beyond abstract curiosity. In a letter to his mother, he wrote about his plans for the men in the upcoming engagement: "You may look for hard fighting, or for a complete run away....I shall compromise nothing in making this attack for I regard it as an experiment."

It was an experiment that Dwight practically guaranteed would fail. On the morning of the assault, May 27, 1863, Dwight was drunk by the time he met with his officers. When Lieutenant Colonel Bassett asked him about the type of terrain the Native Guard would have to travel to reach the rebels, Dwight assured him that it was the easiest of all approaches into Port Hudson. In fact the general had conducted no reconnaissance; otherwise he'd have known that the colored troops would face the most difficult section of the Confederate line.

Opposing the Native Guard were six companies from the Thirty-ninth Mississippi, dug in on top of a steep bluff that overlooked the river. At the foot of this bluff was a two-hundred-yard-wide moat, eight feet in depth, that the rebels had engineered as an additional obstacle. The only approach to the position was along a road below the bluff that ran between sixty Confederate sharpshooters on one side and a battery of artillery on the other, with no cover to be found.

The morning of the assault was all sunshine and blue skies. After eight months of digging trenches and carting supplies, the colored troops were in high spirits as they assembled in a willow forest at the far end of the road. Henry's company, Company C, and five other companies from the First Regiment would lead the charge. In the style of warfare of the day, the regiment lined up in two long rows in which the men would move forward in formation until they were within two hundred yards of the enemy's position — shooting range.

At 10 a.m. Henry and the men of the First Louisiana started down the road at double-quick time. In the lead was Captain André Cailloux, a thirty-eight-year-old ex-slave. Cailloux, of unmixed African blood, liked to brag that he was "the blackest man in New Orleans." His contemporaries described him as a "fine-looking man who presented an imposing appearance" and "a born leader."

The Native Guard had covered about one-third of the distance toward the bluff when the Confederate artillery opened fire with a torrent of shot and shells and foot-long pieces of iron railroad. The sharpshooters began picking off the men from the left, and the two guns positioned on the river raked the right side of the line. One of the first to fall was the color sergeant — who carried the regimental banner that helped soldiers orient themselves in the fog of battle — with a shot taking off half his head.

The surprise and intensity of the slaughter sent confusion through the colored ranks. Soldiers fell back on those coming up behind them

ASSAULT OF THE SECOND LOUISIANA (COLORED) REGIMENT ON THE CONFEDERATE WORKS AT PORT HUDSON, MAY 27th, 1863.
From a Sketch by F. H. Schell.

as they frantically sought cover. Cailloux had taken a musket ball in the elbow, and his left arm flopped uselessly at his side. But in his right hand the ex-slave waved his unsheathed sword, calling to his men, "En avant, mes enfants!" *Forward, my children.* His detachment reached the moat at the bottom of the bluff, where the colored soldiers unleashed a volley of shots upon the white men who would have them and their families enslaved.

It was the only round that the Native Guard got off. And not one of these bullets struck home. On top of the bluff, the Thirty-ninth Mississippi, in its excitement, opened fire on the black troops even before its commander had given the order to shoot. Cailloux was starting across the flooded ditch when a shell caught him in the head. Some thirty or forty of his men continued on, attempting to swim across the deep water with their muskets lifted above their heads. Nearly all of them were shot dead, with only six making it back to safety. The rest of the Native Guard had already retreated to the willow tree forest.

Out of the roughly 540 colored soldiers participating in the battle, 2 officers and 24 enlisted men were killed and another 3 officers and 92 men were wounded. Only one regiment—the 165th New York—suffered a higher percentage of casualties that day. No details of Henry Broyard's particular experience at Port Hudson survive, but six of the fatalities came from his company, suggesting that he and the other members of his unit had been in the thick of battle.

General Banks praised the Native Guard's performance in a letter written to his wife three days after the assault: "They fought splendidly!, splendidly! Every body is delighted that they did so well!" In his official report, Banks offered this assessment: "In many respects their conduct was heroic. No troops could be more determined or more daring....Whatever doubt may have existed heretofore...the history of this day proves conclusively...that the Government will find in this class of troops effective supporters and defenders."

Newspapers across the country began broadcasting accounts of the Native Guard's bravery—a good number of which were wildly exaggerated and distorted by racial stereotyping. But the *New York Times* observed that Banks's report about the men's conduct "settles the question that the negro race can fight with prowess....It is no longer possible to doubt the bravery and steadiness of the colored race, when rightly led."

These accounts helped to change public sentiment about enlisting black troops in the Union army. Before Port Hudson the debate focused on whether arming former slaves would invite too much hostility from Southerners to be worth it. Now the Northern population measured the question in terms of the tactical advantage that the colored troops might bring to the fight. More than 180,000 colored troops would eventually serve the Union cause.

This rush of black volunteers represented a turning point in the war for the North. White enlistment had dwindled, and public support was beginning to falter in the face of the constant casualties. The influx of manpower helped to turn the mood around. The black troops freed up additional white soldiers for combat by taking over much of the guard duty and fatigue work. They also participated in a number of decisive battles themselves—the most famous among them at Fort Wagner in South Carolina.

For the country's African American population, the participation of black soldiers and their honorable conduct in battle called forth a sense of pride that had been beaten down by slavery and race prejudice. With the possibility of freedom around the corner, the community would need leaders, and the men's heroic conduct in war proved them up to the job. Also, the Negroes' enlistment added strength to their political battle. If a black man was willing to die for his country, he should be entitled to the rights of citizenship. He should be allowed to vote.

*   *   *

Unfortunately for Henry and his fellows in the Native Guard, the elevation of their esteem in the eyes of Banks and the Northern press didn't bring about practical improvements in their daily lives. Nowhere was this discrepancy more evident than in the treatment of their war dead. The day after the assault at Port Hudson, white flags appeared up and down the line, and the Confederates ceased their fire so that the Union soldiers could recover the fallen soldiers and bury them. Not only was this pause permitted for honorable reasons, but the stench of decaying flesh could quickly become unbearable for both sides. Yet the dead black soldiers were conspicuously denied this basic decency; their bodies were left on the battlefield to rot in the hot Louisiana sun.

Not until five weeks later, when the fall of Vicksburg forced the Confederates' surrender, were the remains of the dead soldiers retrieved. The decomposed corpse of Captain Cailloux—identifiable only by a ring on his finger—was finally transported back to New Orleans. His funeral was the largest public event in the city since the burial for the first white Louisiana officer slain on the Confederate side. Thousands of blacks, both free and slave, lined the route from the hall where Cailloux's body lay in state to the cemetery. As the coffin passed, borne on the shoulders of six of Cailloux's fellow black officers, the onlookers waved small American flags.

For Paul Broyard, who turned seven that summer, the name André Cailloux would have been inescapable. The boy was perhaps even more inclined to latch onto the martyr's story since his family had received no word of Henry's fate. Union officials had insisted on a news blackout in New Orleans to prevent Confederate spies in the city from gaining any intelligence.

In another few months, Henry Broyard would be home to share his stories with his son firsthand. Banks continued to oppose the use of black officers, writing to President Lincoln in August of 1863 that black men were "unsuited for this duty." One by one the officers were forced out. In late September Emile Detiége, from Henry's company, resigned, citing prejudice as his reason, and a quarter of the men in Company C, including Henry, deserted as a result.

The soldiers were tired of facing attitudes like those held by a white lieutenant who shared this view with a newspaper reporter: "I must not only obey [a black officer], I must politely touch my cap when I approach him. I must stand while he sits, unless his captainship should condescendingly ask me to be seated. Negro soldiers are all very well, but let us have white officers, whom we can receive and treat as equals everywhere, and whom we may treat as superiors without humiliation." In New Orleans the provost marshal under Banks likened the sight of black officers to "dogs in full dress, ready to dance in the menagerie. Would *you* like to obey such a fool?" But with Union victory and the beginning of Reconstruction in Louisiana, some of those "dogs" would seek to become the white men's masters.

One June weekend my brother, Todd, flew down from Boston to meet me in Baton Rouge to attend a conference about the Louisiana Native Guard. It was held at the actual site of the Battle of Port Hudson, giving us a chance to tour the ground where our great-great-grandfather had fought nearly 150 years before. Even more thrilling to me was the prospect of sharing the experience with my brother.

People tended to ask me, after hearing of my efforts to learn about my African heritage, what Todd made of his lately discovered roots. (The question often struck me as a veiled attempt to gauge how "normal" my own avid interest was.) I usually said that as a history buff, Todd seemed to feel most connected to his black ancestry through reading about African American history. The books piled by his bedside included James M. McPherson's *The Negro's Civil War* and Thomas Wentworth Higginson's account of leading a black regiment from South Carolina against the Confederacy. What I didn't mention was the fact that my brother's love of history started with a misplaced affinity for our father's jettisoned roots. As a child Todd developed an interest in the Civil War that turned into an obsession with the Confederate army during his adolescence. One year in his yearbook at Fairfield Country Day, a local private boys school in Connecticut, in the category "most likely to be," he was listed as a "Confederate Rebel."

When I reminded Todd of this description, he shook his head in wonder and said, "Isn't that funny." For the most part, Todd saw his preference for the Confederates as a case of rooting for the underdog. "The South never had a chance against the Yankees," he said, "which made them seem kind of romantic. Also, the Southern generals and leaders were more colorful. Their victories and battles made better stories."

For a white boy in Connecticut with only one child of color in his entire school, for a kid whose history books didn't dwell on the less romantic stories about the slaves, the moral question at the heart of the Civil War—the institution of slavery—had been impossibly remote. I was hoping that this visit to the battle site might leave him feeling more personally connected to our black heritage.

Todd never shied away from disclosing our father's racial ancestry, but his blond hair, green eyes, and pale skin could make a listener second-guess his story. They certainly never squinted at him, as they sometimes did with me, and said, "Yeah, I can see it." As Todd said: "As soon as I tell them my father was African American, I have to point out, 'Well, my mother's of Nordic descent, of course, and I picked up her coloring.'"

Despite Todd's encouragement of my own interest in our Creole history and his immense pride in my career as a writer, I wondered at times if he viewed my compulsion to figure out my racial identity as perplexing, or even a little distasteful. It wasn't that I believed he was racist, any more than I was, but I thought that he didn't quite understand why I was always making such a big deal out of the "black thing."

For Todd the news of our dad's ancestry hadn't altered his sense of himself. As he said, he looked so white that nobody thought to ask him about his racial background. And in his line of business, installing home security alarm systems in wealthy Boston suburbs, the question of what he was never came up. (Although working "in the trades" over the years had brought him into more frequent contact with people whom he generously described as "uneducated"—the type who openly made racist comments.) My brother's wife, Michèle, came from a Scottish and Polish background: she was equally blond and fair, as were their identical twin daughters. Todd took the view that we came from an interesting family, and our dad's ancestry was one more thing that made us stand out from everyone else.

However, in my line of business, a writer whose job required that I place myself in the public eye, the question of what I was *did* come up. In fact even before I published anything about my African ancestry, various editors and producers had already begun deciding my racial identity for me. My first book, *My Father, Dancing*, a collection of stories that didn't deal with race at all, was treated on numerous occasions as if written by an African American author. It was reviewed in the African American general-interest magazine *Emerge*, included in the African American Book Expo in Chicago, and selected for a dramatic reading, also in Chicago, as part of a night celebrating Black History month. My writing shared the bill with work by Alice Walker and Zora Neale Hurston, and a recording of the reading later aired on Chicago's public radio station. (I'm definitely black in Chicago, it seems.) Yet if this exposure ever inspired someone to search out a copy of *My Father, Dancing*, he or she might have been surprised to encounter the image of a blond-haired, pale-skinned girl dancing on its cover and not one black-identified character within its pages. (The characters aren't necessarily identified as white either.)

Beyond needing to address this presumption of my African American identity, I felt compelled to resolve the question about how to define myself because of what I'd learned about our family's history. Unlike my brother, I found this knowledge had altered my sense of myself. I'd begun to feel the stirrings of the "double-consciousness" described by W.E.B. Du Bois in his 1903 book, *The Souls of Black Folk*. Du Bois wrote: "One ever feels his two-ness,—an American, a Negro; two souls, two thoughts, two unreconciled strivings, two warring ideals in one dark body." Entire books have been devoted to interpreting Du Bois's concept, but at its most basic, I understood double consciousness to mean the sense of otherness felt by African Americans — the result of being viewed as different by whites as well as viewing the world differently from them. Because I didn't look black, I didn't have the experience of my "difference" being mirrored back to me the way that visibly black people did. But over the course of learning the history of my father's family, I'd begun to feel a shift in my worldview, away from the "white" one I'd grown up with.

African Americans, according to Du Bois, lived behind a racial veil that gave them a "second sight" to observe the world more clearly by remaining themselves unseen. Ironically, the invisibility of my own African ancestry had given me a uniquely suited vantage point from which to view the current status of Du Bois's veil. I had a chance to hear how white people talked when they thought they were alone — sometimes making overtly racist comments, more often unwittingly sharing observations that indicated a subtle belief in African Americans' inferiority. I'd been privy to the kind of conversations that black people had among themselves — passing remarks that told of the degree of separateness they felt from whites, how far they still remained inside the veil. And while it seemed for African Americans that the day-to-day reminders of otherness — on the job, in a store, with friends — were less frequent and pronounced, I noticed a recurring gulf between white and black perspectives on race matters.

Case in point: During an evening at an interracial artists salon that I'd organized in New York with a friend, I read from this book the chapter about the racial attitudes that I had grown up with in Connecticut, including the passage about my telling racist jokes in my high school cafeteria. There were about thirty writers and artists in the audience, almost evenly mixed between whites and people of color. As I'd hoped, the reading sparked conversation among the group, including this one between my white friend N. and my African American friend J.:

N. [to me]: It's interesting how you've got these two secrets: about your
    father's racial identity and also the secret of racism.

J.: Racism isn't a secret. We've always known it was there.

N.: Yes, but I mean, it's been kept secret. It's not really acknowledged and
    people don't talk about it.

J.: We talk about it all the time, every day when it happens.

N.: But I'm saying, it's not discussed openly in the world.

J.: Depends on whose world you're talking about.

N. [exasperated]: You know what I mean!

When N. and J. walked away, I'm guessing, they were more entrenched in their own positions and less willing to engage in this kind
of conversation again. For my part, I realized that I no longer had a
set position. In learning about the country's history from the African
American vantage point, I'd begun to peer over the racial veil. I was
hoping that Todd's own love for history would similarly lure him away
from his familiar perspective. After all, who could better understand
than my own brother my particular difficulty in answering the question *What are you?* In a world of "us" and "them," perhaps he and I
might join together to form a "we."

About sixty people showed up for the conference on the Louisiana
Native Guard. Outside the Port Hudson State Park headquarters, two
African American Civil War reenactors, wearing full period garb and
carrying antique muskets, replayed the history of the first officially
sanctioned black regiment in the U.S. Army. To a rapt audience, they
described the colored troops' doomed charge on the ridge.

In between lectures about the free people of color community and
archaeological excavations at the battleground site, Todd and I chatted
with the two reenactors. One of them, Murray Dorty, had traveled
around the world telling the story of black troops in the Civil War.
He recalled for us the first time he participated in a full-scale battle
reenactment. He'd been standing on the line, waiting to go in, when

he started to cry. Dorty found that he couldn't stop himself, and then he looked down the line and saw other men crying too. "The guy next to me tapped me on the shoulder and said, 'It's okay. It's their spirit you're feeling,'" Dorty recalled. "In that moment, I understood the significance of [the soldiers'] struggle and their sacrifice."

As we listened I fantasized that Todd would decide to participate in an African American Civil War reenactment to better understand the struggle of our great-great-grandfather Henry. Todd's best friend, who was also a Civil War buff, had taken part in a few living history events — always as a white Union soldier — and Todd had said that he might like to try it himself. But as the day wore on, I noticed that Todd seemed more interested in talking about the reenactors' contemporary lives than the lives of the dead soldiers they'd been resurrecting for us.

We had dinner that evening with some other conference attendees — nearly all of them black. Some were veterans themselves and others were the descendants of Civil War or World War II veterans. Many were involved in trying to establish a special memorial for African American war veterans in Washington, DC, and the dinner conversation ranged from stories about injustices against blacks in the military, to the politics of building memorials in our nation's capital, to the challenges of fund-raising. I was impressed with the men's determination to commemorate their ancestors' largely overlooked contribution. That a large group of the U.S. population had been willing to die for a country that had treated them for much of its history as second-class citizens (or worse) struck me as an act of patriotism certainly worthy of recognition.

On the car ride back to our hotel, when I asked Todd what he'd thought of everyone, he said that he'd found the men impressive too. He started talking about this fellow or that one — but nearly all the identifying details he mentioned were concerned with the men's occupations and lifestyles. One guy was a big union lawyer in DC; another guy had appeared in Hollywood movies; this one lived in a wealthy suburb near someone Todd knew; that one went to the same college as his buddy.

As I listened, I realized that for Todd, the class line, not the color line, was the relevant problem of the twenty-first century. It made sense that he would think this way. During his twenties my brother had struggled to support himself — knocking on doors of businesses in Boston to sell industrial cleaning supplies on commission, losing a leased car to a repossession for failure to make the payments. The double consciousness he had gleaned from our upbringing was the veil between the haves and the have-nots of the world. On the racial question, though, I was on my own.

Luckily I met other people in New Orleans who could join me in my search; they hadn't grown up aware of their African ancestry either, despite being descended from some very illustrious forebears. Michelle Olinger, a blue-eyed blonde who ran an asphalt company in California, was the great-great-great-great-grandniece of Henriette Delille, a free woman of color who started a black order of nuns in New Orleans in 1842 and was currently being considered by the Roman Catholic Church for canonization. Should Delille's cause be successful, she would become the world's first African American saint. Steve Lanusse-Siegel, a blues musician from Oregon who once thought of himself as an Italian Jew, was the great-great-grandson of the colored Creole intellectual Armand Lanusse. Pat Schexnayder, from Slidell, Louisiana, and her daughter Kara Chenevert, from North Carolina, descended from Antoine Dubuclet, the longest-serving African American elected official during Reconstruction and the richest person of color in Louisiana at the time. My fellow researchers marveled that they had never heard about these people or learned their stories.

In my family too, no one — not even my relatives who stayed in the black community — had any inkling that my great-grandfather Paul had been involved in politics. He was a Republican Party boss in the late nineteenth century, a period when white Democrats began systematically reversing all the civil and political rights won by blacks in the wake of the Civil War. Paul fought against resegregation of schools and public accommodations, the disenfranchisement of blacks, and the reinstitution of the ban against interracial marriages. My aunt Shirley, who spent her life, along with her husband, trying to undo the legacy of Jim Crow, knew nothing of her grandfather's precedent.

One woman I met was an exception to the rule. Ever since she was a child, Julie Hilla, who grew up white in Los Angeles, had heard about her grandfather Arnold Bertonneau, who had met with President Lincoln during the Civil War to ask for the Negro's right to vote. Julie's grandfather died before she was born, but Julie's mother had talked about him often, clearly proud of her father's early civil rights activism. It wasn't until Julie was in her late seventies, though, when she visited New Orleans for the first time, that she learned the rest of the story.

In a bookstore in the French Quarter, Julie decided to look for her grandfather's name in the indexes of some local history books. She was tickled to find an entry describing Arnold Bertonneau's trip to visit Lincoln, but what she read next made her pause. Her grandfather was described as a man of color. Julie showed her husband the reference, commenting that the author had to be mistaken. "My grandfather was white," she said. "Like the rest of us."

But back at home in Palm Springs, where she was living, Julie couldn't stop thinking about what she'd found. She was more curious than anything—her grandfather's civil rights legacy helped to ensure that she'd been raised to believe that everyone was created equal. She decided to call up Mary Gehman, the author of *The Free People of Color of New Orleans*, another book that described Arnold Bertonneau as a colored man. After a long phone conversation during which Julie learned that her grandfather had also served as a captain in a black regiment, she became convinced that her mother and her mother's family had been keeping a secret from her all these years. She decided to return to New Orleans to learn more, with her husband and two grown children accompanying her.

When Julie and I happened to meet a few nights after she arrived, I knew nothing of her recent discoveries. We were at a gathering of people in town for the conference about the Louisiana Native Guard, and I figured the petite older white woman with the short grayish blond hair and bright blue eyes was a professional genealogist or an academic interested in the history of free people of color. But when I told her that my great-great-grandfather had fought with the colored troops, Julie surprised me by clapping her hands and saying, "So you're mixed too!"

We traded our stories. As Julie talked, she chuckled over some of her relatives' responses: one cousin had confessed that decades earlier she had found her mother's birth certificate, with the label "colored," and ripped it up. I remarked on Julie's own enthusiasm for her black ancestry, given that she had lived as white for nearly eight decades, much of it during a time of widespread discrimination in America.

Julie paused a moment before answering. "I sometimes wonder if my grandfather hadn't been so active in civil rights, if he'd been just an ordinary person, whether I would feel any different." She shook her head. "I just don't know." But Julie was so proud of her grandfather Arnold already that a bit of colored blood wasn't going to change her opinion. "In fact I feel even more proud of him," she explained.

For every person like Julie I met in New Orleans, I heard stories about dozens more who turned away from their newfound African ancestry. In my own family, my cousin Gloria's grandparents—who had been living as white for more than sixty years—stopped speaking to their granddaughter because of her insistence on digging up the past. There were also those who simply closed their eyes, hoping that this evidence of Africa in their background would magically disappear.

Yet with the increasing popularity of genealogy facilitated by the Internet and the growing availability of records online, the discovery of a black ancestor can be just a few keystrokes away for people who have gone through life thinking they were entirely white. Generally, the longer someone's family has been in America, the more likely his or her chances of having some African or Native American ancestry, given all the race-mixing throughout the country's history. Since I've started my own genealogical search, three different white friends have discovered racial passing in their own family trees.

In 1958 Robert Stuckert, a sociologist and anthropologist at Ohio State University, published his findings about the frequency of black-to-white passing in the *Ohio Journal of Science*. After analyzing decades of census records and fertility data, he estimated that by 1950 one in five Americans who identified themselves as white had some African ancestry. And he predicted that the percentage of white people with black ancestry would increase as these individuals went on to have children.

Even before Stuckert's study appeared, passing had become a popular topic in American culture. Movies like *Imitation of Life* (1934, remade in 1959) and *Pinky* (1949) and novels such as *Passing* (1929), by black author Nella Larsen, and *Kingsblood Royal* (1947), by white author Sinclair Lewis, stoked curiosity and paranoia about the preponderance of "hidden white Negroes." Folklore beliefs for detecting invisible blackness advised examining a person's fingernails for a bluish tinge to the half-moon. A more "scientific" approach early in the twentieth century involved measuring hair texture and skull size. Nowadays geneticists can analyze a person's DNA to identify the geographic origins of their ancestors. Dr. Mark Shriver, a scientist who grew up white and whose research helped to make such genetic testing possible, only learned when analyzing his own DNA that 11 percent of his ancestors traced back to Africa.

As white people continue to discover their own black roots, the question becomes more pressing: What drove so many individuals to reject their black ancestry in the first place? In the wake of the Civil War, black Americans felt hopeful about their future. When and how did the scales tip so that this hopefulness became outweighed by despair?

When Henry Broyard returned to New Orleans in October 1863 after the battle at Port Hudson, he found Paul Trévigne and the rest of his colored friends engaged in a battle of their own. President Lincoln was eager to bring the conquered Confederate territories back into the Union, a process that had been dubbed Reconstruction, and Louisiana, as the rebel state under federal control the longest, was the obvious starting place. For Lincoln the goal was to establish a state government that would be loyal to Washington as quickly as possible, but the Trévigne camp wanted to seize this opportunity to realign race relations in the South—a divisive issue that would surely cause delays.

The first step in the reconstruction process was the election of delegates to write a new state constitution. These delegates would face many thorny questions, beyond emancipating the slaves. For example, would a reconstructed Louisiana continue to enforce segregation in public spaces? Would blacks be allowed to vote? How would the economy accommodate this sudden transition from slave to free labor? And what about schools to educate the newly freed men and women? Even those whites who recognized the need for abolishing slavery weren't prepared to accept civil and political equality for Negroes.

Paul Trévigne, however, wouldn't settle for half measures. For him the future health of the country depended on finally honoring the Founding Fathers' vision that all men were created equal. Using his newspaper as a platform, Trévigne helped to organize a rally in the beginning of November in support of voter registration of blacks for the upcoming election of delegates to the Constitutional Convention. The colored radicals figured they had some bargaining power. The majority of white Louisianans had supported the Confederacy; the administration in Washington could hardly now turn to these rebels to restore the Union. Since there weren't enough white Unionists in Louisiana to make up a representative electorate, the free colored community was going to be needed for its sheer numbers.

The white Unionists at the rally finally agreed to draw up a resolution requesting the registration of blacks who were free before the rebellion to present to Louisiana's military governor, General George F. Shepley. (They had convinced the Creoles of color that amending their original request, which included newly freed blacks too, would give the petition a better chance for success.) Elsewhere in the country, the question of Negro suffrage had barely been considered.

General Shepley never responded to the petition, and then President Lincoln disappointed the colored men too. Impatient with delays, Lincoln issued his own guidelines for the reconstruction process in early December of 1863. His plan called for the use of existing election laws, thus excluding black voters, and pardoned most Confederates, as long as they swore to uphold the U.S. Constitution and support abolition. Soon enough, Michael Hahn, a German immigrant who had been elected to Congress shortly before the war, won the gubernatorial race on a platform opposing Negro suffrage. At the same time, a labor program instituted by General Banks forced the ex-slaves back onto the plantations and sharply curtailed their movements. It was beginning to look as if reconstructed Louisiana would be indistinguishable from its antebellum days.

Trévigne helped to organize another petition, signed by one thousand colored property owners, twenty-seven veterans from the War of 1812, and twenty-two white radicals, in which the colored men's right to citizenship was demanded on the basis of paying taxes and serving the country. Julie Hilla's grandfather, Arnold Bertonneau, as a captain in the Union army and prosperous wine merchant, was selected, along with Jean-Baptiste Roudanez, the brother of the cofounder of Trévigne's paper, to deliver the petition to the White House and to Congress.

Lincoln had declared his opposition to Negro suffrage during his debates with Stephen Douglas back in 1858, but his meeting with the two colored delegates from New Orleans made him reconsider the question. After hearing their case, the president explained that he could only act if the issue was "necessary to the readmission of Louisiana as a State in the Union." (It went without saying that blacks and the ballot box weren't exactly a unifying cause.) But Lincoln was impressed enough to pen a note to Louisiana's Governor Hahn the following day: "I barely suggest for your private consideration whether some of the colored people may not be let in [to the franchise]—as, for instance, the very intelligent, and especially those who have fought gallantly in our ranks."

Governor Hahn ignored Lincoln's suggestion. When the white delegates convened during the summer of 1864 to draw up Louisiana's new constitution, they failed to grant blacks voting rights. They did establish public schools for black children but ordered their segregation from white schools. Slavery was abolished, as Lincoln's plan required, and some radicals sneaked in a loophole that allowed the Louisiana legislature at some future date to extend suffrage to certain Negroes who had "demonstrated their capacity...by military service, taxation, or intellectual fitness." But the end result guaranteed a two-tiered postwar society, with whites on top and the formerly and newly free blacks below them.

At the same time, General Banks began an assault on Trévigne and his colored cohorts. The general had his eye on the White House, and his success with Reconstruction, on top of his military victories, would go far in furthering his campaign. The Creoles of color's constant agitation over suffrage was interfering with the general's plan.

Bertonneau and Roudanez's trip to Washington had been covered extensively by the New York and Boston newspapers. The colored men's quest for the vote had also gained support from various Northern Republicans, including influential congressmen. Louisiana's readmission into the Union ultimately depended on the approval of Congress, and Banks wanted to prevent Trévigne and his fellow radicals from persuading their new friends in Washington to make universal suffrage a necessary condition.

By mid-July 1864, one of Banks's lackeys had forced Trévigne's paper into bankruptcy. Luckily *L'Union*'s founder was able to fund a new enterprise, the *New Orleans Tribune*. A white radical from Belgium, Jean Charles Houzeau, joined Trévigne as coeditor and launched an English section to reach a wider public. Contributors from Boston, Washington, and Paris began reporting from the national and international fronts. By the fall the expanded *Tribune*—published in the heart of the Deep South in the midst of the Civil War—became the first daily black newspaper in the United States. Copies were sent to every member of Congress.

The paper's launch on July 21, 1864, coincided with my great-grandfather's eighth birthday. To a boy the life-and-death crusade embodied by the newspaper must have seemed both exhilarating and frightening. Paul Trévigne bursting into the Broyard house on young Paul's birthday, the first issue of his new platform in hand, declaring that their cause could not be stopped, would set a much different tone than the mass exodus of friends and neighbors to Haiti and Mexico just a few years before. But as the call for universal suffrage widened, uniting New Orleans's free and newly freed Negroes with black leaders and white radicals across the country, the stakes grew even higher, with opponents of the movement willing to stop at nothing to prevent the colored men from winning the franchise.

*   *   *

On the evening of April 11, 1865, President Lincoln stood on the balcony of the White House and addressed a crowd of a few thousand people gathered on the lawn below him. Two days earlier General Robert E. Lee, the commander in chief of the Confederate army, had surrendered at Appomattox, effectively bringing about the end of the war. When the news reached the nation's capital, cannon fire began booming throughout the city, rousing people from bed and shattering their windowpanes. Eventually the city's residents made their way to the White House, where they gathered on the mansion's lawn and called for their president to speak.

"We meet this evening," Lincoln began, "not in sorrow, but in gladness of heart." He took a moment to acknowledge Ulysses S. Grant, the general who had led the Union army to victory, along with his "brave soldiers"—tens of thousands of whom had died and hundreds of thousands of whom had been injured. Then the president turned to the matter of Reconstruction. "It is fraught with great difficulty," he explained.

Indeed Louisiana's new state government had yet to be restored to the Union, and members of Lincoln's own party couldn't agree about how to proceed. The radical wing of the Republicans argued that the president's plan didn't go far enough in restructuring the South. Thanks in part to the lobbying efforts of Trévigne and the other New Orleans Creoles of color, Congressman Thaddeus Stevens from Pennsylvania and Senator Charles Sumner from Massachusetts had begun to call for Negro suffrage and civil rights as a necessary condition for readmission to the Union.

In his speech that night, President Lincoln focused on Louisiana. He had consistently taken the position that the rebel states must first be returned "to their proper practical relation with the Union" before other concerns about reshaping Southern society could be addressed. Lincoln now posed for his audience: "Concede that the new government of Louisiana is only to what it should be as the egg is to the fowl, we shall sooner have the fowl by hatching the egg than by smashing it?"

But in recognition of the growing movement for universal suffrage, the president declared publicly for the first time what he had expressed in private to Louisiana's Governor Hahn a year earlier. Regarding the vote for colored men, Lincoln told the people gathered below him, "I would myself prefer that it were now conferred on the very intelligent, and on those who serve our cause as soldiers."

For many in the crowd, this was a startling admission. And for one man standing toward the back, a militant white Southern separatist named John Wilkes Booth, it was the last straw. Booth turned to his companions and muttered, "That means nigger citizenship." He'd been plotting to abduct Lincoln and deliver him to the Confederacy, but the war's end was forcing him to amend his plans. Booth now swore: "That is the last speech he'll ever make. By God, I'll put him through." Four days later, on April 15, 1865, Booth sneaked up on Lincoln at Ford's Theatre, placed a pistol to the back of his head, and fired.

In New Orleans the *Tribune* mourned the passing of the president, who had "willingly jeopardized [his] life for the sacred cause of freedom." Despite Lincoln's gradualist approach to Reconstruction, his death dealt the Negro suffrage movement a severe blow.

President Andrew Johnson, like his predecessor, wanted to restore the Union as quickly as possible — a goal he thought best accomplished with as little oversight from Washington as possible. A Tennessee Democrat and former slaveholder, Johnson was disinclined to force Negro suffrage on the Southern states. Within a few months' time, the new president's priorities became clear when he granted amnesty to nearly all returning Confederate soldiers and officials. In November white voters across the South flocked to the polls to reinstall the rebels in the political offices they'd held before the war.

In Louisiana the Confederates swept the elections with a Democratic platform that was hardly discernible from their secessionist stance: "We hold this to be a government of white people, made and to be perpetuated for the exclusive benefit of the white race....People of African descent cannot be considered as citizens of the United States, and that there can, in no event nor under any circumstances, be any equality between the white and other races."

Across the South and in Louisiana, black codes were instituted to allow the state to seize any freed person lacking proof of a "comfortable home and visible means of support" and hire him or her out to the highest bidder. At the same time, Louisiana lawmakers dragged their feet in establishing public schools for Negro children, despite the provision in the new state constitution requiring them to do so. As a final blow, in March of 1866 John T. Monroe, the Confederate mayor of New Orleans before the war — a man who'd been expelled from the city by Union forces for his refusal to take an oath of allegiance to the United States — was reelected to his former office.

The outlook for Southern blacks was growing bleaker by the day. For those who were already free, such as the Broyards, their standing in society was actually worse than before the war. After a century of occupying a legal and social middle ground, they were now subject to the same black codes as the ex-slaves. Most galling of all for my great-great-grandfather Henry must have been the fact that despite his having risked his life for the preservation of the Union — and belonging to the winning side — the reins of the South were now being handed over to the very men who had started the rebellion.

The colored radicals joined forces with local white Unionists, who were equally alarmed by the Confederates' sudden return to power. Some of the Unionists came up with a plan to use a technicality as an excuse to reconvene the Constitutional Convention of 1864 — the delegates had neglected to formally adjourn it — during which they could disenfranchise anyone who supported the Confederacy while at the same time granting Negroes the vote. There was concern, however, among the *Tribune* staff that the uncertain legality of amending the constitution would taint its validity. Beyond that, they worried that the proposed convention would incite racial violence. The planning continued without the newspaper's support, and the organizers scheduled a meeting of the original convention delegates at the Mechanics' Institute at noon on July 30, 1866.

Events in Washington were helping to push the matter forward. In June, Congress passed the Fourteenth Amendment, which guaranteed the rights of citizenship to all people born in the United States, regardless of their race, along with equal protection under the law. In addition the amendment barred from elected office any Confederates who had been officeholders before the war—which effectively destroyed the existing Democratic power base—while also limiting a state's congressional representation to the percentage of eligible citizens, including blacks, it enfranchised. President Johnson submitted the amendment to the Southern states for ratification (as he was required to do), but he included a caveat advising them to reject it.

Not surprisingly, Johnson also refused to give his support to the reconvening of the Constitutional Convention in New Orleans. When an emissary from Louisiana sought his position on it, the president replied that if the local authorities needed to break up the meeting, he'd make sure the federal troops stationed in New Orleans didn't interfere.

On the morning of July 30, 1866, about an hour before the convention was scheduled to begin, a crowd of local black families started forming outside the Mechanics' Institute, in New Orleans's business district. The men, women, and children had all turned out in their Sunday best. They'd heard that the conventioneers were going to give their race the vote, and they dressed up in honor of the momentous occasion. A Baptist minister, who was white, took to the steps of the hall and urged the onlookers to disperse. "You will only create more trouble by remaining here," he told them. A half a block away, another group was gathering: rowdy white men and boys who'd begun to jeer at the black supporters as they passed by on their way to the institute. The women and children apparently heeded the minister's request and headed home, but their men stayed on and soon had doubled their number.

Inside the Mechanics' Institute, another two to three hundred spectators were assembled, nearly all of them black, in addition to the twenty-seven white delegates belonging to the convention. A handful of the men carried pistols or sword canes, but most had left their arms at home. The convention organizers were determined to keep the peace. They'd assured the local authorities that they wouldn't put up a fight if the police came to break up the meeting. If trouble did start—as talk in town predicted—they were counting on the federal troops to restore order. Unbeknownst to them, the bulk of the Union force was stationed at Jackson Barracks, at least an hour's travel time away. The commander, General Absalom Baird, mistakenly thought that the convention didn't commence until 6 p.m. Anyway his hands were tied. President Johnson had specifically ordered him to stand down.

With the federal troops out of the way, the responsibility of peacekeeping fell to the local police force, nearly two-thirds of whom were Confederate veterans. Barely a year off the battlefield, these rebels were still smarting from their defeat and the economic hardships that came with belonging to the losing side. For their troubles they blamed "the Yankee sons of bitches" along with "the damned niggers," and viewed the efforts to reconvene the Constitutional Convention as nothing short of insurrection.

The white press fanned the racial tension with its sensationalist coverage of black-white relations. Two days before the opening of the convention, one local paper ran a front-page story with the headline "A NEGRO ATTEMPTS TO VIOLATE A WHITE WOMAN," despite the incident's being three weeks old.

The police chief ordered the entire force of 499 men to report to duty on convention morning. New Orleans's sheriff had sworn in an additional 200 deputies, also all Confederate veterans. A few officers were posted at the Mechanics' Institute itself, with the bulk of the men held at surrounding station houses, from where they could be quickly summoned.

By midmorning about 100 policemen were lounging on the grass at Lafayette Square. Although the men were only supposed to carry nightsticks when on duty, all of them had guns, with some carrying two. When a passerby asked an officer if the men were planning on breaking up the convention, he replied, "I won't say, but by and by we will likely have some fun."

The heat—pushing ninety degrees by 10 a.m.—didn't help to calm the men. Neither did the whiskey bottles that were passed around as they waited. Three hours had passed when they heard the alarm that signaled trouble—twelve taps of the fire bell, the same signal used a few years earlier to warn city residents that Union warships were heading their way.

Also out in force that morning were members of Henry Broyard's old regiment, the First Louisiana Native Guard. Between seventy and a hundred veterans had gathered downriver to march to the Mechanics' Institute, armed with pistols, broomsticks, even a slingshot. Three drummers and a fife player led the procession, along with a black veteran carrying a tattered American flag, reportedly the bloodstained one salvaged from the charge at Port Hudson. I don't know whether or not my great-great-grandfather Henry was among them. The exact whereabouts on that day of Henry and of my grandfather Paul remain unknown. Their names don't appear in any of the surviving records, and as with so many other details of my family's past, no mention was passed down of this defining moment in Louisiana's and the country's history.

The trouble began when the Native Guard passed through the gauntlet of hostile whites lining Canal Street. A white boy pushed down a black marcher, yelling, "Go away, you black son of a bitch!"

Blows were exchanged and a few shots were fired, but the procession managed to reach the Mechanics' Institute, where the men were greeted with a roar of cheers. Some of the black spectators had also begun to drink in the hot sun, and their mood was growing increasingly rowdy.

Before long the troublemaking white boy reappeared to continue his taunts. Some black men, by way of reply, began lobbing bricks from a nearby construction site. Then one black man removed his revolver and opened fire. The ensuing shooting match left one black man dead and two others lying bloody in the street. A handful of courageous policemen posted at the hall tried to intervene, but they were no match for the hostile crowd. A few minutes later, the twelve-tap alarm began to sound. The police officers, special deputies, firemen, and bands of armed white citizens who headed to the institute outnumbered the conventioneers and colored onlookers by more than five to one.

Inside the Mechanics' Institute, the white delegates, still hoping to conduct the meeting, urged the black spectators to disperse. The onlookers began exiting the building, but they found themselves surrounded by police and the armed white citizens. Before they could head back inside, the white mob started forward, firing their guns as they came.

In the main hall, a white delegate took charge, commanding everyone to sit down — on chairs or on the floor — to indicate their lack of resistance. The Baptist minister moved through the crowd, telling the men to place their trust in God. The front doors were left open, in another display of submission, but when the policemen burst through the doorway, they opened fire without hesitation. Scrambling for cover, the crouching men cried out, "For God's sake, don't shoot....We are peaceable."

Repeated attempts to surrender were met with more gunfire. When the minister tried to exit the institute, waving a white handkerchief atop an American flag, a policeman shot him twice, causing in-

juries that would end his life six days later. The remaining men inside
started to fight back. With flimsy cane chairs, they tried to fend off
the guns and knives of the police and the white mob. But it was hopeless. When the fighting was over, the wooden floorboards were so wet
with the conventioneers' blood that they squished underfoot.

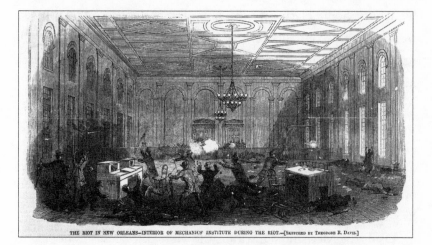

THE RIOT IN NEW ORLEANS—INTERIOR OF MECHANICS' INSTITUTE DURING THE RIOT.—[SKETCHED BY THEODORE R. DAVIS.]

A few white delegates managed to escape the hall and were taken
into custody and protected by policemen who recognized them. Most
blacks weren't so lucky. Officers handed over black prisoners to the
mob, who shot them and beat them to death. My friend Julia Hilla's
grandfather Arnold Bertonneau managed to slip out undetected and
was hiding in an adjacent lot when a gang of whites discovered him. A
policeman spotted Bertonneau and intervened, mistakenly thinking
the light-skinned Creole of color was a white man.

When it was all over, an estimated forty-four black men had been
murdered, with another forty severely wounded. On the side of the
police, only one man died—a young student who accidentally stepped
into the line of fire—and no men at all suffered severe wounds. The
commanding officer of the Union troops, in a report to Ulysses S.
Grant, came to this conclusion: "The more information I obtain of

the affair...the more revolting it becomes. It was no riot; it was an absolute massacre."

The following week a grand jury convened in New Orleans to determine the cause of the violence. None of the twenty-nine witnesses
called were black or had been present inside the Mechanics' Institute
during the massacre. The all-white jury found the convention delegates and black spectators to blame for what they deemed a "riot,"
and refused to charge a single policeman or white citizen for the kill-
ings. As one Unionist observer described the situation: "The rebels
have control here and are determined to maintain it."

The New Orleans massacre proved the error of President Johnson's
claim that the Southern states could be trusted to reconstruct
themselves. Not only had unarmed blacks been attacked, but white
men—loyal Unionists such as ex-governor Michael Hahn and
R. King Cutler, who'd been elected to the U.S. Senate—were badly
beaten; and other whites, such as the Baptist preacher, had died from
their wounds. More practically, rebuilding the Southern states after
the devastation of the war was going to require Northern investment.
But with the safety of Northerners and Republicans in the South uncertain, investors were unlikely to sink their money into the region.

As the November 1866 congressional elections approached, word
about the massacre spread across the country. The cover of the influential magazine *Harper's Weekly* featured an illustration of the Baptist
minister being fired upon while he waved a white handkerchief affixed
to the American flag. A few weeks later, the American electorate—
composed mostly of white Northerners—voted into Congress a
two-thirds majority of Republicans, more than enough votes to over-
ride any presidential vetoes.

With the power of the House now firmly in the hands of radicals
and moderate Republicans, the lawmakers soon passed the Reconstruction Acts of 1867. The bill divided the Southern states into five
military districts, overseen by federal troops who would back up the

authority of the local government. The act also required that every state write universal suffrage into its constitution and ratify the Fourteenth Amendment regarding citizenship as a condition to rejoining the Union.

Three years later Congress wrapped federal protection around the black man's franchise with the ratification of the Fifteenth Amendment, which ensured that the "right to vote shall not be denied or abridged by the United States or by any State on account of race, color, or previous condition of servitude." However, the wording of the amendment left open the denial of the vote on grounds of education level and property ownership, a loophole that would be exploited soon enough.

But for the moment, the reformed Southern society imagined by Paul Trévigne and his compatriots appeared tantalizingly within reach. Back in New Orleans, the radicals began calling for civil equality too — particularly the desegregation of public spaces. The *Tribune* commented: "All these discriminations that had slavery at the bottom have become nonsense. It behooves those who understand the new era...to show their hands, and gain the friendship of the colored population of this State."

Pragmatic whites such as future governor Henry Clay Warmoth assessed the state's changing political landscape, where black voters would soon outnumber whites by nearly two to one, and followed this advice. In 1868 an interracial coalition of delegates, elected by Louisiana's first-ever multiracial electorate, headed back to Mechanics' Institute, where they peacefully wrote Louisiana's new constitution. The conventioneers, including Arnold Bertonneau, granted the vote to all men, except for the Confederate officeholders disfranchised by the Fourteenth Amendment, and ended segregation in schools and public places. Two years later the newly elected state legislature — more than half of whom were colored — ventured into the last bastion of equality, the bedroom, and quietly removed the ban against intermarriage that had been in place since colonial days.

After fifteen years together and the births of eight children (six of whom survived), my great-great-grandparents Henry Broyard and Pauline Bonée saw their union legally sanctioned at last. A few months later, the census enumerator came round to the Broyard house on St. Ann Street. When he was there in 1860, the enumerator had recorded everyone in the family as "mu" for mulatto. But this time Henry let it be known that he was actually white, although his wife and their six sons were mulattoes.

According to his death certificate, Henry was still a white man when he died three years later. It's unclear whether his death from "a violent nosebleed" was sudden (resulting perhaps from a brain aneurism) or the result of a lingering illness, whether his identification as white on the certificate was his last wish or a spontaneous decision made by his wife's nephew when reporting his uncle's demise. Fittingly, after a lifetime of playing racial musical chairs, Henry went into the ground as a white man in the colored section of St. Louis Cemetery No. 2 on the edge of the French Quarter.

After stumbling across the location of Henry's interment during my research, I spent a morning trying to find it, accompanied by my cousin Sharon Broyard. Sharon also lived in New York, where she worked for a financial services company, but the busyness of our lives prevented us from getting together much up north. She surprised me one June weekend in New Orleans by showing up at a genealogy conference where I was speaking about the free people of color. We decided to go look for Henry's vault, to see if it provided any additional clues about his life.

I was also hoping to find Henry's burial place so that he might be included in the local tradition of visiting the tombs of one's ancestors on the first of November, All Saints' Day. Every year, on the days leading up to the holiday, Catholics flocked to the cemetery to repair and whitewash an ancestor's tomb, plant fresh flowers, and clean up the grounds. On the evening of All Saints' Day, when the tombs were decorated with pots of chrysanthemums and lit with votive candles, a priest came to bless the dead.

I'd been to an All Saints' Day celebration at a cemetery in Lacombe, a town across Lake Pontchartrain where another branch of my father's family had lived. There, as in New Orleans, the dead were also interred aboveground. Live oak trees surrounded the small grave-yard, and their twisted boughs trapped the pale glow from the candlelit tombs, forming an eerily beautiful open-air cathedral. As I moved through the ghostly light, scanning the faceplates for my family names, surrounded by other descendants of the people buried there, my connection to my dead forebears had never felt closer at hand.

My cousin Joe, the son of candid Jeanne, was already tending two other family tombs in the "black" section of St. Louis Cemetery. His parents had purchased the second one in the 1960s during a secret meeting with some family members who were living as white. Because the tomb was in the colored section of the cemetery, this family didn't want it anymore. Joe, who works as a fireman, laughed when he told me this story. But it still bothered him that nobody was taking care of a Broyard tomb in the white part of the cemetery. Joe couldn't because of the unspoken code that kept the white and black branches of the family from mixing. He had no better idea than Sharon or I did where exactly Henry Broyard had been buried.

The cemetery's closing hour of noon was fast approaching. I started walking faster up and down the rows, trying to decipher the location of "tomb no. 8, left alley, facing east, upper arch." I wasn't sure why I'd suddenly become so anxious to find Henry's vault. Visiting my own father's grave generally left me feeling hollow and unsatisfied. If anything, the close proximity of his ashes just obscured my sense of him. Henry was an even more elusive character. The contradictory circumstances of his death made it impossible to finally locate him on one side or the other of the color line. I was hoping, improbably, that the wording on his vault might provide some conclusion—

maybe even a reference to his race—and I would then know where the rest of the story of my mixed blood began.

Yet as I scanned the walls of vaults and rows of tombs, I was struck by the tenuousness of all these distinctions—between water and dry land in this cemetery where the dead were buried above-ground; between the blacks and whites of this city who'd been inter-mingling for the last three hundred years; between the legacies of the past and their consequences on the future. If dividing lines existed at all, they were conditional, temporal things.

The cemetery closed. We never managed to find Henry. Too many of the faceplates had been stolen or broken to figure out where he'd been laid to rest.

Unlike the members of his parents' generation, my great-grandfather Paul Broyard had the chance to enter adulthood as an equal to other men, rather than as a colored man subordinate to whites. In his heart Paul may have already felt as good as or even superior to the white kids he knew from his neighborhood—mostly the children of Italian, German, and Irish immigrants. According to one of his grandsons, Paul could understand their languages but few immigrant children mastered his mother tongue, French. Many of his white counterparts were heading toward careers as laborers like their fathers, while Paul was apprenticed in the respected trade of carpentry, showing a flair for drawing and attention to detail that suited him for the practice of architecture. Paul had the Creole community to thank for these advantages. Their long presence in New Orleans and years of freedom had allowed them to create a supportive social network, with a focus on education, a tradition of activism, and a history of artisanship that they passed down to the next generation. That the former slaves lacked these opportunities further elevated young Creoles of color like Paul in New Orleans's social hierarchy.

Paul was also growing up to be handsome, which made him cocky. Of medium height, with long legs and a lean, sinewy build, he was known to strut around. Friends and family began referring to him as Belhomme—"beautiful man"—a nickname that would stick for the rest of his life. He wore his wavy brown hair parted on the side, and added a pencil mustache when he was older. With gently hooded pale green eyes, a long thin nose, and strong square chin, he could have easily passed for white. Only a yellow tinge to his skin alluded to his mother's African ancestry.

If Paul had any fears about his ability to compete with whites, he had a chance to allay them after a judge in 1870 finally forced the city's schools to integrate. While no records exist of my great-grandfather's education, the mixed schools with the heaviest Negro attendance were concentrated in his neighborhood, making it likely that Paul learned side by side with white children. In no other city throughout the entire South during Reconstruction were whites and blacks educated in the same classroom.

A white reporter from the *Picayune* (a paper that didn't usually favor black people) was assigned to cover the horrors of school integration. Instead he found "white ladies teaching negro boys; colored women showing the graces and dignity of mental and moral refinement...; children and youth of both races standing in the same classes, with black teachers pushing intelligently up into the intricacies of high school mathematics." The journalist was almost certainly author George Washington Cable, who later wrote that the experience of reporting on desegregated schools convinced him that blacks and whites must share equally in public rights if the South were to thrive.

While arguing for school integration in the *Tribune*, Paul's godfather, Paul Trévigne, had observed, "The objection 'too soon' is but laughable....When will the right time come? Is it, per chance, after we have separated for 10 or 20 years the two races in different schools, and when we shall have realized the separation of this nation into two peoples?" But many recently freed blacks weren't comfortable demanding full and immediate integration. For ex-slaves living in the countryside, this conciliatory stance was partly a matter of self-preservation.

In 1867, in response to the Reconstruction Acts, some white men in the town of Franklin, a hundred miles west of New Orleans, founded a paramilitary group called the Knights of the White Camelia, designed to intimidate black voters. Other white citizen militias would spring up throughout Reconstruction, including the Ku Klux Klan. Over the next eleven years, between three thousand and ten thousand colored Republicans in the state would be murdered for political reasons, according to estimates by federal investigation committees.

Integration wasn't the only issue dividing the ex-slaves and the free people of color. The colored Creole radicals made a number of missteps that alienated the ex-slaves from the political process. The free men of color insisted on deputizing themselves the leaders of the colored constituency, despite the fact that the emancipated slaves made up the voting majority. While the colored Creoles were committed in theory to securing civil and political equality for everyone of their race — Trévigne, for example, had helped to defeat a bill introduced by white lawmakers that would have granted the vote only to light-skinned Negroes like himself — they often snubbed their recently emancipated neighbors in practice. The *Tribune* had no former slaves on its editorial board, not even in the English section that had been added specifically to address them. One editorial went so far as publicly scolding the ex-slaves for their lack of "discipline" and habit of "boasting."

The so-called carpetbaggers — white Northerners who'd come South as Union soldiers and stayed to make their fortunes — were happy to exploit these rifts in the black community. At the first Republican state convention following Reconstruction, the *Tribune* faction made the unwise decision to support in the gubernatorial race two former slave owners, one of whom had been among the largest Negro owners of slaves in the state. No matter that these men stood on the more radical end of the Republican platform, the newly emancipated blacks weren't about to vote their old masters into office, especially not colored ones. The carpetbaggers, on the other hand, won the primary easily with their shrewdly chosen candidates: twenty-five-year-old white Illinoisan Henry Clay Warmoth, whose service in the Union army made him the face of liberation for bondsmen, and his running mate, Oscar Dunn, an African American barber who was dark-skinned, English-speaking, and the son of a slave.

In his inaugural address, Lieutenant Governor Dunn echoed the sentiments of many former slaves when he remarked: "As to myself and my people, we are not seeking social equality....We simply ask to be allowed an equal chance in the race of life; an equal opportunity of supporting our families, of educating our children, and of becoming worthy citizens of this government." P.B.S. Pinchback, a black politician originally from Mississippi and a supporter of Governor Warmoth's, put it more bluntly: "It is wholesale falsehood to say that we wish to force ourselves upon white people." In his view blacks "could get no rights the whites did not see fit to give them." But the colored Creoles couldn't reconcile this attitude with their urgent desire "to be respected and treated as men."

As the oldest son, my great-grandfather was forced to become the man of the Broyard family when his father died in 1873. At age sixteen Paul was suddenly responsible for supporting his mother and five younger brothers (their sister Pauline had died), who ranged in age from fourteen-year-old Pierre to the baby Octave, just six months old. Paul's trade, carpentry, paid well, but his few years of experience would have made it hard to secure jobs on his own. Over the next few years, the family moved from one rented cottage in Tremé to another, in search of lower rents and closer proximity to relatives who could lend a hand.

The political situation in the state had grown more uncertain too. Shortly into his term as governor, Warmoth had traveled up to Washington to meet with President Grant, whom he assured that he would not let Louisiana become an "African State." To that end he vetoed a bill that would have imposed fines on any Louisiana business or public resorts and conveyances that continued to practice segregation. Warmoth later explained that efforts to "Africanize Louisiana were bound to lead to civil war and to the ultimate destruction of the rights of all our colored citizens."

The blacks who helped put Warmoth into office were outraged by his veto of the enforcement bill. His own lieutenant governor, Oscar Dunn, called him the country's first Ku Klux Klan governor, only to die soon afterward under mysterious circumstances. Warmoth silenced protests from Trévigne and his fellow editors by cutting off the *Tribune*'s main source of funding. The paper had been serving as the state Republican Party's "official printer," but Warmoth convinced party delegates to switch their patronage to the *New Orleans Republican,* a more conservative paper that — conveniently — supported him. After leading the struggle for universal suffrage for seven years, the *Tribune* had to close its doors just a few months after blacks were finally able to exercise their franchise.

While fighting between Warmoth and his detractors tore apart Republican ranks, Louisiana's white Democrats furthered their efforts to reclaim the state offices — a process called "redemption." If the disarray among Republican leadership wasn't enough to discourage Negro voters from heading to the polls, the Knights of the White Camelia gave them reason to stay away.

Prior to one election in the city of Shreveport, sixty merchants and bankers vowed to withhold advancing supplies or money to any planter whose laborers or tenants voted a Republican ticket. If colored Republicans did risk their lives and livelihood to cast a ballot, their votes were often stolen or disregarded. Many northern parishes routinely reported 100 percent Democratic election returns, despite their large black populations. It's not surprising that many blacks took the cash rewards for their votes offered by Democratic Party operatives.

To combat the Democrats' tactics of corruption and violence, Republicans began resorting to fraud themselves. Election results in the state were regularly contested. In the 1872 gubernatorial race, both Democrats and Republicans claimed victory, leading to the bloodiest episode in Reconstruction history, where 3 white and 150 black Republicans were killed when trying to defend their claim to the parish seat in the northern town of Colfax. In New Orleans a white paramilitary group stormed the city and seized control of the statehouse, until President Grant called in federal troops to restore order. A few months later, gangs of white boys traveled from school to school for three days, ejecting colored children from the classrooms. Students like Paul, whose black ancestry wasn't obvious, were able to escape detection by sitting quietly and not calling attention to themselves.

In 1876 Louisiana produced conflicting election returns yet again—this time throwing the outcome of the presidential race into question. Neither the Democratic presidential candidate, Samuel Tilden, nor the Republican, Rutherford B. Hayes, had a majority of electoral votes without the results from Louisiana or the two other contested Southern states, South Carolina and Florida. In Congress, Democrats kept blocking attempts to resolve the dispute, and when President Grant reached his last week in office, still no successor had been named. There was talk of another civil war if Tilden wasn't declared the victor.

With just a few days to spare, Hayes met with a group of Southern representatives with whom he hammered out the famous Compromise of 1877. The Republicans agreed to remove the remaining federal troops from South Carolina and Louisiana (the only Southern states that had not yet been "redeemed" by whites), so long as the Democrats would let them have the presidency. In effect, the Southerners chose to regain local sovereignty in exchange for giving up their candidate as president, and the Republicans opted to sacrifice the cause of the Negro in exchange for the peaceful possession of the White House. Two days later the Democrats ended their filibuster, the vote counting continued, and Hayes was declared the country's nineteenth president. On April 24, 1877, the last of the federal troops pulled out of Louisiana, and the fifty-year reign of the "Solid South" began.

As part of the deal, Democratic candidate Francis T. Nicholls was declared the winner of Louisiana's gubernatorial race. Nicholls, who'd lost an arm and a leg for the Confederate cause, had run on a platform that promised to respect black rights secured by the Reconstruction amendments. But when New Orleans's children, including three of Paul Broyard's younger brothers, headed back to school in September 1877, the superintendent began segregating them into separate black and white facilities. Paul Trévigne, who'd been on the school board during Reconstruction, immediately filed a lawsuit, alleging a violation of the equal protection clause of the U.S.'s Fourteenth Amendment, along with the article in Louisiana's state constitution that forbade establishing separate schools for the races. The judge dodged the case, saying it was too late to hear it once school was in session. Also, Trévigne's children weren't directly affected by the law.

Arnold Bertonneau, whose two sons had been turned away from the white public school down the street, quickly followed with a suit of his own. After a year-and-a-half delay, his case was also dismissed, with a ruling that no discrimination had been practiced. The opinion read: "Both races are treated precisely alike. White children and colored children are compelled to attend different schools. That is all." Eventually this "separate but equal" ruse would drive Bertonneau from his hometown to California, where he and his family, including the mother of my friend Julia Hilla, would begin living as white. That a man like Bertonneau—who'd met with Lincoln to argue for the

Negro's vote — would resort to passing is a measure of the desperation felt by New Orleans's colored community in coming years.

Over the summer, my great-grandfather had turned twenty-one, which meant that he no longer had to watch this fight from the sidelines. In the election the following November, Paul would be able to finally exercise the franchise that his father and godfather had fought to obtain. Given the departure of the federal troops, it remained to be seen whether Paul's vote would carry any meaning. By election time Paul was responsible for a family of his own, with his first child on the way and a wedding around the corner, which made his own stake in the outcome even higher.

Paul Broyard married Rosa Cousin in New Orleans on December 9, 1878. The couple eventually had eleven children—seven of whom survived to adulthood—including my father's father, Paul Anatole, born on January 21, 1889. While researching in the city's archives, I'd found out that Rosa was born in 1852 in St. Tammany Parish, across Lake Pontchartrain, in the village of Lacombe, and that her mother was a mulatto woman named Marie and her father was a white man named Anatole Cousin—the source for my father's first name. In June of 2000, I spent a few days across the lake trying to learn more about Rosa's background.

The Cousin name was well known in these parts. The family's progenitor, a white man from France named Pierre François Cousin, helped to settle St. Tammany back in the 1740s, when the only other inhabitants were Choctaw Indians. As a reward the Spanish crown granted four thousand acres to Pierre's son, Jean François Cousin, making him the largest single landowner in the parish. By the time of the Louisiana Purchase, the family had a prosperous business making bricks and milling lumber, along with a fleet of six schooners to transport their wares across the lake to the booming city of New Orleans. All the work was performed by slaves, and by 1850 the Cousins owned nearly two hundred people. I had a hunch that Rosa's mother, Marie, had been one of the Cousin family slaves.

Several clues pointed to this fact, starting with Marie's name.

I'd seen her listed in records as Marie, Mary, or Marianne, but she always used the surname Cousin, despite the fact that she and Anatole Cousin never married. At the same time, I couldn't find any reference to Marie's maiden name, suggesting that she didn't have one of her own. Also, "Mary" Cousin was listed on the 1870 census as born in Virginia in 1825 — a state where fewer than 10 percent of blacks were free at the time. I speculated that Marie had been sold to a slave trader who sent her downriver in the hold of a ship or as part of a slave coffle to the New Orleans market, where Anatole Cousin had picked her out for his "fancy girl."

Anatole was twenty-one when the first of his six children with Marie was born. During the antebellum era, it wasn't uncommon for a young white man, especially one from a wealthy family, to take a slave mistress before marrying a white woman and producing legitimate heirs. Any children born to the union were also slaves, which helps to explain why by 1860 almost half of the people owned by the Cousin family were of mixed race according to the slave schedules. From some birth certificates I'd found for her children — issued a few years after their birth but before emancipation — I knew that Marie and her children had been freed before the Civil War began. (Slave births weren't recorded in civil records.) But I was hoping to discover the date of their manumission to know whether my great-grandmother Rosa had once been a slave too.

My father wouldn't have remembered his grandmother Rosa: he was just shy of his first birthday when she died in July 1921. But as I drove out to St. Tammany Parish, across the twenty-four-mile causeway spanning Lake Pontchartrain (the longest bridge of its kind in the world), I imagined the types of contact the pair might have had: Rosa picking up my father from his crib, my dad squirming in her lap during Sunday dinner, she giving him a bath — all the things that my father had done with me. And I tried to feel this sense of proximity bridging the generations, from my great-grandmother to my dad to me.

It had been nearly a decade since my father had died, since I'd learned of his—and my—African ancestry, since I'd begun reading and learning and talking about race. And despite my glimmerings of double consciousness, I didn't yet *feel* black. I was still waiting for an "Aha!" moment, an affirmation of this identity down deep in my bones. I hoped that proof that my great-grandmother had been a slave would call forth something buried inside my DNA and I'd have my visceral confirmation at last.

Looking back now, it's surprising, and discomfiting, how much I equated slavery with black identity. But I was hardly the first person to arrive at this formulation. In his book *One Drop of Blood: The American Misadventure of Race*, Scott Malcomson traces the correlation between African ancestry and bondage back to fifteenth-century Portugal and the beginning of the Atlantic slave trade. Writing in 1453 Portuguese royal chronicler Gomes Eanes de Zurara called upon the "Curse of Ham" story in Genesis to justify his countrymen's enslavement of Africans, the race cursed "to be subject to all the other races of the world."

Slavery had been going on since the ancient civilizations, but Zurara's explanation marked the first time that enslavement was seen as a matter of biological inheritance rather than a conditional state brought about by war or an economic transaction. The notion that servitude was passed down through blood became particularly expedient as the plantation societies in the New World required more and more labor. Not only could the workforce continually regenerate itself through reproduction, but a seemingly infinite supply of new slaves were available for purchase on the Dark Continent. While African states had long been selling war prisoners to their Muslim neighbors, the Europeans, armed with their quasi-religious, then quasi-scientific rationale, elevated the practice into an international institution.

In the American colonies, the concept of the African's natural servitude helped European settlers reconcile their allegiance to personal liberty with their reliance on slave labor. It also provided an entity against which a disparate collection of immigrants—from different social classes, geographic regions, and cultures—could unify as one society. To be American was to be white and free. A century and a half after slavery ended in the United States, the association of bondage with blackness remained potent enough to have implanted into my brain the belief that to be black in America necessarily meant to have been enslaved.

Most of the records for St. Tammany Parish were housed in the basement of the courthouse in Covington, a small city of 8,400 people in rural Louisiana. A nondescript concrete building, the courthouse sat at the intersection of two main streets on the edge of a grassy square. In nice weather the benches lining the square were filled with (mostly white) workers on lunch or cigarette breaks. These people would nod hello as I walked back and forth to my rental car or across the street to the Conveyance Office, where the indexes of property sales and purchases—including slave transactions—were kept.

Most visitors to the courthouse basement came requesting marriage licenses or birth certificates, but a few metal stools were pulled up to the counter for people doing genealogical research among the probate and property records, wills and court documents, and marriage licenses for parish residents dating back to 1810. My first day there, I sat down on one of these stools, pulled out my laptop, and searched in vain for a place to plug it in. A computer felt out of place among these yellowing records and the old-fashioned uniforms of navy skirt, white shirt, and plaid necktie worn by the two female clerks. As the women chatted with each other or on the phone, I listened for evidence of their obsolete attitudes too.

But when I told the younger clerk that I was looking for a slave ancestor, she hardly batted an eye. After all, whites in these parts had been mixing with blacks and Choctaw Indians for centuries. There were lots of people like me, although they didn't tend to go around looking for evidence of it. But, the clerk told me, the former archivist—an older woman by the name of Bertha Neff—had combed through all the public records in her spare time to put together a set of index cards on which she kept track of who was what. The young clerk pulled out a thick stack for the Cousin family and handed them over. "Apparently Miss Neff either liked you or she didn't," the clerk said.

I glanced through the index cards and guessed from Neff's close scrutiny of the Cousins' bloodlines that the family wasn't among those she favored. One card for François Cousin—the son of Jean François (who'd received the land grant) and father to my dad's great-grandfather Anatole Cousin—indicated that he'd cohabited with two different "squaws" from a local tribe of Choctaw Indians. The second, Eugenie Judissé, born of a "half breed woman and white man," was Anatole Cousin's mother. So I was part Native American too.

The clerk told me that when Neff started working at the courthouse in the 1960s, the archivist was already in her seventies. She stayed for twenty years and was well over ninety when she was finally forced out. During Neff's lifetime Louisiana changed the legal definitions of whiteness and blackness and amended the miscegenation laws at least seven different times. It was up to clerks like Neff in parish courthouses across the state to interpret and implement the latest rulings, a job over which some of them exercised an obsessive despotic authority.

Neff's counterpart in New Orleans had been a punctilious woman named Naomi Drake until she was fired in 1965 for, among other things, acquiring a backlog of nearly six thousand requests for certified copies of birth or death certificates on which she deemed the racial designation suspicious. Her office kept a list of 250 family names—mostly old French ones, with Broyard surely among them—that automatically triggered an investigation by her or one of her "race clerks" into an applicant's racial background.

According to the clerk in the Covington courthouse, Miss Neff, by the end of her reign, had come to think of the records there as her personal property. On packing up her things, she even took some of the ledgers home with her for "safekeeping." Most of them were eventually retrieved, but every so often a book would turn up missing, spirited away by Neff or someone else who wanted a fact about his or her family to disappear.

I tried to imagine the trepidation that my Creole cousins must have felt when facing Neff or Drake. For much of the state's history, race determined almost every aspect of a person's life: whom you could marry, where you could live, where you went to school, whether you could vote, the copy of the Bible you'd swear on in the courthouse. If someone in Miss Neff's position didn't like you, she could make your life very hard indeed. I had trouble envisioning this woman lording over her records just twenty years earlier, while I was blithely playing badminton at my prep school in Connecticut. Perhaps most telling about my degree of removal from such racial paranoia was my current eagerness to uncover slave ancestors in my own family's past.

I'd spent the last three days looking through the probate records for every Cousin family member to see if a young mixed-race slave named Marie was included in anyone's estate. I'd searched through hundreds of pages of property transactions for her purchase or emancipation. While there were plenty of documents for the Cousin family that involved slaves, none so far concerned anyone who seemed like Marie. Then, on my last day in Covington, the last day of this research trip in Louisiana, I found something.

At the Conveyance Office across the street from the courthouse, I came across a reference to a sale made by Anatole Cousin to Marie E. Cousin on December 28, 1859. The entry was handwritten and barely legible, causing me to miss it the first time I'd looked through these indexes. I'd seen Marie listed with the middle name Evaline, which would explain the middle initial. My heart began to beat faster as I copied down the page number for the corresponding ledger back in the courthouse basement. As I gathered my things to go, I wondered if it had been Marie's own freedom that she purchased from Anatole or the freedom of their children.

I walked outside into the glaring noonday sun. The people on the benches nodded hello as usual and I stared back, feeling as if I'd never seen them before. My senses were strangely heightened: the heat of sunshine on my shoulders, the rustle of paper lunch bags, the smell of cigarettes on the warm air, all recorded precisely in my brain, as if I anticipated returning often to this moment. I entered the courthouse and headed down the metal stairs, wondering how different I'd feel when I ascended.

As I filled out my request slip for the ledger, I told the young clerk about my discovery. She offered a neutral nod. But I could sense her watching me as I started to search through the ledger's pages. She'd already told me about a girl who'd run crying from her twin sister when she realized what the yellowing record of a slave emancipation she was looking at meant. I located the referenced page and searched the handwritten entries for Anatole's or Marie's name. The transaction wasn't there. I flipped back and forth to the surrounding pages.

"You can't find it?" the clerk asked.

I shook my head.

"Maybe the page number was transcribed wrong." She stood up and walked over to the counter. "See if there's an index in the back of the book."

There was another index. I scanned it for Marie's name. "Nothing," I said, and then, "Wait a minute. Here's something for a Marianne Cousin in 1870."

I found the entry and started reading the details of a land sale of two hundred acres to Marianne Cousin...*fronting the bayou...measuring one hundred chains on one side...ninety-five chains on the other side...adjacent to the lot owned by Marie Evaline Xavier, also known as Marie Cousin.* My stomach dropped. It dawned on me for the first time that there was more than one woman with a name resembling "Marie Cousin" and I might have been chasing the wrong person.

My Marie seemed to have a maiden name after all, and enough money to purchase a lot of land before 1870, which was sounding less and less like someone who'd been a slave. I checked my watch. If I hurried back to New Orleans, I'd have a couple of hours to look for information about the Xavier family in the library before heading to the airport to catch my flight.

I raced back to the city, across the twenty-four mile bridge, riding all the way in silence, shaking my head every so often and swearing under my breath. The leaps of logic I'd made and the clues I'd missed in researching Marie's genealogy were suddenly distressingly clear. The thought of how blinded I'd been in my obsession to find a slave ancestor made me feel sick with shame.

Xavier wasn't a very common surname. The first probate record I looked up belonged to François Xavier, who died in 1839, leaving behind a wife and five children, including a daughter named Marie Evaline, my great-great-grandmother, who was born free in New Orleans in 1824. I quickly read on, discovering that both of Marie's parents had also been free people of color. They'd arrived in the city as children, among the wave of refugees fleeing the slave revolt in St. Domingue. Marie's father was educated and was a successful shoe-maker. At his death his holdings were valued at roughly $4,100, placing him well above the average net worth of $3,000 for free people of color at the time.

Among the property that François passed along to his wife and children, including my great-great-grandmother Marie Evaline, were three different lots of land, two buildings, a collection of furniture, the inventory of a shoe store on Bourbon Street, and two slaves: a twenty-eight-year-old Negro named Marie, and a twenty-year-old "griffe" (three-quarters black, one-quarter white) named George. I swore out loud this time—drawing an annoyed glance from the woman at the adjacent microfilm reader—and copied the rest of the document before hurrying off to the airport.

Once the plane was aloft, the events of the day began to sink in. In a few short hours, I'd gone from believing that my great-grandmother was born a slave to discovering that she'd grown up in a family of black slave *owners.* Sometimes free blacks purchased their own family members, particularly when the laws regarding emancipation tightened, but these relatives remained slaves only in name. That scenario didn't seem to be the case in the Xavier family. In the years after François Xavier died, the slave Marie was put up for auction numerous times. According to the probate record, she was "addicted to intoxication," which made it hard to fetch her appraised price. The family held on to George longer. My great-grandmother Rosa was six when her grandmother finally sold him, at a 50 percent return on the original investment. That my white Louisiana ancestors had owned slaves wasn't surprising, but the fact that my black ancestors had also partaken in the "peculiar institution" astounded me. These weren't the noble tragic figures I'd been expecting to encounter. My claim to an authentic black identity felt more distant than ever.

I sat back in my seat and looked out the plane's window. A thick bank of clouds obscured the landscape below. Normally I enjoyed the feeling of disorientation when flying, the idea that I could be anywhere, but right then I wanted something concrete to hold on to. Each time I thought I'd finally tracked the path of the color line through my family's past, it twisted out of sight. First I hadn't been able to place my great-great-grandfather Henry Broyard on one side or the other. Now my great-great-grandmother was confounding my grasp of what African American identity was supposed to be. I was nearing the end of my research in New Orleans and I was worried. If I couldn't pinpoint the place from which my father had fled, was he going to elude me too? As I kept discovering, nothing in New Orleans was as simple as black and white.

A natole Cousin's father owned a town house in the Tremé neigh-borhood of New Orleans, around the corner from the head-quarters of the family's brick-making operation. Wealthy families living in the countryside often made lengthy stays in the city, espe-cially during Carnival season. When Anatole was growing up, it was likely that he visited the family's pied-à-terre a few times a year, either accompanying his father on business or to celebrate the holidays. In 1843, when Anatole was fourteen, a widow moved across the street with her five children. There was a boy, François, who was Anatole's age, but Anatole was more drawn to the eldest sibling, Marie Evaline, who was five years his senior. Although she was colored and Anatole was white, their families weren't that different from each other: the Cousins and Xaviers were both French-speaking Creoles, and they both belonged to the propertied class — owning land, buildings, and slaves. So when Marie Evaline's pregnancy started showing in 1851, a few months after Mardi Gras, perhaps it wasn't much of a surprise for anyone to learn that Anatole was the father.

Before the baby arrived, Marie Evaline moved across Lake Pontchartrain to Bayou Lacombe, where she and Anatole began to live as man and wife. My great-grandmother Rosa was their second child, born almost exactly a year after the first one. Perhaps the difficulties of these back-to-back pregnancies made Marie Evaline begin to shy away from Anatole's advances; or perhaps their five-year age difference became more apparent after the physical toll of childbirth on Marie Evaline's body. In any case, by the time Marie Evaline reached her midthirties, Anatole had begun to stray with twenty-year-old Margaret Ducré, the daughter of an emancipated slave, who would eventually bear thirteen of his children. Bayou Lacombe was a small community; Marie Evaline must have known about the infidelity. Yet a colored woman with little means didn't have much recourse, and she continued to allow Anatole into her bed.

By the time the Civil War broke out, Marie Evaline was pregnant with her and Anatole Cousin's fifth child, and he had another two children with Margaret Ducré. Legislators for St. Tammany Parish had initially voted against Louisiana's seceding from the Union, but once the war started, all the local men were expected to volunteer for the Confederate cause. In the summer of 1862, Anatole and his brother Octave set off for Camp Moore, up near the Mississippi border, to join the Ninth Louisiana Partisan Rangers. Marie Evaline had no family in Lacombe other than Anatole's kin, who may have been disinclined to look after her, especially when he had a second colored family living down the road.

After New Orleans fell to Union forces, getting food and supplies to St. Tammany Parish across the federal blockade on Lake Pontchartrain became nearly impossible. Deserters from both sides raided a nearby Indian village for food, killing or displacing hundreds of Choctaw, many of whom later died from illness or starvation. Lincoln's proclamation freeing the slaves in the rebel territories made life more difficult still.

Anatole Cousin owned about fifteen slaves, one or two of whom may have been assigned to help Marie Evaline. Cousin family lore describes a group of happy workers who stuck by the family throughout the war, even helping them to evade capture by Union soldiers. The story went that when some Yankees came to the door of the Cousin family's homestead in a neighboring town, a slave convinced the marauders that everyone inside was sick with yellow fever and sent them on their way. Nevertheless, in the weeks following Lincoln's proclamation, when thousands of slaves from the parishes surrounding New Orleans were making a dash for Union territories, some of the St. Tammany slaves must have seized the opportunity to flee as well.

Sometime after the birth of her fifth child, Marie Evaline sneaked across the lake herself to wait out the duration of the war in New Orleans. After the conflict ended, Marie Evaline saw Anatole at least one more time, for she became pregnant with their sixth (and last) child in February of 1867. But the war laid bare the fact that more differences existed between them than a few shades of skin color. During the Battle of Port Hudson, Anatole's Confederate unit had faced off against Marie Evaline's brother François, who belonged to the Louisiana Native Guard. The Partisan Rangers had supplied the sharpshooters who struck down so many of the colored soldiers that day.

After impregnating Marie Evaline for a final time, Anatole returned to Lacombe, where he would live out the rest of his years with Margaret Ducré. But he didn't completely disappear from Marie Evaline's life. A few years later, a family friend of Anatole's arranged for the sale of a few tracts of the Cousin family land in Lacombe to Marie Evaline and two other colored women who'd been mistresses of his brothers, the records of which I'd come across in the basement of the Covington courthouse. Leasing the acreage to farmers or lumbermen provided the women with some regular income. And so even if Marie Evaline's children didn't see their father very much (or appear as beneficiaries in his will), they continued to have ties to Lacombe, even becoming friendly with some of Anatole's other children. In fact after Rosa and Paul married, they built a summer home in Lacombe, which my father used to visit as a child until his family left Louisiana.

Over the years, Marie Evaline was forced in various legal transactions to admit to her unmarried status, but she maintained the fiction to her friends and family that she and Anatole had been married. She went by the last name Cousin, and around the time of Rosa's wedding, she began referring to herself as Widow Cousin, even though

Anatole was alive and well, residing in Lacombe with Margaret Ducré. It must have been particularly painful for her to learn that Anatole eventually married Margaret—making their children legitimate— during the brief window in Louisiana when intermarriage was legal. But still Marie Evaline's last word, on her memorial card, described her as Mrs. Anatole Cousin.

Paul and Rosa had probably known each other since childhood. His father and her uncle served in the same company of the Louisiana Native Guard. Their extended families belonged to the same circle—people who worshipped at St. Augustine's Church, attended Republican political meetings, and belonged to the more exclusive of the Creole benevolent associations. Compared to Paul, Rosa enjoyed a childhood of relative comfort despite her mother's precarious connection to Anatole. During the antebellum years, when they lived in Lacombe or at her grandmother's place in New Orleans, there'd been slaves to help with the cooking and cleaning. Even with the upset of

the war, Rosa had been able to attend school, where she learned to read and write. And there was money enough for frivolities such as photographic portraits and elegant clothes to wear in them. Rosa's Choctaw ancestry gave her straight dark hair, broad high cheekbones, and deeply set eyes. Neither she nor her siblings looked much like Negroes, which allowed them more freedom as the city became more segregated.

At the time of the 1878 national election, Rosa was nearly eight months pregnant with her and Paul's first child. The months leading up to the election had been marked by unprecedented violence, particularly in the cotton parishes along the Mississippi, as colored men attempted to register to vote. In New Orleans election officials first stalled on supplying the special deputies needed to assist in the registration and election processes, and then appointed only Democrats, wrecking any shot at fairness. On election day itself, the Republican U.S. marshal reportedly got drunk, allowing the Democratic deputies in the city to swing votes their way with impunity. No matter that blacks outnumbered whites in the majority of Louisiana's parishes, all six of the state's U.S. congressional seats went Democratic.

Up in Washington, President Hayes received a day-by-day, parish-by-parish catalog of the colored Republicans who had been murdered:

On Oct. 16th, William Henry was shot in Tensas Parish and Richard Miller was hanged at Lake St. Peter. On Oct. 17th, Louis Postewaithe and James Starier were shot at Wren's store in Tensas Parish....On October 18th, Bob Williams, Peter Young, and Monday Hill were hanged and Hiram Wilson was shot, all in Tensas Parish. On October 19th, Charles Bethel was shot and had his throat cut on a plantation just above the town of Waterproof in Tensas Parish....In Concordia, on October 17, Charles Carroll and Wast Ellis were killed, and Commodore Smallwood, a preacher, was whipped, weighted down with an iron cogwheel and thrown in the lake and drowned. Dickey Smith was hanged on Oct. 18th....

The list went on and on. Hayes sent federal prosecutors down south to investigate, but they couldn't secure convictions in any of the cases. Those few witnesses who didn't sympathize with the perpetrators were either killed before they could testify or were too afraid to come forward.

✻   ✻   ✻

The disastrous results of the November election forced the different factions of Louisiana Republicans to mend their rifts. The Democrats were convening another constitutional convention, where they would surely try to repeal some of the rights secured for Negroes at the last one. Republicans needed to work together to ensure that some of their delegates were elected if they wanted to have a voice in the process. To that end fifty white and black party leaders gathered at Antoine's Restaurant in the French Quarter. In a great show of cooperation, ex-governor Warmoth and *Tribune* founder Louis Roudanez shook hands, agreeing to end the dispute that had been begun ten years earlier with the paper's refusal to back Warmoth's gubernatorial nomination.

The Republicans' united front paid off. Out of 134 delegates at the convention, 32 were Republicans, including 17 blacks. Sure enough, the Negroes' franchise was debated, but white planters feared that taking away the black vote would drive too many of their laborers from the state. So Governor Nicholls moved on to the next goal: segregating public institutions and businesses. In order to pass the amendment, he needed the support of the Negro delegates. In exchange for their votes, he offered to establish a separate state-funded black institution for higher learning, which eventually became Southern University. P.B.S. Pinchback, a colored Republican who had always stuck by Warmoth, convinced the other black delegates to accept the deal.

Pinchback later explained himself: "I have learned to look at things as they are and not as I would have them....This country, at least so far as the South is concerned, is a white man's country....What I wish to impress upon my people, is that no change is likely to take place in our day and in general that will reverse this order of things." But many in the Creole of color community never forgave Pinchback for his acquiescence to segregation. The national black leader Booker T. Washington would advocate a similar accommodationist position in his 1895 speech dubbed the Atlanta Compromise. In effect, these colored politicians agreed to forgo integration in exchange for the funding of their own institutions. It marked the beginning of a style of race relations that would persist in Louisiana, and throughout the South, until the 1960s.

My grandfather Paul Anatole Broyard was born in his parents' home on January 21, 1889. His name—invoking his father and his mother's father—was typical of an eldest son's, but Paul Anatole was actually the sixth child, and third boy, born to Paul and Rosa. They'd lost their first male child, christened Anatole Paul, in 1880, and were apparently too superstitious to recycle the name for their next son. By the time my grandfather came along, the curse had worn off, or else Paul couldn't wait any longer for his namesake. My grandfather must have felt his name to be cursed in a different way. To be the "junior" of a man like Belhomme was a lot of pressure for a young boy. When he was twelve or so, my grandfather nicknamed himself Nat, although his father persisted in calling him Paul Jr., and as an adult he reversed his name to Anatole Paul, which further distinguished him from Paul Sr.

By the time Nat was born, Paul was clearly the patriarch of the extended Broyard clan. With neither a father or father-in-law present, he was the oldest male in the family. He'd already been serving for the previous fifteen years as the surrogate father for his five younger brothers. When all of their families gathered for Sunday dinner, Paul occupied the head of the table, carving the duck that Rosa prepared and doling out the wine—two fingers apiece for Nat and his cousins. Paul's construction business was steadily growing, particularly after his carpentry skills were showcased at the World's Cotton Exposition held in New Orleans in 1884. Creoles of color and whites alike were hiring him for bigger and bigger buildings, for which he employed his younger brothers and cousins.

During the early 1890s, Paul also became involved in politics, joining the new generation of Creole radicals who'd begun to fight back against the ascendance of white supremacy in the state. For most of the decade, Paul served as Republican president for the Fifth Ward, which included the Creole neighborhood of Tremé. In this elected position, he participated in every aspect of the political process: from electing delegates to the Republican state convention, to leading party meetings and setting party platforms, to securing polling sites and running the primaries. Paul also served on the Republican Party's state central committee, which was responsible for assembling the state tickets.

During his period of political activity, Paul focused particularly on uniting the disparate parts of the Republican Party. The Reconstruction-era division between American blacks and the Creoles of color had persisted. At the same time, white planters, unhappy with the Democratic Party's antiprotectionism policies, began entering the Republican fold, along with poorer whites who were fed up with a governing style that favored the wealthy. Although the white newcomers to the Republican Party had to be coaxed into supporting the Negroes' fight for equality, Paul worked to make room for them, recognizing that an interracial coalition was the party's only chance to win back control of the South. His efforts very nearly paid off.

When Nat was grown and had children himself, he often told stories about his father, but he never mentioned Paul's political activity. The ultimately disappointing outcome might have made him reluctant to share these memories, or else he was too young to understand anything more than that his father seemed to be always busy.

By day Paul was supervising hundreds of men (black and white) in the construction of some of the most elegant and modern buildings the city had ever seen. A few weeks before Christmas in 1893, when Nat was four, Paul completed the Grunewald, New Orleans's first "modern" luxury hotel. The 250-room property boasted two elevators, its own electric plant, steam heating, an interior finished in carved cypress, and a roof garden big enough to accommodate three thousand people. The following year Paul was hired to build the southern headquarters for Liverpool & London & Globe Insurance, the largest insurance company in the city.

By night Paul ran from one political rally to another, meeting with everyone from other colored Republicans to the recently converted white planters to U.S. senators who came to New Orleans as representatives of the national Republican Party. As a ward president, Paul also played a hand in doling out federal patronage, such as jobs at the post office and customhouse or contracts for federal buildings or roads. Along with the work generated by his construction firm— which oversaw budgets up to $250,000 (almost $5 million today) and crews of as many as 250 men—my great-grandfather was in the position to improve many people's fortunes.

Even without knowing the specifics of his father's activities, Nat would be able to see from his father's example that being colored didn't necessarily prevent a person from being respected and treated as a man, no matter how much the segregation imposed by southern whites might try to convince him otherwise.

Ever since federal troops had pulled out of Louisiana, Democrats had been trying to repeal whatever gains blacks had secured during Reconstruction. In his inaugural speech on May 19, 1884, Governor Samuel McEnery declared: "That many of our best citizens, who have given thought and attention to public affairs, are practically disfranchised by a larger class of citizens who are unacquainted with the operations of the government, and are absolutely ignorant of passing events, is evident....I believe that public opinion imperatively demands that the right of suffrage be restricted to those who can intelligently exercise it." While the federal constitution prevented Governor McEnery from legally disenfranchising blacks, the Democrats' tactics of intimidation, bribery, and fraud gave the party control of elective offices across the state.

In 1890 passage of the Separate Car Law, which segregated travel on state railroads, presented the Creole radicals with their chance to call a national referendum on the declining state of southern race relations in the form of the court case *Plessy v. Ferguson*. Rodolphe Desdunes, Paul Broyard's friend and a fellow Creole of color, came up with the idea. While studying for his law degree at an integrated law school in the 1880s, Desdunes had concluded that the U.S. federal courts offered blacks their best option to contest the loss of their civil and political rights. In response to the Separate Car Law, he proposed setting up a test case in order to force the U.S. Supreme Court to rule on its constitutionality. Another Creole lawyer, Louis Martinet, started a Republican newspaper, the *Crusader*, to publicize the legal fight, and a group of leading Creoles formed the Citizens Committee to raise money for the defense. The white civil rights lawyer Albion Tourgée, from upstate New York, signed on as legal counsel.

The judicial battle wasn't going to be easy. Even if the Supreme Court agreed to hear their case, the Creole radicals had no guarantee of winning the decision. Since the end of Reconstruction, the mood in Washington had turned against African Americans. In 1883 the Supreme Court had ruled that the Civil Rights Acts of 1875, which ensured equal access to public buildings and conveyances, was unconstitutional. So far federal courts weren't objecting to the appearance across the South of "Jim Crow" laws (named after a popular minstrel show character, an old crippled black slave), despite their clear violation of the Fourteenth Amendment.

On February 24, 1892, Rodolphe Desdunes's son, a thirty-year-old musician named Daniel Desdunes, boarded a train headed for Mobile, Alabama, and took a seat in a "whites only" car. The idea was to first test the constitutionality of train travel *between* states. Since only Congress had the power to regulate interstate commerce, this case presented a better chance for a favorable ruling. Desdunes hadn't traveled two miles when the conductor stopped the train and a private detective stepped forward to arrest him. This had all been arranged beforehand with the railroad company, which disliked the Jim Crow law as much as the colored men. Maintaining separate cars for blacks and whites was expensive and inconvenient. Also, if a conductor wrongly accused a white person of being colored, he ran the risk of being sued for damages.

While waiting for Desdunes's case to come to trial, the Citizens Committee launched a second, more challenging, legal battle to test train travel *within* the state. One of the younger members of the committee, a thirty-year-old shoemaker named Homer Plessy, volunteered as the rider. A Creole of color, Plessy looked white enough to enter the "whites only" coach without calling attention to himself, but was black enough—one-eighth—to get himself arrested. On June 7, 1892, he boarded a train for Covington, across Lake Pontchartrain. Again the railroad company was in cahoots with the Creole activists, and the train had barely pulled out of the station when the conductor confronted Plessy. After the young shoemaker was arrested, his case was placed on the docket of Judge John H. Ferguson of the New Orleans Criminal Court.

In June of 1892, the Creole radicals celebrated their first victory. As they had anticipated, the court threw out the charges against Desdunes's son, holding that the Separate Car Law when applied to passengers traveling between states was unconstitutional. But in the Plessy case, concerning travel within Louisiana, Judge Ferguson ruled against them: "There is no pretense that [Plessy] was not provided with equal accommodations with the white passengers. He was simply deprived of the liberty of doing as he pleased." In other words, the white and black cars were separate but not unequal, and therefore the law didn't violate the equal protection clause of the Fourteenth Amendment.

The ruling didn't come as a complete surprise, nor did the decision of the Louisiana Supreme Court to uphold the decision on appeal. The Creole activists had always expected that they would have to take their battle to the federal courts. But by the time the case was placed on the U.S. Supreme Court's docket, their prospects for success had changed considerably. Democrat Grover Cleveland's victory in the 1892 presidential election had brought about a change to the court's political complexion. By the count of attorney Albion Tourgée, five of the eight justices would be against them. In Tourgée's view their best option was to try to rally support for the cause in the press. If each of these justices "hears from the country," perhaps one of them could be convinced to change his position.

Accordingly, Louis Martinet stepped up publication of the *Crusader.* In 1894 the paper became the only black daily newspaper in the United States and the sole Republican daily in the South. But the country at the moment wasn't feeling receptive to political action on behalf of colored people. Many northerners blamed blacks for the failure of Reconstruction. Also, the country was in the middle of a depression: hundreds of banks had folded, thousands of businesses were in bankruptcy, 4 million people were out of work, and farmers across the South and West were teetering on the edge of ruin. Even well-meaning white Americans were too concerned with putting food on their table to rally for racial equality. For many of the country's colored citizens, Booker T. Washington's focus on job training and accommodation to white prejudice made a lot more sense than the New Orleans committee's push for integration.

In his famous Atlanta Compromise speech in September of 1895, Washington declared: "The wisest among my race understand that the agitation of questions of social equality is the extremest folly, and that progress in the enjoyment of all the privileges that will come to us must be the result of severe and constant struggle rather than of artificial forcing." Washington's reasoning that "the opportunity to earn a dollar in a factory just now is worth infinitely more than the opportunity to spend a dollar in an opera-house" obliquely criticized the New Orleans committee for being out of touch with the realities of most black people.

It was true that the relative economic security of my great-grandfather and his New Orleans compatriots afforded them the luxury to fight for equality on other fronts. But this battle meant much more than earning the right to sit next to whites at the opera. Louisiana's general assembly had already outlawed intermarriage and was in the process of trying to pass a suffrage amendment that would impose property and education requirements on voters. My great-grandfather and his fellow Creole radicals recognized that the Democrats were on the verge of turning back the clock on race relations in the South to the preemancipation days.

While waiting for the ruling in *Plessy v. Ferguson*, Paul was hard at work helping to assemble a compromise ticket to challenge the incumbent Democratic candidate in the April 1896 gubernatorial election. For the first time since the state had been redeemed, the Republicans actually had a chance of their man's winning the election. An interracial coalition of disgruntled white Democrats and colored Republicans joined together to support a white sugar planter named Captain John N. Pharr, who was running on a Populist ticket. Further uniting the disparate group was opposition to the suffrage amendment, which would disenfranchise poor whites and blacks alike.

At the Washington Artillery Hall, Pharr announced to a crowd of nine hundred — half of whom were black — his willingness to run against the amendment and for equal rights, "especially for the nigger," who he declared had no bad traits except for what he'd learned from white people. His speech drew cheers, especially from the black contingent, but Pharr's base of support was far from solid. In the weeks leading up to the election, Paul and other Republican leaders had to repeatedly thwart efforts by one faction or another to establish a splinter ticket that would siphon off votes.

Pharr ended up winning every white parish in the state. In the black parishes, however, the Democrats—by alternately stealing and buying black votes—returned an outstanding number of ballots for their candidate, resulting in his victory. The close election results demonstrated the ability of black voters to decide a race when whites were divided. The sugar planters, in particular, feared the potential power of future cross-racial alliances among blacks and small white farmers, and set about eliminating colored voters altogether through jury-rigged reforms of state election laws and then the amendment of the state constitution. (The number of blacks on Louisiana's voter rolls would eventually drop from 154,000 in 1896 to fewer than 500 in 1908.) Just a month after this blow came a second one. On May 18, 1896, the U.S. Supreme Court upheld the lower court's decision in the *Plessy v. Ferguson* case with its finding that segregated facilities were not unconstitutional because separate did not necessarily mean unequal.

During the preparations for the *Plessy* trial, the Creole newspaper publisher Louis Martinet had written to Albion Tourgée about the stakes for New Orleans's colored population: "You don't know what the feeling is…knowing that you are a freeman, & yet not allowed to enjoy a freeman's liberty, rights, and privileges unless you stake your life every time you try it. To live always under the feeling of restraint is worse than living behind prison bars." Martinet had told the lawyer that he wasn't willing to raise his child in the "prejudiced southern atmosphere." Neither, apparently, was my great-grandfather.

Over the next few weeks following the *Plessy* decision, Paul finished up his various construction jobs and gave a local lawyer power of attorney to conduct his business affairs in his absence. Then he boarded a train with Rosa and their six children for California. No matter that the Broyards had lived in New Orleans for the last 150 years, no matter that Paul owed everything he was to the city's Creole culture, my great-grandfather was willing to leave if it meant that his children could grow up believing themselves to be equals. One way to ensure that would be for the family to live as white.

The Broyard kids were all pale enough that they could probably get away with it. Perhaps Paul had even bought tickets for the white compartment of the train as a trial run of sorts. Los Angeles at the turn of the century was nowhere near as race conscious as the Deep South. A thriving agriculture and the recent discovery of oil were drawing people to California from across the country. The Broyards would have been one of many families who were trying to start over. But something made Paul decide to come back to New Orleans in time to start the school year in September. It's possible that he didn't have the necessary connections to find work; at least in New Orleans, Paul could hold his head up as one of the biggest builders in town. Or maybe he found that he didn't like living as white. After expending so much energy fighting against them, jumping to the other side of the color line wasn't so simple or appealing. But I think the most likely explanation for his return is that he simply felt homesick. Out in California, Belhomme was just another lonely immigrant lost inside customs and a culture that were mysterious to everyone else.

My grandfather Nat was seven that summer, old enough to remember the transcontinental train travel, the daytrips to the Pacific Ocean, the relative freedom from racial discrimination, and his father's somber moods. One day he would make a similar trip, leaving New Orleans in search of a better life for his children, when his son, my father, was just about the same age as Nat had been. The one difference would be that when Nat left his hometown, he would make a point of vowing never to return.

-24-

During my visit to New Orleans, Keith Medley, the proprietor of the guesthouse where I was staying, secured me some invitations to a couple of Mardi Gras balls. Tourists tend to associate Mardi Gras solely with Fat Tuesday, but Carnival season actually begins in early January, and the weeks leading up to Lent are filled with dances and parades put on by krewes and social clubs throughout the city. Both of my invites, to the Plantation Revelers and Bunch Club balls, were known particularly as Creole events.

The divisions in New Orleans's black community had been smoothed over to some extent during the civil rights movement. Although the city's first African American mayor, Ernest "Dutch" Morial, came from an old Creole family, neither he nor his son Marc, who succeeded him eight years later, identified as Creole. However, in some of the older customs such as the balls, the legacy of this segregated culture continued. African Americans had their favorite event too, thrown by the Zulu Social Aid and Pleasure Club. The most well known among the black balls, Zulu generally fell on the same night as the Bunch Club dance, but tickets to the Zulu party weren't easy to come by.

Keith had also asked our friend Bev to the Bunch Club Ball, but as the date grew closer and he didn't reiterate his invitation, she became convinced that he didn't really want her to go. She'd heard the rumors about the Bunch Club members employing the "paper bag test" to screen partygoers at one time, and Bev thought Keith was worried that her darker skin and dreadlocks would make her unwelcome. I tried to suggest, gently, that Bev's insistence on constantly referring to the party as "the light-skinned nigger ball" might have given Keith the impression that *she* was the one who didn't want to go. In any case, she wasn't coming. I was worried about fitting in too, but my main concern was about what to wear.

The Bunch Club Ball required a formal gown, and the invitation for Plantation Revelers called for "Strictly Plantation Attire," with special instructions for ladies of "no pants or skirts above the knee." Keith offered to ask his sister, who was about my size, if I could borrow one of her gowns from a previous Mardi Gras. But the "Strictly Plantation" dress code presented more of a challenge. For starters, I wasn't sure if that meant dressing up like the slaves or the masters.

More like slaves, suggested Keith. "You know. It's supposed to be Saturday night on the plantation." I wondered out loud why a group of people who neither typically descended from antebellum slaves nor seemed eager to associate with that legacy would choose a plantation theme. Keith shrugged. He had a theory that many of the more theatrical aspects of the balls and parties originated from the movies. "I bet a bunch of Creoles saw *Gone with the Wind* and got to thinking, 'Now, that looks like fun! Let's dress up like slaves on a plantation and have a hoedown!'" he said.

Keith wasn't able to offer any more advice on the plantation attire beyond the fact that red seemed to be popular, particularly red check, and that people wore a lot of denim. "But not cowboy," he said. "They hate cowboy outfits." And with that, I headed off to the French Quarter to go shopping.

Since I'd been in New Orleans, I'd heard locals grumbling about Carnival—the noise, garbage, stink, and throngs of college kids who'd begun descending upon them. As Fat Tuesday drew closer, residents of the Quarter were forced to shutter the bottom-floor windows of their homes during the day to keep out unwanted guests and grease the poles that supported their balconies to prevent rabble-rousers from shimmying up to their second floors at night. Despite the hassle, however, it seemed impossible to escape the contagion of excitement in the air.

Everyone bustled around, buying beads and masks, punch bowls and party mixings, booze and outfits for all the parades and parties. They complained about being too spent, hungover, stuffed, exhausted, to attend one more thing, then went anyway, and ate and drank as much as the last time, or more. Along with a spot on a parade float or a place to watch the procession in the stands of Gallier Hall, an invitation to a Mardi Gras ball was the hottest ticket in town. I wandered in and out of stores, griping to the shop clerks about having to find outfits for *two different balls,* feeling just like a native.

In a costume shop on Decatur Street, I told the saleswoman that I needed something for the Plantation Revelers dance. I thought she might recognize it as a Creole affair and wonder why a white woman was going to a black party. I found myself wanting to tell her my story. Covered in tattoos and piercings, the salesclerk, who was white, looked like someone who could understand another person's struggle over her identity. But she didn't ask me any questions, except if there was something in particular I had in mind.

"It needs to be plantation attire," I said. "You know, something that the slaves would wear on a Saturday night."

The saleswoman nodded, unfazed by the potential minstrel show I'd just described, and started sorting through the racks. "What about this?" She held up a red-checked shirt.

"That could work," I said, glancing at the tag. "Hmm, it says it's 'hillbilly' style."

The saleswomen held the shirt against me. "But it could totally go plantation," she said. "Tie a kerchief around your head. You're done."

The Plantation Revelers dance was held in a convention center in Chalmette, a suburb south of New Orleans once known as David

Duke territory because of its concentration of supporters for the former Ku Klux Klan leader's 1991 gubernatorial campaign. Chalmette
also had a reputation as a place where many Creole of color families
had moved during the early twentieth century to pass as white. The
fight in town against school integration had been particularly fierce,
fueled in part by mixed families living as white who didn't want black
children with the same last names suddenly showing up as their kids'
new classmates. Yet Keith told me on the way to the dance that he'd
never had a problem when he'd had a job in Chalmette.

I'd ended up in the red-checked shirt, a denim skirt (below the
knee), a kerchief tied around my head, and some red tube socks,
which Keith insisted were a key part of the outfit. Walking in I quickly
surveyed the women in camisole tops corseted at their waists, long
blue-checked skirts with aprons tied over them, and cotton shawls
draped around their shoulders, and felt completely out of place. The
only thing I had in common with the other women was my kerchief,
although mine was red while theirs were white or blue. Keith had been
right about the dance taking its inspiration from *Gone with the Wind*.
The other women looked like sexed-up, light-skinned versions of
Mammy, while I looked like somebody auditioning as an extra for
Hee-Haw.

Keith gave me a sheepish smile. "You look fine, baby," he said. (It
turned out that the dance committee picked a new theme color every
other year. For the last two years, it had been red; this year, it was blue.
But throughout the night, I kept spotting other folks in red who also
apparently hadn't gotten the memo.)

Rows of picnic tables surrounded the dance floor, with two assigned to each party. Keith found our group and introduced me to the
dozen or so men and women. "Bliss just found out she's Creole," he
explained. "So she's down here searching for her roots."

They turned to me, gave me an appraising look.

I smiled, offered a little wave.

"She's a Broyard," Keith said.

"Oh!" Now people were nodding and smiling back. "A Broyard. Sure. I went to school with some Broyards." They shifted around to make room. "I hope you're hungry, bay." A stack of plates was pushed my way. "You had any Creole cooking yet?" "Make sure you get some of them crab legs now, 'fore they're all gone."

Keith and I filled our plates from the spread of garlic-sautéed crab legs, jambalaya, andouille sausage, gumbo, rice and beans, spicy deviled eggs, and something called hog cheese, which I didn't care for at all. Keith made us each a stiff rum and Coke, sharing another of his pet theories: that all the spice in the food counteracted the effect of the alcohol. I squeezed into one end of the table, next to our host, Ray. He was a tall, pot-bellied, barely tan-colored man, whose posture in his folding chair — feet planted before him, hands resting heavily on his knees — brought to mind Abraham Lincoln seated on his monument.

Ray leaned his head down to be heard above the din. "So your daddy was passablanc?"

I nodded, my mouth full of food.

"And you're down here looking for your family?"

I smiled, nodded some more.

Ray laughed heartily and lifted his big hand to clap me on the back. "Isn't that something?"

That was all of my story that I had to share that night. My fellow revelers could fill in the rest of the blanks them- selves. We talked, drank, and ate. Then the band came on, and it was time to dance.

Plantation Revelers didn't have a court the way some of the more formal balls did, but they held a "call out," where the members lined up in two long rows and took turns strutting with their partners down the aisle toward a photographer who snapped their photo. I got up to head to the dance floor with the rest of the table.

"Hold on a minute, bay." One of Ray's daughters stopped me. "Let me fix this." She took hold of my kerchief, which was tied in back at the nape of my neck Grateful Dead–style, and rotated it so the knot sat at my brow. "Much better."

After the call out the band traditionally started a "second line" number. "Second line" referred to the row of stragglers who tagged along behind brass bands in parades, but it also was the name for the type of music that followed a funeral. During the procession to the cemetery for the burial, the band would play a solemn dirge, but on the trip home, the members would break into a sprightly number, with the second liners in tow, dancing and strutting, their spirits lifted by the music.

Two long notes on the trumpet announced the start of a second line number. At that cue everyone still sitting at the table hopped up and flooded the dance floor. They began waving handkerchiefs in the air, stepping up their feet as if marching in place, and snapping their fingers in time to the music.

"You look like you've been dancing to the second line all your life," Keith marveled while we stomped across the floor.

I thanked him while keeping to myself the observation that it wasn't exactly hard to keep up with this crowd. One stereotype about African Americans that I was quickly abandoning was their supposed superior dancing skill. Not only did I see plenty of people at the ball who appeared to lack natural rhythm, but the partygoers seemed on the whole as reluctant and self-conscious about getting down as attendees of most all-white affairs I'd been to. The only other song, besides the second line, that got people truly enthused was "Electric Boogie," the theme music for the Electric Slide.

Keith likened the number to the black national anthem. Indeed there was something duty-bound about the way everyone lined up in rows and moved in unison through the dance's steps. After four or five rounds of the same routine, I grew bored and sat down. Alone at the table, I watched my fellow revelers. Notwithstanding my inability to grasp their penchant for line dancing, I felt as if I fit right in.

For my other Creole event, the Bunch Club Ball, I was fortunate in that I didn't have to rely solely on Keith for fashion advice. His sister had brought by the guesthouse a big plastic crate with a dozen gowns to choose from. I selected a floor-length one made out of dark blue sequins with golden braiding crisscrossed over the bodice. It was by far the fanciest dress I'd ever worn. Then Cherry, a waitress at the Italian restaurant where I often ate, offered to style my hair for me.

Cherry was a preoperative transsexual who was training to become a beautician. The money was better than waiting tables, she said, and she was trying to save up for sex-change surgery. On the afternoon of the ball, Cherry, along with her friend Sissy, came over, bearing a big bag of styling supplies. I showed them my dress and we decided on a hairstyle.

The elaborate "Egyptian princess" updo required Cherry to curl my hair piece by piece and pin it to the top of my head. It was a slow process that left plenty of time to chat. They wanted to know about the ball and my date for the evening. During my visits to the restaurant, I'd never gotten around to telling Cherry what I was doing in New Orleans, and so I shared my story.

If anyone could understand what it was like to grow up as one thing, then realize you are something else, it was Cherry and Sissy. But it became evident as we talked that our experiences had been different. While neither of them had any doubt that they'd been born into the wrong bodies, my attachment to my blackness felt tenuous. While they weren't waiting for anyone to give them permission to be female, I wanted someone to tell me it was okay to call myself something other than white.

For Sissy and Cherry, their external transformations were occurring in degrees—from wearing women's clothing to taking hormones to surgically altering their bodies—but internally they'd felt themselves to be feminine for a long time. My experience was nearly the opposite. By acquiring enough knowledge about African American culture and my own Creole history, and meeting the kind of people and having the sorts of experiences that went with growing up in this community—by putting on the right clothes—I was hoping to transform myself from the outside in.

As transsexuals, Cherry and Sissy were vulnerable to ridicule or even violent attacks, but they went about undeterred from living as they felt themselves authentically to be. I remarked that it was a courageous choice, but they didn't seem to view their lives as ruled by choice at all. "It's who I am," Sissy said. "It would just make things harder if I didn't accept it."

I, on the other hand, was hesitant to proclaim myself as part of the black community, for fear of offending someone or stepping on a racial land mine or having to field accusations of being an impostor. Just a few days earlier, when describing what had brought me to New Orleans, I'd been dismayed to hear myself backpedaling in the face of opposition once again.

I'd been at a club called Café Brasil, down the street from Keith's place. A friend from New York, Laura, had come to visit for the weekend, and we headed out to have a few cocktails, hear some live music, and do some dancing. The place was packed. It didn't take long after we hit the floor for two young men, both African American, to claim us as their partners.

Laura, a tall European beauty with silky black hair and striking eyes from her Chinese grandmother, was paired with the cuter of the two guys, who we soon learned was named Deforest. He was also tall, and dark and handsome, with long dreads that clouded his face and a remote demeanor (no doubt from the "blunts" he kept disappearing to smoke) that added to his sex appeal.

My guy, Edwin, was equally long and lean, but he looked sort of nerdy behind his Malcolm X horn-rimmed glasses. And he insisted on making conversation while we danced, which he seemed to think was a better mode of seduction than just keeping quiet and letting our bodies try to find some common ground.

Glancing over at Laura, I saw her and Deforest engaged in a sexy pas de deux: he was pantomiming her form, his hands held off at a respectable distance but alive and shaking at the fineness of her body. I felt jealous and thought (uncharitably) how that should really be me. Laura seemed to be enjoying herself, and she looked truly gorgeous, but she just wasn't giving Deforest much to work with. Their dance had no dialogue to it.

Finally the band took a break, and we headed to the bar for a refill. Edwin was bursting to talk now that he could be heard. He quickly made it known that he and Deforest weren't from New Orleans originally, saying something about the natives being a sorry collection of colored people. Edwin wondered how such a fine pair of women as ourselves had ended up at Café Brasil.

"Our friend Keith told us about it," Laura said. "We're staying at his guesthouse down the street."

"In town for pleasure then?" Edwin asked, cocking an eyebrow toward me.

"I am," Laura said, "but Bliss is here working on a book."

"A book?" Edwin repeated, glancing at me again. Clearly books were a subject about which he had much to say. "Fiction or nonfiction?"

"Nonfiction." I hoped that my tone would discourage further inquiries. Particularly because these guys weren't locals, I expected that they might feel judgmental about my dad's story. But Edwin insisted on hearing more, and Laura looked suddenly apologetic, realizing perhaps the potential awkwardness of my having to explain myself.

"Well." I took a deep breath. "Actually you guys might find this interesting." I launched into my spiel about how when my father passed away, I learned about a secret... "And so I came down here to find out more about my ancestry."

Edwin shook his head, gave a little grin. He turned to Deforest, who hadn't been paying attention, and said something I couldn't hear. Deforest rocked back on his heels, arms crossed, and looked me up and down. It was impossible to tell what he was thinking behind his forest of locks and glassy-eyed gaze. He directed a comment my way with a lift of his chin. "So you saying you're a sister?"

"Well, I didn't say that *I* was. I said that my father was a—you know, black, or Creole, whatever." I struggled to match the challenge of Deforest's stare. "But if I'd been born here, I would have been considered black, legally at least."

"What *do* you consider yourself?" asked Edwin.

"Biracial," I said, trying to keep the question out of my voice.

Edwin saved me, unwittingly, by embarking on a discourse about how there was no such thing as race. "It's a social construct with no basis in biology." He began pontificating about the Atlantic slave trade and African essentialism.

"Right. Right," I said. I waited for Edwin to take a breath so that I might demonstrate that I too grasped the finer points of this conversation. But the band had started again, and Deforest had moved closer to me, and I was having trouble concentrating.

Deforest stood at my left shoulder. The smell of shea butter from his dreads filled the space between us. I tried focusing again on Edwin, who was now expounding on the one-drop rule and the practice of hypodescent, designed to increase the slave population.

Deforest bent toward my ear. "I don't believe you're black," he said. "I saw you on the dance floor and you don't move like a black girl." I turned to him, protest rising: *Well, if your friend here would have just shut up for a minute.... Plenty of other men, black men, have disagreed.* But Deforest had moved closer still; I could feel his breath on my neck. Edwin was directing his oration—Frantz Fanon, *Black Skin, White Masks*—to Laura in the vacuum of my attention. "You want to prove you're black?" whispered Deforest. "Then come home with me and let me fuck you, and we'll see what kind of a black girl you really are."

I jerked my head up. A smile was sneaking across Deforest's face. I knew that he was playing with me, but his proposition also contained a real dare: Could I follow him? Could I do whatever was required to convince him of the lack of separateness between us? I knew that I couldn't, not because he was black—by then I'd dated a few African Americans and hadn't felt distanced by our outward differences—but I couldn't get any sense of this guy, behind his shield of hair, smoke, and posturing. He'd unnerved me so much that I could barely muster a comeback.

"Well, that might work with some of the other Creole girls, but..."

Deforest burst into laughter, as if he'd been joking all along, then wandered off outside. With his wingman gone, Edwin seemed to lose his game and soon excused himself too. I never got around to telling Laura what Deforest had said, but she seemed to sense that my mood had shifted, and before long we called it a night.

Recalling this moment days later still sent a surge of heat roiling through me—anger mixed with anxiety and shame. I hated the image of myself in Deforest's eyes—a silly white girl making a big fuss over nothing. I hated how uncertain I became when trying to locate myself on this racial landscape or even recognize its terrain. Torn between trying to pinpoint the boundaries between black and white and an urge to deny their existence at all, I was caught in a dialectical tug-of-war. The futility of my efforts reminded me of a skit I once saw in which a man kept moving a wooden chair around an empty white room, unable to find a spot that suited him, despite their being all the same.

I tried to explain my confusion to Cherry and Sissy. But as I heard myself voicing various complaints and objections, I imagined that I just sounded like someone mired in denial. And perhaps I was hesi-

tant to separate myself from my white-girl roots because I feared losing some social advantage. Maybe Skip Gates had been right when
we'd argued about his writing the piece about my dad: I *was* afraid of
being stigmatized by calling myself black. Sissy, reclining on the bed,
smiled benevolently as I babbled on. Stretching her arms out to her
sides, she gave a big yawn. "I hear you, girl," she said. "The whole
coming out thing is really really hard."

"All finished," Cherry exclaimed, coming around to face me. She
clasped her hands at her chest. "But wait till you see how fabulous you

look! Now put on that dress and let's
take some pictures!"

There's nothing like hamming it
up for the camera, coached by two
transsexuals, to make you stop taking
yourself so seriously. Heading over to
the party in a taxi, I got to thinking
that maybe Sissy, Cherry, and the
folks at the Plantation Revelers all had
the right idea. Identity *was* a performance of sorts; I was just arriving late
to rehearsal. Perhaps before Deforest
turned into a Jamaican "rude boy,"
he'd been a choirboy in New Jersey.
Maybe Edwin picked up his racial politics at Howard after a childhood in white suburbia. Sissy and Cherry had certainly found expression for their femininity through the theatrical side of womanhood,
with their interest in fashion and makeup and penchant for *Sex and the
City*–style girl talk. We were all straddling fences of one kind or another. We were all in the process of becoming the person whom we
felt ourselves most to be.

At the Bunch Ball, Keith's services as a dance partner were in high demand, since single men seemed in short supply. I spent much of the

night sitting at the table, feeling like an overlooked Cinderella. Then at the stroke of midnight, everyone started to leave in a big rush, heading off to the Zulu party, to which I hadn't been invited.

Luckily the writer Toi Derricotte, who was in town teaching at a local university, had come too, so we could keep each other company. I'd met Toi after reading her thought-provoking memoir, *The Black Notebooks*, in which she explored her racial identity as a light-skinned black woman who sometimes, consciously or unconsciously, had passed as white. While I could relate to the many awkward moments in the book when someone realized Toi's "true" identity, she wasn't questioning what she was. She described her intermittent flights from blackness as moments of denial or experiences of being an impostor.

In conversation with Toi, I had the impression that she viewed the Creoles' tendency to distinguish themselves from African Americans as similar rejections of their black roots. When I first came to town, that's certainly how I saw the insistence of some relatives on calling themselves Creole rather than black or African American. Despite their explanations about the unique Creole culture and history, I still interpreted their clinging to this designation as a way to set them-selves apart—and above—the rest of the African American popula-tion. To avoid accusations that I was dodging my own African heritage, I'd avoided the label of Creole myself.

Yet learning the history behind the distinct Creole of color and African American cultures in New Orleans had made it harder for me to write off someone calling himself Creole as self-hating or a bigot in denial. Certainly comments about their neighborhoods "being in-vaded" and the problem with "the niggers" revealed prejudice on the part of some Creoles. But to judge them solely in terms of their dis-tance from an African American identity seemed to miss a larger point. What had brought people together at these Creole balls was more than an agreement about what they were not. Rather they were united by all they held in common: their gumbo mix of European, African, and Native American ancestries; their French language and

Catholic faith; and their legacies as artisans and activists. They shared family recipes, holiday traditions, a love for storytelling. They attended the same high schools and churches. And they were united by a complex kinship in a community that, for better or worse, had been culturally, geographically, and legally segregated from both whites and African Americans for more than a century and a half. After so many intermarriages in the Creole community, everybody was to some degree cousins with everybody else.

Home has been described as the place where people understand you. The people at the Bunch Ball made sense to each other. They could even make sense of me. Being among them did make me feel at home.

Toward the end of the evening, before everyone left for the Zulu Ball, the band started up a second line number. As at the Plantation Revelers Ball, the partygoers flocked to the dance floor. Toi headed off with someone too, leaving me alone. I was debating getting up myself, when I noticed a group of women rushing toward an older man seated in a wheelchair at the table next door. "It's your song, Grandpa," I heard someone say. One of the women pulled the wheelchair back from the table, and everyone closed around the old man, his face lit with joy and anticipation.

The women began to clap and step their feet in time to the music. The old man raised one hand, waving the traditional napkin, and with the other rotated the wheel of his chair back and forth. Delighted by this familiar trick, the women laughed, egging the grandfather on. He swung the chair forward and backward, angling it one way and then another. One of the younger women began to wag her behind, hands on hips, and turn in circles before him. The old man thrust out his chest and gyrated his shoulders, dipping them up and down. He took the girl's hand and twirled her.

Watching the young woman dance with her grandfather brought my own grandfather to mind. He had also been confined to a wheelchair at the end of his life. He died from bladder cancer in 1950, long before I was born, but I knew some details about his death from a few autobiographical stories that my father had written. One of them is about a son visiting his father in the hospital. His dad is seated in his wheelchair, alone in a corridor, as the narrator watches him for a moment through a small window in the door. "Throwing his head back, [Father] closes his eyes and listens again to something only he can hear. He stays like that for a while and then he opens his eyes and claps his hands. I can hear it through the door. He's beating a rhythm, and when the chair starts to move again, I understand that he's dancing."

I fantasized briefly about joining the group at the next table, imagining that I'd be welcomed into their circle. They would see that I knew the joy of dancing with your family; that I understood how this atavistic pleasure could give a person a sense of her rightness in the world. But I stayed seated. When my father's family had moved away, they'd left behind these people and their music and rituals, forfeiting my spot along the cultural continuum.

In his writings my father described his father in Brooklyn as a "displaced person." I was beginning to understand what he meant. No one in New York could grasp the particulars of my grandfather's life. He'd become a man without a context, which left his children adrift to chart their own courses in the world.

During the first half of the twentieth century, the blunt force of Jim Crow cut through New Orleans's colored Creole community, scattering people on opposite sides of the color line, threatening their livelihoods, insulting their manhood, and toppling the institutions that had always sustained them. Every trip to the movie theater, beach, or opera house; every ride on the streetcar or visit to a hotel or restaurant; every stop in a public bathroom and drink from a water fountain posed the question: Was a person "colored" or "white"?

For those Creoles whose appearance made clear their black ancestry, there was no decision to make. They headed to the back of the streetcar or the balcony of the movie theater, where they sat alongside the American Negroes, who made up the majority of the city's black population. Other Creoles who could have passed for white joined them there—people who didn't want to abandon their friends and families or to deal with the trouble that could come from bucking the city's color line. Over time some of these Creoles not only resigned themselves to the label of Negro, but they began taking on aspects of the lifestyle that went with it. They stopped teaching their children how to speak French. Because the public schools offered instruction exclusively in English, a new generation of Creoles grew up unable to understand what their elders were saying. On the political front, they joined forces with the American Negroes in the local chapter of the

NAACP, after its opening in 1915, where they worked together to fight discrimination.

Many other colored Creoles, however, saw the bifurcation of the racial order in the city—and its elevation of a person's blood over his culture and accomplishments—as a crude American invention. Obeying it meant conceding to the gradual effacement of their Creole identity. Already their claim to the term was threatened by the white Creole population, who since Reconstruction had been trying to redefine "Creole" as strictly Caucasian, lest the northern newcomers suspect them of being "tainted by the tarbrush." And so many colored Creoles—rather than relinquish the sense of themselves that had fueled their self-worth over the last century—put off choosing between "white" and "colored" for as long as they could. They turned inward, to their church and clubs, to their Creole neighborhoods, and most of all to their families. In this way Jim Crow at once crystallized the colored Creole identity while also fracturing it. It encouraged Creoles to set themselves apart, where they stood proud, protected, and finally sidelined by history. The trajectory of my great-grandfather's life—from a proud Creole businessman to a man who, in his grandson's words, "was as shabby as shabby can be"—echoed the colored Creoles' demise.

In the early decades of Jim Crow, Paul Broyard and his family could avoid situations where they'd be reminded of their second-class citizenship. When my grandfather Nat rode the streetcars, he might head past the white and colored sections to stand on the back platform. Or if he or his sisters went to Canal Street to go shopping, they could make sure to use the toilet at home rather than having to choose between the different public restrooms. And in Tremé or the Seventh Ward, it was pretty much business as usual. While Paul was no longer the Republican ward boss doling out treats from his goody bag of patronage, his successful construction business still earned him a respectful "Monsieur" from his neighbors.

With most blacks shut out of skilled work in factories and from jobs in white-collar professions, many colored people were beginning to feel the economic sting of Jim Crow. But the Creoles of color continued to dominate the building trades, of which carpentry was considered among the most prestigious. With a construction firm and an architect's office in town, Paul was doing better than most. In the first two decades of the twentieth century, he was regularly hired, mostly by whites, to build residential housing and rental properties, with as many as three jobs going at once. By 1905 he was able to purchase a two-story home on a nice block in Tremé, with plenty of room for his seven children.

In his house Belhomme could be assured of receiving the treatment due the man of the family, no matter how low his standing in the world might fall. My grandfather Nat, along with his two brothers, worked for the family business, while the four girls helped out with chores and tended to their father. My grandfather liked to describe for my father how on hot evenings Paul would retire to the porch, where one daughter would bathe his feet in a tin of lemon-scented water, another would wind the gramophone to play his French opera records, the third would bring him a cold drink and the paper, and the fourth would ply him with a fan.

At work Paul would have had to act respectfully to his white employers: taking off his hat in their presence, calling them "Mister." But white people had always expected that treatment. Only one building contract out of three dozen secured by the Broyards in the two decades following the *Plessy* verdict stipulated that the construction be supervised by a white man. Otherwise the white men hired Paul, paid him his money, and left him alone.

On the job site the color line worked a little differently. All the skilled workers under Paul's hire—the carpenters, lathers, plasterers—were Creoles of color, while the laborers—the men digging foundations, sawing boards, nailing up shingling—were American blacks. The two groups didn't mix. During lunch hour they sat apart. They headed to different water barrels when they were thirsty. Posing for a photo, Paul and his brothers stood, while the darker-skinned laborers were seated beneath them. Compared to these men, the Broyards were the bosses, the ruling class, the whites.

In oral histories collected by the historian Arthé Agnes Anthony about the Creole of color community during the early twentieth century, an interviewee recalled the Broyard family as belonging to a "high class" group of Creoles. That meant that my grandfather and his siblings grew up speaking French at home, the family's bookshelves displayed their Francophile tastes in literature, they visited the French Opera House to hear the latest performers. And as a general rule, they didn't socialize with darker-skinned American Negroes.

Unlike the situation in previous generations, a formal education wasn't needed to belong to the upper crust of Creole society. Following the resegregation of public schools in 1877, many Creole families opted against sending their children to the "colored schools," which were seen, according to another of Anthony's interviewees, as "for the poor and those with limited backgrounds." Yet few people could afford private schools or tutors. Many in my grandfather's generation left the classroom after the eighth grade. In Nat's case, rather than continue on to secondary schooling, it made more sense for him to begin apprenticing in his father's business, given that carpentry was the best occupation available to him.

Creoles with social aspirations were also expected to conform to a certain standard of respectability. Mothers made sure their children were outfitted in clean, neatly pressed clothing, with their hair combed and shoes shined. Families were to be seen in church on Sunday. Daughters must be kept close to home until they were married, young children were expected to mind their elders, and no one in the family should ever have babies out of wedlock or engage in extramarital affairs. Families whose members began to stray might find themselves snubbed at a Creole dance or church services. They could run into difficulties when trying to court a girl from a good family or they might become the subject of gossip among the grocers at Tremé market. Many believed that by continually improving his character, the colored person might even one day convince whites of his worth in the world.

In the early days of Jim Crow, black leaders around the country were also stressing the importance of respectability. Ida B. Wells, famous for her crusade against lynching, encouraged blacks to "strive for a higher standard of social purity" through her activity in the National Association of Colored Women. Booker T. Washington suggested that African Americans, through hard work and the demonstration of their Christian virtues, would "give lie to the assertion of his enemies North and South that the Negro is the inferior of the white man." Even the educator and activist W.E.B. Du Bois's push for higher learning and acculturation for African Americans contained a note of moral uplift.

Still, a decade into Jim Crow, it became increasingly clear that no matter how useful to the economy or inoffensive to society southern blacks strove to be, whites weren't going to get rid of segregation or restore universal suffrage anytime soon. They had too much economic self-interest to voluntarily concede their superior position. If anything, the separation of the races was making white prejudice more deeply entrenched. The formation of the NAACP in 1909 and the subsequent ascendance of Du Bois over Washington as the leader of the country's black community signaled a change in tactics. Agitation, not accommodation, was the only way to win back their rights. It would take almost fifty years of fighting before the Supreme Court would finally acknowledge in the *Brown v. Board of Education* decision that separate status had never been equal.

By 1920 the Louisiana legislature had passed the bulk of statutes that formalized the legal wall between the black and white population in the state. Now blacks were lawfully prevented from moving into predominantly white neighborhoods. Prisons, mental institutions, and circuses too all drew the color line. In 1916 the Catholic Church segregated worshippers in downtown New Orleans with the inception of Corpus Christi, an all-black parish in the heart of the Creole Seventh Ward. Many Creoles, including my great-grandfather Paul, stopped attending services in protest.

Between the clampdown of Jim Crow laws and the stiffening of the moral code in the community, a man like Belhomme was left with little room to move. He had always lived best by living large. And the more white southerners tried to make him feel small, the bigger his personality became.

In 1915 Paul Broyard had given over his house to his oldest daughter and bought a second home on a mixed block of whites, Creoles, and a few blacks in the Seventh Ward. This house was even bigger than the first, with seven large rooms, two fireplaces, a wide arched hallway, and a side porch. Out back was a stable for his horses, above which were the servants' quarters. The sight of these people working in the kitchen, who appeared phenotypically black compared to the nearly white-looking Broyards, helped Paul and his family to maintain their sense of occupying a middle position.

Belhomme was nearing sixty but didn't show any signs of slowing down. For much of his adult life, he'd been known as a ladies' man. His grandsons—including my dad—would grow up hearing stories about their grandfather's exploits: how he liked to say that if you spread a woman's hair on the pillow and kiss her on the lips, she will open her legs like a Bible. Or that he would head to the Tremé market with six baskets on his arms—one to fill for each of his girlfriends.

The women in the family clucked about Belhomme's "outside children," many of whom took the Broyard name. His son Jimmy, visiting a girl he liked across the river one day, spied a picture of Paul on her mantle. When he asked the girl why she had the photograph, she explained that the man was her daddy! Retelling the story sixty years after Paul's death, Jimmy's son, Jimmy Jr., laughed, explaining how his father had hightailed it out of there.

It's hard to know what Rosa made of her husband's adulteries. During their forty-two years of marriage, Rosa bore eleven children and likely miscarried a few more. She might have looked past Paul's transgressions because she simply didn't want to be pregnant anymore. But she couldn't stop the neighbors from gossiping about Belhomme's excesses; nor could she prevent that talk from tainting the family's good reputation.

For Nat, having a father like Paul must have been both a badge of honor and a mark of shame. As a young man, he could either compete with his dad's lothario behavior or reject such shenanigans completely, a choice between vice and virtue that was echoed by the city itself. In 1897 New Orleans's city council voted to establish a legalized red-light district in a corner of Tremé in an attempt to regulate the rampant prostitution. The district was nicknamed Storyville after Sidney Story, the unlucky alderman who suggested the plan.

When Nat was twelve, his father ran a saloon as a side business on the edge of Storyville, where people could stop off for a drink before heading to a gambling den, brothel, or cabaret. To entertain his customers, Paul might have hired a "professor," one of the black piano players who were flocking to Storyville at the turn of the century, where they experimented with playing a new musical form, jazz. Segregation wasn't strongly enforced in the red-light district; men and women of all races drank and flirted side by side.

For a colored boy on the edge of puberty, the scene in Paul's bar offered a shortcut to manhood, compared to the strategy of patience and virtue endorsed by the world at large. But this underworld was threatening too. These pleasures of booze and sex could anesthetize a young man, content him with the status quo, and condemn him to becoming the image drawn by his accusers.

When it came time for Nat to begin courting, the consequences of his father's behavior would make themselves known. If Nat's marriage to my grandmother Edna Miller in 1917 was any indication, he was forced to look outside his family's social circle. While the Millers were also Creoles of color, they didn't belong to any of the community's elite benevolent societies. Edna's father was a laborer, and her mother hired herself out as a cook. By age thirteen Edna had quit school and gone to work rolling cigars in a factory and sewing for a local tailor to help make ends meet—another sign that her family wasn't as refined as her future husband's.

There were also whispers that Edna's grandmother had been a prostitute, and that her mother was the offspring of a white Confederate general. Whether or not the rumors were true, the fact that

Edna's grandmother had consorted with at least four different men, not all of whom she married, would have raised eyebrows. After a childhood like hers, Edna may have been inclined to look past Belhomme's proclivities. Also, Nat had begun to get his own construction jobs: in their first three months of marriage, he landed contracts totaling almost $9,000 ($130,000 today). Edna must have been relieved to let someone else support the family for a change.

When my father was born, on July 16, 1920, Nat and Edna were living in half of a shotgun house on St. Ann Street in Tremé. Edna's mother lived there too, which made life in the three small rooms rather cramped for the young family. My father's sister Lorraine was two years older, and Shirley arrived three years after my dad. My father's few recollections of New Orleans paint an atmosphere that was congenial and cozy. In the evenings the neighbors sat out front of their houses and chatted with the passersby. Weekends were spent visiting with family. The days ran into one another, all hot and humid, wrapping my father's childhood in a tropical sultry innocence.

But there were tensions in the Broyard household too. While both Nat and Edna were playful and loving with their children, their differences in temperament grated on their affection for each other. Nat told wonderful stories, embellished with improbable details, while Edna clung literal-mindedly to facts. He wasn't much of a con-

versationalist and she was sociable, making friends easily. He walked quickly—a man with a purpose—yet with style, arching his back and kicking out his heels. She moved slowly, "like a glacier," because her feet were bad and she was always in pain. My grandfather shared a bit of his father's fondness for excesses—he smoked a long pipe, wore his cap pulled down over one eye, pulled his pants up toward his chest to show off his long legs. Edna summed up life with the precision of an accountant and had a talent for advising people how to solve their problems.

The real conflict, however, lay between Edna and the Broyard family. She was unused to such a patriarchal culture. Her childhood had been mostly dominated by women: her mother, aunt, and grandmother. As a Broyard wife, she was expected to wait on her husband, make all of his clothes (even his underwear), and defer to the men of the family. After working and earning her own money for so long, she didn't take easily to this subservient role.

And her father-in-law was such a domineering presence in their lives. Every Sunday the family was expected at Belhomme's house for supper. Because Nat depended on his father for his paycheck, the family didn't have control over their own purse strings. It was Paul who headed to the registrar to record the birth of my father in 1920. After his wife's death, in the summer of 1921, Belhomme became even more overbearing.

Rosa had always managed the household, watched the finances, and ensured that her husband's peccadilloes didn't interfere with the family dinner. But her death left Belhomme without a leash at the very moment that the city's racial wardens were cracking down. Over the next ten years, he veered toward ruin.

The story in the family went that after becoming a widower, Paul began spending the down payments from his construction contracts on "fast women and slow horses." When he needed to buy materials for the jobs, he'd seize his sons' savings to replace the squandered sums. Nat couldn't stop his father because he had granted Paul power of attorney, but he probably would have given him the money anyway. Since Paul was sixteen, he'd taken care of everyone: his mother and five brothers, then his wife and seven children. Paul had provided jobs for his sons and looked after all of his kids' families. He'd earned a little paying back. And he was the measure by which the fortunes of the rest of them rose and fell, so it was in their best interests to protect him.

Nat would have been motivated to help his father by love and sorrow too. He must have seen how Paul's life had become circumscribed by loss—of his wife, his Creole culture, and his place in the world. And so Nat indulged his father's gambling and women—pastimes that could make Paul feel like a man again, at least for a night. But Belhomme's indulgences began to hinder Nat from being a man himself. Besides his three kids with Edna, he had to support another daughter, Ethel, from his first wife, who'd died back in 1915. And so when Edna began to nag her husband to move up north, where there was plenty of construction work and Nat would be able to hold on to his own earnings, he let himself be talked into the idea.

Since World War I blacks had been fleeing the South in huge numbers in search of better economic opportunities and a break from Jim Crow segregation. During the Great Migration, as the movement was called, roughly 1.5 million African Americans moved to urban centers such as New York, Chicago, and Detroit. For Edna the decision to join them, like so many things in her life, was practical. Anyway, she didn't have the same attachment to New Orleans or its Creole culture that her husband did. She wasn't raised speaking French. Her people hadn't been active in the Republican radical movement. Her sense of self-worth didn't depend on the fading Creole legacy.

Nat was thirty-eight when he finally agreed to leave New Orleans. By this time, he might have realized that he had no choice at all—the world of his childhood was heading toward extinction. While he kept to his promise to never go back—although my grandmother and my aunts made a few trips down south during his lifetime — Nat remained nostalgic for the city he'd loved. He also was faithful to its Creole legacy, including the disdain for blacks, feelings of betrayal by the Catholic Church, and notions of manhood that had characterized the community in its waning years.

If Nat also held his father and his extravagances responsible for the decision to move north, he kept these criticisms to himself. My father grew up hearing only romantic stories about the "operatic character" Belhomme. But neither, apparently, did Nat blame Jim Crow for his father's decline in society. To acknowledge the effect of the color line on his family would mean acquiescing to its black-and-white depiction of the world, and Nat held fast, even up north, to the Creole's intermediary position in the racial order.

It was winter, early in 1927, when my father boarded the train for New York City with the rest of his family. He was six and a half years old. Any excitement he felt about the prospect of an overnight train ride to a fabled northern city may have disappeared on entering the Jim Crow car that his sister Shirley recalls taking. These coaches were typically positioned directly behind the locomotive, and the air stank of smoke from the engine's exhaust. Baggage belonging to white passengers often occupied the seats, leaving little room for the colored riders. Bathrooms rarely worked, and the coaches were infrequently cleaned. Since blacks were excluded from dining services, families had to bring enough food for the forty-hour journey, adding to the smell and garbage. It's not unlikely that this train ride was my father's first foray into a "colored" facility.

The world of my father's childhood in New Orleans had consisted of his house, his grandparents' house, his block, church, and school, and occasional trips to the Creole market in Tremé. He spent most of his time with people like himself: family members and other Creole kids from his neighborhood. If he'd been shielded from the contingencies that the South forced upon colored people, the trip north would have made them clear, especially after crossing the Mason-Dixon Line and arriving in Washington, DC. There Jim Crow service ended, and the family was able to move to the more pleasant cars and sit in the company of white people.

The journey from South to North was my father's first trip from black to white. He saw that crossing the color line could be as simple as walking a few steps down the platform of Washington's Union Station and as devastating as his father's mood on arriving in New York City. Looking back on this moment, my father later wrote, "[My father] had left the French Quarter a popular man, but he got off the train in Pennsylvania Station to find snow falling and no one there waiting for him." Ten years later my father would himself eventually have to choose between the world of his family and childhood and a new world where he could create his own history, with all the contradictions that implied.

III.

Avenues of Flight

-26-

Back in Brooklyn I started to look for my father. It was a strange notion—searching for a dead person. For the first few years after my father died, I used to dream that he wasn't really dead: he was just off somewhere and I hadn't looked for him hard enough. In the dream he'd leave a message on my answering machine, or send me a postcard telling me where to find him. But always the message would be garbled or the directions would be unclear, and I'd wake up with a start, my sense of loss redoubled.

When you lose a family member or close friend, people tell you, to console you, that your loved one will always live on in your memories. They act as if this process occurs involuntarily: a biological trick to offset your grief, just as the brain suppresses traumatic memories that are too difficult to handle. Your friends don't tell you to record everything that you remember about the dead person because you will indeed forget many things over time. Nor do they warn you that your memories will become irreversibly mortared into a monument of the "dearly departed"—some myth that you fashion to help organize your recollections to better retrieve them. Nor are you told about the contaminating influence of other people's stories, which seem all the more vivid compared to the familiar old statue in the corner of your brain. And absolutely no one will suggest that you might begin to wonder how well you knew your family member or close friend in the first place, now that it's too late to learn anything more firsthand.

*   *   *

I looked first for my dad in his large collection of writing: the essays and short fiction that he published in his twenties and thirties that established his literary reputation; the memoir about his life in Greenwich Village during the 1940s, when he first became a writer; his collection of articles about family life in exurban Connecticut that originally appeared in the *Times* in the 1970s; his book, published posthumously, about his experience of being critically ill; and even the 1,500 or so book reviews he wrote during his thirteen-year stint as a daily book reviewer. I also read the many drafts of stories that he wasn't able to publish and the journals and notes he kept for the novel that he could never finish.

Surprisingly for someone who was supposed to be concealing his identity, much of my father's work focused on himself and his family. His first published story, in 1954, dealt with his father's death four years earlier, when my father was twenty-nine. Based on its positive reception, my dad secured a contract for a novel expanding the story of his father's death against the backdrop of leaving his childhood home of Brooklyn for Greenwich Village. After his mother became widowed, my father began increasingly to include her in his stories and essays, although he saw her less and less frequently. In his articles about domestic life for the *Times,* my father often recalled his youth, contrasting it with my brother's and mine. In his journals my father jotted down scenes from his family's life, from his refusal at age five to hand over some flowers that he'd been instructed to lay upon the church altar to the first forlorn Thanksgiving with his mother and sister Lorraine after his father's death.

I recognized the father I'd known in these writings, but the colored boy from New Orleans and Brooklyn was harder to locate. Even in his private journals, my father never referred to himself directly or indirectly as black. In some instances he wrote about black people — or Negroes and "colored," as he called them in the 1940s and 1950s — but they were always "them," people different from himself. In the late

1950s he made an observation about a "spade" at the Village Gate who says to a white girl, "I'm a very ethereal cat," and the difference grew.

At the same time, his writing contained clues that he wasn't exactly white: listening to gospel on the family radio; taking on American jazz as his subject during a time, the 1940s, when it was considered the special province of African Americans; and displaying an intimate knowledge of Negro life — their social pastimes, slang, and attitudes about themselves — that a white person either wouldn't know or dare to write about with such authority.

I sought out the people who knew my father to find out what race they thought he considered himself. To his friends from his youth, he was just another one of the guys in their happy tight-knit gang of middle-class Negroes growing up during the 1920s and 1930s in the Bedford-Stuyvesant section of Brooklyn. They knew him by his childhood nickname Bud, and remembered him as handsome, a good dancer, a big tease, and popular with the young ladies. My mother, on the other hand, maintained that my father wasn't "really black," a position that backed up his right to define himself and distinguished him from the kinds of black people — poor, criminal, angry — that she encountered on the news. Yet the late writer Harold Brodkey recalled that my father himself, during a discussion about his racial identity in the early 1980s, had insisted that he was "really black." Brodkey's subtle grasp of the complexities of human nature, as displayed in his many short stories appearing in the *New Yorker*, made him not only one of my father's favorite contemporary writers but also an insightful confidant. Harold had told my father that he didn't believe he was black, or at least he didn't believe that my father knew anything about the sort of lives that most African Americans lived.

My father's own record on the question of his race didn't clear up the confusion. When he was seventeen, he completed an application for a social security number on which he had to identify his race for the first time. Marks appear next to both WHITE and NEGRO, and there's a mysterious *C* in the space following OTHER, leaving me to guess at the circumstances that produced such a muddled response.

Even the degree of secrecy that my father maintained about his background was unclear. My father's best friend in his later years, the noted psychologist Michael Vincent Miller, who authored *Intimate Terrorism*, about the crisis in contemporary love, and has lectured widely on the topic of disappointment, would certainly have been a sympathetic audience, but the two men never discussed the subject. Although Mike had heard the gossip, he assumed that my father didn't want to talk about it and therefore respected his wishes. Yet another writer, Michael Mewshaw, who hardly knew my dad, recalled being at a cocktail party together at the home of his editor in Westport, Connecticut, in the 1970s, where he heard my father reveal to a group of writers and publishing folk that he was a colored man according to his birth certificate.

My aunt Shirley takes the most definitive view: my father was raised black and became white. When she talks to me about her and my father's childhood, she doesn't refer to him as Bud or Anatole or the more distant "your father," but "my brother." As Shirley repeats "my brother" over and over—as if she must remind herself of their connection—she reclaims him and the truth about her family's identity. As the only survivor, she has earned this right. Also, after forty-five years of marriage to a civil rights lawyer and a lifetime of thinking about race issues, Shirley had no question about what she was, and she seemed unable—or unwilling—to imagine herself or her family members as ever feeling otherwise.

To reveal the young colored boy that my father had been, I had to carefully strip away the father that I had known. It was like uncovering a pentimento, the part of a painting that is hidden beneath the surface of the paint, the artist's first try. My father's portrait contained hints of this earlier picture: in some places, the underlying image matched up perfectly with my sense of my dad; elsewhere it had been obscured completely. And then every once in a while, both portraits came into focus simultaneously, and I could see how each version of my father had informed the other.

I found him after all, although he was different from the person I remembered: more vulnerable to others' opinions and less self-assured about the choices he'd made. He seemed both needier and more self-ish, less heroic and more human. I imagined him impatient with my eagerness to figure him out. It would bruise his ego to think that a problem he wrestled with all his life could be resolved. I imagined him defending himself, and I imagined him wanting to be forgiven.

My father's family settled in the Bedford-Stuyvesant section of Brooklyn, which in 1927 was known as Stuyvesant Heights. It was middle-class, 90 percent white, and "one of the most attractive home sections in the entire boro," according to the *Brooklyn Eagle*. By the time I moved to Brooklyn, in 1996, Bed-Stuy had long been recognized as one of the country's worst urban ghettos. Its name — synonymous with poverty, gang violence, teenage mothers, and crack — served as shorthand for the hard lot of African Americans. Most whites, along with many blacks, wouldn't dare to go there.

When someone asked my father where he was from, he answered simply "Brooklyn" or offered nearby Brownsville (a neighborhood that, ironically, has since developed a similar reputation to Bed-Stuy). He may have justified his evasion by reasoning that the integrated middle-class environs of his childhood *weren't* the same place as the notorious Bed-Stuy. But he was also trying to distance himself from the events that had brought about Bed-Stuy's transformation — events that conflated blackness with desperation in white America's imagination, that circumscribed the dreams and opportunities for a bright colored boy growing up on those streets, that made the desolation of Bed-Stuy inevitable. To my father's mind, leaving behind this hard lot necessarily meant leaving behind his hometown and the people he'd known there too.

✳   ✳   ✳

Blacks have lived in Brooklyn since the midseventeenth century, first as slaves, then as free people of color after slavery was phased out in New York State in 1827. By the time my father's family moved to Brooklyn, the borough had developed a reputation as home to a better class of colored people, but it didn't offer much of a black community. By far in the minority, blacks were scattered across a half-dozen different neighborhoods. In the early years of the Great Migration, most southern Negroes who came to New York City were heading to Harlem, considered the "Negro Capital of the World."

During the 1920s alone, nearly 100,000 blacks streamed into Harlem, more than doubling its population. The influx of so many newcomers—who arrived with few resources and no jobs—quickly led to overcrowded slums, which helps to explain why my grandfather chose Brooklyn instead. Also, after growing up Creole, living in the center of American black life wouldn't hold much appeal for Nat. Stuyvesant Heights, on the other hand, had enough black people that his younger daughter, Shirley, who was turning out to be browner than the rest of them, wouldn't cause anyone to look twice, and plenty of whites among whom the family could get lost if they ever needed to.

My grandfather found construction work right away. For $50 a month, he rented the family an apartment on the top floor of an apartment building on a busy avenue. At age six my father became a city boy. The double-laned roads filled with cars and lined with tall brick and stone buildings were nothing like the narrow streets and one-story wooden cottages of Tremé. In New Orleans my father had run around outside in

his bare feet, eaten fresh figs from a tree in the backyard, sat under the overhang of the shed's tin roof listening to the thrum of rain during storms. In Brooklyn he and his friends played stickball in the street, and he had to ride his bike to Prospect Park if he wanted to walk around without his shoes on. Anyway, it was usually too cold.

The people in the neighborhood were different too. Russian, Jewish, Irish, and Italian immigrants lived among a handful of southern Negroes and transplants from the West Indies. My father's parents knew only one other Creole family, and they lived way out in Queens. My father later recollected: "In the 1920s in New York City everyone was ethnic.... We found our differences hilarious. It was part of the adventure of the street and the schoolyard that everyone else had grown up among mysteries."

My father's two best friends during childhood were both "colored," meaning that their families were mixed-race and tended more toward a middle-class lifestyle than "blacks." The family of one of the boys, Carlos deLeon, became friendly with the Broyards and often shared Sunday meals with them. My father and the other boy liked to gang up on Carlos. My father would ask him how to spell a word, and Carlos would answer correctly, but my dad and his sidekick would insist that Carlos had gotten it wrong, enraging him in the process.

Carlos was darker than my father, which introduced a subtle subtext into their play. As small as the Negro population in Stuyvesant Heights was, it contained a rigid hierarchy, with the light-skinned descendants of free blacks or Caribbean emigrants on one end and the darker sons and daughters of former slaves on the other. The fathers in the uppermost class were all professionals — dentists, doctors, or lawyers. Their wives didn't work, except as volunteers at the National Association of Colored Women or the Brooklyn Urban League. These families owned their own houses and drove their own automobiles. During the summer they vacationed at one of the black resorts: Oak Bluffs on Martha's Vineyard or Sag Harbor in Long Island.

While this class thought of themselves foremost as Negroes—

striving for the betterment of *all* their people—they didn't mingle with the more disadvantaged among their race. The singer and actress Lena Horne, who has been described as America's first black movie star, came from the colored bourgeoisie of Stuyvesant Heights. In her book about her family's history, Horne's daughter, Gail Lumet Buckley, described her maternal grandparents as representing "the upper class of America's 'untouchable' caste—the small brown group within the large black mass."

No matter how light their skin or esteemed their profession might be, however, the white world still didn't want any Negroes living or working near them. As Buckley points out: "Although members of the black bourgeoisie were vastly more successful than their poorer and blacker brethren, they rarely had opportunities to make *real* money....Who you were and where you came from—'roots'—meant more than money."

In New Orleans the Broyards, by virtue of who their people were, had belonged to the better set of black people. But in Brooklyn they didn't quite measure up. Their pale skin was all right, but neither Nat nor Edna had more than an elementary school education. Also, while the white side of the Broyard family tree had been in Louisiana since the colonial era and the African side had arrived from St. Domingue as free people, there weren't any other Creoles around to attest to the illustriousness of their connections.

The Broyards had been in Brooklyn for two years when Nat received word that his father's house in New Orleans had been seized by the sheriff for failure to pay back taxes. Fourteen years before, Paul had put the property in Nat's name to protect his investment should his construction business ever run into trouble. Paul's "slow horses and fast women" had finally caught up with him, and he needed to sell the house to pay his debtors. One May morning in 1929, Nat headed to a notary in downtown Brooklyn to get power of attorney authorizing his father to unload the property.

Nat must have been grateful that he didn't have to witness his father's final fall from glory, but the sale of the house was also a loss for him. His dad had owned it since before Nat was married; it was where the family had always gathered. Nat likely celebrated his wedding there and the baptisms of his children. Even if my grandfather wanted to go back to New Orleans, he no longer had a home to return to. At the same time, Nat didn't feel at home in Brooklyn.

My father, reflecting on his childhood, noted that his father turned into a "silent and solitary figure in New York," after being "dislocated by moving...from the intimacy and immediacy of the French Quarter to an abstract and anonymous city." In New Orleans, Nat had six siblings and a dozen aunts and uncles. He was kin one way or another to almost everyone he knew. In Brooklyn he had no one with whom he could share all the Creole customs that had shaped his first thirty-eight years, no one with whom he could speak the French patois of his childhood. Yet there was no denying that living up north had improved his family's chances for success in the larger world.

My father and my aunts were attending a good integrated elementary school down the street. In New Orleans black people had to send their children to one of the private colored schools to get a decent education. If they couldn't afford the tuition, the only other option was passing for white. In a few years, one of Nat's cousins would change his last name — to avoid being associated with any black Broyards — in order to enroll his kids in a white school. His wife had never learned how to read in the city's black schools and she was determined to secure a better future for her children.

In Stuyvesant Heights, a person could go where he wanted without having to confront signs for coloreds and whites. While prejudice and de facto discrimination certainly existed — blacks of all shades were routinely refused service in local restaurants — white supremacy wasn't always presumed to be the natural order. When the ushers at the Bedford movie theater tried to Jim Crow some patrons, charges of discrimination were reported in the Brooklyn paper. A local Episcopal minister who sent letters to his black congregants discouraging their attendance was met with a national outcry. White clergies from around the city publicly censured him while opening their own doors to his colored worshippers. Despite these improvements over the racial attitudes in New Orleans, a mood of loss and longing lingered beneath the cozy surface of the Broyards' family life.

At night my father and his sisters would do their homework around the dining room table, while Nat sat in his armchair, smoking his pipe and reading the paper. Nearby in the kitchen, Edna prepared dinner. Sometimes she brought out a bowl of peas for the girls to shell or a pot of potatoes for her husband to mash. In minutes Nat had the potatoes whipped into a high fluff, his arm moving up and down as fast as a piston. After dinner they listened to radio dramas, *The Shadow* or *The Lone Ranger*, or they played a few hands of fan-tan. Sometimes my dad made them laugh by putting on a record of the Cuban music that he loved and trying to imitate the dances.

Edna doted on her son, worrying that he was too skinny, and regularly chased him around the dining table, trying to force Scott's Emulsion or cod liver oil down his throat. During the summer months, she bribed him with Tarzan books to stay inside during the hottest part of the day, and his lifelong love of reading was born. Lying on his bed inside the dark apartment, the curtains drawn against the sunlight, my father could escape his father's silences as he swung from vine to vine through the jungle.

Eventually my father graduated to reading Alexandre Dumas, whose complete works, including *The Count of Monte Cristo* and *The Three Musketeers*, lined one shelf of the family's dining room. Dumas' father was the son of a Frenchman and slave woman in St. Domingue, a legacy that gave the writer a common history with Creoles. For my dad and his sisters, Dumas' books, their mother's unique recipes, and the strange French their parents spoke when they didn't want the kids to understand them were everyday reminders of their Creole identity.

Yet neither my father nor my aunts were exactly sure what Creole was. Shirley only understood that it was a different kind of African American.

My father and his sisters weren't taught to speak the language themselves, nor did they grow up hearing about the history of Creole activism and their own family's contribution. From Nat's perspective his father's political career was a series of defeats. Nat was seven when the *Plessy* challenge was lost, nine when blacks were disenfranchised by the new state constitution, eleven when his dad was ousted from the Republican Party, and thirteen when Paul stopped voting in elections. Rather than recount these failures, Nat regaled my dad with tales of the impressive buildings his father built, his conquests of the ladies, and the stylish and charismatic figure he cut as Belhomme, the beautiful man.

Perhaps it was these stories—or Nat's animation in telling them—that sparked my father's interest in his roots. As a teenager he decided that he wanted to learn how to speak Creole too. Maybe he could follow these foreign words to his father, the same way that he'd followed Tarzan on those jungle vines. But the Brooklyn public schools didn't offer Creole instruction, and my father's parents weren't inclined to teach him themselves. What was the point of their son learning this vestigial language? Even with all its immigrants, New York was an American city that offered a chance at the American dream. Better that my father focus on his studies, so he could do well on the civil service exam and get a good job at the post office, with a steady income and a pension. Even if their place in society *had* fallen since leaving New Orleans, and even though Nat's removal from the Creole culture had left him heavyhearted, Nat and Edna could console themselves that New York offered the chance to make a better life for themselves and their children. But then came the Depression.

The stock market collapse in 1929 made things difficult for everyone in New York, but as the "last hired and first fired," blacks were particularly vulnerable. There was no recourse for job discrimination during the worst years of the Depression—President Franklin Roosevelt didn't establish the Fair Employment Practices Commission until 1941—and newspaper want ads regularly specified "whites only" among their hiring specifications. Even jobs as maids or laborers, once considered the exclusive domain of African Americans, started going to European immigrants. When blacks did get work, they were routinely paid less than whites. Trade unions traditionally blocked the entrance of African Americans; in 1930 only one in twenty black workers belonged to a union, compared to one in five whites.

My grandfather had joined the carpenters' union when he first arrived in New York by passing as white. Membership qualified him to work on bigger commercial buildings, and his experience earned him a foreman's grade, just one step below the superintendent. It was his job to translate the architect's plans into orders for his crew of carpenters to carry out. Between this responsibility and his respectable paycheck, my grandfather was very proud of his job. On the work site Nat kept a hammer in the belt of his overalls, and regularly whipped it out to demonstrate how something was done. My father often bragged how his father could drive home a two-inch nail with two strokes of his arm. Nat had built an elaborate wooden toolbox outfitted with slots and compartments to carry his tools back and forth to the job site. In the neighborhood he could often be seen walking down the sidewalk with the long toolbox balanced on one shoulder, his other hand on his hat, ready to tip it for the ladies.

But even passing as white couldn't protect Nat during the Depression. He was out of work for much of the 1930s, losing his dignity as much as his income. Over an eight-year period, the family moved five times in search of ever cheaper apartments. In one place, Edna tended the building's furnace to offset the rent. The next apartment was a railroad flat adjacent to the El—Lexington Avenue's elevated trolley. For three years my father's sisters slept in a room whose window was eye level with the train tracks. Finally, in 1934, my grandmother took a job ironing six days a week at a commercial laundry. The owners hired Edna because they thought she was white.

Even before the Depression, utility companies, department stores, factories, hospitals, hotels, and New York City's transit companies had all practiced racial discrimination in hiring. For the paler Negroes of Stuyvesant Heights, passing for work was commonplace and acceptable. Everyone knew that most of the salesgirls and elevator operators at the Abraham & Strauss department store in downtown Brooklyn were really light-skinned blacks. Other colored people often applauded these racial infiltrators, happy to see one of their own "getting over." Some of the darker blacks even encouraged the practice, since it meant less competition for the few jobs available to their race.

In New Orleans the phenomenon had been even more widespread. The ubiquity, however, didn't make passing any easier. In the early 1970s, the historian Arthé Agnes Anthony collected oral histories about the practice from septuagenarian and octogenarian New Orleans Creoles. As a man who passed in order to work at a printing company explained, "The whites would be talking about Negroes and you'd have to take it. Once I had been seen at night...and I was later asked what was I doing with all those niggers. I told them that it was none of their damn business who I was with. They never asked me that anymore, but I didn't like it." This fear of detection and the stress of distancing oneself from one's coworkers—you couldn't socialize with them or ever invite them to your house—compelled many Creoles to return to colored employment, no matter the loss of wages.

But as the Depression worsened, colored employment in New York City wasn't an option for my grandparents. Nat worked mostly in Manhattan, where he ran less risk of bumping into someone who knew about his background. For Edna, whose job was only a half mile from the family's home, the threat of discovery was greater.

Other blacks tended to protect people who were passing—by not acknowledging the person when in public—but a white neighbor wouldn't be as inclined to keep a black person's secret.

My grandmother was well known around Stuyvesant Heights. She often stood by the front gate of the yard, chatting with passersby. She had a talent for drawing people out about the difficulties in their lives and would freely offer advice about what someone should do in any given situation. She also had a habit of unconsciously mimicking a person's accent. Before long she'd fall into an Irish brogue, Caribbean lilt, or the Yiddish inflections of a neighbor, which made her daughter Shirley worry that people might think her mother was mocking them.

While visiting my aunt Shirley, I try to ask, gingerly, what it was like for her to grow up under these circumstances. The subject is uncomfortable for the very fact that Shirley, unlike the rest of her family, couldn't pass for white. In New Orleans I heard stories about Creole families who rejected their own children because they were too dark. Sometimes these families justified their decision by the fact that the child made it impossible for them to live as white at a time when passing was one of the few means of survival. Other times a family had simply absorbed the prevailing attitudes about skin color to such a degree that they willingly betrayed their own flesh and blood.

Shirley acknowledges that her childhood was probably very different from her brother's and sister's. On the street or in school, people knew what Shirley was by looking at her, which made her prey to the kinds of subtle prejudice—a waiter ignoring her at the lunch counter, a white classmate rebuffing her overtures of friendship—that black people experienced all the time. My father and Lorraine, on the other hand, could go through their day unharmed by such offhand cruelties. But I wondered if these differences in experience extended to their home life too.

We sit at Shirley's kitchen table, where we always sit during our visits. Post-its decorate the cabinet doors, with reminders about upcoming appointments, calls to be returned, bills to be paid. In her early eighties, my aunt still goes out most nights, to meetings of her book club or performances at Lincoln Center or the Brooklyn Academy of Music—but I recognize these reminders as the efforts of a proud woman to resist the tide of aging. My aunt isn't the type to talk easily about her vulnerabilities.

"Do you think that your mother or father ever had any close calls at work?" I ask. "It must have been sort of stressful for them. And for you."

Shirley dismisses the question with a shake of her head. She says that she doesn't know for sure, but she doubts that her parents ever worried about being found out. "I never worried about it myself," she adds.

"But you knew, for example, that you couldn't visit your mother at her job."

"I had no desire to go to the Laundromat. It didn't interest me."

Shirley explains that after school she and Lorraine would do the grocery shopping and start dinner, and when their mother came home, she would finish the cooking. Their home life was just like other families'.

I tell Shirley that my father described the experience a little differently to a friend. He said that one day his father had sat the family down in the living room and announced that they were no longer going to be black. Because Nat and Edna had to pass as white for work, the kids had to be white now too. "Imagine having someone say that to you!" my father had exclaimed to his friend.

"Well, if it happened, I wasn't there," Shirley says flatly. I can see why she might doubt this account. How, after all, could her father have acted as if race was elective, when for his youngest child it obviously wasn't?

Shirley tells me that she was never treated any differently in her family. "The only thing I can remember," she says, pausing, "is them teasing me about being the cookie they left in the oven too long."

I can't help laughing. "They said that?"

Shirley laughs too, in amazement. "Yes, I was the brown sugar cookie or the ginger snap."

"That must have hurt a little."

Her face clouds. "Well, I still remember it, so I guess it made an impression."

It's clear from talking with Shirley that there wasn't much conversation in her family about racial identity. It seems possible that my father and his sister could have grown up under the same roof with vastly different understandings about what race they were supposed to be. Neither my father nor his sisters were advised, for example, about how they should present themselves when applying for a job or meeting new classmates. Shirley doesn't know how my dad and Lorraine were perceived in high school. "We never discussed it," she says.

The example set by their parents had to be confusing. While the family visited with black people, attended black social events, and remained in the neighborhood even as white people moved out, Nat and Edna avoided being labeled as "black" themselves. Shirley remembers how the family sat apart from the other black families at the beach in Coney Island. In 1930, when the census taker came around, Edna claimed that her mother was born in Portugal, and Nat reported that his parents came from Mexico. Despite these attempts to explain away their dark hair and tawny complexions, the census taker recorded the family's race as black anyway. When I ask Shirley about the deception, she shrugs and says, "Still trying to keep up the fiction."

Around the time of the 1930 census, Nat's brother James and his nephew Jimmy Jr. arrived in Brooklyn from New Orleans. Jimmy Jr. moved in with my father's family until he found a place of his own.

When I track him down in Louisiana, Jimmy, who is eighty by this time, tells me that my grandfather was never colored in New York. Jimmy knows that this was true, because Nat and Edna had told him so. Yet he also recalls black people visiting the Broyard house, which seems unlikely if the family was trying to pass among its neighbors.

Kathy Jeffers, who was my aunt Lorraine's best friend during the latter part of the 1930s and was herself recognizably black, also has the impression that Nat was passing both for work and around home. One day in the early 1940s, she saw Mr. Broyard in the street and said hello, but he kept walking without acknowledging her. She confessed the incident to Edna and Lorraine, and she recalls being told that Nat was trying to protect his employment. But again this explanation didn't quite make sense, since Shirley, and later her brown-skinned husband, was living in the Broyard household.

When it came to race, however, Nat wasn't known for being logical. Shirley describes her father as "the biggest racist you ever set your eyes on," adding that he hated everyone: blacks, Catholics, and Jews alike. Every night my grandfather read William Randolph Hearst's newspaper, the notoriously conservative *Evening Journal.* She remembers her father agreeing with everything the paper said and even saving the front page each day for posterity. When the editors of the *Brooklyn Eagle* suggested that the influx of blacks into Stuyvesant Heights was bringing down the neighborhood, Nat agreed with them too. His disdain for African Americans underscored his feeling of separateness from them—a line of distinction that only deepened as the complexion of his neighbors darkened.

With the onset of the Depression, residents of Harlem began relocating to Brooklyn to escape the worsening ghetto conditions. But those same problems followed them across the East River. The deteriorating economic climate forced black homeowners in Stuyvesant Heights to take out second mortgages and then take in renters to pay for them.

In 1931 the *Brooklyn Eagle* first described the central Brooklyn neighborhood as Bedford-Stuyvesant, linking together Stuyvesant Heights and adjacent Bedford Corner. Over the next ten years, the moniker gained currency—usually with negative connotations—as the boundaries of Bedford-Stuyvesant were increasingly defined by the presence of black people.

Ironically, federal policies implemented by Roosevelt's New Deal hastened the neighborhood's downfall. In 1933 the Home Owners' Loan Corporation (HOLC) was established to stem home foreclosures and bank failures. The agency developed lending guidelines to help ensure that struggling financial institutions would get back on their feet. To that end grades of A, B, C, or D were assigned to a neighborhood based on condition of its housing stock, transportation and utility services, maintenance of homes, and "quality" of the population. Specifically, federal agents looked at the percentage of blacks and foreign-born residents in a community and whether either population was on the rise. Needless to say, Bedford-Stuyvesant earned the worst grade, D.

The historian Craig Steven Wilder, in analyzing the HOLC's "Residential Security MAP" for Brooklyn in his book *A Covenant with Color*, found that while a heavy concentration of Jews, Irish, or Italians risked bringing a neighborhood a negative rating, the presence of African Americans absolutely guaranteed it. "Bensonhurst and a portion of Flatbush, with sizable Italian populations, managed at least B− grades, just as a number of Jewish areas received B or better ratings. In contrast, not one of the eighteen neighborhoods that received a B− or better had any black residents, except for Crown Heights, where the black population was described as 'Nil,' meaning '2 or 3 families.'"

Neighborhoods with D ratings appeared in red on HOLC's map, which led to the infamous term "redlining." By deeming these areas bad investments, the federal government helped to make them so. The difficulty in obtaining loans to buy homes or maintain existing properties in Bedford-Stuyvesant further decreased property values. Trying to cut their losses, whites sold their homes, often to unscrupulous white investors, who would then break up the houses into apartments, which they would rent out at inflated prices to blacks who found themselves unwelcome elsewhere.

As the black community in Bed-Stuy grew, class conflicts sparked between the old "colored" group and the new "black" population, with the flash point often occurring among the teenagers. The lower-class kids knew, if perhaps implicitly, that my father's family, for example, fared better than their own because his parents could pass as white. Despite rough times there was never any shortage of food or serious deprivation for the Broyards. Edna continued to make her apple pies and yellow cakes throughout the worst years of the Depression. One December, when my grandfather hadn't worked for a while, it looked as if the family would have to forgo Christmas. But at the last minute, Nat landed a job and surprised them by coming home with a tree and a bag full of presents.

During high school my father and his friends had the leisure time and pocket change for a jam-packed social life. In the summer they played tennis at the courts down on Fulton Street. In the winter they skated at the rink on Atlantic Avenue. On the weekends they took their dates to the movies at Lowe's theater and then to Bruggerman's for ice cream afterward. On any given night they could be found at one of the girls' houses listening to records—Duke Ellington, Ella Fitzgerald, Coleman Hawkins—and polishing their moves for an upcoming dance.

Most dances were sponsored by private clubs and were invitation only. The Guardsmen, a social club started by the black bourgeoisie in Brooklyn, held three parties annually, often at the Savoy Theater in Harlem, at which the Duke Ellington band regularly played. The biggest event of the year was the formal Christmas dance thrown by the Comus Club, usually held at the St. George Hotel in Brooklyn Heights. Young men and women from the best black families in

Washington, Philadelphia, and Boston flocked into town to attend the annual party.

Meanwhile, by 1938 the Brooklyn Urban League was reporting that 90 percent of black Brooklynites depended on some kind of relief. Many children had to drop out of high school to look for full-time jobs. Their families were crammed into one-bedroom apartments, and they had no hopes of attending college. Needless to say, they weren't invited to the Comus Christmas dance.

"Other blacks were jealous of us. We got into a lot of fights," remembers Robbie King, one of my father's friends. These other kids called Robbie and my father's circle the four hundred, after Lady Astor's four hundred—the members of New York society deemed worthy of an invitation to her annual ball. Marjorie Costa, a childhood friend of my aunts, tells me how in high school a gang of darker-skinned, poorer kids targeted their crowd. "Your aunt Lorraine was beaten by one of the gangs," she explains. "They were going alphabetically." With her turn coming, Marjorie got a rival gang to fight for her, but she understood the roots of the tension. "Many of our group were snobs and didn't want to talk with [other kids] if they weren't the right color and didn't dress the right way." The hard-off boys particularly resented that the girls in my dad's clique wouldn't go out with them. At the same time, lighter-skinned boys, including my father, were fooling around with the girls in their crowd. "They only wanted them for sex," Marjorie says, disapprovingly. "They wouldn't take them to a movie or to Bruggerman's ice cream parlor."

My dad once told a friend in whom he had confided about his racial background that he'd become such a fast runner from being chased by black kids during his childhood. Sometimes these kids caught up with him and he'd come home with his jacket torn, but his parents never asked what happened. Perhaps Nat didn't want to acknowledge that his passing for white and superior attitude toward blacks had contributed to his son's problems. Or he simply viewed these street scuffles as a boy's rite of passage. Nat had probably gotten into fights with the American blacks in New Orleans when he was a kid. But for my dad, his father's feigned ignorance was so painful that recalling it to my mother fifty years later made him break down into tears. It was the second and last time my mother ever saw my father cry. (The first was during his best friend's funeral.) During childhood, though, it was easier for my father to turn his hurt into anger, which he eventually redirected toward black people.

Learning about my father's experiences growing up made sense of a story that my father liked to tell from my own childhood. When my brother was eleven or so, my dad took him to the movies in Oak Bluffs, a town in Martha's Vineyard with a large number of African American vacationers. After the film my father had to use the bathroom and sent Todd outside to wait for him. When my dad exited the theater, he found my brother in a doorway down the street, having a fistfight with a black kid a head and half taller and three or four years older. My father, who had taught my brother how to box, would jab and feint at this point in the story, demonstrating how his son had knocked down this kid twice his size.

The detail that always struck me was not Todd's prowess at boxing but my father's disconcerting glee that my brother had trounced a "tough black kid." Todd couldn't remember anymore what started the fight, but he did recall that our father had stood back and watched him rather than breaking it up. People say that having children gives you the chance to relive your own childhood. With his victory Todd had unwittingly settled an old score for our father.

In a similar vein, Todd was taken out every month or so for "father and son nights," while I had no special dates with our dad. Since my brother, particularly as a teenager, was himself a fairly silent character, my father claimed that if he didn't hold Todd captive at a dinner table once in a while, he would never learn anything about him at all. My father was hoping that he and my brother could learn to talk as friends the way he and his father never did.

My grandfather had trouble simply looking my father in the eye. In his spare time, Nat liked to make furniture in a workshop that he'd set up in the basement of their building. As a young child, my father followed his father downstairs and tried to place himself in the way so that his father was forced to meet his gaze. Sometimes Nat would talk to himself as he worked, and my dad would strain to listen, in case his father mentioned his name.

As an adult my father blamed New York for turning his father into this taciturn, evasive man. In New Orleans his father had been "a popular figure, a noted raconteur, a former beau, a crack shot, a dancer, a bit of a boxer." He was the kind of man who would suddenly throw himself upside down and walk on his hands over to a friend's house for a laugh. But after moving north, Nat became preoccupied, always listening for something, "some New Orleans jazz, or a voice telling him a story." My dad decided that his father "lived in New York under protest, a protest that he never admitted even to himself. He was ashamed to think that he had been pressured into leaving the city he loved."

What my father didn't acknowledge was that in Brooklyn, Nat was just another light-skinned black guy who could only make it in the larger world by presenting himself as something that he wasn't. My grandfather was reacting not only to New York but also to the question the city forced on him: Was he black or was he white? Yet for my father to see the box that race had forced Nat into, he would have had to recognize that he was similarly hemmed in.

My father attended Boys High, located in Stuyvesant Heights, not far from where the Broyards' apartment overlooked the El. Although no tests were required for entrance, the high school had a reputation for being where the smart kids went. The students, who came from across Brooklyn, were mostly the sons of Jewish emigrants from Poland, Russia, and Germany. A handful of my father's friends from the neighborhood also attended Boys High. In the 1930s there wasn't much racial tension, and the black and white students mingled easily with each other. A white classmate, Harold Chenven, assumed that my father was white too until their junior year, when my dad leaned over during a break in Ms. Wilson's literature class and whispered that he was a Creole from New Orleans.

Recalling this conversation sixty years later, Harold says, "I guess I was worldly enough then to know that he was telling me he was of mixed racial parentage." In hindsight Harold surmises that my father wanted to pass for white and that his confession "was like trying it on for size." Harold didn't answer, but he thought to himself that Bud Broyard didn't look like a Negro. His skin was as pale or even paler than his own.

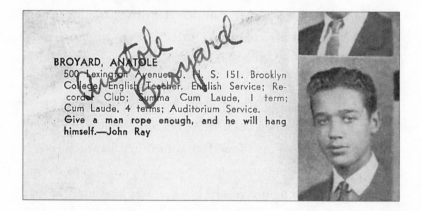

BROYARD, ANATOLE
500 Lexington Avenue. J. H. S. 151. Brooklyn College English Teacher. English Service; Recorder Club; Summa Cum Laude, 1 term; Cum Laude, 4 terms; Auditorium Service.
Give a man rope enough, and he will hang himself.—John Ray

Not everyone was as worldly as Harold when it came to understanding that Creole suggested mixed race. By describing himself that way, my father could avoid the black/white question and let people draw their own conclusions. But this was more than a tactic of obfuscation. Just as this heritage could momentarily lift the fog of distraction and defeat surrounding his father, it also offered a way for my

dad to explain himself to himself. In the absence of any real knowledge about his legacy, my dad turned New Orleans into a mythical
city filled with irreverent characters: the swashbuckling pirate Jean
Lafitte, romantic adventurers lifted from the pages of an Alexandre
Dumas novel, and his own lady-killing grandfather. At college my father discovered how his New Orleans roots could even put an exotic
spin on his difference from everyone else.

When my father entered Brooklyn College in January 1937, the first thing that people noticed about him was how out of place he seemed. He was only sixteen, having skipped two grades during elementary school, and one of the very few students who wasn't Jewish. His classmates had never met someone named Anatole before; they'd never known anyone who was Creole or from New Orleans. He was also completely apolitical, while the rest of the students were swept up in the radicalism of the 1930s—reading the *Daily Worker*, holding antiwar rallies, and debating the relative merits of various socialist ideologies. My father later explained that he regarded politics as an "uninteresting argument with the real." I imagine also that he couldn't very well stake out a position on these social issues without first claiming his position in society, which was something he was unwilling to do.

My father dressed differently from everyone else. Back then men put on dark suits and somber ties for school, and women wore knee-length skirts and plain sweaters. On top of the custom-tailored three-piece suit my father had bought with his earnings from delivering newspapers, he added a porkpie hat and short gray overcoat with hidden buttons that looked like the kind of cape someone might have worn to a nineteenth-century duel. A classmate later observed: "Anatole was the mysterious subject of many conversations, with everyone speculating about where he belonged."

The question weighed on my father too. After his first semester, Brooklyn College relocated from its rented office buildings in downtown Brooklyn to a new forty-acre campus on Flatbush Avenue, complete with colonial redbrick buildings and the beginnings of ivy trailing up their fronts. There the cafeteria became the meeting place and testing ground for the student body. It was, in the words of my father's future best friend Milton Klonsky, "a crowded, bustling, feud-ridden, volatile, and at times cacophonous place that had a continuous life of its own apart from that of the college itself." A person was identified according to where he sat: there was a table for the Trotsky-ites, the Stalinists, the Socialists, the Communists, the jocks, the Orthodox Jews, the Catholic girls of the Newman Club, the handful of Wasps, and the even smaller handful of black students.

When Vincent Livelli first spotted my dad, he was standing alone in the cafeteria, looking for a seat among the crowded tables. "Nobody seemed to want his company," Vincent recalls. "That coat was the problem. It was much too big for him—it must have been his father's from New Orleans—but this was still the Depression, so I was willing to make allowances."

Vincent was a bit of an oddball himself: an Italian Catholic from the largely Scandinavian neighborhood of Fort Hamilton. After being turned away by various fraternities, he ran for student council and lost, losing his interest in politics along the way. When he encountered my father, Vincent was peddling penny cigarettes in the cafeteria. Hoping to sell him a "loosie" after his meal, Vincent invited the odd fellow in the cape coat to sit down. My dad accepted reluctantly—lest he appear resigned to a future among misfits—and then ignored Vincent for the rest of his meal.

But the pair bumped into each other again riding home on the subway. Shouting over the loud clacking of the train across the ties, they discovered a mutual interest in Cuban music. From the time he was a kid, my father had listened to Xavier Cugat on the radio. Such was his love for the Latin bandleader that he was allowed to hog the family radio each week during Cugat's program. Vincent impressed my dad by mentioning that he'd met some of the musicians who played on Cugat's show in the nightclubs of Spanish Harlem.

Before long Vincent and my dad were stopping off on the way home at a bookstore in downtown Brooklyn that sold Afro-Cuban records. After winding up the Victrola, they crowded into a listening booth to decipher the lyrics full of puns and sexual innuendos. One of their favorites was "El Plato Roto" (the broken plate), about the girl who was made pregnant during the encounter that broke her hymen. Another man was tricked into paying for her abortion, which my father and Vincent thought was bad luck indeed.

One day Vincent came to my father's house to loan him a record and was invited to stay for dinner. It was during this visit that Vincent realized, with a bit of a shock, that my father's family was Negro. Over the years other friends of my dad's would learn of his racial identity this same way. Yet this revelation didn't induce them to start viewing Anatole as a black person. They all offer the same explanation: people didn't think in racial terms back then, in spite of — or perhaps because of — the persistence of segregation. Anyway Anatole didn't look or act like most black people. Vincent says that he was simply happy to have found a kindred spirit — someone more social than political and equally passionate about music, dancing, and women.

Flora Finkelstein at Brooklyn College was my father's first real girl-friend. She was Jewish, although after growing up in a socialist commune in the Bronx, she wasn't religious, particularly interested in politics, or conventional in the least. Another classmate, the writer Pearl Bell (who is the sister of Alfred Kazin and the wife of Daniel Bell, two leading New York intellectuals), remembers: "Flora wore her bangs down to her eyes and had a way of taking her shoes off and dancing in the grass in the spring, which nobody did in those days. She was eccentric and so was Anatole."

Flora knew that my father was part black — he'd told her so — and

it didn't matter to her in the least. She was under the impression that it didn't much matter to him either. The young couple could be seen walking hand in hand across the quad or hunched over a table in the cafeteria deep in conversation. They talked mostly about literature—not the dusty canonical texts, *Beowulf* and Swinburne, assigned for their English literature course—but the erotically charged works of D. H. Lawrence, the brutal nihilistic vision of Céline, and Kafka's disturbed symbolic universe. Flora had a keen analytical mind, and her unusual upbringing gave her the courage of her own convictions. She listened closely to my father's opinions, which made him phrase things more carefully in order to impress her. When he showed her the poems and bits of stories he'd begun to write, she encouraged him.

My father had known some classmates at Boys High who had interesting things to say about books, but he'd never before had someone with whom to share his love of literature—someone who could join him in deciphering the secret codes that unlocked these imagined worlds and celebrating the patient exquisite precision that it took to create them. For my father and Flora, books and each other were their first loves, their true loves, with each feeling redoubling the other.

In English class my father started to draw attention to himself. Pearl Bell remembers him as having a "wonderful capacity for hitting at the center of whatever it was that was being talked about." The acuity of my father's insights helped to erase the distance between him and the other students who were also "aware" about literature—which were the only people he cared about. In the cafeteria he took his seat beside the other literary men. Books became the place where my father could belong: his sole allegiance, his primary ethnic, political, and religious affiliation. They provided a refuge from all the boxes in his life, an opportunity to escape into himself, literally.

Back in Bedford-Stuyvesant my dad wanted to spread the news. He loaned Shirley his collection of Kafka stories. After dutifully reading *Metamorphosis,* she opined that a guy turning into cockroach was pretty weird. "But you see that it's operating on more than one level?" my father pressed. Shirley was still in high school, reading Hawthorne and Mark Twain, and didn't know anything about different levels. Anyway, who talked like that—and to his kid sister! No one Shirley knew.

My father couldn't share his newfound enthusiasm with his neighborhood friends either. Many of them were bright, with some also earning spots at one of the free colleges, but they had more practical concerns on their minds, such as who would hire them when they graduated and what would their place in American society be. As they ventured farther from Bedford-Stuyvesant, my father's friends had begun to experience discrimination for the first time—being turned away from clubs in Manhattan or refused service in a restaurant—and this had drawn them into the fight for racial equality.

An old classmate from Boys High, Alfred Duckett, had also been passionate about writing, publishing his poetry in the school's literary magazine, but when he got older, he turned his attention to politics—joining the local chapter of the NAACP, canvassing the neighborhood for signatures to demand that businesses hire blacks and picketing those that wouldn't. Duckett's writing career increasingly reflected his concerns—he published his poetry in Negro anthologies and eventually became an editor at the *New York Age*, a black newspaper.

Being a black writer was exactly what my father feared. Given his racially indeterminate upbringing, he wasn't exactly equipped to represent the black experience. Anyway, he wanted to write about the *human* condition—the existential problem of being, how to find meaning in an irrational world, and the possibilities of transformation; the subject matter of his literary heroes. My father saw himself as special—isn't that what his classmates at Brooklyn College thought?—so why should he voluntarily consent to the indiscriminating smear of discrimination? Especially if he didn't have to.

In the evenings and on the weekends, my dad hung out in the neighborhood with his friends as usual, but more and more, his real life seemed to be taking place somewhere else. My father's regular partner at the weekend dances, Lois Latte, remembers him as seeming very distant. "Bud wasn't like the other fellows, who were raucous and loud and always carrying on, except for that he really loved to dance."

My father taught Lois steps that he had worked out to Artie Shaw's hit version of "Begin the Beguine." "I remember feeling so proud that your father wanted to dance with me," she says. "He could have asked anybody he wanted." Lois wasn't surprised when she heard a few years later that Bud Broyard had gone to the other side. During the time they'd known each other, Lois's mother had been supporting Lois by passing as white to waitress in a fancy hotel up in Westchester, making Lois inclined to defend my father's decision. "There were times when you had to do what you had to do to live," she reflects. And then she ventures a guess that the rest of their friends would have done the same thing if they could have.

Shirley suspects that her brother was passing as early as Brooklyn College. To his parents and sisters, he certainly seemed to change around that time. But then again, going to college was unlike anything that had ever occurred in their family. Neither of their parents had even made it to high school. And Lorraine, who was the oldest of the siblings, had opted for secretarial school instead, so she could start earning money and contributing to the household income.

"College could have meant that this is how you behave," Shirley says. "You make new friends, you're busy, you have homework, you have all these classes, and you have to make your way to Brooklyn College, which is not exactly around the corner." You also learn things that make you discontented with the world that you've always known.

It's hard to say when my father started presenting himself as white, if he ever explicitly did so. What's more likely is that he didn't identify himself as black, neglecting to mention that he lived in Bedford-Stuyvesant and avoiding the colored students' table at lunchtime. But his transformation wasn't as sudden or absolute as that of Kafka's Gregor Samsa, who woke up one morning to find that he'd changed into a cockroach his parents couldn't recognize or understand.

As my father became more articulate with his friends at Brooklyn College, he did grow less intelligible to his family — purposefully so with his father, using words that Nat wouldn't know to pay him back for his years of silence. But his conflict wasn't between black and white as much as it was between provincial and sophisticated, old world and modern, literal-minded and literary-minded. And this struggle wasn't exactly uncommon among his college friends, as they too grew mysterious to their immigrant parents.

My father's situation differed in one important aspect. Besides the universal question Who are you? that all of them were asking themselves, my father had to confront the question What are you? on occasion too. In March 1938, when he was seventeen, my father visited the local field office of the Social Security Administration to apply for a social security card. While his responses on this application concerning race represent the first tangible evidence I have of what he considered himself, the form raises more questions than it answers.

I've studied the muddled notations on the small sheet of paper countless times, spent hours wondering about my father's train of thought as he completed the application. And while I don't think that this visit to the social security office necessarily demarks a turning point in my father's life, the occasion has become the repository for all my imaginings about the different moments over the years when he had to make a calculation about how to describe his race.

Bud retrieves an application from a stack and finds a spot at one of the counters to fill it out. In his carefully rounded schoolboy print, he answers the questions: name, address, birth date, place of birth, full names of father and mother, sex, and then question number twelve: COLOR, with the choices WHITE, NEGRO, or OTHER.

Bud has never faced a form like this before. He's never had to answer this question. He hesitates, trying to imagine the future of this slip of paper — where it will go and who will see it; how question number twelve might affect his life. He knows very well, from his parents and people in the neighborhood, that he won't be able to get any kind of decent job if an employer thinks that he's black. But he also knows that no white person is going to suspect that he's any different from themselves. He decides that identifying his COLOR on this form is merely a formality of the modern age, and whatever shadow self that is created from it will live on only in the dusty file rooms of federal warehouses. Convinced that his answer to question number twelve doesn't matter, he touches his pencil to the piece of paper. . . . But what should his answer be?

Bud knows what "they" think: that his COLOR should be NEGRO, even though the arm resting on the counter before him is no darker than the arm of the young Italian guy to his right. For that matter, his hair is no curlier than the Jewish girl's across the room. His lips are no bigger than the lips of her father. And his nose is no wider than the broken one on the Irish thug over there. But "they" have already decided this question for him on other slips of paper stored in dusty file rooms. Bud's birth certificate identifies him as "colored" and that's how the census taker recorded him and his family too. If a person accepted the one-drop logic of race that seemed to be the law of this irrational land, then Bud was colored, thanks to his great-granddaddy falling for the beautiful island girl from Santo Domingo . . .

And what was so wrong with that? These distinctions between black and white were exactly that, arbitrary distinctions that had been imposed by "them" with no basis in fact or science. Any intelligent person knew that whatever differences existed between the races were caused by social conditions, such as poverty. Professor Otto Klineberg, student of the "father of American anthropology" Franz Boas, had just lectured at Brooklyn College on that very topic. If Bud opted against electing NEGRO *on question twelve, then he would appear to be giving credence to the "crackpot race theories" that Klineberg had just exposed.*

And yet . . . and yet . . . Bud drums his fingers on the countertop. These slips of paper have a way of trailing a person around — like a piece of toilet paper stuck to your shoe. Hadn't he heard stories his whole life in which a person's "papers" figured as the punch line? There was the one about his uncle Jimmy, when he got into a scrape with the police down in New Orleans. They were going to lock him up in the colored part of the jail — which, needless to say, was full of roughneck lowlifes and not where his uncle belonged — until Jimmy protested that he was white and pulled out his driver's license to prove it. The cops apologized, addressing him as "Mr. Broyard," and let him go. Ha. Ha. Ha. His father slaps his knee. Just because Jimmy had those white papers . . .

Bud shifts his pencil in his grip. Anyway, he wasn't really a Negro like "they" thought of them — the sullen toughs that were moving into his neighborhood; the poor, downtrodden, uneducated masses. His people had never been slaves; they'd never bowed and scraped before white people. What did "they" know about the wide variety of Negroes — that they ranged in color from ebony to alabaster; that some of them spoke French or Spanish in their homes; that their history had taken them across not only cotton fields but battlefields, barricades, and fields of knowledge too? And who were "they"? Where were "they"? These invisible authorities with their nonsensical rules were like something out of Kafka.

Recalling the author gives Bud a warm feeling in his chest, like the memory of a lover. Perhaps literature could provide an answer to number twelve. Bud thinks of the penultimate section of the brilliant Wallace Stevens's poem "The Man with the Blue Guitar," which had just been published. Yes, he would recite that to the clerk as his response to the question of his COLOR.

> *Throw away the lights, the definitions,*
> *And say of what you see in the dark*

That it is this or that it is that,
But do not use the rotted names.

How should you walk in that space and know
Nothing of the madness of space,

Nothing of its jocular procreations?
Throw the lights away. Nothing must stand

Between you and the shapes you take
When the crust of the shape has been destroyed.

You as you are? You are yourself.
The blue guitar surprises you.

The young Italian glances over. Bud has been mumbling under his breath. As he turns his attention back to the form, his father's voice pops into his head: "Get your head out of your books for once, Bud. Check off WHITE, hand in the slip, and walk away. That's how people see you, and that's all there is to it."

But it's one thing to be mistaken for white and something else to actually present himself that way. Yes, the color line is shot full of holes, and crossing it could be as easy as crossing the East River. Every day people from his neighborhood who are black when they enter Fulton Street station become white just by taking the subway to Manhattan and going to their jobs. Bud knows that people's perception of him changes according to his context—among his colored friends from Stuyvesant Heights he's viewed as colored; sitting with his white classmates at Brooklyn College, he's seen as white. But he also knows that people can become exiled on the other side of the color line. He thinks of Ethel, his half sister.

When she arrived from New Orleans with her new husband, Walter, it was as if his father had woken from a long nap. Bud was ten, and Uncle Jimmy and his son, Jimmy Jr., had just come up to New York too. All of a sudden, there was a burgeoning Broyard clan in Stuyvesant Heights, and their house was its center. One Sunday his dad made a big show of having to fetch from the basement the extra leaf he'd made for the dining room table, but everyone could see how delighted he was to have so much family around.

Watching his dad at the head of that table, carving the roast, telling his stories about the French Quarter, puffing away on his cigar after the meal — sending up regular clouds of smoke, like a miniature train locomotive — Bud felt himself shaking off a sort of slumber too. After supper he found on the radio some of the Latin music that he liked, and he began to imitate the Cuban dancers — braiding his steps as fast as lightning with his arms crossed in front of his face, snapping his fingers, and spinning his head left and right. He meant it as a joke — but then when everyone quieted and began to watch him, he started playing off the beat of the claves, stalling then rushing the tempo. When he was done, they laughed, but he could see that he'd impressed them too with his witty interpretations. Walter offered him a nickel to dance again.

After Ethel gave birth to Charmaine, things started to change. His parents began talking in Creole all the time, so that he and his sisters couldn't understand them. When his mother took care of the baby, sometimes Bud would catch her just staring at Charmaine's face for minutes at a time. Then one day Ethel came home with her hair tamed into neat waves and a new set of clothes, which she referred to as her traveling outfit. She explained that they were going away for a while.

"But where?" Bud asked. "When are you coming back?" He worried that his father's newfound vitality would disappear with them. Ethel promised to write when they got settled and that Bud could come visit soon. Then she knelt down and hugged him hard, saying, "You'll understand when you get older."

He still remembers the day that they left. His dad wanted to take a picture of Ethel — usually he made everyone go up to the rooftop because he didn't think there was enough light on the sidewalk — but Ethel said there wasn't time. Besides, she didn't want to soil her traveling outfit by climbing up to the dirty roof. His father became insistent, nearly yelling that he wasn't going to have his only photo of his eldest daughter ruined. Finally they compromised by walking to the street corner, where at least they weren't under the shadows of the buildings.

His father was right — the picture didn't get enough exposure. Ethel's face under her hat lies half in darkness. Her skirt blurs with movement, as if she has already begun to walk out of the frame. Sometimes Bud would take the photo out from his

mother's drawer and try to read his sister's expression. Had she already made up her mind to
disappear?

By that time Bud was aware that life was
easier for people who lived as white, but he couldn't
understand why Ethel should have to move across
the color line so absolutely. They didn't even know
where she was, whether she was alive or dead. No
one would think anything if they saw her with
him, or with his father or mother for that matter.
It was almost as if she was ashamed of them, as
if she believed all the things "they" thought about
Negroes.

The Italian guy has gone. Bud needs to go too. "Don't make this so complicated,"
he thinks. "It's just a slip of paper." He closes his eyes and asks himself, What are
you, Anatole Broyard? After a moment he opens his eyes and on the line following
OTHER, he writes in his careful print a faint C.

The clerk is a young woman, just a few years older than Bud. As she looks at the
young man standing across the counter from her, she feels her cheeks coloring slightly.
He's very handsome, she notes. Then she sees the corner of his lips raise slightly, as if
he knows what she is thinking.

"So Mr. . . ." She pauses, puzzling over his name.

"Broyard," he supplies, rolling the r's slightly. "It's French."

"Right. I see here that you are from New Orleans, which of course was a French
territory."

He cocks an eyebrow. "Very good. You'd be surprised, Miss. . ." He glances around
her desk area.

"Watkins," she says, touching her chest. "My nameplate hasn't arrived yet. I've just
been here for two weeks."

"Miss Watkins." He croons her name, making it his own. "As I was saying, you'd
be surprised by how many people don't know anything about the history of our country. Or maybe you wouldn't be surprised—you must have met so many different

people, working here for even a short time—that you have, as they say, seen it all." He whispers this last bit.

"Mr. Broyard," she says reprovingly. "I don't wish to take up any more of your time than is necessary. If I may...?"

"Of course." He rests his chin on his hand and stares at her intently.

But she is more flustered than ever. The young man's efforts to engage her in conversation have turned their interview more intimate than she would like. She frowns at the form, clarifies a few points, makes some addendums, and then says, "About number twelve, COLOR, you indicate C. That stands for..."

"Creole," the young man says confidently.

She shakes her head, indicating that she doesn't know what that means. When he doesn't explain further, she asks, "Is that black or white?"

"Well, what do I look like to you?"

His tone tries for affront, but he doesn't quite pull it off. The clerk takes his question literally. He doesn't really look black, but there's something about him—a slight insolence maybe—that makes her think of Negroes. "Mr. Broyard, I can help you fill out the form," she says, "but I can't provide the answers for you."

"Very well, Miss Watkins. Creoles are from New Orleans. They are descended from the original settlers and date back to before the Louisiana Purchase."

"And so Creoles are...?"

"French."

"I mean are they white or black," she says, resenting the exactitude he has forced upon her.

"Well, they can be either. I myself am mostly white."

Miss Watkins raises her eyebrows.

"I also have a little Indian blood as well as some"—he pauses—"Caribbean influences."

"Meaning that you're colored?"

"Well..."

"Is that what it says on your birth certificate?"

"Yes," he says quietly.

And the clerk feels like she's won something, something that she fought hard for, only to discover that she didn't really want it. She looks down at her desk, ashamed of her own tenacity. She reflects unhappily that the young man must think she's prejudiced.

She taps her pen on the paper, trying to think. She can't risk running into trouble with her supervisor before her nameplate has even arrived. She's lucky to have this job, given all the people out of work. "Well, it's important for the success of the social security program to try to be as accurate as possible," she says. She begins to make a check next to NEGRO and then changes her mind and starts to write "Creole" in the space instead. Let them — the powers that be — decide what that meant.

"Miss Watkins," the young man says, beseechingly. With his confidence gone, he looks his seventeen years. She notices that the shoulders of his jacket stand out beyond his narrow frame, making his head look small and delicate. He must have bought the suit a few sizes too big, to stretch more use from it. Or maybe it was his father's, borrowed especially for this trip. Life, she knew, was very hard for Negroes.

"Is there a problem here?" Her supervisor is suddenly standing beside her. He nods to the long line that has formed in front of her desk.

"No, sir." Where did all these people come from? "I was just helping Mr. Broyard complete his form." She cuts her eyes at the young man.

"And what's taking so long?"

"We had just a little confusion on number twelve. Mr. Broyard is Creole, which are the group, as perhaps you know, who originally settled Louisiana. They were there since before — oh, what did you say?" She glances at the young man for help.

"Miss Watkins," the supervisor admonishes, "the Social Security Administration is not in the business of conducting genealogical surveys. This gentleman's color is white. That's as plain as the nose on your face." He turns to my father standing at the counter. "I'm sorry, sir, for the delay. I'm sure Miss Watkins's overzealousness can be explained by the fact that she is new and therefore eager to prove herself."

The supervisor looks on as the clerk scratches out "Creole" and makes a check next to WHITE on the young man's application. On the top of the form, she records the next available social security number and then fills out the card for the fellow to keep. She hands it over, mumbling an apology, and the young man with a wave of his hand indicates that all is forgiven. After he has turned to go, Miss Watkins places the young

Form 88
TREASURY DEPARTMENT
INTERNAL REVENUE SERVICE
(Revised July 1937)

U. S. SOCIAL SECURITY ACT
APPLICATION FOR ACCOUNT NUMBER
EACH ITEM SHOULD BE FILLED IN. IF ANY ITEM IS NOT KNOWN WRITE "UNKNOWN"   133-07-4189

Anatole   Paul   Broyard
402 Decatur Street   3. Brooklyn   New York
None
17   7. July 16, 1920   8. New Orleans, Louisiana
Anatole Paul Broyard   10. Edna Miller
SEX: MALE ✓   FEMALE   12. COLOR: WHITE ✓   NEGRO   OTHER
no
3/2/38   16. Anatole Broyard
DETACH ALONG THIS LINE 009-01-7671

man's application in her outbox to be sent to the main office in Baltimore and gestures
for the next person on line to come forward.

Of course I don't know what actually transpired in that social security field office to explain the cross-outs and mysterious *C* that constitute my father's answer to question number twelve. It looks to me as if a different hand made the check next to WHITE — likely the same person who made the other corrections on the form. But there's no way to be certain. The original application was destroyed in the 1960s, after its image had been filmed for storage — not in a dusty file room but a defunct salt mine in Kansas, chosen for the aridness of its environment.

I doubt that my father walked away feeling that he'd redirected the course of his life. Unlike his half sister Ethel, my father continued to travel back and forth across the color line — journeys that were often unconscious and inconsequential. As he came to be defined more and more by his intellect, the fact that he was part black became less and less important to him. By extension he made it unimportant to everyone else — or to his white friends at least.

☆   ☆   ☆

According to Flora Finkelstein, their crowd of aspiring intellectuals didn't think of my dad as a black student or a white student, just a bright one who was a talented writer. In the late 1930s, there weren't enough blacks at Brooklyn College to create anything like racial conflict. The factions of communists dominating the cafeteria were eager to demonstrate their solidarity with Negroes and would have happily embraced my father as a comrade-in-arms had they known about his background. But most people didn't know, because my father didn't tell them and they didn't guess it on their own.

"If someone came up to me in the course of my being there and said, 'Did you realize that Anatole Broyard is part black?' I would have said, 'You're crazy,'" observes Pearl Bell. "I also would have said, 'Why is this important?' [Race] just didn't have the enormous significance that it came to have later on in the sixties." The poet Harold Norse, who edited the college literary magazine and was a friend of my dad's, insists that my father couldn't have been black. "He didn't look black," Norse says. "Besides there weren't any black students at Brooklyn College back then."

Well, none who registered on Norse's radar. But among the small number at the "black" lunch table was at least one fellow who knew the details of my father's background quite well. My dad's best friend from childhood and the brunt of his teasing, Carlos deLeon, started Brooklyn College in the fall of 1938, six months after my father's trip to the social security office. When deLeon spotted my father in the cafeteria, he went up to say hello, but my father took him over to a corner and said: "I didn't tell you, but I've decided that I'm going to be white."

When I reached him by phone in Cleveland, Dr. deLeon — he became a psychiatrist and a professor at Case Western Reserve medical school — was in his late seventies. Age and health problems made his conversation difficult to follow (Dr. deLeon has since passed away), but his bitterness about this long-ago slight from his childhood friend was unmistakable. Harder to decipher was the rest of the story. Dr. deLeon also said that my father avoided him because he thought that Carlos was stupid. "But I graduated at the top of my class at medical school," he insisted. "And I have many white friends."

To gain admittance to Brooklyn College in those days, Dr. deLeon had to have been bright, but he excelled in courses like math and chemistry. He wasn't literary like my father's new pals, which may explain in part why my dad was reluctant to welcome Carlos to his lunch table. But Dr. deLeon interpreted his rejection as a judgment against his intellect — those childhood spelling games left a deep impression — and then further extrapolated that my father had reached this conclusion because Carlos was black.

That Dr. deLeon linked his racial identity to assumptions about his intelligence wasn't simply paranoia. After he graduated from medical school in 1946, deLeon was interning for a black doctor located down the block from my father's family's apartment. By this time my dad had moved to Greenwich Village, but he bumped into Carlos outside the doctor's office during a visit home. My dad said to him, "What the devil are you doing in a white coat with a stethoscope around your neck?" And Dr. deLeon answered, "Well, man, what would you think if you saw anyone else with a white coat and a stethoscope?" It was a reasonable question.

If my father believed that being black held a person back — because of the general limitations imposed on the race, such as job discrimination, or the specific ways that being black hindered a person's development, such as inferior schools and lower academic expectations — then he could feel better about avoiding a black identity himself. But African Americans who succeeded despite these obstacles forced him to rethink his equation. Was my father unwilling to claim a black identity because he simply refused to go along with the prevalent notion that blacks and whites were different in an essential way? Had the confusing racial climate of his upbringing left him feeling racially neutered? Or had he to come to believe what "they" thought about black people: that they were necessarily inferior?

Was my father's choice rooted in self-preservation or in self-hatred? Did it strike a blow for individualism or for discrimination? Was he a hero or a cad? And how did he justify his behavior to himself?

For many years my father had a recurrent dream that he was on trial for a crime that he may or may not have committed. He would never learn the nature of the accusations against him, but each time he elected to defend himself, making a speech "so moving that I could feel myself tingling with it." When the jury foreman rose to deliver the verdict, my father would feel certain of his acquittal, but he always woke before learning of his fate.

At the end of his life, my father interpreted this dream in light of his illness: "Now cancer is the crime I may or may not have committed, and the eloquence of being alive, the fervor of the survivor, is my best defense." But he never shared any prior readings, so I must draw my own conclusions about what it meant and where it came from. Of course I wonder if the guilt manifested by the dream was connected to my father's racial background. Did he feel remorseful about living among whites after being raised in a black community? Was his crime that he dared to treat his racial identity as if it were elective? Or was the accusation against him blackness itself? These racial interpretations gain currency when considered alongside the dream's parallels to Kafka's *The Trial.* The novel, which my father recognized as a great influence in his life, first appeared in English around the same time that he paid his visit to the social security office.

The Trial relates the story of Joseph K., a bank clerk who on his thirtieth birthday is charged with a crime whose nature he never learns. Joseph K.'s attempts to mount his defense keep failing amid the vast enigmatic procedures of the court, the inaccessibility of the judges, and the unknowability of his crime. He learns that "in fact, defense is not really allowed under the law, it's only tolerated, and there is even some dispute about whether the relevant parts of the law imply even that." Joseph K. can never complete his plea "because to meet an unknown accusation, not to mention other charges arising out of it, the whole of one's life would have to be passed in review, down to the smallest actions and accidents, clearly formulated and examined from every angle." At the novel's end, Joseph K. learns that he's been sentenced to death. He reflects: "The logic cannot be refuted, but someone who wants to live will not resist it. Where was the judge he'd never seen? Where was the high court he'd never reached?" He is stabbed in the heart and dies.

The mysterious enforcers behind the one-drop rule were not so unlike Kafka's invisible authorities. While a verdict of blackness in 1930s America certainly wasn't death, it could significantly diminish someone's life. And there was little chance of a person's individual merit mitigating his sentence. But the parallels between my father's situation and *The Trial* weren't just metaphorical. His racial identity was also a matter of law, the jurisprudence of which was as murky and irrational as anything that Kafka might have dreamed up.

On the day that my father was submitting his social security application, neither the U.S. government nor his birth state of Louisiana had a law on their books that defined my father as colored, according to his one-quarter of black blood (give or take an ancestor or two).

Legal definitions of blackness (which also defined whiteness by default) began appearing in southern states during the latter half of the nineteenth century as a part of their passage of antimiscegenation and segregation statutes. Equations of how much "black blood" made a person black ranged from "one drop" in North Carolina to 50 percent or more in Ohio, with the most common definition among the states being one-eighth.

Louisiana legislators passed their share of laws barring blacks and whites from marrying or sitting next to each other, but they were reluctant to define exactly what a Negro was. A 1908 act forbidding "concubinage between a person of the Caucasian or white race and a person of the Negro or black race" originally contained a clause defining a person of the "Negro race" as someone "who is as much as one thirty-second part Negro," but it was struck out at the last minute. Two years later a legal case landed in Louisiana's supreme court that hinged on the question of whether an "octoroon"—someone with one-eighth African ancestry—was a "person of the Negro or black race."

After an exhaustive survey of newspapers, encyclopedias, literary sources, and the jurisprudence of states across the country in which not one definition of Negro could be found that contained "octoroon," the court encouraged the general assembly to be more specific. Their amended act forbade concubinage between whites and a "person of the colored or black race," which didn't exactly clear up the confusion. Presumably the state's history of race-mixing explains the white lawmakers' unwillingness to specify a percentage, lest their own pedigrees not pass muster.

In the absence of any legal definition, a person's race was left in the hands of the registrars who issued the birth certificates, marriage licenses, and death certificates that determined the school a person could go to, whom he could marry, and the cemetery where he could be buried. Without any guidance from the courts, these deputies exercised an even more anarchical rule than successors such as Miss Neff in Bayou Lacombe and Naomi Drake in New Orleans, who were—so they claimed—trying to carry out the law that was eventually passed.

In my father's case, his old French name along with the facts that his family lived in a colored Creole neighborhood and that so many of their relatives were already "colored" on various records made the designation "col" on my father's birth certificate a foregone conclusion. But it wasn't until November 1938, eight months after my father's visit to the social security office, that Louisiana's supreme court finally ruled on the question of how much black blood made a person black, in a trial that involved my father's own second cousin.

If my father didn't know his cousin Verna Cassagne directly, he certainly knew about her family. Verna was three years older; her people also had ties to Bayou Lacombe, the town across Lake Pontchartrain where my father's grandmother Rosa was born and where his grandparents had a country home that he visited as a child. There, among my father's playmates, was a big group of cousins from his grandmother's side that included Verna and her younger brother. Like my dad, these children were also the great-grandchildren of Anatole Cousin, but they came from his second family—the one Anatole had with Margaret Ducré, daughter of an emancipated slave. That Verna's great-great-grandmother had been a slave would come back to haunt her.

After growing up in Lacombe, Verna's mother moved to a white neighborhood in New Orleans, married an Italian man, and raised her daughter and son as white. During her senior year in high school, Verna met an Italian boy named Cyril at a dance. The next day, when Verna got out of class, Cyril was waiting for her in his brother's yellow roadster. After dating for six months, the couple eloped to a neighboring parish and got married.

Verna and Cyril moved into an apartment on the second floor of Verna's mother's house and soon started fighting. Verna claimed that Cyril wanted to engage in "unnatural acts" and that when she refused, he beat her. Cyril claimed that his wife was a tramp. After about a year, Cyril was either kicked out or moved out—depending on who was telling the story—and Verna went to juvenile court to force him to pay alimony. After falling behind in his payments, Cyril was hauled back into court and slapped with a hefty fine. He responded by filing a countersuit to annul his marriage on the grounds that his wife was a "person of color, having a traceable amount of Negro blood." In the ensuing trial, it came out that someone had told Cyril that his wife was colored on her mother's side, and he'd gone up to Lacombe and found some people who knew her family to confirm it. In which case their marriage had never been lawful and Cyril didn't owe Verna one dime.

The legal battle between the young couple dragged on for four years. The case rested upon the racial identity of Verna's great-great-grandmother Fanny. That she'd once been a slave wasn't in contention—her emancipation papers proved that her owner (after he "took her for a wife") freed her in 1837. But Verna's lawyer argued that being a slave didn't necessarily mean that Fanny was a Negro. During Louisiana's colonial period, Indians had been enslaved too.

Fanny had died at least fifty years prior to the trial, but Cyril's lawyer managed to round up nearly two dozen residents of Lacombe—most of them mixed-race or black and in their seventies and eighties—who remembered her. They dutifully made the trip across Lake Pontchartrain to the New Orleans courthouse, but getting them to provide admissible testimony about Fanny's "real" racial identity was another story. Despite the rather bullying efforts of the lawyers and court to treat black and white as distinct and apparent, the trial's transcript makes clear the difficulty, and absurdity, of trying to retroactively sort people into categories that hadn't formerly existed.

One witness, in trying to answer a question about what Fanny was, replied that she'd been a midwife. Another witness ventured that Fanny's daughter was from "up country" when asked about her race. The lawyers ran into more confusion when trying to determine Fanny's appearance. Some witnesses remembered her hair as kinky. Others recalled that she had "tolerable fair hair hanging down on her head." Her color was described alternately as yellow, as black as the hat on a spectator's head, and "like an Indian."

Apparently no photos of Fanny could be dug up to let the court judge for itself, but the defense supplied a picture of her daughter and two granddaughters, who, it was admitted in the record, looked like white people. Cyril's attorney produced records from the health department to remind the court that in Louisiana a person's looks can be deceiving. Copies of Verna's birth certificate and the marriage licenses of two of her aunts indicated that they were colored. Although the racial designations on these documents had originally been white, the registrar's office amended them after coming across evidence of their slave ancestor Fanny. The court noted that while this practice of altering the certificates was illegal, it was persuaded by the evidence that had caused the change to be made in the first place.

In his opinion, the trial judge declared that if Verna's great-great-grandmother was an emancipated slave, she must have been "a full-blooded Negro." Ruling in favor of Cyril, he stated that although Fanny might make the defendant only one-sixteenth black, "there is nothing in our law which permits of the intermarriage of people of the white race and people with any appreciable degree of Negro blood." After two unsuccessful appeals, Louisiana's supreme court upheld the lower court's decision. Verna's marriage was annulled, she lost her right to collect alimony, and she had to pay the court expenses too. More damaging perhaps was the public nature of the trial, which meant that Verna and her mother could no longer live as white in New Orleans.

The "traceable amount" standard remained in force until 1970, when the Louisiana General Assembly amended it to one thirty-second percentage of black ancestry. Then in 1983, after a sensational trial splashed this equation (and the fact that Louisiana was the only state that continued to measure percentages of blood) across the national news, the assembly did away with definitions altogether. In the case, a woman who insisted that she'd been raised as white — and who looked white — was legally determined to be black because of an ancestor who lived 222 years earlier.

When my father read the headline LOUISIANA REPEALS BLACK BLOOD LAW in his *New York Times* over breakfast, he must have felt satisfied to see the denunciation of such draconian thinking about race. But he had reason to feel angry too. He was sixty-three by that time. The one-drop rule that was codified into law had decided his racial identity long ago, and he'd spent the majority of his life protesting the answer—an effort that had indelibly shaped him.

I often wonder how my father would have explained the way he negotiated his racial identity. His recurrent dream about being on trial suggests that he anticipated, if not feared, being called upon to offer a defense. My father could imagine no worse fate than Joseph K.'s silence at the end of *The Trial.* Encountering the two "unspeaking, uncomprehending men" who have come to execute him, Joseph K. thinks to himself that he is grateful "that it's been left up to me to say what's necessary." But when the moment comes, he can only utter, "Like a dog," to describe his fate. If my father's time ever came, he intended to be ready with a "speech so moving" that he could be sure of his acquittal.

Justifications, however, would come later. In the beginning my father's decision was rooted in practical concerns. Some months after getting his social security card, my dad went out looking for a job. There was no question that he would present himself as white. Not only was there his parents' example, but Lorraine had recently been hired at a dentist's office by passing as white. Shirley, on the other hand, had been told by the clerk of the state employment office when applying for a summer position, "Sorry, no jobs for colored girls."

My father was hired as an office clerk by a syrup manufacturer in downtown Manhattan. Between this job and his classes at Brooklyn College, my father spent more and more time among people who didn't know about his racial background. The corresponding shifts required in his behavior—subtle changes in the way he spoke; an evasiveness about his home life; indifference to racist comments—turned him into a kind of impostor, whether he felt like one or not. Was there anyplace where my father could feel authentically himself? Would it be among the middle-class blacks of Bedford-Stuyvesant? With the swashbuckling French Creoles of his mythical New Orleans? Or the Jewish intellectuals at Brooklyn College?

When he headed back to school in the fall of 1939, this question took on a greater urgency. Hitler's forces marched into Poland on September 1, and France and England declared war on Germany. It seemed only a matter of time before the United States got involved too. Significantly, the Third Reich's Nuremberg Laws, which defined full Jews as anyone with three or more "racially" Jewish grandparents and mixed Jews as anyone with at least one Jewish grandparent, mirrored the United States' attempts to measure blackness by fractions of blood.

In the college cafeteria, the conversation was always the same: blitzkriegs and nonaggression pacts, peace rallies and the possibility of a draft. But one day at the lunch table, a fellow named Chester Kallman changed the subject. He told the rest of them about hanging out in Greenwich Village with his new friend Wystan. Those who'd heard the rumors knew that Chester meant the poet W. H. Auden, with whom he'd recently become lovers.

Chester shared stories about drinking and arguing aesthetics with the likes of Stephen Spender, Louis MacNeice, and the editors of the *Partisan Review,* the magazine that served as literary manifesto for my father and his friends. In the Village bars and cafés, men traded lines of poetry in verbal duels, sometimes coming to actual blows, defending the honor of their favorite writers. There were midnight jaunts up to Harlem to hear jazz, secret nightclubs where you had to know a password to get in, parties where men and women who had just met retired to a bedroom to get better acquainted.

Although Chester's audience was made up of aspiring writers, it didn't occur to most of them that they might lead this life too. The New York intellectual Norman Podhoretz, who grew up in Brownsville in the 1930s, began his memoir *Making It* by observing that "one of the longest journeys in the world is the journey from Brooklyn to Manhattan." How could these young men and women forgo the tidy lives that their parents had planned for them? How could they leave behind their neighborhoods and families, especially now when their counterparts in Europe were coming under siege? They seemed doomed to experience Chester's life the same way that they gained so many life experiences — vicariously, through stories.

But from one end of the table, my father spoke up. He'd been listening to Chester the most closely of them all — asking questions, planning strategies, making calculations. Now he told his friends that he'd made a decision. In a voice whose timbre took the full measure of his being, he announced that he was going to move to Greenwich Village.

-30-

During the first half of the twentieth century, Greenwich Village became a haven for writers and artists. With Midtown executives and Wall Street bankers to the north and south, and New Jersey factory workers and Brooklyn shopkeepers to one side and the other, that square mile in lower Manhattan provided refuge from the daily grind of dollars and cents. As my dad's friend Milton Klonsky put it, "The Village, with its unpredictably digressive streets and twisting free-associational byways, was divided from the straight and square-away world uptown like the ego from the id."

In the Village, a cold-water flat could be had cheaply. Barkeepers let a person sit for as long as he could nurse a beer. A ten-cent plate of spaghetti and meatballs from the Waldorf Cafeteria on Sixth Avenue could fend off hunger for most of the day. Among the artists and writers who hung out in the San Remo Bar, the Cedar Bar, and the Minetta and White Horse taverns, conversation was the only currency that mattered.

Nobody cared where a person was from; nobody asked about your family. They wanted to know what you thought — about Freud, Surrealism, the Modernists. Had you been to Paris?...Were you in analysis?...What did you make of the Stevens poem in the latest *Partisan Review?* Everyone in the Village had run away — from conventional backgrounds and burdensome family histories, from petty lives short on grandeur and futures that would leave them as normal and discontented as everyone else. It was in Greenwich Village that my father could figure out the person he most felt himself to be.

It would be a while, however, before he made it across the river. The same fall that Hitler invaded Poland, my father dropped out of Brooklyn College, explaining to his friend Vincent Livelli: "It doesn't coincide with my frame of mind." The college administrators may also have encouraged him to leave. His grades had never risen above Cs and Ds (except for one B in Hygiene). Vincent doesn't remember ever seeing him carrying books or studying. "I don't think he was very serious about college," he says. But my father continued to hang around the campus in his spare time, and one day he noticed a pretty girl and struck up a conversation with her. Her name was Aida Sanchez and she was Puerto Rican, which made her almost as much of an outsider at Brooklyn College as he was. Before long Aida replaced Flora as my father's constant companion.

While today there's much cross-pollination—cultural and otherwise—between Puerto Ricans and African Americans, that wasn't the case in 1940. The Puerto Rican migration to the United States had barely begun, and the new immigrants didn't tend to settle in black neighborhoods. Shirley says that her parents didn't know what to make of Aida when Bud brought her home for dinner, figuring only that she was an extension of his obsession with Latin music. But in fact Aida's family and the Broyards had more in common than any of them realized.

Like that of New Orleans, Puerto Rican society during the eighteenth and nineteenth centuries was characterized by three distinct racial groups: whites, slaves, and free people of color (which included the native Indian population), with much blurring of the boundaries between them. As a result the majority of Puerto Ricans were mixed, but the absence of Jim Crow laws meant that black and white identity had never been measured in blood as in the United States. Class dictated a person's side of the color line.

In the United States, Puerto Ricans, and Hispanics in general, remained outside the one-drop standard applied to mixed-race African Americans. For example, up until 1960, census enumerators were instructed to record mixed white and black people as Negroes no matter how small the black component. Hispanics, on the other hand, were generally classified as white unless their appearance was too black for the enumerator to ignore.

For my father's friends in Bed-Stuy, his decision to marry Aida marked the beginning of his living as a white man. Indeed, both he and Aida described themselves as white on their marriage license. When I track down Aida in a nursing home in Los Angeles, she says that my father wasn't being dishonest. She describes the pale skin and wavy hair of her former in-laws, insisting that there was very little black in the Broyard family. Aida has a daughter with my father, which might explain her reluctance to acknowledge his African ancestry. Also, by the standards in the Puerto Rican community, my father *was* white.

My father used to say that he married Aida because with the war around the corner, everyone was getting married to have someone to write home to. Shirley suspects that her brother may have also wed and impregnated his wife as a way of avoiding going to war altogether. When I ask Flora Finkelstein what she made of my father's decision to marry Aida, she says simply, "Well, she was very beautiful." Aida was vibrant, smart, and fun too. But it's also true that marrying a Puerto Rican woman was a way for my father to postpone committing to a specific racial identity. For a mixed-race person, the choice of a mate is often viewed as an indication of the world—black or white—in which a person locates him- or herself. Whenever I tell my aunt Shirley I'm dating someone new, she asks about the fellow's race. I imagine that an answer of black would convince her that I'd truly embraced my African American heritage.

While Aida defended my father's subversion of his racial identity, she wasn't so happy about the rest of his unconventional behavior. After finding them a cold-water flat on Gay Street in Greenwich Village, he painted a love poem that he'd written to Aida on the bedroom door, but on most nights, he could be found out dancing with another girl in his arms. During the daylight hours, when he wasn't working, he spent his free time studying art at the New School, browsing the bookshops along Eighth Street, or arguing the relative merits of Baudelaire and Mallarmé in a café. Six months after the couple wed, the Japanese attacked Pearl Harbor and the United States entered the war. It wouldn't be long before my father was drafted, and he didn't intend to spend what little time he had in the Village staying home with his new bride.

After Aida became pregnant, the couple moved in with my father's parents to await his orders to ship out. Six months before their daughter was born, my dad headed off to basic training at Camp Edwards in Massachusetts, as a white man. By then checking off that box was getting to be old hat. Or perhaps, as happened with his buddy Harold down the block, the clerk at the draft board simply looked at him and marked him as white without my father having said a word. As a white man with some college, he was tapped for officer training school, and in a twist of fate that would help to set his course on his return, my father was placed in the command of a Negro stevedore company.

More than I million African Americans served during World War II, but they were segregated from their white counterparts for much of the war. Overwhelmingly, black servicemen were assigned to noncombat roles: they cooked meals, drove trucks, and loaded and unloaded ships, like the men in my father's company. Aside from the famed Tuskegee Airmen, few units saw any action.

In the war stories that my father occasionally told, he would mention that he'd commanded black troops. One time I asked him why—I had the sense that the assignment was unusual—and he said that his senior officers must have figured that as a city boy, he was better able to understand them. Ironically, this answer may not have been so far from the truth.

A few black units had black officers, but the majority were led by white men. Part of the problem was logistical: at the beginning of the war, there weren't enough existing Negro officers to supply the necessary command—only five in the army in 1940, three of whom were chaplains. The military also had a longstanding bias that blacks didn't make good leaders. But the War Department soon discovered that white officers didn't effectively lead black troops either.

Initially the department followed a policy of tapping white southerners to command black units, with the rationale that these men had more experience with the race. Not surprisingly, many of these white officers resented being assigned to a Negro unit. Not only did maintaining segregation impose extra duties, but discrimination in the world at large meant that black soldiers entered service with less education and technical preparation than their white counterparts, which made training them more difficult. And then some white officers were simply prejudiced. Fairly typical was the opinion expressed by this commander when writing to a friend that black soldiers "are for the most part afraid and the few smart ones have no desire to fight." Another officer seeking transfer to a white unit described his "disgust for [black soldiers'] inherent slovenliness, and their extreme indolence, indifference and frequent subtle insolence." Of course, these attitudes didn't exactly encourage confidence in their leadership among the black soldiers. Neither did the constant turnover, from all the white officers who managed to get themselves reassigned.

By 1942 the War Department realized that morale in the black units was abysmal and set about trying to improve the caliber of their commanders. When my father was assigned to the 167th Port Company in Noumea, New Caledonia, in March 1945, the department had implemented standards for officers of Negro units. They were supposed to possess demonstrated leadership ability, along with evidence of maturity and patience. Efforts were made to ascertain whether an officer would be amenable to working with black troops, either through personal interviews or by reviewing the candidate's personnel file. For the previous three years, my father had been a drill instructor stateside and then a troop commander for an antiaircraft unit stationed in New Guinea. This experience, along with the fact that he'd grown up in New York City—perhaps he even mentioned living in a mixed neighborhood—apparently qualified him for the assignment.

The French colony of New Caledonia, after throwing off Vichy rule early in the war, became a staging area for American operations in the South Pacific. My father was hardly off the boat before he began trying to chat up some of the native women who were hanging around the dock, quoting lines in French from Baudelaire. To the amusement of his new fellow officers, these women, who were mostly prostitutes, burst into laughter, and my father's nickname Frenchy was born. The long workday didn't leave much time for extracurricular activities. My father and the other lieutenants served ten-hour shifts, overseeing the crews of black stevedores as they loaded and unloaded ships.

Two of my father's fellow officers remember my dad having some trouble getting the black soldiers to take his orders. Normally the company was run like a combat unit, with orders passed down through the chain of command. When an officer wanted a ship unloaded or a truck moved, he relayed instructions to a sergeant, all of whom were black, who then got the enlisted men to execute the order. This system, explains Edward Howard, who was a second lieutenant like my father, limited opportunities for the noncoms to regale the commanders with their complaints. "Because as long as they were talking, they weren't working," says Howard. Receiving orders from other blacks also helped to keep the morale high. Ellis Derry, who'd been a first lieutenant in the 167th, tells me that not all companies ran as smoothly. In another port company, the white officers were forced to go around armed.

One day not long after my father arrived, First Lieutenant Derry received word that the men had gone on strike and were refusing to work. When Derry arrived at the dock, he found all the stevedores hanging around on top of the ship and the new officer, Second Lieutenant Broyard, leaning on the gunnels alongside them.

Derry approached one of the black sergeants and asked him if he was planning on working that day. The sergeant had to say yes or risk being court-martialed. When Derry told him to get into the hold, the sergeant tried to protest that no one else was down there, and Derry said, "I didn't ask you if there was anyone else there or not, I told you to go to work." The sergeant went into the hold, and after a moment the rest of his men followed.

Derry attributes this episode to my father's inexperience in commanding black troops. But I wonder. It hadn't been so long ago that my father was being chased through his neighborhood by gangs of darker-skinned boys. Some of his men may even have suspected his black ancestry—his curly hair and tawny skin, a certain ease my father had around blacks, or his slightly "pimp roll" style of walking—which could lead them to make subtle challenges. It's possible too that my dad heard out their complaints because he knew firsthand that blacks received a bad deal and he felt compassionate toward them. Unfortunately I haven't been able to track down any of the soldiers who were under my dad. The records for individual military units only contain the names of officers, and, unlike many whites who served in World War II, the stevedores weren't inspired by their experiences to hold regular reunions.

For African Americans who didn't grow up under Jim Crow, military service was often their first experience with formalized segregation.

During his time with the 167th, my father had a chance to witness such humiliations up close. He would have heard the kinds of remarks that whites felt free to make when blacks weren't around. He would have seen black soldiers barred from entering USO clubs by armed white soldiers. While his fellow officers in the 167th seem to have genuinely respected their black enlisted men, there was no getting around the fact that simply because of their race, the whites gave the orders while the blacks sweated in the ships' hold beneath them.

Novels about racial passing often feature a pivotal scene where the light-skinned protagonist witnesses some mistreatment of blacks that convinces him or her to cross to the other side. In James Weldon Johnson's *The Autobiography of an Ex–Coloured Man,* the narrator decides after watching a lynching that he will never again identify with a group of people who could be treated worse than animals with impunity. I wonder if my father saw something during his time with the 167th that helped him make up his mind about how he would live his life when he returned to New York.

Was he there on that scorching day when the men were unloading a freighter that was anchored offshore? At break time the black men headed for the ship's water fountain—they'd been working for four hours in a hot, cramped hold—where they were met by a white crewman armed with a loaded pistol. Ignoring the demands of the presiding officer, the man prevented the stevedores from getting a drink for hours, until the Coast Guard finally arrived to arrest him.

There was also the story that my father told about the black soldier who suddenly went crazy and slashed open another enlisted man's belly with a jungle knife. The perpetrator fled into the woods, with my dad—so he told my brother and me—right behind him, in hopes of reaching the deranged man and convincing him to give himself up before the white guards got to him. As my father ran through the forest, did the shouts of "catch that crazy nigger" make him fear for his own life? I have no way of knowing.

*   *   *

While my father's service in the army probably made him feel more distanced from blacks than ever, I suspect that it left him mostly determined to live outside a world where roles were predicated on race, because he didn't necessarily draw any closer to white soldiers. He told another story about sitting on the ship's deck very early one morning during a transpacific crossing. With his arms hugged around his knees, he stared onto the ocean, adrift in the loneliness of being surrounded by a thousand strangers. A shipmate walking by commented, "Feeling anthropomorphic this morning?" My father nearly jumped up and hugged him—he was so grateful for someone who could recognize his "existential absurdity." (He discovered later that the guy was being discharged on a Section Eight; he was considered crazy.) But for the most part, my father didn't know anyone who could remind him of the person he'd been at home.

Instead he had a collection of poetry by Wallace Stevens. One night while standing watch on the dock in Yokohama, my father began reciting all the lines he could remember — "The windy sky cries out a literate despair," "These days of disinheritance we feast on human heads"—and the idea suddenly hit him that when he returned stateside, he'd move back to Greenwich Village and open a bookstore.

The question of what he would do had suddenly become real. It was the fall of 1945; the United States had dropped the atom bomb on Hiroshima and Nagasaki, and Japan had surrendered. In Yokohama the weather had turned cold, and much of the city was bombed into rubble. The Japanese who were left wandered the streets, their remaining possessions tied to their backs in filthy blankets.

As my father watched his men unload pallets of milk, he pictured a secondhand bookstore, specializing in twentieth-century literature. The idea made him feel warm, and he took his hands from his pockets and squeezed them. In a few months he would be back at his parents' apartment in Bedford-Stuyvesant, biding his time until the rest of his life began.

*   *   *

The Broyards' household had changed since my dad went overseas. Aida, who had been living with Nat and Edna, moved out, taking her and my father's baby daughter with her, after intercepting some love letters from an American nurse that had beaten my father home on a different Liberty ship. She might have forgiven him if he hadn't been so determined to open the bookstore. Aida wanted her husband to get a job in an office, with a dependable salary. "I loved Anatole," Aida tells me, "but my mother convinced me that I would never be happy with him." The couple filed for divorce a few months later. (In a few years, Aida would remarry and move to Texas, where her daughter would grow up calling a different man father and never meet her biological father's second family.) In the meantime Shirley and her new husband, a young NAACP lawyer named Franklin Williams, had moved into the apartment upstairs.

My dad spent his days canvassing Greenwich Village for a place to live and a space to open his bookstore. Vacancy rates hovered near zero immediately following the war, making an affordable rent hard to find. At night he was back in class at the New School. But on the weekends, he joined his family for dinner. Shirley says that she doesn't remember anything unusual about those meals, but I can't imagine that conversation came easily.

My father and his brother-in-law actually had a lot in common. Both men were bright and handsome, which made them a little arrogant, and they could be extremely charming. Each thought of himself as special—someone for whom the regular rules didn't apply. My father and Frank even looked a bit alike, with the same close-cropped hair, tall forehead, and deep, penetrating eyes.

Frank also grew up among middle-class blacks. He lived in a big brick house in Flushing, Queens, that belonged to his uncle, the first black doctor in the borough. Frank was raised mostly by his grandmother, who was very light-skinned and looked more American Indian than African American, which initially confused him about his family's identity. He used to tell a story from grade school about the

time that the teacher asked all the students about their background. One kid said that he was Irish from Ireland; another answered that he was Polish from Poland. When it was Frank's turn, he said that he was an Indian from Indianapolis, which was his grandmother's hometown.

By the time Frank met Shirley, however, he knew exactly who he was: a black man who was dedicated to the betterment of his race. And he couldn't understand how any thinking African American wouldn't feel the same way.

Frank and Shirley had been living upstairs from the Broyards for a year and a half when my father returned from the war. By this time Frank had grown used to the family's ambivalence about their racial identity. He knew that his father-in-law didn't approve of him, because Frank was too dark and too insistent about being a black man. Because Nat had spent his first thirty-eight years in the South, Frank might have overlooked some of his father-in-law's old-fashioned attitudes, but Shirley's brother didn't have that excuse.

I can imagine the scene of my father's arrival home. In his letters he has complained to his parents about ruining his teeth from a diet of candy because he couldn't stand the army food. Edna has spent the morning in the kitchen, where she prepares all his favorite dishes: roast chicken, mashed sweet potatoes, string beans, and fried banana fritters for dessert. Nat picks up some Rheingold beer and a copy of the *New York Times.*

Frank knows from Shirley that Bud served in the army as a white man. But he's also heard about his brother-in-law's sophisticated taste in literature, his love of jazz and French films, and his skill on the dance floor. Bud has stirred this family from its somnambulistic existence, and Frank can't resist getting caught up in the excitement of the return of the prodigal son.

Everyone admires how handsome my father looks in his officer's uniform, although Edna insists that he's grown too skinny. In Bedford-Stuyvesant, there are a lot of young men in uniform, but not too many with officer's insignia on their sleeves.

When Bud sees the spread of food, he teases his mother that she's made enough to feed the entire army. And he adds how if only *she'd* been cooking for them, they'd have won the war long ago. Edna hugs Bud again before scurrying back to the kitchen. Shirley introduces Frank, and the two men shake hands with a decisive grip, as if they are boxers greeting each other before the opening bell. Nat opens a beer for Bud and offers a toast to "the veteran."

Over dinner my father tells his war stories. The one about taking a ride in a fighter with a friend and coming upon a Japanese warship. Seated in the bomber's position, he razed the deck with machine-gun fire. He tells them how the men looked like ants swarming the ship, which made it easier to squeeze the trigger. And then there's the story about the crazy guy who slashed open the stomach of another stevedore, and how the victim caught his guts as they fell out into his hands. Maybe Shirley or Edna objects that this isn't dinner table conversation, but my father goes on, explaining how after the soldier was sewn up and the wound was healed, the doctor removed the bandage, taking the man's belly button with it. My father laughs a little condescendingly, recalling that the soldier had become hysterical and wouldn't calm down until the doctor promised to reattach it. My father subtly indicates the stevedores' race by imitating their voices or mentioning a detail about hailing from rural Georgia. Frank watches his brother-in-law for some recognition that he also has roots in an African American community, but my father gives away nothing.

Frank also has some war stories he could tell. He might start with his arrival with some white friends at Fort Dix for basic training, where he was separated from them and made to line up with the other black soldiers. It was his first experience with formalized segregation, and from then on Frank could sense his white friends' acceptance of the new racial order. He could have told his wife's family how he arrived at his camp in Arizona to find that the black soldiers had to sleep in tents, while the white men were housed in barracks. After a few weeks of marching in circles and cleaning toilets, he realized that the fort was nothing more than a holding pen. The officers, all white southerners according to army policy, had no intention of letting the black men fight, lest proving themselves on the battlefield might lead them to expect equal treatment at home. But this kind of talk — political, indignant, racial — wouldn't be welcome at the Broyard table.

At the end of Frank's life, Enid Gort, a colleague and close friend, recorded his oral history in preparation for writing his biography. She tells me that Frank gave her the impression that he could pick up the phone and call his brother-in-law anytime he wanted, but because Anatole wasn't interested in civil rights, they had nothing to talk about. "There was a lot of tension there too," adds Enid, "that started with a sort of unspoken competition when they were young." I can imagine Frank silently fuming at the dinner table as he watched my father receive the hero's welcome befitting a returning first lieutenant — all because he'd passed as white. (In the war stories he told my brother and me, my father returned home with a captain's rank, another example of his bending the truth.)

If my father felt embarrassed or self-conscious in front of Frank, he didn't show it. During their rare interactions, he was always friendly with his brother-in-law, but in private he referred to him as a "professional Negro." Had they ever discussed their views on the race question, the men might have agreed that blacks shouldn't accept being treated as inferior. But unlike my dad, Frank didn't have the choice to opt out. He had to try to change the system instead.

During the three years that my father was stationed overseas or on the West Coast, his childhood neighborhood had deteriorated significantly. In 1944 the health districts were redrawn, and Central Brooklyn officially became Bedford-Stuyvesant. A few years later, the *Brooklyn Eagle* sealed the neighborhood's fate as the bastard child of the borough with its declaration that Bedford-Stuyvesant was "one big, continuous slum, largely populated by Negroes."

The decline of the neighborhood gave my father one more reason to escape. After months of searching for a place in Greenwich Village, he finally met a woman at a party who told him that she had two adjacent apartments in a tenement building on Jones Street, and that one of them might be available. The woman, Sheri Martinelli, was an abstract painter and a protégée of Anaïs Nin's. The next day, when my father went to see the apartment, he found it jammed full, with an old printing press and piles of canvases, half-empty boxes, and clothes. Confused, he turned to Sheri and asked if the apartment was available. The way she smiled at his question led him to understand exactly what she was offering. "I'll take it," he said, meaning, of course, that he'd take her.

My father went home, packed his things, and kissed his parents good-bye. They didn't know what to say. Since he'd returned from the army, Nat and Edna had been treating him differently — calling him Anatole instead of Bud, asking no questions as he came and went at odd hours. When he told them he was moving out, they simply said, "You're a veteran now," as if his war experience had turned him into a stranger. As his taxi pulled away, Nat and Edna stood waving on the curb. Although he was only moving across the East River, a sense of finality marked the occasion. Nothing had been said out loud, but everyone understood that my father was embarking on a new life. His parents must have wondered if that meant that he, like his half sister Ethel, would disappear from their lives forever.

Living in Greenwich Village was everything my father dreamed it might be during those nights standing watch in the South Seas. The GI Bill provided a small stipend and paid for his classes in modern art and psychology at the New School. And Sheri gave him the chance to apply his professors' abstract theories about avant-gardism and neuroses firsthand. He later wrote that she required a process of continual adjustment, "like living in a foreign city."

Sheri was unlike anyone my father had ever known. Dressed in dirndl skirts (to hide her heavy thighs) and no underwear (to my father's consternation), she had a wide tall forehead, large pale blue eyes set under high arched brows, and a thin pointed chin. Among the piles of unopened mail that covered the ironing board perpetually set up in her kitchen were unopened checks for lingerie spreads she'd done for *Vogue* magazine. In a voice that placed equal emphasis on each syllable, as if she were speaking an unfamiliar language, Sheri offered her pronouncements: she didn't trust what she read in books, she wasn't interested in having orgasms, my father would never be a man as long as he expected to understand everything.

Sheri liked to create mysteries. Not long after they moved in together, two different friends of my father's came over to tell him that they were better matches for her than he was. After the second one, he realized that Sheri had put them up to it. Then she announced that a doctor had diagnosed her as having a defective heart and that she

could no longer climb stairs.
For the next few months, anytime they visited friends (who
all seemed to live in top-floor
apartments, which were cheaper
and offered the painters more
light), my father dutifully carried her up the five flights. He
later realized that she'd made
up the condition. Even as he

loved her, he secretly believed that she was weird, while he worried
that she thought he was too conventional.

Yet they had things in common. Sheri had also left behind a failed
marriage and young daughter. Her mother was born in New Orleans,
so there was no need for my father to explain his Creole identity. And
they were both drawn to the new trends in art and culture. Sheri introduced my dad to Anaïs Nin, who later described him in her diary
as "New Orleans French, handsome, sensual, ironic." The couple
passed their evenings with friends at the San Remo bar—derided by
one poet as "the restlessly crowded hangout...and catch-all for whatever survived of dedicated Bohemianism in Greenwich Village."

Before long my father found an old junk dealer's shop on Cornelia
Street for his bookstore. After clearing out all the old boilers, pipes,
and radiators, Nat helped him to make bookshelves for the front
room. But my dad never had enough stock to fill them, and the few
dozen copies of Kafka, Céline, Kenneth Burke, Paul Valéry, and
García Lorca that made up his selection sat on a table near the door.

Customers were few. Most of the serious readers in the Village already had more books than money, and my father tended to dissuade
the nonserious readers who wandered in from buying books that he
considered above them. He wasn't being protective of potential clients
but of authors. It would be a betrayal of his literary heroes to allow

them to be read by someone who might not appreciate or understand them.

While the bookstore was a financial failure and my father would eventually be forced to close it, it served as a hangout for the writers and intellectuals in the neighborhood. My father and his visitors would sit around a large potbellied stove in the back and talk. There were his friends from Brooklyn College Milton Klonsky and Vincent Livelli; the writers William Gaddis and Chandler Brossard (both of whom would later publish romans à clef negatively portraying my father); and art students such as Larry Rivers from Hans Hofmann's Expressionist classes down the street. After hours, on a mattress pushed into the corner, there were clandestine visits from a parade of different girls.

If it weren't for books, my father later observed, the young men of his crowd would have been completely at the mercy of sex. Books gave them balance, gravity, something else to fill the waking hours. But literature wasn't just a diversion from the corporeal pleasures of the real world; in some ways it comprised the real world. My father and his friends didn't know where books stopped and they began. My dad's favorite writers became his adopted family. "With them, I could trade in my embarrassingly ordinary history for a choice of fictions. I could lead a hypothetical life, unencumbered by memory, loyalties, or resentments."

It was a project he took very seriously. Vincent Livelli recalls my dad's rehearsing his observations about a painter or memorizing lines of poetry to insert into dinner conversation at the San Remo later that evening. Together Vincent and my dad worked out a strategy to ensure that they controlled the topic of the conversation, so as to benefit from their prepping. Vincent might bring up the novel *Tropic of Cancer*, which would lead my father to mention Baudelaire's influence on Henry Miller, spouting a few lines from the poet and Miller's prose to make his point.

Because Vincent wasn't as intellectually inclined as the other young men, he welcomed this advantage. For my dad conversation was a sport and required training to be competitive like any other. Even with his best friend from college, Milton Klonsky—to whom he remained unceasingly loyal, even as Milton grew increasingly difficult and hermetic and lost most of his friends—my dad would try to verbally pin him to the floor. And Klonsky was no lightweight opponent. As he later said of himself: "I'm famous, not so much for what I've written...as for the cyclotron of my personality." His literary contributions were limited to a few volumes on William Blake, but his intelligence was legendary.

I recognize my father's conversational style from my own family dinner table: his refusal to give up center stage, impatience with topics that he didn't know anything about, and aggressive tactics even when he was clearly on top. Sometimes when I was in the middle of a story, he would interrupt me with such little regard that I would doubt for a moment that I'd been speaking at all. When I protested, he would silence me with the complaint that I was being "boring"—the worst imaginable crime.

It's tempting to blame this behavior on those nights at the San Remo. My dad, with his hangover of black intellectual inferiority, when seated among the other men—who were mostly Jewish and assumed by him to be naturally bright and analytical—turned into the runt of the litter, forced to bite and kick his way to the teat. But it's just as likely that my father was simply as competitive as the next guy: determined to win the argument, get the girl, earn the others' admiration at any cost.

In some ways he never gave up his compulsion to be the most charming person in the room. Yet when my father was in his twenties, the figure he cut in the world was more than just a means to an end. It was all he had. Like an orphan who must make his way on his wits alone, my father no longer had family or community to fall back on. He literally dined off the strength of his personality, and it paid off.

After a few years in Greenwich Village, writers and painters were crowding around the booth that the bouncer saved for him at the San Remo. From his job giving poetry lessons to a crazy millionaire, my dad always had money to buy a round or pick up dinner. Cover girls and daughters of famous men appeared on his arm at parties and later joined him in bed. Jay Landesman, the editor of the short-lived but influential magazine *Neurotica*, remembers the girl from the Midwest who hated Greenwich Village and kept complaining that she wanted to go home. "Someone finally asked her why she didn't leave already," Jay says. "And she said that she wouldn't leave until Anatole spoke to her." And most significantly for my father, the editors of those magazines that he'd read so religiously in college—*Partisan Review* and *Commentary*—began to publish his writing. This life was a long way from his upbringing as a colored boy in Brooklyn. Ironically, it was his knowledge of that world that helped him to secure his reputation.

Greenwich Village had long been a place where people fled to make themselves over, but the postwar years were a particularly good time for reinvention. The New York intellectuals who crowded the neighborhood's apartments and cafés had become disillusioned with their political idealism in the wake of the Hitler-Stalin pact of 1939. While use of the atomic bomb had abruptly ended a conflict that they expected to drag on for decades, the Soviet Union's development of nuclear technology meant they now had to live with the knowledge that they could be extinguished in an instant. Add to that the dawning horror of Hitler's Holocaust, and the world had become a much more serious place. Nobody knew what to believe in anymore.

In the classes that my father was taking at the New School, all the professors—many of them Jewish exiles from Germany—focused on what was wrong: with the world, with America, with the relationships between people. The very dependability of reality was called into question. The art critic Meyer Schapiro demonstrated how Picasso in *Les Demoiselles d'Avignon* had fractured the picture plane. At the

Cedar Tavern, the burgeoning group of Abstract Expressionists talked about ridding the canvas of any verisimilitude and focusing on the action of making the painting itself. French existentialism, by way of translations of Sartre and Camus in the *Partisan Review*, landed on the Village's newsstands. Understood originally as more an emotional response to the war in Europe than a formal philosophy, existentialism's emphasis on individual freedom and absurdity appealed to the prevailing zeitgeist. As Irving Howe, a contributor to the *Partisan Review* in the early cold war years, observed, "Ideology crumbled, personality bloomed."

Onto this unexplored frontier a new cultural hero appeared—the hipster. Famously portrayed by Norman Mailer in his 1957 essay "The White Negro," this latest incarnation of the American individualist rejected all pressures to conform, ignored society's expectations and traditions, and lived only for the moment and according to the "rebellious imperatives of the self." Found in New Orleans, San Francisco, Chicago, and especially Greenwich Village, Mailer's hipster took inspiration from "Negroes," particularly those associated with jazz. Although the hipster was a fleeting phenomenon—subsumed by the end of the 1950s by the Beats—he was crucial in cementing the link between counterculture and African American communities.

Mailer's essay may have preserved the hipster for posterity, but he wasn't the first or only person to note his arrival on the Village scene. Nine years earlier, in 1948, my father described the hipster's aesthetics in the *Partisan Review* in an essay titled "Portrait of the Hipster." He was twenty-eight years old at the time, and the piece—his second publication after a short book review—was his attempt to establish himself among the Village intellectuals. The poet Delmore Schwartz, who was working as an editor at the magazine, gave him the assignment. He knew my dad through Milton Klonsky, who almost certainly shared with Schwartz why Anatole Broyard was particularly suited to this topic.

Indeed my father portrayed the hipster's hero—the black jazz character who hung out at the Savoy Ballroom—with a scientific specificity that only an insider could know: the thirty-one-inch pant leg of his zoot suit and the two-and-seventh-eighths-inch brim of his hat; the white powder streak he wore in his hair and the Ray-Ban sunglasses that perpetually covered his eyes; his secret handshake of brushing palms and preferred greeting of a raised index finger; and the shorthand of his jive speech. *Solid* "connoted the stuff, the reality of existence"; *nowhere,* "the hipster's favorite pejorative, was an abracadabra to make things disappear"; and *in there* "was, of course, somewhereness," which was the place the hipster longed to be.

But it was into the hipster's existential crisis that my father demonstrated the most insight. The hipster's status, "always of the minority—opposed in race or feeling to those who owned the machinery of recognition," made him especially anxious to relate to the world in a socially acceptable, meaningful way. Yet the alienated position into which he was born or had found himself made such acceptance nearly impossible. My father suggested in an early draft that the hipster "became a criminal because he was not allowed to become a citizen."

My dad's recent change in circumstances offered him a front-row seat to observe the black model for the hipster. He and Sheri had broken up, and when he couldn't find another apartment, he was forced to move back to Bed-Stuy and live with his parents. During his jaunts to the dance halls of Harlem with his childhood friends, he became an undercover anthropologist, making observations and collecting the data that would help him make his name back on the island of Manhattan.

Soon after the essay appeared, my father ran into Delmore Schwartz in the San Remo bar. Sitting with him were Clement Greenberg, the leading proponent of Abstract Expressionism, and Dwight Macdonald, a famous communist and critic of American culture. The men were talking about the "primitive"—Picasso and Hemingway, bullfighting and boxing—and they invited my father to join them.

He sat down reluctantly, worried that his hipster piece would typecast him as "an aficionado of the primitive." He wanted to be a literary man like them. Yet he couldn't resist showing off his knowledge of the city's rawer pleasures.

He told Delmore and his friends about visiting the Park Plaza, a club in Spanish Harlem where a man nicknamed Midnight, for the color of his skin, and another called Electrico, for the speed of his feet, engaged in acrobatic face-offs for the unofficial title of best dancer. At another club he watched a group of men stomp to death a stranger who had tried to gain free entry by wielding a knife. Afterward the men wiped the blood from their shoes with their handkerchiefs before returning to the dance floor. His stories whetted the intellectuals' appetites. They wanted to see the primitive for themselves. My father suggested that they go to the Park Plaza that very evening; he hailed a cab and they headed uptown.

My father later wrote that although he admired the New York intellectuals for their talent for "high abstraction" and ability to "see life from a great height," he also pitied them for losing touch with the "raw data of actuality." Because they'd read themselves right out of American culture, these writers needed people like my father to show them around. But I'm surprised at my dad's eagerness to play along. In his *Partisan Review* essay, he scorns the hipster for becoming the darling of the Village intellectuals, who hailed him as the "great instinctual man" and demanded that he interpret the world for them. My father notes that recognition by the literary establishment gave the Negro hipster real somewhereness at last and subsequently ruined him: "His old subversiveness, his ferocity, was now so manifestly rhetorical as to be obviously harmless....He let himself be bought and placed in the zoo."

But how was my father's willingness to pimp some Harlem primitive for Delmore and his friends any different? He even found them girls to dance with. Having cast himself as native tour guide, he looked upon the men's inability to mix with the locals with the con-

tempt of the colonized. Only Dwight Macdonald, "a permanent revolutionary," seemed at home.

Yet my father persisted in acting as a bridge between the uptown
(black) world and the (white intellectual) Village. He started to bring
a group of disciples up to Spanish Harlem every Thursday night. He
continued to write about the jazz world, Afro-Cuban music, and the
sexuality of dancing—none of which were typical subject matter for
the average white intellectual. (Milton "Mezz" Mezzrow, a Jewish
jazz clarinetist, was often described as passing for black after embracing the music and culture.) And my father didn't shy away from
"primitive" pastimes, even working out with George Brown, the boxing coach who was reputed to have trained Hemingway. While in
hindsight it might seem that my father was exploiting his access to the
black world for his own personal gain, I think he might have argued
that he was simply being himself and wasn't inclined to accommodate
his interests to those of the white intellectuals around him.

As it was, most everyone in his circle already knew about his mixed-
race ancestry. The writer Herbert Gold, who lived in Greenwich Village then, says that it was the first thing you heard about Anatole
Broyard. (Gold, who has written many fiction and nonfiction works,
described my dad as "his spade friend, Leroy" in his fictionalized
memoir about those years, causing a rift in their friendship.) *Neurotica*
editor Jay Landesman concurs: "Everyone knew Anatole was a Negro.
He didn't deny it in any way. He didn't affirm it either."

The novelist Anne Bernays dated my father in the early 1950s.
She'd been forewarned by Milton Klonsky's girlfriend, who introduced them, that Anatole was black although he looked white. After
learning that Anne's father, Edward Bernays (who is often described
as the father of public relations), was handling the PR for the
NAACP, my dad volunteered that his brother-in-law also worked for
the organization. Otherwise he rarely mentioned his background. For
Anne's parents the fact that my father was "downtown" worried them

as much as his racial identity. Not only might he give their daughter a black baby, but he wouldn't be able to support her and the child either. Anne, however, was more concerned with reading all the books that my father gave her and coming up with intelligent things to say about them over dinner.

Of the ten women I spoke with who dated my father during the forties and fifties, all but one were aware of his racial identity—learning it either from someone else or from my father himself. Among my father's correspondence, there is one terse note from a girl he'd recently dumped who reveals that she'd learned from a mutual friend that my dad was "partly colored." She writes that she was sorry that my father didn't trust her enough to tell her himself. But the rest of his old girlfriends, all of whom were white, insist that his racial identity made no difference to them.

Of course these women had styled themselves as rule breakers by moving to the Village and taking up with one of its more notorious denizens. Dating across the color line was just another way of bucking convention. But since my father neither looked nor identified as black, there wasn't much risk of public censure. The women could be daring and modern without being truly radical. Even in this bohemian haven, interracial couples still attracted the ire of passersby on the street. In public, blacks and whites kept mostly to themselves.

On many nights the writer James Baldwin and the artist Beauford Delaney, both African American, could be found at their own booth at the San Remo. And they might have been joined on occasion by Delaney's good friend W. F. Lucas, also black, who happened to have grown up with my dad in Bedford-Stuyvesant. I doubt that my father would have ignored Lucas—other black friends from the neighborhood say he was friendly when they bumped into him at jazz clubs—but Lucas, who eventually became a scholar and dramatist, later sniped that my dad was black when he entered the subway in Brooklyn and white when he got out at West Fourth Street in Manhattan.

The conversation at the Baldwin booth wasn't so different from that at my father's table—also revolving around modernism, the avant-garde, and aesthetics. But these men (and occasionally women) had to deal with the additional burden and responsibility of being seen as "black artists," even as they weren't sure what that label was supposed to mean. Baldwin's biographer, David Leeming, recounts how the young writer struggled with this problem early in his career: "The question of his identity obsessed him. What was a homosexual? What was a Negro? Was it necessary to live by these 'presumptuous labels'?"

On a visit to a writer's colony during the summer of 1948, Baldwin wrote in his journal about his desire to conceive of himself, in Walt Whitman's formulation, as "containing all roles, classes, ethnic groups, and orientations." He also realized that he must accept his condition in order to be "free," inspired perhaps by Sartre's recent essay in *Commentary* on the Jew's need to accept his irreducible difference in the eyes of non-Jews in order to live authentically in the world. Having shelved his identity crisis for the time being, Baldwin wrote in one night "Previous Condition," his first published work of fiction.

Published in *Commentary* in October of 1948, the story concerns a young black man who is evicted from his Village apartment because of his race. To his well-meaning white (Jewish) friend who had secretly rented him the apartment, the narrator says, "I know everybody's in trouble and nothing is easy, but how can I explain to you what it feels like to be black when I don't understand it and don't want to and spend all my time trying to forget it?" A month after publication, Baldwin left for Paris, where he would be better able to forget his blackness. Delaney, who also had to contend with being labeled a "Negro artist," no matter his affinity with the Abstract Expressionists, followed his friend to France five years later.

From Baldwin and Delaney's vantage point, my dad, laughing at the next booth with Delmore Schwartz and Dwight Macdonald, had his identity all figured out. He was passing as white, end of story. This observation wasn't made with particular judgment, but it did make being friends with Anatole difficult. On the other hand, two African American writers who *were* friendly with my father, Ralph Ellison and Albert Murray, didn't view him as dodging black people or black culture. Murray recalls the time he and Ellison spotted Anatole at a party: "He had this blond chick all bent over doing the one-butt shuffle. Anybody could see that he wasn't denying identification with that particular style, lifestyle, outlook, and whatnot." Murray says that neither he nor Ellison saw any need for my father to declare himself one way or another.

Yet the question of what he was did weigh on my father's mind. The focus of his writing and his intellectual inquiries during the late 1940s and early 1950s suggests a preoccupation with black identity in general and his own identity specifically. My father had always been very deliberate in how he presented himself to the world, fastidious in his appearance, careful in his manner of speech, nearly abstemious because he didn't like to lose control. His relationship to his racial identity would be no less carefully fashioned, resting upon a sound philosophical base.

At the New School, he took course after course in psychology: "Approach to Personality," "Psychology of Adjustment," "Toward Knowing Oneself," and even a semester on the Rorschach method. At age twenty-six my father entered into the first of many analyses that he would undertake over the next forty years. And in his writing, he returned to the examination of social type that he'd begun in his hipster piece, placing next under his lens the Anglo-Saxon, whom he satirized as "so perfectly in harmony with things as they are that when he isn't laughing his face is expressionless." Sartre's essay "Portrait of an Inauthentic Jew" in the May 1948 issue of *Commentary* provided my father with the necessary framework to explore his ideas about blackness, and he began to work on a similar analysis of Negro inauthenticity.

In Sartre's formulation, "authenticity for [the Jew] is to live to the full his condition as Jew; inauthenticity is to deny it or to attempt to escape from it." In other words, a Jewish person had to accept the reality that others saw him as a Jew, with all the prejudices and my-thologies that went along with that identification, before he could truly be himself. The alternative, according to Sartre, was pursuing "avenues of flight" that made the Jew complicit with anti-Semitic stereotypes. For example, the Jew's reputation as excessively self-analytical, particularly among the intellectual class, was not, in Sartre's opinion, an inherited tendency but an avenue of flight. Other exam-ples were feelings of inferiority, acute anxiety, Jewish anti-Semitism, and altruism (in reaction to the Jew's supposed money hungering). By recognizing the prejudice that defines his relation to the world, opined Sartre, the Jew can begin to short-circuit his defensive reactions.

In his article "Portrait of the Inauthentic Negro," which appeared in *Commentary* in July 1950, my father also identified various avenues of flight: there was "minstrelization," symbolized by the grinning Negro who seemingly acquiesced to his minority status; "romantici-zation," represented by "Negro artists" and others who made a career out of being society's scapegoat and martyr; the "rejected attitude," wherein refusal of the Negro's supposed gaiety and spontaneity re-sulted in an exaggerated aloofness; and "bestialization," in which Ne-groes exploited their reputation as more primitive and sexualized beings. In his recommended cure, however, my father parted ways with Sartre's model. For the Negro he prescribed a "stubborn adher-ence to one's essential self, in spite of the distorting pressures of one's situation." By essential self, my father meant "[the Negro's] innate qualities and developed characteristics as an individual, as distin-guished from his preponderantly defensive reactions as a member of an embattled minority."

Unlike Sartre, he saw no benefit in the minority person's recogniz-ing that the rest of the world viewed him as irreconcilably different. In fact my father suggested that Negroes could best "authenticate themselves" by proving that they were "fundamentally 'different' [from whites] only in appearance." My father conceded that while the physical fact of blackness could still strike terror into the hearts of white people, especially the prospect of having a "black baby," he counseled: "The falsity of such physiognomic discrimination becomes immediately apparent when we realize that thousands of Negroes with 'typical' features are accepted as whites merely because of light complexion."

It's impossible not to read this essay as my father's attempt to justify the way he was living his life. After all, he could hardly be accused of passing after publishing in one of his crowd's most widely read magazines a piece that demonstrated his intimate knowledge of the American Negro—a situation, his author biography observed, "which he knows at first hand." But the essay is more than a blanket apologia. My father truly believed that there wasn't any essential difference between blacks and whites and that the only person responsible for determining who he was supposed to be was himself.

For much of my childhood, a copy of the July 1950 issue of *Commentary* magazine sat within arm's reach of our dinner table, but I didn't pull it out and read "Portrait of the Inauthentic Negro" until a few years after my father died. When I finished I remembered what he'd said when I first learned about the existence of a secret on Martha's Vineyard: *If you want to know me, then why don't you read more of my writing?* Perhaps he'd been thinking of this essay. Yet if I had opened the magazine while he was still alive, I would have been left with more questions, such as why there was a neatly razored hole on the bottom left-hand corner of the first page, where the contributor's note describing his firsthand knowledge of the American Negro should have been. Apparently his view of black identity was acceptable to share, but the editors' view on his black identity was not. Once again here was my father picking and choosing about how he would be presented to the world. Here he was hiding in plain sight. I don't know whether to feel thankful or regretful that I never stumbled on his secret while he was alive.

*   *   *

Few among his Greenwich Village friends seem to have read the "In-authentic Negro" piece. At least they couldn't remember it years later, although they recalled other essays my father published during this period. This is particularly curious given the popularity of Sartre and existentialism at that time. It was no small thing for a young, relatively unknown writer to take on the venerable French philosopher. Consid-ering that my dad was addressing the subject of black identity, after all the intrigue about his own background, it's even more surprising that so little attention was paid to the essay's publication.

Perhaps "Portrait of the Inauthentic Negro" wasn't memorable because it wasn't particularly good. Despite his supposed intimate knowledge, my father dismissed the everyday realities of black peo-ple's lives without a backward glance. It was easy for *him* to suggest that African Americans forget they are Negroes—the world didn't throw that identification in his face again and again. It was easy for *him* to recommend that blacks resist the distorting effects of white prejudice—he wasn't bombarded by it every day.

At a moment in American history when blacks were having trouble finding work and gaining admission to restaurants and clubs, where any good or bad thing they did was chalked up as a credit or embarrassment to their race, when the possibility of being seen with a white woman or getting lost in a white neighborhood could lead to spurious—and life-threatening—conclusions, my father's prescrip-tion of a "stubborn adherence to one's essential self" was, at best, very weak medicine. Try telling that to his brother-in-law Frank, who the year before had been chased by the Ku Klux Klan after leaving a Florida courthouse, where he'd been consulting on the trial of three black men accused of raping a white woman. After two hours at high speeds, his driver, who was a local African American man, managed to shake their pursuers in a black ghetto in Orlando. Two of the defen-dants weren't so lucky: while the sheriff was transferring them to an-other jail, they allegedly tried to escape and were shot to death.

No matter how many classes my father had taken with the Freud-ian revisionist Erich Fromm, whose focus was the role of society in shaping the individual, no matter how closely he studied Freud's thesis in *Civilization and Its Discontents* about the tension between a man's freedom and the conformity imposed by civilization, my father still couldn't see how the hand of the world pushed upon the Negro's back and how that pressure might make a person want to push back. Yet when someone pinned my father's race on him— "Look, a Negro!" in the formulation of Martinican writer Frantz Fanon in his essay "The Fact of Blackness," published in 1952, also in response to Sartre's analysis of Jewish identity—my dad wasn't able to turn the other cheek either.

Around the same time that my father was analyzing inauthentic Negroes, his pal Chandler Brossard was writing his roman à clef about the 1940s Greenwich Village scene. My father was under the impression that he was Brossard's closest friend; after all, he'd served as best man at his wedding a few years earlier. So it must have come as a surprise when word got back to my father that he was the model for the protagonist in Brossard's novel—a smooth-talking hustler named Henry Porter. And that surprise must have turned to hurt and anger when he received a copy of the manuscript from Brossard's publishers, who wanted him to sign a release before publication. The novel's opening paragraph read:

> People said Henry Porter was a "passed" Negro. But nobody knew for sure. I think the rumor was started by someone who had grown up with Porter in San Francisco. He did not look part Negro to me. Latin, yes. Anyway, the rumor followed him around. I suspect it was supposed to explain the difference between the way he behaved and the way the rest of us behaved. Porter did not show that he knew people were talking about him this way. I must give him credit for maintaining a front of indifference that was really remarkable.

My father refused to sign the release, and Brossard was forced to change identifying details. In the version that was published, Henry Porter is instead illegitimate, which didn't carry nearly the same stigma as blackness. Needless to say, the men's friendship was over. (Twenty years later my father would nearly sabotage his new position as the daily book critic for the *New York Times* in the process of settling the score.)

My father certainly had reason to feel betrayed. By singling out his racial identity, Brossard made him an exception to the prevailing Village credo that they were all free to discover themselves without being encumbered by familial or ancestral histories. In my dad's case, the past could never be forgotten, because contrary to what he'd asserted in his essay, it made him fundamentally different from whites, no matter how much he might resemble them. In Brossard's formulation, my father wasn't inventing himself like everyone else; he was pretending to be something that he wasn't. He was a "passed Negro," which was how my dad's friends from Bed-Stuy and his family saw it too.

In the postwar years, the rest of my father's family were growing more accepting of their black identity. Edna quit her job at the Laundromat, which meant that she no longer had to pass for work. Lorraine stopped considering whites-only positions. Even Nat showed signs of relaxing his antiblack attitudes. While he still had to pass at the construction site — as late as 1959, building trade unions in New York City remained segregated — he chose Sag Harbor, a popular black resort area on Long Island, when he bought a plot of land on which to build a weekend home.

My father explained himself to Lorraine by saying that he wanted to be a writer, not a Negro writer. The critics may have hailed Ralph Ellison's *Invisible Man* as a great novel about the human condition, but it was still praised in the *New York Times* as "the most impressive work of fiction by an American Negro" that the reviewer had ever read.

After five years in Greenwich Village, however, the majority of what my father had published did concern black people and black culture. In 1951 *Commentary* ran the essay "Keep Cool, Man," in which my father explored how jazz music had begun to adopt the "rejected attitude" avenue of flight that he'd described in "Portrait of the Inauthentic Negro." This time the contributor's note described him as "an anatomist of the Negro personality in a white world."

It's not the case that my father was assigned these pieces; he came up with them himself. The sociologist Nathan Glazer, who later led the charge against affirmative action and then reversed his position, was an associate editor at *Commentary* at the time. He recalls that Anatole Broyard wasn't thought of as an American black writer in the same way that James Baldwin was, although it was common knowledge that Broyard wasn't entirely white. Mostly, according to Glazer, he was seen as someone who was "au courant" on cultural matters. Yet when he tried to publish an essay that ventured outside the black world, "Marginal Notes on the Anglo-Saxon," neither *Commentary* nor *Partisan Review* wanted it. More to their liking were Chandler Brossard's tongue-in-cheek observations about how the gentile intellectual, finding himself New York City's latest Alienated Man, had begun to mimic his Jewish friends.

Eventually a subject that could transcend race presented itself to my father in the form of his father's stiff neck. When the pain didn't subside, Nat consulted a doctor, who diagnosed him with metastasized bladder cancer that had spread to his bones. He was dead within two years. Four years later, in the summer of 1954, my father published his first short story—a slightly fictionalized version of his father's death called "What the Cystoscope Said."

In his exacting descriptions of the physical and metaphysical devolution that occurs at the end of a person's life, my father conveyed the terror, love, and wonder of a son attending his father's death. Everything he felt about his dad was poured into the story—his inability to talk with him; his desire to see him as heroic and recognition that his life was not; the gaps in generation, education, and sophistication between them; and the well of tenderness that rose up at the end — without mentioning the family's racial identity. In the final scene, the son returns one night to his Greenwich Village apartment to find a package on his doorstep. It's the box containing his father's ashes. After bringing it inside and placing it on the bookshelf, he thinks to himself: "I'd heard that ashes were supposed to be scattered from a hilltop to the four winds, or poured into the headwaters of a river going out to sea, but as I looked at the box on the shelf, I knew that those were not our ways.... It was my job to sift those ashes and sift them I would, until he rose from them like a phoenix." In real life the ashes would be moved from one closet to another over the next forty years.

A few months after "What the Cystoscope Said" appeared, my father published a second autobiographical story, "Sunday Dinner in Brooklyn," about the estrangement that a young man from Greenwich Village feels from his parents during his weekly visit to their apartment in Brooklyn. The narrator's mother and father keep his picture on the mantel next to the clock, but he forgets about his parents each time he says good-bye. "Always, without realizing it, they were wondering what I was, whether to be proud of me or ashamed, whether my strangeness was genius, sickness, or simply evil, whether I had sold my soul like Faust or was still learning to walk, whether I was a hero or an abortion."

The theme of both stories — the painful, necessary process of separating from one's family — resonated with many people. By year's end every major publishing house in New York had contacted him to inquire about expanding these stories into a novel. Eventually my father signed a contract for a sizable advance with Seymour Lawrence at the Atlantic Monthly Press, who was responsible for publishing such writers as Katherine Anne Porter, Pablo Neruda, and Kurt Vonnegut. People in the literary world began waiting for Broyard's novel. In *Advertisements for Myself,* Norman Mailer finds some complaint about nearly all contemporary writers except William Burroughs, whom he mentions in a footnote, and my father, about whom Mailer writes: "I've read two stories by Anatole Broyard. They are each first-rate, and I would buy a novel by him the day it appeared."

But that day would be a long time coming. My father had planned for the novel to chronicle a young man's journey from a provincial Brooklyn boyhood to sophisticated Greenwich Village alienation, with all the discontinuities of self and culture that accompanied that transition. However, trying to capture the life of a young intellectual in the Village led to murky waters. In straining to be hip and smart, his writing started to come across as labored and abstract. After reading a story from this new material in a literary journal, Sheri Martinelli wrote to my father that he was trying too hard to impress other men. I think she was right.

Like many young writers who receive a lot of praise too early in their careers, my father seems to have become paralyzed under the weight of everyone's expectations. His journals from this period are filled with notes for the book—ironic dialogue ("My personality costs me so much money that I'm obliged to take it seriously"), elaborate metaphors (a character "opens his ego like a newspaper, puts it on in the morning like a necktie, blows his nose in it like a handkerchief"), and telling observations (a small boy's dog urinates on stacked paintings at an outdoor art show)—but my father never managed to corral all this luster (or bluster) into a cohesive thing. Years later he confided to his friend Michael Vincent Miller that his problem with writing the novel was that he didn't know how to get his character into and out of a room. There was no way to make that kind of scene setting brilliant or lyrical. And he couldn't accept the idea that not every sentence had to be special, that *he* didn't always have to be special, especially as other peoples' expectations—and scrutiny—grew.

"Sunday Dinner in Brooklyn" was included in a popular anthology of Beat literature, and my father's photo ran in *Time* magazine as a representative of that generation. Arna Bontemps wrote to

Langston Hughes, "His picture...makes him look Negroid. If so, he is the only spade among the Beat Generation."

For my father, trying to write honestly about his childhood without being honest about all its particulars was rather like trying to write one of those lipogram novels that never use the letter *e.* Reading these drafts, one gets the feeling that everything is disconnected from the "raw data of actuality" and shot through with dead ends. In desperation my father returned to the ground he'd covered in his early stories and tried to mine it again, managing in the process to suck out any remaining vitality, so that even the scenes in his father's hospital ward lost the sharpness of their tragedy. Rejection letters from literary magazines began piling up. While his publisher remained committed to the novel for almost fifteen years, people in the literary community stopped holding their breath.

According to his notebook, my father planned for the book to end with his father's death, which represented his final break from the past. While he had trouble achieving this narrative arc on the page, he made progress in real life. An analyst whom my father saw during the mid-1950s tells me about my father's relationship to a man named Ernest van den Haag, who was a Dutch-born professor of sociology about six years my father's senior. My dad, in the analyst's view, came to view Ernest as the ideal father, after he came to terms with how disappointing his own father had been.

While Nat had never shared any of his son's interests except for boxing—once they'd relived punch for punch the most recent bout, they had nothing left to talk about—Ernest had "a mind as clear as light" and could engage my father in conversation for hours. My dad

particularly admired how precisely his friend could express an idea, especially since he'd arrived in the United States in 1940 speaking no
English. But my father's choice of Ernest as a surrogate father seems a
rejection of more than his dad's inarticulateness.

After meeting literally on the street shortly after the end of World
War II, my father and Ernest began a daily habit of taking a walk
around Greenwich Village. A close friendship soon developed that
would last for the next forty-five years. After a few months, my father
invited his new friend home to Brooklyn for dinner, where Ernest met
my father's family. "I was somewhat surprised," Ernest told me before
he died in 2002, "because they were all blacks, of course, and Anatole
had not warned me of that."

Despite this omission Ernest never had the sense that my father
was conflicted over his identity. "In my recollection he never tried to
hide the fact that he was black," he said. "But he never liked discussing
it, because it wasn't important to him." For his own part, Ernest said,
my father's racial identity didn't make any difference to him, which is
rather hard to believe given the political positions he'd begun staking
out at the time.

In 1956 Ernest published *Education as an Industry* (an expanded version of his doctoral thesis completed six years earlier), in which he
laid out his argument against school integration, claiming it amounted
to "compulsory congregation." The following year Ernest launched
the first of a series of attacks on the famous doll tests conducted by
the African American sociologist Kenneth Clark, which were cited in
the recent *Brown v. Board of Education* decision as proof that segregation
indeed affected the self-esteem of black children. Just as my dad was
describing to his analyst why Ernest would have been a better father,
his friend was proselytizing about why the races should be kept
apart.

For the next two decades, Ernest served as an expert witness
against desegregation, appearing before U.S. House and Senate sub-
committees and the U.S. Supreme Court. Among his arguments was

his conclusion that black children would be *more* harmed by sitting in the same classrooms as whites, since their historical deprivations meant that they couldn't measure up. The harmful effects of prolonging this injustice apparently didn't concern him. For his finale, he testified before the World Court in The Hague about the benefits of apartheid in South Africa for the black population.

When I was growing up, Ernest was a frequent presence in our house, sometimes joining us for Thanksgiving or Christmas dinner. My brother and I knew him as Uncle Ernest, and it wasn't until I was eight or nine that I realized he wasn't actually a blood relation. My father didn't ignore Ernest's more difficult traits: his penchant for holding unpopular opinions—he later became a leading proponent for the death penalty—and his general fastidiousness—he tortured my mother with his culinary requirements. But my dad always defended his friendship with his pal, saying that if it weren't for him, Ernest would have no friends at all. The implication was that once you made a friend, you were stuck with him. Your family, on the other hand, was disposable.

I didn't learn of Ernest's racial politics until after both he and my father were dead. I imagine, though, that if I'd had a chance to ask either of them about it, they would have dismissed it as immaterial to their friendship. In my conversations with Ernest, he described my father as his best friend and one of the brightest minds he had ever known. And my father gave the impression of being so secure in his own identity and intelligence (and so uninterested in any questions of race) that he was immune to feeling hurt or influenced by his friend's antiblack positions.

Yet my father's adoption of Ernest as an ideal father had to involve some repudiation of himself and his background. And I'm not convinced that Ernest could completely ignore my dad's racial identity, as he claimed. For starters, when my father proposed to my mother, Ernest tried to exploit my father's blackness to scare her away.

I can't help feeling sad, and slightly sickened, by the thought that my father would choose such a man to become his—and my—surrogate family. It felt almost as if he had knowingly invited a robber into our house, someone who would rifle through our family albums and keepsakes, stealing and defacing things. But I can also see—from my father's perhaps unconscious perspective—how Ernest helped to shore up his defenses by providing yet another bulwark against the mixing of whites and blacks. With him in his life, my dad had one more reason to keep the family in his past apart from the one in his future.

A t my mother's house in Martha's Vineyard, there are three big boxes containing nearly every letter that my father ever received. The collection spans forty years, but the bulk of them date from the 1950s, when my father was living in Greenwich Village.

Sitting on the floor of the living room, I sort the letters into piles: the ones from his mother and Lorraine; the ones from his first wife, Aida, and their daughter; the letters from friends—Ernest, Milton Klonsky, Michael Vincent Miller, Vincent Livelli, and a junkie named Stanley Gould who writes from prison to thank my father for sending him some cash and a change of clothes for his release. There are notes from fans about stories and essays he'd written, professional correspondence from editors at literary magazines and New York publishing houses, and letters from girls. Before long, the ones from girls overtake every other type.

There are hundreds of them: dozens from a single woman and solitary notes from girls who never appear again. Most of the letters appear to be written in the midst of a romantic interlude between my dad and the author. Sometimes the girl has gone back to college or she is away for the summer. Or else she simply wishes to communicate things that are too delicate or risqué to say out loud. It's clear from their letters that my father wrote these women back. I ran a query in the pages of the *New York Times Book Review*, asking to hear from people who knew my dad, and while I was contacted by some

old girlfriends who remembered him vividly, none held on to his correspondence. I imagine that his letters were the sort that a woman
burned, reluctantly, in some private ritual, before heading off to say
"I do."

More than one of my father's friends suggests to me that perhaps
Anatole couldn't finish his novel because he spent all his creative ener-
gies on seducing women. His analyst from the mid-1950s remembers
that my father would often start a session by mentioning that he'd
"made a new discovery," meaning that he'd met a new girl. He picked
them up on the street and in Washington Square Park, in bookstores
and museums, and in the San Remo and Cedar Tavern, where men
were said to follow him in hopes of getting lucky with a disappointed
girl after my father had made his selection for the night. Writing was
another kind of seduction—you had to entice your readers to enter
your imagined world—but it took longer and required more work.
With writing, my father wasn't as sure of being successful.

Significantly, my father was attracted mostly to blondes. The analyst was unaware of his ever having a relationship with a girl who
wasn't white. If my father was worried about fitting into his adopted
world, each woman who said yes—to an invitation for dinner or a request to make love—offered the warm embrace of social acceptance.
Each woman who wanted him was a validation of his self-made man.
His relentless womanizing, which persisted for most of his life, was
also a way to keep his connection to the Broyard legacy and his grandfather Belhomme alive.

The girls in the letters have sturdy American names like Ann or
Susan or Sarah or Barbara. A few sign off with more exotic, boyish-
sounding nicknames like Jae, Lou, or Mel. They write in curlicue
handwriting on light blue stationery or in hurried-looking cursive on
sheet after sheet of plain white paper. Some of them type their letters,
carefully, with no cross-outs or corrections. One girl, a particularly
young one, misspells "renaissance" three times—ranaissant, rana-

sance, ranaissance—before she gets it right. (She is writing a paper about renaissance art for her freshman year art history class and has asked my father to recommend some books. I imagine he dismissed this request: he's twenty years the girl's senior and has been contributing articles to the country's most respected journals for over a decade. But to my amazement, the girl's next letter thanks him for sending the lovely art books.)

There are letters written in choppy English from girls who live in Denmark or Sweden; a few dozen written in French, and one written in Italian, a language that I didn't know my father could read. These girls are dancers, models, students, potters, writers, or rich daddy's girls who complain about the boring office jobs they've taken to pass the time. A few of them are married. A few others are deeply troubled. They write from mental institutions, thanking my father for his faithful correspondence; he is, they tell him, their one true friend, the only one who understands them.

In one of the boxes, I also find an envelope containing all the photographs of themselves that the girls enclose (at my father's request), along with their little apologies—that their nose is too big, their legs are too fat, or they didn't have any better pictures lying around.

Occasionally someone writes something about black people. One girl whom he dated on and off for a year or so tells him how she tried to talk to some Negroes after reading a James Baldwin story. "However it was a flop because they were Ethiopian nobility, extremely blasé, feeling not at all oppressed because they were black." Another girl who is working for a few months in the Virgin Islands describes the black men who "creep all over...most of them act as tho' they just let go of the limbs of a banana tree..." And then she adds, "One nice thing, most of the Negroes walk like you except for the ones who are pregnant which is about 95%." My father is apparently undeterred by her observations, because her next letter responds to his urging her to come home for Christmas.

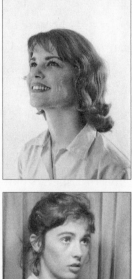

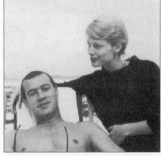

I read through every last one. I like best those letters written during courtship, especially the ones where the women reflect on their most recent rendezvous with my father. How courageous these young women seem! As Joyce Johnson describes in *Minor Characters*, her memoir about the Beats in the 1950s, "[Sex] was the area of ultimate adventure, where you would dare or not dare." The girls who write my father seem amazed by their own boldness, especially when recounted from the calm distance of their dorm rooms or childhood bedrooms, for those still living at home. They share their feelings with the guilelessness and vulnerability of children, as if through the experience they have been born anew.

One girl tells my father that she has always felt less feminine than other girls because she is big-boned. She writes: "So it made me so happy when you picked me up in your arms for a moment and lifted me off my feet." Another girl says how glad she is that my father is a writer, because then she can always keep him near, reading his words or imagining what he would say if they were walking together. Yet another girl writes about the "numinous quality" of their lovemaking and of her gratitude to my dad for introducing her to sensual pleasures that she'd begun to believe didn't really exist.

From the women's letters comes some suggestion of my father's end of the conversation. He writes to them about their clothing styles and their figures — their "quattrocento" beauty or their scrubbed midwestern faces; one girl has "sturdy Israeli knees." He fits them into categories: whether they are "sleepers" (which I gather means that they are good to actually sleep next to) or have the qualities of wholesomeness that make them "Pure Food and Drug Act" types. Sometimes he corrects them — their use of certain words or their grammar, or scolds them about the books that they are or are not reading. He signs off his letters with "affection," or occasionally with "love"; there's the ironic "you know what comes here," or an old favorite, "pornographic kisses."

It's obvious too that my father often cautions them, in between seducing them, that they will never be the only one. Sometimes he offers that he hasn't graduated yet from "charm school" and therefore isn't ready to settle down. Other times he's more frank, saying that he tends to lose desire for a girl when he becomes too friendly with her. Some of the women respond to his warnings with bravado, insisting that they knew all along that this was the score and they like it better that way too. Others confess their worry that they're going to be hurt, as if this confession will protect them. Few, however, seem to have actually taken my father at his word. For many, he is the first man they have slept with, and they imagine that this offering has earned them the right to expect something in return—to be the one who is the exception to the rule.

And so the second most frequent type of letter is the bitter reexamination of the relationship in the wake of its end. Now the girls let loose their resentment about having their looks, clothing, and taste in literature critiqued. They confess to chafing at my father's corrections and constant lecturing about books, art, and life. Sometimes they revisit the scene of their seduction, which strikes them in hindsight as calculated and formulaic. One woman accuses him of following the same program with all his conquests:

1. *mood talk*
2. *favorite little bar*
3. *present Journey to the End of the Night (maybe you have 100s of them)*
4. *do it with clothes on*
5. *do it with clothes off*

(As far as I can tell, she was right, although it's hard to imagine Céline's misanthropic tale of a French doctor during World War I as a successful tool for seduction.) These former girlfriends denounce my father as shallow and callous for his inability to settle on a single woman. They describe feeling tricked, betrayed.

My father appears to have answered these letters too, for some of the women write next to offer their forgiveness, and a few of them turn into true friends. They begin writing with news of their next love affairs, and counseling my father on his own. To some my father confides that he is growing bored with his own routine. In 1960, around the time of his fortieth birthday, he begins to write about wanting to get married, to this one or that one perhaps, but to someone sometime soon.

*   *   *

"As a bachelor, Sundays were lonely," my father later wrote, "and I began to wish for children around." Actually he was lonely much of the time—or so he confided to his women friends—despite all his female companionship and his friends down at the San Remo. He began to question, in the guise of the narrator of his novel-in-progress, whether spending one's day reading and thinking constituted a real life. One of the character's friends who gets married, has a child, and moves to Kew Gardens tells him: "This is how it goes: your life is there and you live it. You don't read it in a book or take a walk through it or dream it, and you don't think it up either—it's there." In his notes for the book, my father imagined the story would drive toward a "terrific nostalgia for normalcy." Perhaps if he himself lived a more ordinary life, he'd be able to let go of his crippling perfectionism and finally finish his novel.

He shared with Ernest his vision of family life. He imagined a house in the country and a wife who played the piano. He'd be writing in his study, with the soft sounds of piano music and children's laughter floating up the stairs. In 1961 letters from a twenty-three-year-old dancer named Sandy Nelson began to appear. To the shock of almost everyone who knew him, my father could be domesticated after all. But some of his friends, Ernest in particular, weren't ready to give up their favorite perennial bachelor.

In many ways my mother was a perfect match for my father. She was his type, thin and blond (and played the piano), and while my father described himself as a metaphorical orphan, my mother was a literal one. Both her parents were dead by the time she was twenty years old, and she was estranged—emotionally at least—from her brother, Brook, and sister, Barbara. They didn't approve of her pursuit of modern dance. When she told them how in class one day Martha Graham had put her hands on her shoulders and told her she was a dancer, Brook had scoffed: *She has to say those things. It's good for business.*

It was January 1961. My mother was riding the uptown Lexington Avenue subway to Grand Central after getting out of class at the New School when an attractive man started talking with her. Telling the story of meeting my father now, my mother shrugs and says, "We grabbed the same pole." It was no accident. My father spotted my mother leaving the New School—her dancer figure caught his eye—and he followed her to the station. Watching her pose on the subway steps, as she stretched out her calves, which were tight from a dance class that morning, he made up his mind to ask her out.

My father introduced himself as a professor at the New School. On hearing his name, my mother remembered running across his of-fering in the course catalog: something about popular culture that sounded rather lightweight. But he was handsome and charming, and she had some time before catching a train back to Westchester, where she had grown up and was now living. So when my father asked her to join him for a drink, she agreed.

Over martinis at the Vanderbilt Hotel, my mother's impression of her date improved. She learned that my father played in a regular vol-leyball game up at Columbia University with a former religion profes-sor of hers. And he was an intimate of Greenwich Village, which was a world apart from the one my mother had grown up around, the one that her siblings still frequented—drinks at the Stork Club, dinners at '21,' husbands who bought their wives mink coats and played golf at the country club. My mother told my father that she'd just returned from a year in Europe and was hoping to move to the Village too.

My father was impressed by my mother's Nordic beauty and glam-orous past, her old-fashioned innocence and sophisticated poise. She had such confidence in her ability to recognize what was fine and beautiful in life—the best churches in Europe, the right cut of steak, the kind of dress that best suited her figure. She'd performed a nightclub act in cabarets in Europe, where she was obliged afterward to *faire la salle,* or dance with the male customers. At the Jockey Club in Paris, she'd sold more glasses of champagne than any other girl. But she also knew how to knit woolen caps and sew buttons on jackets and refinish furniture. Perhaps with my mother in his life, the ordinary could be extraordinary. After dating for five or six months, he asked her to marry him, and she said yes.

My father was seventeen years older than my mother, but she'd never thought to ask about his age. (He often lied about it anyway.) Nor did she know anything about his family background. Such auto-biographical inquiries were considered square in the Village. Anyway, she wasn't eager to divulge her own past, although it had been haunt-ing her more and more, because at the heart of my mother's story lay a secret tragedy too.

When she was nineteen, her father was diagnosed with multiple myeloma. At the start of her junior year, my mother transferred from Mount Holyoke College, in Massachusetts, to the Juilliard School of Dance, in New York City, to be closer to her parents, who lived just outside the city. A month after her classes began, her father died in their dining room, in a hospital bed that occupied the place where the dinner table usually stood.

My mother had been a religion major at Mount Holyoke, where she'd met her boyfriend, a Dartmouth graduate who was studying to become a minister. She leaned on him now, their shared interest in faith giving her great comfort. She'd just turned twenty, and she began to hope that this boy would ask her to be his bride.

Over Christmas break my mother was having dinner in the room where her father had recently died when someone knocked on the front door. It was her boyfriend's fraternity brother. He had come to tell my mother that the young man she loved was dead, killed in a car accident outside of London. As my mother listened to this news, she smiled slightly, a gallows grin, and then she started to weep.

In the months that followed, my mother felt that she and her mother were drifting apart in their separate pools of grief. My mother proposed that they take a trip together to Norway, where some cousins lived. The second day in Oslo, they picked up a rental car—a squat convertible. My mother, who always drove on long car rides, slid behind the wheel for the three-hour trip to their relatives' house.

The weather was mild and clear, and so they put the top down to better enjoy the view of mountains and fjords. My mother came upon a truck lumbering down the highway. With no cars approaching, she accelerated and moved into the passing lane. But just then the truck driver pulled out to pass an even slower-moving truck in front of him. He didn't see the little car in his side-view mirror.

For years the thought that if only she had beeped would torture my mother. It would play over and over in her brain, disturbing her sleep and her waking hours too, as if the repetition and intensity of this regret could one day burst a hole in time through which she could reach back, press the palm of her hand against the center of the car's wheel, and sound that horn at last.

My mother veered off the side of the road, and the car flipped. She and her mother were thrown through the air. After a minute my mother stood up, stunned and shaken but uninjured. Other cars had pulled over, and a man was hurrying toward her. My mother could see her mother lying in the grass twenty feet away, but this man had caught her in his arms and she couldn't move. In his accented English, he was saying: *She is dead. She is dead.* My grandmother had had a fatal heart attack in the air. On the edge of the roadway, standing in this stranger's arms, my mother began to scream.

The police took her to the station, where they nicked her ear for the blood alcohol test that was customary in all traffic accidents. My mother hadn't been drinking, but this cut made her feel marked with blame. At the airport, waiting for her flight back to New York, she caught people looking at her, knowing that she'd been in an accident.

My mother's sister and her best friend went to JFK to meet her. They didn't recognize her at first as she walked down the corridor from the plane. Her blond hair, which she normally wore long around her shoulders, was pulled back into a tight bun. She was carrying a large red shopping bag, and my aunt remembers thinking it odd that my mother had the time or inclination to go shopping. And then Barbara, and my mother's friend too, noticed the bulky square shape of the bag's contents and realized that what my mother was carrying— what in fact had rested between her feet for the last seven hours—was the ashes of her mother's body.

My mother never cried about the loss. Not once that anyone witnessed. And that's the end of the story, as my mother's friend and her sister tell it. But at night my mother began to have dreams that made her afraid to go to sleep. Sometimes, during the daytime hours, she would burst into tears or begin to tremble for no apparent reason. Today she would be diagnosed with post-traumatic stress syndrome. A therapist might help her to revisit the scene of her mother's death so they could understand together that it wasn't her fault. My mother would have the support of psychotropic drugs and a community of other people who'd also suffered great losses. She'd be encouraged to talk about her feelings.

In the late 1950s, however, that wasn't how things were done. Back then people suggested having a drink if you were feeling anxious, taking a pill if you couldn't sleep. So my mother had a drink. She took a pill. And it worked, for a while at least.

It was my father who first gave my mother the sleeping pills; he struggled with insomnia himself. When she began staying overnight at his place on West Tenth Street—there was no one to tell her not to— and he saw how much trouble she was having falling asleep, he offered her some pills from his supply. The summer after they became engaged, my father went off to Europe to "exhaust the last of his romantic restlessness," and my mother, left alone in his apartment, started taking the pills every night.

During their two months apart, my parents wrote to each other almost daily. In her letters my mother attributes her insomnia and bouts of depression and anxiety to her frustration about the progress of her dance career. She tells my father that she is counting on their marriage to provide the strength and stability that she needs so badly in her life. For my father's part, he confides: "I rely on you with all my heart to make me happy and productive." They write to each other of their "infinitely romantic domestic plans."

In my father's absence, my mother had been turning his bachelor pad into a home. She found an old wooden rocking chair that she spent her evenings restoring with wax and furniture stain. She made curtains for the windows, bought a GE steam iron to press their clothes, hung a small chalkboard in the kitchen on which to note things to pick up at the store—all of which, recounted in my mother's letters to him, filled my father with delight.

This trip, he predicts in one letter, will be his last experience of loneliness. When he looks at her picture, he writes, tears well up in his eyes, something that happens to him about once every ten years. "It's not really because I miss you though, but because you make me so happy and I never expected to be happy that way. I feel more like a bride than a husband, if you can understand that, because I'm so unused to this tenderness."

My mother rescued my father from his role of being a spectator on the world and enticed him to participate in the everyday dramas of real life, while he became, she writes, "the object of my affections— my salvation, my inspiration—all that and more."

I'm surprised and touched by the abundance of genuine romantic feeling in my parents' correspondence. It's hard to believe that all my father's years of bachelorhood hadn't corrupted his store of affection, and all my mother's tragedies hadn't scarred over her ability to love.

They put so much hope into each other, they had so much riding on the success of this union, that I find myself worrying for them, even as I know how everything turns out.

My father hadn't returned from Europe before cracks began appearing in their snow-globe vision of the future. For starters, my mother's siblings disapproved of the match: Sandy was too young and too naive for my father. She would get hurt; he would never make her happy. What did he do for a living anyway? They wondered if he was after my mother's money. She was living off a small trust from their parents' estate, but she was due to inherit a much larger sum after their grandmother's death, which was looking rather imminent.

My uncle Brook went so far as hiring a private detective to investigate my father, which was something that had been done to Brook himself by the father of a girl that he'd been dating. But my father's report — as my mother never tires of saying — came back spotless, which makes me wonder about the skill of this private eye. He didn't even turn up the information about my dad's racial background. That piece of news my mother would learn from his friends.

In her letters to my father, my mother discloses that his pals have been taking good care of her in his absence. One woman in particular — an ex-girlfriend of my dad's named Sue Freeman — had been particularly friendly, inviting my mother to dinner, planning outings to the beach. Then my mother writes that she's had an interesting conversation with Sue the night before — mostly about my father — but she wants to think about it more before saying anything else.

In fact Ernest van den Haag had roped Sue into telling my mother that her fiancé was a Negro. In 1961 a black man marrying a white woman was still shocking — the U.S. Supreme Court didn't outlaw state miscegenation laws until *Loving v. Virginia* in 1967 — and Ernest had convinced Sue that my mother had a right to know. Sue only realized later that he was trying to break up Anatole's engagement. "I think Ernest was as in love with your father as I was," she tells me. "But frankly, I didn't want to lose him either."

During her conversation with Sue, my mother brushed off the revelation as gossip, but she couldn't quite put it out of her mind. Sue had mentioned that my father's daughter from his previous marriage was quite dark; Ernest claimed to have seen her picture. (In fact, my half sister doesn't look discernibly black.) My mother asked herself whether she was prepared to have a black baby, and the answer was no.

Before she met my father, my mother had dated a South American man who was very dark-skinned. This man came from a wealthy family and took her to the kinds of places that would meet with her brother and sister's approval. One night they were riding home in a taxi after another elegant dinner when the driver, realizing that they were a couple, made up an excuse to pull over and asked them to leave his cab. "My date had incredibly good manners, but I think he was profoundly embarrassed," my mother says. "I never went out with him again." She began to worry that having a black child would feel like being back in that taxicab.

My mother wonders now whether having a supportive family behind her would have given her the courage to withstand the hostility and isolation that mixed-race couples could face. When she was growing up, her father, who worked in international banking, had an African business associate from Liberia who frequently visited their home with his French wife. Based on their warm reception of this couple, my mother guesses that her parents might not have objected to her marrying a black man, depending on his education level and the kind of work he did. But her parents were dead, and Brook and Barbara definitely weren't in favor of her fiancé, for reasons that had nothing to do with race.

＊   ＊   ＊

While my father was away, my mother was charged with the responsibility of planning their wedding, which they hoped to hold a few weeks after his return. Since they hadn't discussed the arrangements, she tried to work out the particulars by mail. But when she suggested holding the ceremony at her sister and brother-in-law's house in Westchester, my father vetoed it, saying that he was unwilling to get married surrounded by strangers in a hostile house. He was adamant that just as her family had been unwelcoming to him, he wasn't prepared to welcome Brook and Barbara into their lives. "The more I surround my marrying you with ties, obligations, compromises, false politeness and artificial responses, the less I'm going to like it. You must remember that I've been an independent, undomesticated animal for 37 years." (Actually, my father had just turned forty-one.)

But my mother wasn't willing to get married by a justice of the peace in some anonymous city hall without any friends or family around. She was too old-fashioned for that, which was part of her attraction for my father. He used to say when I was growing up that he'd married my mother because she was the last woman left who really believed in marriage; she had enough belief for the both of them. Yet he was making it virtually impossible to plan a traditional ceremony.

The matter of the invitations was particularly awkward. My mother hadn't met anyone in my father's family. In a letter my mother points out: "It would be very strange for a mother to receive an invitation to her own son's wedding to a girl she's never met *from that girl.*" She suggests that perhaps she could arrange a meeting with his mother while he's away. But my father nixes this idea too.

> As far as your meeting my mother and sister, I might as well tell you that I really don't want you to meet them at all. For my mother's sake, I suppose I'll have to give in on this, but I don't want to. I really don't see what they have to do with it. The only part of our lives we've ever shared is our history — and that's one of things I want to climb out of in marrying you.

Although I love my family pretty much as other people do, they've never been anything but an embarrassment to me. It's as though I'm forced to love a completely incongruous person or persons just because we grew up together. They're really very nice, my mother and sister, but they connote to me all the misery of my childhood, and I don't see any reason to store those ghosts in our attic.

It was the middle of September 1961, and my father was due home in less than ten days. After a month and a half apart, it wasn't as easy for my mother to feel the strong certainty of their love. Alone in the apartment, unable to sleep, muzzy-headed from the cycle of sleeping pills and beer she sometimes drank in trying to feel drowsy, she began to have doubts. She realized that she'd never asked for God's sanction of their marriage and felt ashamed.

My mother decided to seek out the rector at Grace Church down the street. She'd gone to the services there once before and been impressed by his sermon. Seated in his office, she presented her problem: she'd recently learned that the man she was due to marry in a few weeks might be a Negro, although he was very light-skinned, and she was concerned about the possibility of having a dark baby. The rector smiled, laid a hand on her arm, and told her not to worry. It wasn't possible for her to bear a child any darker in color than the darker one of the two of them. Recounting this later, my mother laughs and shakes her head. "I think that rector was a little out of his league." But she left his office feeling greatly relieved.

Walking home she headed back down Tenth Street, one of the prettiest streets in the entire Village, with its charmingly crooked skyline of pastel-colored brownstones, tall brick apartment buildings, and squat wooden town houses. All the brightly painted doors sparkled in the sun, the glossy black window shutters lay open to the morning light, and the late-blooming flowers spilled from window boxes. How beautiful the world could be! How full of life and possibility!

Crossing Fifth Avenue, she reached 39 West Tenth Street... Anatole's apartment... their apartment. She thought back to when she first started visiting him there. She'd round the last of the five flights to find him sitting on the top step waiting for her, and as she ran up those last few stairs, he would stand to catch her. Flying into his strong arms, she'd think to herself, "I'm home."

She had written my father that when he got back, their home would be "very warm & very beautiful—just like everything else is going to be from now on." More than ever she was convinced that getting married was the solution. The fog of anxiety and sadness that had been hanging over her would lift. She would finally be able to get some sleep.

Two weeks after my father returned, my parents were married in a friend's apartment on another beautiful street in Greenwich Village. It was a small wedding, just forty people. My mother's friend made deviled eggs, and my mother splurged on a $32 wedding cake from a local bakery. My father's mother and his sister Lorraine attended;

Shirley and Frank were out in California, for which my father must have been privately grateful.

My mother's siblings, however, missed the ceremony. Brook's boat had suddenly sprung a leak, and they had to stop off at the country club to prevent it from sinking. Among the pictures that eventually ended up in our family album, there are none of the traditional portraits that mark the union of two families. Instead my parents' relatives appear in the background of candid shots, as if their photos had to be taken when they weren't looking. If the gathering has a slightly grim and perfunctory air—as if the people there have been herded together against their will—there is also a resoluteness to their appearances, for they all know the unlikelihood of this particular group's ever being assembled again. My parents were setting off for a new world, united by their great hope in the future and their desire not to look back.

Two years after they were married, my parents moved from New York to southeastern Connecticut, where they bought and sold a series of antique farmhouses over the next twenty-five years. The house where my parents were living when I was born had been a tavern during the American Revolution—the curved wooden bar still stood in the front room—and George Washington was supposed to have stopped there for a drink. All of these houses had a central "keeping room" with an oversize stone fireplace that provided heat, light, and fire for cooking. Over the years my mother acquired the hearth and kitchen accoutrements that a colonial family would have used: a big black cast-iron pot, a row of wrought iron spoons and forks, bellows, a butter churn, and a long wooden paddle to remove the bread from the beehive oven. When I was little, I would pretend to cook in the fireplace and imagine that we were Pilgrims trying to make our way in a foreign land.

Indeed my parents had come to Connecticut as hopeful settlers, looking to secure for their children a contemporary version of the American dream. When my mother was pregnant with my brother, they bought a ten-room house with a pool and a tennis court in a rural neighborhood, miles from any friends or family. The exceptions were Robert Pack, a Barnard professor and Wallace Stevens scholar who played in my father's weekly volleyball game, and his wife, Patty.

My parents' social life consisted of having dinner with this couple every Wednesday night at alternate houses.

But then in July 1964, Todd was born, providing reason for their self-imposed isolation. By this point my mother had asked my father about his racial background. He'd mostly evaded the question, saying something vague about "island influences." But my mother had gotten to know Lorraine — the three of them traveled together in Europe for three months the previous summer — so she didn't have reason to feel that my father was hiding his family. If either of my parents had any lingering apprehension about how a baby would come out, my brother's appearance must have put them at ease. Towheaded, blue-eyed, and pale-skinned, he looked like a pre-Raphaelite angel. Two years later, I arrived, with more of my father's darker coloring, but not so much to make anyone wonder about my ancestry.

My father may not have thought of the move to Connecticut as a conscious decision to pass as white, but it did settle the question of which side of the color line his children would be raised on. While the fact that he was mixed race was common knowledge in New York, the rumors didn't follow him outside the city. In Greenwich Village he had never seemed bothered, or even aware, that people were gossiping about his background, but once my brother and I were born, the stakes were higher. Part of Connecticut's appeal might have been the unlikelihood that we'd accidentally discover the truth. It was also, in my parents' opinion, a wonderful place to raise a family.

My father had been greatly looking forward to having children—fueled perhaps by regrets over his neglect of his first daughter—but he was unprepared for the depth of his feelings for my brother and me. He told a friend: "You think you've been in love in your life, and then you have children, and you realize that you've never really been in love before." Like any parent he wanted us to be happy. And it seemed, from what he said to my mother and various friends over the years, that he thought living in Connecticut and living as white were our best shot. With rigorous schools that combined high expectations and mollycoddling to coax forward our best selves, wide-open spaces in which to exercise our growing bodies and exhaust our youthful spirits, and neighbors whose friendships could one day prove beneficial, our exurban life offered all the advantages that my dad's upbringing had lacked. Yet my father still indulged a predilection for viewing our childhood as marked by narrow escapes.

When we were young, he would entertain vainglorious fantasies of rescuing us. The scenarios he concocted were usually far-fetched: he'd yank us at the last minute from the path of a Bengal tiger or snatch us out of the surf, away from an incoming tidal wave. He seemed to view the role of father as a kind of homespun Superman.

He reveled in the physicality of the job. My brother was a colicky baby who required constant motion to keep him from fussing. My dad happily rocked him for hours on end, even playing tennis in the after-noons with his racket in one hand and Todd's carriage in the other. He delighted in parading me through the house after my bath, seated naked on his large palm, perfectly balanced, like a waiter with a tray.

The games he played with us involved small, exhilarating risks. We would toboggan down a rarely used country lane that led into a busy intersection. Near the end of the ride, my father would leap out of the sleigh and stop it before it ventured too close to traffic. Or we would run down a blanket chest that he'd placed like a diving board at the foot of my parents' bed and fling ourselves torpedolike at our father, who sat against a barricade of pillows piled against the far wall. Every time he would catch us in midair.

By saving us, could he begin to save himself? By appearing heroic in our eyes, could he feel more like a hero? I suspect so. Just as he'd managed to divert the outward signs of his black ancestry with the infusion of my mother's Nordic blood, he could deflect the inward turmoil he'd felt growing up through providing us with a childhood of "ideal experiences."

What my father didn't seem to realize was that the world was changing. Being black or mixed race when my brother and I were growing up wouldn't have marked us with social inferiority the way that it did in the 1930s. But out in Connecticut, snug in our antique farmhouse, the clocks might as well have been turned back a generation or two. The evolution in civil rights that was rocking the country didn't upset life along our country lane. Given that blacks made up less than 5 percent of the population in Fairfield County in the 1960s (and most of them lived in Bridgeport), it was almost possible to put African Americans out of one's mind entirely if it weren't for the nightly news.

In 1963, the year that my parents left the city, image after image from the civil rights movement scrolled across the television screen every evening: water hoses and attack dogs turned on black teenagers in Birmingham, Alabama; Martin Luther King Jr. leading hundreds of thousands of men and women in the March on Washington; four little girls killed by a bomb in a church basement. The following summer the focus moved closer to home, with riots sweeping through

Harlem and Bed-Stuy following the fatal shooting of a black boy by a white police officer. If my father tuned in to these events, he didn't talk about them, and despite the fact that some of it was taking place on the streets where he grew up and his mother still lived, he never gave any indication of relating them to his own life.

Martin Luther King, lunch counter sit-ins, protests and marches — my father didn't like any of it. He was opposed to turning race into a movement that collapsed affiliation and identity, requiring adherence to a group platform rather than to one's "essential spirit." While many African Americans would argue that the civil rights movement was a bid for recognition of the Negro's humanity — after all, one of the most popular picket signs was "I am a man" — my dad only saw the ways that such collective action could become an avenue of flight, distorting a person's sense of self.

In the late sixties, Michael Vincent Miller began to notice an edge in my father's attitude about race that hadn't been there before. My dad started regularly using terms like "spade" and "jigaboo" and making derogatory comments about black people. Another friend from that era and his future colleague at the *Book Review*, the novelist Charles Simmons, later hypothesized that this stance was ironical on my father's part — almost a way to test the listener's own racial attitudes. But in hindsight Mike understands it more as a reaction against the rise of black nationalism.

Black pride certainly complicated my father's already fraught relationship to his racial identity. On the one hand, it made his ambivalence about his background seem misplaced and embarrassing, leaving him the lonely defender of a debunked position. On the other hand, the movement narrowed the acceptable ways that my father could be black, if he had been encouraged by the advancement of civil rights to head in that direction. Anything short of growing an Afro and donning a dashiki might not have measured up.

Mike suggests that my father found the African American identity that emerged during the Black Power movement sentimental and false. After all, for his entire life, he'd been against their basic principles — that blacks were and should be different and separate from whites. "He wasn't racist as much as he was opposed to a certain liberal embracing of an idea of blackness that struck him as inauthentic," Mike observes.

Indeed my dad was particularly put off by the way white liberals had taken up race as their cause. Kit Blackwood, who dated my father in the late fifties, remembers telling him how bad she felt about the state of affairs for black people in New York and that she wanted to find a way to help them. Growing up in Texas, she'd been mostly raised by her family's black housekeeper, which had sensitized her to racial injustice. Since she and my dad had talked openly about his background — he'd even introduced her to Lorraine — Kit expected him to encourage her impulse, but in fact he'd come down hard on her. "He said, in essence, that white people don't understand and they should stay out of it," she recalls.

Luckily for my father, people didn't tend to move to Cheever country to proselytize for progressive causes. They came to wrap themselves in the safety and comfort of bourgeois trappings. Of course this good life required money.

After Todd was born, Greenwich Hospital wouldn't release him until my parents paid the bill — $500, which they didn't have. My dad's advance for the novel was long gone, and my mother had been swindled by a dishonest uncle out of her inheritance from her grandmother. What little she could access from her father's estate had been used for the down payment on the house. If my mother asked her siblings for the money, it would only confirm their suspicions about my father's inability to provide for their little sister. My dad called a friend from the Village, Albie, who was a jewel thief and always seemed to have a lot of cash on hand. When telling this story later, my father would portray Albie as a Robin Hood figure: he took from the rich and gave to the poor. That was us, the poor, living in the big house with the pool and the tennis court.

After bailing out my mother and brother, my father took the train back into the city and got his first full-time job, as a copywriter for a New York advertising agency. To the shock of his old friends, he stayed for seven years, working on accounts of Time-Life Books and Columbia Record Club. Anatole, the consummate Village bohemian, had become a company man, a daily commuter! But as the pal of his novel's narrator said, "Your life is there and you live it." Which didn't leave much time for anything else.

During my father's first year in Connecticut, away from the diversions of the city, he managed to produce more writing than he had in years. Living an ordinary life could be fruitful. He published a story in *Playboy* and another one in the *New Yorker,* and wrote a handful of new chapters for the novel. But that period of productivity soon ended, and my father found that he had traded in one set of distractions for another.

During the summer months, he convinced Tim Horan, his boss at the ad agency, who'd read his fiction back in the fifties and was as anxious for the novel as everyone else, to give him an extra ten days of vacation. "He'd always say that was all he needed, a few more weeks," Tim remembers. "Then he'd come back and say, 'Well, I got it pretty well finished. I'll certainly finish it by next spring.'"

In fact he wasn't making any progress at all. Going by the dates on his notebooks and drafts of stories, he seems to have ground to a halt not long after he started at the advertising agency. The sustained concentration required to produce literary fiction wasn't easy to come by for a man with a full-time job, two children, and a house in need of constant repairs—and those weren't my father's only problems.

Bob Pack, my parents' neighbor, says: "At that time, there were two fictions that were a part of your dad's psychology. One was that he was working on the novel and was going to finish it. The other was the fiction of his white origins." About the book, Bob, like Mike Miller, guessed that my father had set his standards to a paralyzing height. About my father's background, Bob says: "The assumption that I made, and everyone else I knew made, was that people are entitled to see themselves the way that they want to. They have the right to make public what they want to make public, and keep private what they want to keep private." Bob adds that for my father's friends, his racial identity didn't make a damn bit of difference.

But it did make a difference for my dad when it came to writing an autobiographical novel with a coming-of-age theme that centered on his relationship with his father. "He didn't use the word 'blocked,' but it was a very painful business," Miller says. Although Mike never talked directly with my dad about his background, he sensed that unresolved issues concerning my father's identity were preventing him from gaining the required perspective for his theme.

It was only in my father's conversation that Mike saw all the aspects of his background coming together: his vast knowledge of European and American literature and his ironic—normally Jewish—take on the world, combined with the raw earthiness of funk and the graceful improvisation of jazz. "If he could have turned this loose in his fiction, it would have been marvelous," Mike says. "He would have synthesized the best elements of American culture." But my dad was never able to write with the spontaneous elegance that was in his speech. Something kept making him tongue-tied whenever he faced the blank page.

That my father should feel compelled to make the subject of his novel the one subject in his life that he couldn't address was the kind of irony that he appreciated. He greatly admired, for example, the idea at the center of Freud's *Civilization and Its Discontents:* since our human nature makes us want to have sex with everything in sight, all civilizations, in order to prevent themselves from falling into anarchy, must incorporate repressive rules about who a person can and can't be intimate with. Such tensions demonstrated human beings' selfish and selfless extremes. But while theoretically fascinating, living within an irresolvable contradiction could wear a person out.

Just as domestic life hadn't loosened my father's writing block, neither did it solve my mother's problems. Her insomnia and anxiety only increased after the wedding. At my father's suggestion, she entered analysis, a style of therapy that is now understood to be the worst possible treatment for post-traumatic stress syndrome. After suffering a breakdown in the analyst's office, she only escaped hospitalization through the intervention of a progressive psychiatrist who put her on one of the first-ever antidepressant medications. But in the meantime she'd stumbled on a powerful elixir of her own—bourbon and sleeping pills—that could lift her out of her pain, and consciousness, for stretches at a time. Having babies and fixing up houses kept her distracted for a while, but after a few years in Connecticut, the old nightmares reemerged, and my mother began knocking herself out more and more frequently.

A wife who spent her days wrapped in an old blue bathrobe on the couch in the den, alternately crying or drinking some more until she passed out again, was a Cheeveresque aspect of exurban life that my father hadn't anticipated. Beyond driving around to the local liquor stores and asking them to please not sell alcohol to his wife, he was at a loss about what to do. Just as he'd tried to avoid the problems of the city by heading to the country, he escaped his troubles in Connecticut by fleeing back to Manhattan, where he took refuge many nights at a pied-à-terre that he rented with a friend. No doubt the women in whose arms my father had always distracted and reified himself offered an additional palliative.

And so while my father may have succeeded in rescuing us from the pain of his childhood, we were left to deal with the pain of our *own* childhoods by ourselves. It wasn't until a few years after my mother quit drinking, with the help of some therapists who specialized in trauma, that my dad recognized his misguided belief in the protective powers of the good life. In an essay he wrote in the late seventies for the *Times,* he wondered if being raised in the country was any better than a city upbringing. The wounds in exurban life "are too exclusive, too internal, too often originating in the family." Perhaps it would have been healthier for us to have been hurt by the outside world instead.

Yet my parents kept on buying and selling houses in Fairfield County, as if the solution was simply a matter of finding the right environment. And actually the strategy sort of worked. With each new location, they allowed themselves a fresh start; as if struck over and over again by sudden amnesia, they continued to believe in the possibility of happiness. Finally, in 1976, shortly after my mother became sober, my parents moved to the last of their eighteenth-century farmhouses, where we would stay put for the rest of my childhood.

My father had also changed jobs, which helped matters. Since moving to Connecticut, the one kind of writing he'd been able to produce quite successfully was literary criticism. A couple of page-one reviews he wrote for the *Times Book Review* brought him to the attention of the paper's cultural editor, Arthur Gelb, when a position for a daily book critic opened up in the winter of 1971. The job was arguably one of the most influential in publishing. Two to three times a week, the daily reviewer's column could make or break an author's career. Landing it meant that my father could spend his days doing what he liked best: reading books and thinking about writing. But he nearly took himself out of the running in his eagerness to settle an old score.

A few months earlier, my dad had gotten word that his ex-friend Chandler Brossard had a new novel coming out. Over lunch one day with Tim Horan from the ad agency, my father mentioned that he was thinking of offering to review the book for the *Times Book Review.* Wouldn't it be nice if Chandler finally had a hit, my dad had said, which Tim found curious, since he'd heard the story about how the passing Negro in Brossard's first novel was based on my father. In any case, my father submitted the review long before the book critic position was even on the horizon, though the piece hadn't yet been published when he learned that he'd gotten the job.

According to Gelb, the competition had come down to my father, the critic Alfred Kazin, and the Irish writer Wilfred Sheed. Neither Kazin nor Sheed particularly wanted it, and my father did. He was also seen as someone who could lend a bit of hipness to the paper's rather staid image. Kazin later likened my father's arrival in the *Times*'s offices to that of an ambassador for Greenwich Village sophistication. After his seven years of commuting back and forth from Connecticut to the advertising agency, it was a role my father was delighted to reprise.

His appointment was announced in the paper on a Monday. The following Sunday his Brossard review finally ran. It began: "Here's a book so transcendently bad it makes us fear not only for the condition of the novel in this country, but for the country itself." Within weeks articles appeared in the *Village Voice* and the *Boston Globe* denouncing my father for using the Gray Lady as his bully pulpit. The *Book Review* was forced to devote an entire letters section to the ensuing firestorm: Brossard's charge, my father's countercharges, and a chorus of bystanders weighing in. Tim Horan, then in frequent contact with *Times* editors regarding a business deal, heard talk that Broyard might be fired.

Again and again the history of the feud was laid out in print, except for one crucial detail: exactly what my father had found so offensive about Brossard's characterization of him. In person, however, Anatole Broyard's racial background became fodder for speculation once more. In the *Village Voice*, the columnist Nat Hentoff had included the first line of the French translation of Brossard's novel, which had been published in the original version: *Le bruit courait qu'Henry Porter avait du sang negre.* Among my parents' neighbors in Connecticut, some of whom were *Voice* subscribers, were people who caught the reference to black blood. Irving Sabo, who lived next door, recalls the article being *the* topic of conversation for a period.

Could my father really have believed that Brossard would remain silent? The recklessness of his behavior suggests that he was too blinded by his desire for revenge to think through the possible consequences, or else he didn't feel that he had anything to hide. What's very clear is his determination to defend his right to be the sole arbiter of his own identity at any cost.

If his new bosses hadn't heard the rumors about Broyard before, they had now. My father managed to quiet the brouhaha with his assured dismissal of Brossard's charges in the letters section of the *Book Review*. However, some of his collegues noted a trickster tendency about the new critic, which they never completely forgot.

The culture editor, Arthur Gelb, who was responsible for actually hiring my father, maintains that he had always known about his racial identity, while Abe Rosenthal, the managing editor at the time, told me a few months before he died that he only learned after my father joined the paper. Years later, both men took the position that it didn't much matter to them and that they even felt sympathetic to my father's situation. Gelb remembered discussing it with my dad in relation to a book that Gelb was working on about self-hating Jews, while Rosenthal said that he was delighted to learn about the "addition of his background," but the idea that my father had to declare himself as white or black was ridiculous. Still, given the climate at the *Times*, it was easier for my father's bosses if he let people go on assuming he was white.

Mel Watkins—the first African American editor in the Sunday section, which included the *Book Review*, Arts and Leisure, and the magazine—explains that it would have been difficult for the higher-ups to acknowledge having hired a black reviewer in the early seventies because of "an abiding assumption in America at the time that blacks were not capable of the kind of objective analysis that was necessary to be a critic." Watkins, who worked as an editor at the *Book Review* between 1965 and 1985, had actually been told that by a senior editor at the paper.

During his tenure Watkins made an effort to suggest black reviewers for books by white writers to correct what appeared to him to be a major inequity. "Although no one would think twice about having Norman Mailer review James Baldwin," he observes, "no one at the *Times* would have easily accepted the idea of Angela Davis reviewing William Buckley." But his efforts were rarely successful, which served to perpetuate the belief that black writers could only write about black subjects. Another African American editor at the *Book Review*, Rosemary Bray, recounts in her memoir, *Unafraid of the Dark*, how she was turned down for the job of daily book critic in the early 1990s. After looking at her clips, the hiring editor determined that she wasn't ready yet: too much of her writing was about black people and she needed to expand her range.

During his nineteen years at the *Times*, that accusation would never be hurled at my dad. From the beginning, African American writers and intellectuals believed that he was particularly hard on black authors. It's true that he was harshly critical of any writer whom he judged to be sacrificing aesthetic concerns for a political agenda. About Toni Morrison's otherwise well-regarded fourth novel, he wrote: "*Tar Baby* may be described as a protest novel, but the reader might have a few protests too," and then went on to pick apart Morrison's book. At the same time, Mel Watkins remembers my father defending *Soul on Ice* by Eldridge Cleaver, leader of the Black Panther Party in the late sixties, because the memoir delivered its message with inimitable style. What's certain is that my dad didn't use his platform to promote black literature, a fact that made some African Americans who knew about his ancestry very angry.

Among many readers, however, my father's high-toned pronouncements earned him a devoted following. The novelist Evelyn Toynton, who later became his student and close friend, recalls discovering my father's column. "It was so amazing to read anything so literary in a newspaper. I still think it was some of the best literary journalism we've ever had in this country." In his criticism my father was finally able to find the fluidity and confidence that had been evading his fiction. Mel Watkins comments: "What I found fascinating was his ability to take the strict academic or intellectual approach that at the time was presumed to be a part of white culture and combine it with the looseness, vividness, and spontaneity of black culture." Yet my father still couldn't synthesize these different aspects of himself in his more personal writing.

After my dad had spent a couple of years on the job as book critic, it became apparent to his publisher that he wasn't going to finish his novel anytime soon. His editor canceled his contract, and my father had to pay back the advance he'd received fifteen years earlier. But he himself still didn't give up hope of finishing the book. During his vacation that summer, my father took out the manuscript for the first time in nearly a decade. He started revising the last thing he'd been working on: a chapter about the narrator visiting his newly widowed mother, who has begun to act as if she is dying too, although there's nothing physically wrong with her. At first the son suspects that she's trying to shame him into being more attentive, but then he wonders if she's launched her campaign out of concern for him, as if to say, "Here, feast on me, fill up while you can."

When my father began this chapter back in the mid-1960s, his mother was as far from death as the mother in the story. But in the intervening years, Edna had suffered a series of small strokes that left her unable to take care of herself. As my father started the new draft, the idea of his mother's mortality was no longer abstract. Neither was his guilt about their relationship. Except for lending a hand with the arrangements to move her into a nursing home a few years back, he hadn't seen his mother much since my brother and I were born.

Say, Mom, what's this all about. You're not dying.

I want to have time to say goodbye, Paul. You know I never could move

fast.

The previous fall Edna, accompanied by Lorraine, had come out to Connecticut to pay her single visit. I had just turned seven and Todd was nine. In my memory I can see an old unfamiliar woman reclining in a lawn chair, with her feet propped up on a pillow. After spending an hour or two sitting in the backyard, we all had an early dinner at the country club next door, and then Lorraine and Edna drove back into the city.

Last suppers. Meals as elaborate as bequests...she drank me in as if she expected never to see me again.

Among my father's correspondence, I found a note from his mother dated a week or two prior to this visit. Over the years, she'd sent birthday and holiday cards and letters. Always they struck the same note: chatty and nonconfrontational, with a teasing admonishment of her rascally son and a motherly pride underneath. This note was written in shaky penmanship, and Edna had used a Christmas card, although it was late August. It read: "Dear Anatole,...I am [not] that young and gay and would love to see the children for once in my life. Why don't you bring [them] or come get me for a day. I would love that very much. I am getting 76 in Dec....Love, Mom."

Her old-person handwriting and the skipping record of her brain, along with the straightforwardness of her appeal, as if she no longer had time for diplomacy, must have scared my father, for Edna came out a week or two later. Afterward another note arrived, this one addressed to my mother, thanking her for the visit. Edna mentions how pleasant the yard had been to sit in, and how adorable Todd and I were. Perhaps, she writes, she can come again before the weather gets too cold.

But there would be no more visits. My mother was drinking heavily at this time, and she suggests that my father wouldn't want to risk his mother and sister seeing his wife drunk. And by the time **my mom** was sober, Edna's health had deteriorated to the point that she couldn't leave the nursing home anymore. But for Edna that single trip could at least silence any doubts about what her son was doing out there in Connecticut. She could tell anyone who dared to ask (and no one would, except perhaps Shirley or Frank) that Anatole had even taken her and Lorraine to his country club for dinner.

As Shirley points out, being seen in public with her mother or Lorraine wouldn't have caused a problem for my father; she and Frank, on the other hand, weren't invited. But Edna wasn't inclined to dwell on how my father was living his life, as long as she could maintain some kind of relationship with him. "She never raised a question about why you didn't know that we existed," Shirley tells me. "It might upset something."

Over the next few summers, my father kept writing and rewriting the chapter about Edna, each draft slightly different from the last, each one increasingly marked by cross-outs and additions, each mother a little less tangible than the last one. But he never managed to bring the story line to some satisfying conclusion.

> *If [Nat] resembled his blueprints — a pale diagram of a father — she was like her cooking, palpable. She wasn't going to "pass away." She'd spill and splash, flounder and putrefy. She might even make a scene…*

In the end Edna simply devolved into vagueness until she no longer recognized her son. And it was my father who made the scene, tearing apart the refrigerator on Mother's Day. I can still recall the surprise and hurt in his voice when he told me about visiting her at the nursing home. "She didn't recognize me," my father had said. "She didn't even know her own son." It hadn't occurred to him that just as a son could forget his mother, so too could she forget him.

> *I'm dying, too, I'm next. . . . Have you anything to say, Paul, something*
> *you've forgotten to do? I hope you won't put if off too long.*

A shadow of resentment obscures my recollections of my grandmother during our single meeting. There'd been a quality of formality
to the day—my brother and I were made to dress up and sit quietly.
I had trouble understanding my grandmother's strong New Orleans
accent. I think, too, I found something vaguely threatening about her
presence, as if these strangers who had appeared out of the blue
would take my father with them. I'd only ever known him as my dad,
and in the blunt logic of my seven-year-old brain, I didn't understand
that he could be a son and brother too.

I imagine that my mistrustfulness made me taciturn and stand-
offish with my father's mother. The few times I'd been around old
people—mostly the grandparents of my friends—their frailty, me-
dicinal smells, and incongruous turns of conversation had made me
keep my distance. I wonder, did I let Edna hug me? Did I call her
grandma? Did she look at me as if to drink me in?

After his mother's death, my father began to second-guess some of
the choices he'd made, often in the *Times* column he had recently
started writing about our life in Connecticut. He wondered if the
"excessively sheltered" upbringing that he'd provided for my brother
and me might prevent us from developing the necessary toughness or
tolerance to survive in the larger world. Also, although he liked the
Wasp lifestyle for the security and advantages it promised, he hadn't
necessarily counted on his children becoming Wasps themselves. Was
he raising my brother and me to be as innocent and uniform as sheep,
lacking any irony or a tragic sense of life? Was he guaranteeing that we
would grow up to be dull? He questioned whether his creative energy
had become stagnant in this picturesque setting, ensnared by rose
vines and ivy into complacency. Perhaps he could have finished his

novel if he'd been more anxious, more desperate. A view of skyscrapers, empty lots, and discarded mattresses might have been more conducive to the modern sensibility. Was this life worth everything that he'd forsaken?

In April 1979, six months after my grandmother died, my father recounted in his column how as a young man he'd run away to Greenwich Village, "where no one had been born of a mother and father." There he and his friends had "buried our families in the common grave of the generation gap." But now that he was a father himself, he had begun to reconsider his relationship to his parents. "Like every great tradition, my family had to die before I could understand how much I missed them and what they meant to me." He wondered if my brother and I would ever try to put him behind us. Or did we understand that "after all those years of running away from home, I am still trying to get back?"

A year or so later, my father was waiting for an elevator with Evelyn Toynton in a friend's apartment building when he mentioned, almost out of the blue, that there was a *C* on his birth certificate. When she asked him what it meant, he told her it stood for "colored." Then the elevator doors opened, ending the conversation.

After that my father would occasionally raise the subject with Evelyn, but always when they were about to arrive somewhere or walking back from lunch and there wasn't time for much discussion. He told Evelyn about his father sitting the family down in the living room and telling them they had to be white. Another time he mentioned that he'd been beaten up by the darker-skinned kids in the neighborhood. Evelyn recalls: "He stopped walking and said, 'You don't know what it was like. It was horrible.'"

Looking back now, Evelyn thinks that my father may have been probing to see how people would respond to the revelation of his background. "And it almost felt like, when he realized that people wouldn't care—certainly people like me didn't care—that it was weird for him," Evelyn says. "Because if nobody would care, then why had he done it?"

It was around this time, the early 1980s, that my father toyed with the idea of going public about his racial identity. One evening he visited Harold Brodkey and his wife, Ellen Schwamm, at their apartment in Manhattan for help with his novel. After listening to him read from various sections, they gave him the same feedback he'd been hearing for years from other friends and editors: the writing was too controlled and distant; he needed to let go to get back to the immediacy of his earlier fiction. Harold told him that it seemed like he wasn't being honest, and if you evaded the truth, this was what you got. My father wondered out loud if he should try to write about being black.

Harold and Ellen had heard the rumors, but they'd never discussed my father's racial identity with him before. Ellen, who is also a novelist, thought that writing about it was a wonderful idea. She suggested that such a book would free him. But Harold said that he didn't believe that my father had lived it. That he was *really black* wasn't the truth either. If my father had felt himself to be actively passing as white, Harold surmised, there would have been more of a gulf between my dad and my brother, my mother, and me, that the act of keeping a secret would have made my father seem more different.

Harold and Ellen asked him why he needed to be secretive about his background in the first place—almost everyone seemed to know already, and wasn't it just one black relative somewhere in his past anyway? My dad told them that in fact both of his parents were black. He said that he had never had anything in common with his family; they didn't understand him. When he started Brooklyn College at age sixteen, he'd felt more at home among the Jewish students. Sometimes it seemed to him that he'd been born into his family by mistake.

When I talked to Harold and Ellen in 1994, Harold described my father wearing a "shit-eating grin" when he talked about being black. "He said how well a book like that would sell," Harold recalled. "How he could make a lot of money." My father's writer's block wasn't only frustrating creatively; my brother and I were about to start college, and my dad needed a book advance to help pay for our tuitions. Harold also thought that my father told him because he knew that Harold would out him one day and then he would be forced to explain himself. But my father died before Brodkey got around to exposing him, and then Harold was diagnosed with AIDS and busy finishing up his own life.

My father eventually told Brodkey that he didn't want to write about being black because he simply didn't want to be viewed as a black writer. Also, he didn't want Todd and me to be seen differently. Harold kept encouraging him to tell us about his background, but my father always refused, insisting that it had nothing to do with us. We were white.

My mother had also begun pressing my father about the need to tell the children. She felt that we had a right to know, both for ourselves and for the sake of our own children. But my father would immediately grow angry whenever she brought up the subject. To end the conversation, he would agree to tell us one day, but we didn't need to know yet.

When was the right time, though? When we were so secure in our white identities that the revelation wouldn't change our conception of ourselves? When the world no longer made distinctions between black and white? When we stumbled on the secret by accident? If he'd ever actually tried to imagine our reactions, he might have been scared. Perhaps he'd done such a good job raising us as white that we'd be upset or angry. Maybe the wall he'd erected between our lives and the colored world of his childhood would prove so high that we'd lose sight of him across the divide.

Equally troubling might be the possibility that we'd embrace our father's background. To his mind, if we started to identify as black, then all the advantages he had worked so hard to provide us — and everything he'd sacrificed along the way — could prove for naught. Through the force of his personality, my father had managed to thwart any racial stereotypes' being "pinned" on him by people who knew about his identity, but he couldn't be certain that we'd have the same sureness of character to deflect the distorting influence of prejudice.

My father might have wondered how springing this news on us would be any different from what his father had done to him as a kid. He knew firsthand how confusing it could be to grow up thinking of yourself as one thing only to be told you're another. His father had also been trying to make a better life for his family, but he'd hijacked his children's sense of themselves in the process. My aunt Lorraine suggested to my mother that she'd never married because of the mixed messages she received as a child about her racial identity. Could my father expect us to keep his secret for him? Would forcing us into becoming his coconspirators be any better than withholding the truth?

My father could have come up with a million excuses about why he shouldn't tell us. Perhaps the simplest explanation is that he was afraid we'd be disappointed in him. He might have gone on postponing forever, but then he got sick and his time ran out.

In a talk about having a critical illness that my father gave at the University of Chicago Medical School six months before his death, he mentioned the need to develop a style for finishing up one's life. He'd always viewed a person's style as the literal embodiment of his personality. For him style extended far beyond fashion to include how a person moved, the language he used to express himself, the angle of his observations. In his view we could deliberately cultivate these aspects of our character by paying very close attention to our instinctual likes and dislikes, our innate prejudices when responding to the world. As if we were each uniquely made instruments, our job in life was to continually tune ourselves, tightening this and loosening that until we hit upon our most natural, most authentic sound. My dad often spoke of life as a rhythmic process—"When I was happy, my rhythms, my tuning were good...and when I was unhappy, I didn't have any rhythm at all." Finding his unique sound allowed him to dance.

In finishing up *his* life, my father adopted a style that defied and disparaged his illness. When his oncologist suggested that the most effective remedy for prostate cancer was an orchiectomy—removal of the testicles—my father told him that losing his balls might depress him, and that depression could kill him quicker than cancer. He entertained us with stories about his hospital roommate, a thug who'd broken his jaw during a bar fight. After having a catheter removed, my father couldn't make it to the bathroom in time and peed all over the floor, and this man, who had drawn blood in anger, leaped onto his bed and began dousing the room in air freshener.

Just as my father had counted on his style to protect him from the diminishment of self that came from being black in the 1930s, he expected it to safeguard him against the diminishment of self that accompanied having a fatal illness. Rather than wasting away, he would become a crystallized version of Anatole, more insistently himself than ever before. As cancer disfigured his body and disoriented his mind, this tactic would keep him in love with himself, which was crucial to maintaining his will to live. And it would also allow his family and his friends to continue loving him as he became more and more unrecognizable.

If my father told my brother and me about his racial background, how could he have remained himself while also revealing that he wasn't who he seemed to be? Even if he convinced us that his few drops of black blood didn't mean that he *was* black, would we nonetheless feel alienated by the drops of secrecy and conclude that he'd become a stranger?

*   *   *

In the final months of his life, my father agreed to see a family therapist with my mother. They'd been fighting a lot because my father
wouldn't go along with the macrobiotic diets and vitamin cures that
my mother wanted to try now that they'd exhausted the treatments
available through Western medicine. In the session, my father tried to
explain to my mother that he was in too much physical pain to tolerate the taxing side effects of these alternative cures. When the therapist asked him about other moments of pain in his life that went
unrecognized, my father began talking about his childhood and broke
down sobbing. He described feeling caught between two worlds, and
how much he blamed blacks for acting in a way that invited prejudice.
He talked about being beaten up because of his white looks and black
identity, and how his parents had pretended not to notice. And he
railed against his father, dead now for forty years, for protecting him
neither from those bullies nor from the turmoil of growing up in this
racial limbo.

In three decades of marriage, my mother had never heard her husband talk about his childhood or internal strife about his racial identity with such honesty or anguish. She was deeply saddened to learn
that he'd been carrying around this burden by himself for all this
time. Both she and the therapist suggested that sharing this pain with
the people who loved him could ease his suffering. Telling my brother
and me would not only help us to understand him better, but it might
make my father feel less alone at the end of his life.

I remember visiting my parents at their house after that therapy
session. My father took up what had become his constant position in
recent weeks—reclined on his side on the couch in the living room.
But as he lay there, with his head propped in his hand, he held forth
with such enthusiasm that I could almost view him as simply relaxing.
He spoke optimistically about the efficacy of the alternative treatments and how he would give them another try. He mentioned writing projects that he was eager to finish and all the work that he could

still get done. And he raved about this magician of a therapist who had accomplished in a single session what forty years of analysis had not. "I feel as if I've been completely recalibrated," he said to me, without explaining what he meant. "Like a brand-new man." In the therapist's office, my father had glimpsed a way to reveal himself without betraying who he was or changing the way that his children saw him.

But in Martha's Vineyard with Todd and me a few weeks later, the right words failed to come. In my father's dream about being on trial for an unspecified crime, he'd made a speech in his defense that was so moving that even in his sleep he could feel himself tingling with it. The style in which he'd lived his life was a conviction he felt in his bones. But even though my brother and I were made from those same bones and blood and flesh, he couldn't be sure that we'd share his feeling about the rightness of what he'd done. As he grew more sick, the frailty of his spirit couldn't tolerate anything short of transcendence.

A few months before my father died, my friend Chinita and her boyfriend Mike paid another visit to my family's house on Martha's Vineyard. One early evening we all headed down to some nearby tennis courts. None of the three courts were occupied, and we spread across them, volleying back and forth. My father started out hitting with us, but he was too weak to play, and after a minute he said that he'd rather watch. Mike and my brother began a game, and my dad took a seat, leaning up against the wire fencing beside them.

Two courts away, Chinita and I had been playing for a half hour or so when the exhortations of my father caught our attention. We stopped to see what the commotion was about. Mike and Todd were both good athletes who could have been great tennis players if they'd ever put their minds to it, but Mike became a competitive rower while Todd took up running. Now Chinita and I watched Mike sprint to the net, scoop up a drop shot, and send it in a lob over Todd's head, and Todd turn and race to the baseline, leaping to slam it back with a high backhand. The rally continued on like this, with neither of them able to make a bad shot and my dad exclaiming after each one: "Keep your eye on the ball!" and "Don't think!" and then just calling out their names or hoots and cries of admiration.

The light started to fade but the match went on, and still they kept making improbable shot after impossible get. Chinita and I abandoned our game and sat down to watch on the other side of the court, adding our shouts of praise to the mix. Neither Todd nor Mike had played as well before, but they didn't seem to be trying to win, because that would mean the end of this match and the spell that had come over them, and the end of the astonishment of Anatole, without which they would never play as well again.

I remember glancing over at my father, who sat with his knees tucked into his chest and his arms wrapped around his legs, the only movement his head tracking the ball back and forth across the court. He looked completely enthralled, as if he had a front-row seat for the finals of the U.S. Open. And he seemed so happy to be celebrating this evidence of vitality, strength, and panache in the world. How graceful life could be! How extraordinary were human beings! No matter the shadows stretching across the court, we could all live on through the immortal magic of this evening.

A few nights later, my father celebrated his seventieth birthday. His illness had reached a stage where it was apparent to everyone present that he wouldn't live to see seventy-one. Michael Vincent Miller came down from Boston to join a collection of my father's closest male friends from Martha's Vineyard. Before dinner everyone sat upstairs in the living room, drinking wine and eating hors d'oeuvres. My father had been feeling nauseous and weak all day, but he insisted that my mother go ahead with the party. After chatting for a while, he announced that he was going to lie down in his bedroom but he wanted everyone to continue celebrating without him. His friends started protesting that he could lie on the couch, that he should try to eat something, that maybe they better leave so he could rest in peace, but my father silenced them with a raised hand as he paused in the door-way of the bedroom.

Never has a man been so rich in friendship, he began. He went around the room, describing the particular talents of each man there: this one's ability to fix anything and find his way to anywhere; that one's skill at deciphering the most mysterious human behaviors; another's sophistication after living in a dozen different countries; someone else's mix of subtle humor and exalted conversation. He talked about each friend at length, making sure that they knew that their best selves had been seen and appreci-ated. The men didn't say anything in response, but I watched each of them nod slightly or sit up taller in his seat, as if to acknowledge ac-ceptance of my father's pact. They would carry on being their best selves in his absence, with even more wit and animation than be-fore, and they would look past the hollow-cheeked figure who needed to lie down and recognize my father's best self too.

Someone raised his glass and said, "To Anatole."

"To Anatole!" came the answer.

My dad raised his eyebrows and smiled. Then he shut the door and didn't come out for the rest of the night.

During a visit with my aunt Shirley in the late winter of 2002, I raised the subject of disposing of her parents' ashes. They represented one piece of my father's unfinished business that I felt I could put to rest. For a while I'd been looking for the right moment to tell her that they were still sitting in their boxes in a closet in our house. Shirley had been telling me how at the end of my grandmother Edna's life, my father hadn't been involved in her care other than arranging for her funeral. Since all of their mother's friends were dead, there was no service, just a private cremation.

"Actually, the ashes, we still have them," I said. "And your father's too. My dad never did anything with them."

Shirley made an annoyed face.

"I know," I said, shaking my head. "I was thinking that perhaps you might want them back. Since they were your parents, and you had a relationship with them…"

"Well, what am I supposed to do with them?" Shirley asked.

"Do you have a family plot or somewhere you could bury them?"

She shook her head. "There's no room." Shirley explained that the vault where the ashes of her husband and Lorraine were stored had a limited number of spaces and they were all spoken for.

I could see that she resented having the responsibility of yet another thing her brother had neglected thrust upon her. We sat there in an awkward silence. Finally she asked, "What do you think your father intended to do with them?"

"I don't know for sure," I said. I told her about a chapter that my dad had written for his novel in which his character headed to the Brooklyn Bridge to scatter his father's ashes and then changed his mind just as he was about to toss them into the East River. I shrugged and said, "So maybe he couldn't bring himself to part with them."

"Then why don't you bury them next to him," she suggested.

My heart beat a little faster. I said, "I think that would be really nice." I told Shirley about an idea I'd been entertaining—that she and Frank and Denise and the kids could all come up to Martha's Vineyard, and we could hold some kind of ceremony to bury the ashes. "Since our two families have never gotten together, it would give us a chance to talk," I said. "It could be healing."

Shirley nodded; she seemed to like the idea. I offered to call Frank and extend the invitation to him as well.

After leaving Shirley's house, I headed for the subway on Central Park West, but when I reached the avenue, I decided to walk through the park instead. It was the middle of the day during the middle of the week, and the park was nearly empty. The air held the damp clinging cold of late winter, but with my hat pulled over my ears, my scarf wound around my neck, and my fantasies about this weekend on Martha's Vineyard, I felt snug and warm.

I pictured us in the living room after dinner. Shirley is talking about her father—how he used to wear his pants high under his chest (he thought he had unusually long legs), which would draw sarcastic remarks from her mother. Frank recalls his grandmother's dating advice when he was in high school, and her prediction when Denise came along that she was the one. Todd and I share the little we know from our father's stories, delighted each time Shirley corroborates a detail. But mostly we listen. Maybe Frank's kids are hearing some of these stories for the first time too.

The conversation moves on to the family's racial identity. Shirley describes the confusing climate of her childhood and her own process of becoming politicized about civil rights. Frank mentions all the gains for blacks that his parents helped to secure, and Denise talks about their efforts to instill in their children a sense of pride in being African American. They all share how my father's rejection of their family hurt them. Perhaps my mother tries to explain my father's decision from his perspective, and while Shirley and her family don't offer their forgiveness, there is a sense of satisfaction that comes from everyone having their say. My brother and I emphasize that we hope to be in their lives now, that we would like to be a family moving forward together.

I had walked seven or eight blocks, lost in my thoughts. Near the Eighty-first Street entrance to the park, I came upon some massive outcroppings that called to mind the boulders pocking our yard in Martha's Vineyard. We'd moved a smaller one to the cemetery down the road to mark my father's grave site. I paused to lean up against the rock face and looked up at the gray sky. I thought how my mother's potter friend could make urns for Nat's and Edna's ashes—as she'd done for my father's ashes a decade before—and that hundreds of years from now, the clay of the different urns would break down and the ashes would migrate through the dirt to mingle together. I thought how I could bring my own children to the grave site and tell them the complicated story about their grandpa Anatole and his ancestors and the wide-reaching effect of racism. But there would be a happy ending, because here were his parents: my father's family belonged to us too.

The stone grew cold against my back, pulling me from my reverie. I never went to my father's grave now—the public nature of its setting and the orchestrated tenor of the visit usually made me too self-conscious to feel any connection to my dad. As I straightened up and headed for the subway, walking briskly, I shook my head as if to clear it. Perhaps my fantasy about what this weekend might accomplish was a little far-fetched, but still, spending time with Shirley and Frank could bring some welcome closure.

Throughout the spring I called Shirley every month or so to try to arrange the visit. Frank had agreed to the idea as well, but the uncertainty of his kids' camp schedules and various vacation plans kept preventing us from setting a date. Then one day, while I was at the New York Public Library, my cell phone rang. It was my aunt calling to say that she and Frank had changed their minds.

I had been working in the Allen Room, a workspace on the second floor available to authors. I stepped into the hallway to take the call, and stared out the window at the buses gliding down Forty-second Street as Shirley broke the news.

"This may come as a surprise to you, but we want to bury the ashes in New York," she said. "Frank and I had a long conversation. He was very close to his grandmother, and we think that makes sense. They were New Yorkers, after all. They belong here." But she stressed that the decision wasn't final and that I should talk it over with my mother.

"But I thought that you didn't have room for them," I said.

"Well, we do."

"But you agreed they should be buried next to my father since he couldn't part with them."

Shirley laughed a little bitterly and said: "I don't think it was the case that he couldn't part with them." She explained that she had always felt uneasy about burying her parents on Martha's Vineyard, only she hadn't realized it until she talked to Frank.

"So I guess this means that you don't want to come visit," I said.

"It's not that we don't *want* to come. It's just that there's no point if we aren't going to bury the ashes there."

Outside, the streetlights started to sparkle and blur.

"But," Shirley continued, "you should talk it over with your mother, and then we can discuss it again."

I mumbled an answer, not trusting my voice to speak. We hung up and I lowered my head and began to cry as hard as if I'd just learned that a beloved grandparent had died. I turned from the window, and the library's grand white marble hallway stretched before me.

Even then I knew Shirley was right. Her parents' ashes didn't belong on Martha's Vineyard. They hadn't been welcomed there when they were alive, and my father hadn't earned being reunited with them in death. Frank had actually been a part of his grandmother's life. His kids, not mine, deserved to visit wherever Edna ended up and hear stories about their ancestors. But I couldn't get past my sadness over having to give up the one connection to my father's parents I had.

The next time my mother came to New York, she brought the boxes of Nat's and Edna's ashes with her. I'd made a plan with Shirley to drop them at her apartment, and then the three of us would have brunch in the neighborhood. After my mother and I parked, she retrieved the vinyl shopping bag containing the ashes from the backseat. I tried to take it from her — it was heavy and we had three or four blocks to walk — but my mother insisted on performing this ritual herself.

On the way to Shirley's, we talked about the other ashes that my mother had transported in her life: her mother's from Norway to New York and my father's from Cambridge to Martha's Vineyard. In her midsixties, my mother still performed modern dance and did the chainsawing and brush cutting on her property. She carried her burden with her shoulders squared and her back straight. I realized that I had no idea where her parents were buried; I'd never asked.

After handing over the ashes, we headed for brunch. My mother and her sister-in-law hadn't seen each other since my father's memorial service twelve years earlier — the only other time they'd met — yet the conversation never flagged during the meal. We discussed opera, the current Bush administration, how much the Upper West Side had changed, with my mother and Shirley nodding continually in agreement.

When my mom got up to use the bathroom, I seized the chance to tell Shirley that I was hoping to be included if she and Frank were going to have a ceremony. She shook her head, and I wasn't sure that she understood what I was asking.

"It would mean a lot to me if I could participate in disposing of the ashes," I said, my voice low and urgent. "I just really want to be a part of this family."

Shirley gave me a sad, curious smile. "But you didn't know them, Bliss," she said gently. She gestured at an envelope of photos of my brother's new twin daughters that my mother had brought along. "And you have a big family of your own." Well, not exactly.

My mother returned to the table and sat down. I was quiet while we paid the bill. We accompanied Shirley to her corner on the way back to the car. Just before we parted, she clasped her hands to her chest and said: "I can't wait to call Frank and tell him we have the ashes back!"

I've continued to visit Shirley or talk to her on the phone a couple of times a year. Her warmth toward me always takes me slightly by surprise. When I tell her that my boyfriend and I are thinking about having a baby, she exclaims excitedly about having another grandchild. "Grandniece or nephew," I correct her, smiling broadly. She answers my endless questions about her parents and her childhood and digs through files in her basement for family photos and birth certificates to help me in my research. "When are you going to finish that book?" she pesters. "I can't wait to read it." And despite my father's rejection of her, she often comes to his defense, alerting me to some favorable mention of him in the press and commiserating when he has been portrayed badly or unfairly.

Yet while Shirley knows that I don't have any other close relatives nearby, I have never been invited over for Christmas or Thanksgiving or even a Sunday dinner. She tells me news of Frank's kids—how they're faring at college, whom they're dating, what they're doing for the summer—but she doesn't encourage me to see them. Whenever I suggest all of us getting together, she makes an excuse about Frank's and Denise's busy schedules. My efforts to make plans myself with my cousin and his family were always greeted enthusiastically, but somehow the follow-up call to arrange the logistics would never come. Eventually I just stopped trying.

Talking with my mother in her car after brunch that day, it occurred to me for the first time that my father's family might not want me in their lives. My mother suggested that Shirley and Frank could be unconsciously keeping their distance to protect me from their anger.

"But it wasn't my choice not to see them growing up," I said. "And it's not fair to hold what Daddy did against me."

"It wasn't Shirley and her kids' choice either," my mother reminded me. She suggested that I had to respect their wishes, just as they had respected my father's wishes for all those years by never showing up on our doorstep.

"But wouldn't coming together as a family now be a way to get over this?" I said. "Wouldn't it be better to try to put this pain behind us?"

My mother put the key in the ignition and turned over the motor. She looked at me and said, "Some wounds can't be mended."

The extended Broyard clan has shown more interest in connecting with their estranged relatives. For these second and third cousins, my father was just one of a number of aunts, uncles, and cousins who'd become lost to the family after crossing over the color line. His rejection of them wasn't viewed as anything personal. In June of 2001, my mother, my brother, his wife, and I attended a family reunion in New Orleans that I'd helped my cousin Gloria to organize. There I encountered many relatives who sought the kind of reconciliation that I'd been hoping to achieve with Shirley and her family.

Gloria had contacted me after reading about my father in the *New Yorker*. She'd also recently discovered her African ancestry, and she was eager to meet the family members whom her grandparents had cut off after moving out west to live as white. I mentioned the idea of a large-scale reunion that some of the California cousins and I had been tossing around, and Gloria took the initiative of coordinating it. After two years of planning and hundreds of letters, phone calls, and e-mails, ninety-seven Broyards assembled in a historic, old-world-style hotel in downtown New Orleans.

People came from around New Orleans and across Louisiana; from Massachusetts, California, Georgia, New York, Arizona, and Utah; from as far away as Hawaii and Germany. Raised as African American, Creole, or white, some had pale skin and blue eyes, others were dark with brown eyes and black hair, then every shade in between. Later many people admitted that they'd been hesitant to attend the reunion because they didn't know which side—the white or black one—was throwing it. For three brothers from Florida, the weekend was confirmation of what one of them had already suspected—their mother wasn't part Mexican as she used to say to explain their dark skin tone.

The first night, we gathered for a cocktail party in a small banquet room. The family tree, dating back to Etienne Broyard's arrival in 1753, covered the tables lining the walls. Everyone leaned over the sheets of paper, looking for their own name, tracing the crooked branches until they found another name they recognized. Sometimes their paths crossed with the person beside them, and they straightened up, extended a hand or opened their arms, and said, "Looks like we're related."

When I explained how I fit into the family, people nodded and said, "So you're Anatole's daughter." Even before his story became public knowledge, many of my relatives knew about the Broyard who wrote for the *New York Times* and was living in Connecticut as white with his family. No one openly criticized his choice, and many were quick to point out that they didn't judge him, citing the lack of opportunities facing blacks at the time and "your father's understandable desire to better the lives of your family." But there were also stories like the one told by my cousin Janis, who was raised as black in Los Angeles among my other California cousins.

When Janis was growing up, her uncle Emile once came over to her house with clippings of cousin Anatole's writings. When Janis asked if she could meet my dad, she was told that she must never contact my family, because we were living as white and we didn't want to know her. "It made me think there was something about myself that I should be ashamed of," she said. As an adult, Janis understood the economic rationale for passing. Yet whenever she came across any Broyards in the phone book or on the Internet and thought about getting in touch, that admonition repeated in her head: *They don't want to know you.*

I told Janis in a quiet voice that I would have liked to know her if I'd just been given the chance. I hoped that my yearning now to be part of this family could make a small amends for what my father had done.

Unlike some families, for whom seeing each other feels more like a duty than a pleasure, the attendees at the reunion couldn't wait to get together again. For so many of us, even those who stayed on the black side, the color line had come between people in some way, and we were eager to get past it. The New Orleans Broyards began having lunch once a month. When I was in town, I would meet up with them too. The clan in California began to include more of the extended family at their gatherings. The handful of us in New York got together as a group or one-on-one on occasion. And Gloria kept us posted on the milestones in people's lives with a family newsletter.

Everyone clamored for another reunion. The natural choice would have been 2006 — five years after the first one — but then Hurricane Katrina devastated the city that had been home to generations of Broyards and scattered many family members across the country.

The majority of my New Orleans relatives' homes were located in the flooded neighborhoods. My cousin Sheila, who started me on my family research, her aunts Nancy and Jane, and her grandmother Rose managed to leave in time, but all of their houses were destroyed. The nursing home where my outspoken cousin Jeanne had moved because of her worsening asthma had no provisions to evacuate its residents. She arranged a ride to the Superdome herself and then spent three days and nights praying that the emergency generator would continue to power her respirator. Eventually Jeanne was airlifted to a hospital in Baton Rouge, where a nurse contacted me after spotting my inquiry on a Red Cross list.

In the weeks following the hurricane, a network of cousins and I managed to locate all the New Orleans Broyards who had attended the reunion to ensure they were safe. More than a year later, however, I'd lost track of many people's whereabouts. Some were headed to Austin and Houston; others planned on settling in Baton Rouge or Lafayette; still others spoke of going to Atlanta. I only know of two family members who returned to New Orleans. One of them, my father's second cousin, O'Neil Broyard, was the proprietor of the Saturn Bar, an infamous dive in the lower Ninth Ward that was popular with locals and visiting celebrities for the surrealistic murals that covered every inch of its walls and ceiling. After being forcibly evacuated to St. Louis by state troopers, O'Neil came back to reopen his bar and then died of heart failure in the midst of cleaning it up.

The city's black middle class, to which the majority of my family members belonged, has mostly disappeared. Thousands of city employees and schoolteachers — the bulk of whom were black — were laid off, which meant that the black lawyers, doctors, dentists, and businesses that served them lost their clientele. Despite the celebration by the national press of the first post-Katrina Mardi Gras, my friend Keith Medley, whose guesthouse was spared by the hurricane, pointed out the absence of black Carnival balls compared to twenty or thirty in the past.

The uncertain future of New Orleans East—where many family members and other middle-class blacks lived—makes deciding whether to return particularly difficult. In large areas city planners are waiting to see who comes back before committing to providing basic services such as working sewers or police patrols. Those who decide to rebuild anyway risk having their houses demolished if their neighborhoods don't attract a critical mass of residents. These sections would then be turned into "green spaces" that would provide flood drainage for the rest of the city. Better schools, more job opportunities, and less crime in the evacuees' newly adopted hometowns give them other reasons to stay away.

The demise of these black middle-class neighborhoods threatens the future of what remained of Creole culture in New Orleans. The community's previous diaspora, in the beginning of the twentieth century, spawned Creole outposts in Chicago, Houston, and especially Los Angeles. But the circumstances of Katrina not only made it hard for members of the community to relocate near each other, it destroyed their cultural touchstone in New Orleans too. Louisiana-based Creole genealogical groups such as the Creole Heritage, Education, and Research Society (CHERS) and the Louisiana Creole Research Association, Inc. (LA Creole), along with organizations such as the Louisiana Creole Heritage Center based at Northwestern State University in Natchitoches, Louisiana, are working to preserve the culture, but the state grant-making institutions and local residents they rely on for funding and support are struggling too.

The situation of the displaced Creoles brings to mind my grandfather's departure from New Orleans eighty years earlier. I wonder whether some of the evacuees will also turn into silent figures, preoccupied by a vanquished existence that survives only in their imaginings.

For me the Creole culture of New Orleans provided the backstory for my father's relationship to his racial identity. It explained why the label of black or African American was an uncomfortable fit for him, and it expanded my understanding of the black American experience outside the narrative of Middle Passage, slavery, and sharecropping. The constant shuffling of the Creoles of color between the categories of mixed, black, and white made it hard to believe in the legitimacy of any racial labels. It was in New Orleans that I finally understood the dilemma that history had created for my father.

Of course he never acknowledged being plagued by any dilemma; he clung to the belief that his actions were governed exclusively by choice. My father told himself, and me, that he didn't see his family because he had nothing in common with them, that sharing blood with people didn't obligate you to them. However, the other relationships in my father's life suggest that he didn't actually feel this way. Over the years, he often voiced his disdain for drunks, yet he stuck by my mother through the worst years of her alcoholism. After bemoaning my decision to attend the University of Vermont—rather than the type of prestigious Ivy League school that he expected for his progeny—he came to praise the school's "quintessential New England college experience." Todd's fascination with home security alarms was as incomprehensible to our father as his own love of literature had been to his father; nevertheless my dad applauded the zeal with which my brother applied himself to his chosen career.

None of these are heroic gestures. All parents must reconcile their fantasies for their children with the choices their kids actually make. But I believe that my father was able to put aside his disappointments because he loved us; and that he loved us because we were his family; and that family mattered to him because he'd loved his parents and siblings too. Still, he left them, which perhaps explains why he seemed so determined to prevent us from ever leaving him.

When I was in high school, he proposed turning part of the second floor of our house into an in-law apartment and building a garage with another apartment above it. That way, he told Todd and me, we could save money on rent while starting out our careers. And then when we got married and had children, he went on, he and my mother would be on hand for babysitting. He'd catalog all the advantages to having some grandparents around. *Dad*, I'd groan. *Don't you want us to have our own lives?*

My father couldn't argue with a desire to make one's own way in the world. But to his mind, the life that he'd provided for us hadn't contained any disadvantages. He didn't recognize how his very overprotectiveness might give us a reason to want to get away. Of course his parents had also been trying to do their best for their children, and that they "failed" by being identified as Negroes hadn't exactly been their fault.

My husband, Nico Israel, and I are about to become parents ourselves, and I've begun to appreciate the complexity and responsibility of legacy. What values and traditions will we pass down? And what accidental flotsam from our pasts will float down unconsciously? Will our child have dark hair and dark skin like some of our ancestors? If our son or daughter asks, *What am I?* how will we answer? *Daddy is a Sephardic Jew with roots in Spain, Greece, and Turkey, and Mommy is Norwegian, French, black, and Choctaw Indian?* Will our child's birth certificate, school applications, and all the other bureaucratic forms encountered during life allow for the record of this complicated history? Since 2000, people have been able to check more than one box under the race question on the federal census, but many states are still following the single-box approach on school forms. What parts, if any, of this ancestral inheritance will our child want to mark down? And will these questions of origin even matter in the future?

From my own father, I inherited a legacy that connected me to the worst and best American traditions: from the racial oppression spawned by slavery to the opportunities created through becoming self-made. Recognizing my forebears' place in the continuum of history has made me appreciate my own responsibilities as a citizen—of my community, my country, and the world—in a way that simply paying my taxes or casting a vote never did.

As T. S. Eliot put it in his poem "Little Gidding": "We shall not cease from exploration / And the end of our exploring / Will be to arrive where we started / And know the place for the first time." I began this journey with the revelation of my father's racial ancestry. After sixteen years of exploration—and being by turns impressed and dismayed by my father and his choices—I feel I have only now, with a child of my own on the way, begun to know the dilemma for myself.

I may never be able to answer the question *What am I?* yet the fault lies not in me but with the question itself. And with that realization, that letting go, I can finally say good-bye.

Every year on the anniversary of my father's death, I have made a ritual of playing audiotapes of his voice. In none of the tapes I have is he speaking directly to me: one is a lecture he gave on Martha's Vineyard about his frustration with the way Americans talk to each other; another is the address he gave at the University of Chicago Medical School about what he wanted in a doctor. But the way he offered his elaborate metaphors in a slow satisfied growl or his habit of stalling as he poked fun at himself, then exploded into a hoot of laughter recall his presence more vividly than any photograph or piece of his writing.

The one tape I could never bring myself to play after my father died was recorded at the funeral of Milton Klonsky, my father's best friend from Brooklyn College. The only other time I listened to it I was fifteen. After overhearing my mother on the phone tell someone that my dad, in the middle of eulogizing Milton, had broken down, I noticed one day a tape labeled with Milton's name lying on the desk in my father's study.

I'd seen my dad lose his temper lots of times, and I saw the aftermath of his losing control that Mother's Day after my grandmother Edna died. Sometimes he'd hinted at a deep sadness in his life before our family came along, and I sensed that he was plagued by vague unspoken regrets, but I'd never seen—or heard—him cry. And I'd thought that hearing such unrestrained emotion would reveal something essential about my father's character that had been withheld from me so far.

This year, on October 11, the anniversary of his death, I retrieve the tape of Milton's funeral from the shoe box where I keep my mementos of my father. I place it into a boombox and fast-forward until I come upon my father's turn to speak, just as I did twenty-four years ago when I first stumbled across the tape. I listen to my dad recount visiting Milton in the hospital. A stroke had left him unable to speak except for a few words. Milton said to my dad, "Do what you have to do," and then blurted out the word "debauchery." My father describes trying to make sense of his friend's enigmatic message. Of all people, Milton understood the bargain that my dad had made: he had introduced him to the literary life that my father eventually chose over his family.

In his typical crowd-pleasing fashion, my father's portrait of his friend comes out sounding effortlessly artful; he pauses on certain particularly nice turns of phrase that capture the extraordinary qualities of his most luminous companion. And then he pauses for a longer moment, and the next phrase comes out sounding less certain, and his voice cracks as he tries again to speak.

I remember back to when I was fifteen, standing there guiltily in my father's study, waiting to hear the sound of his tears. I'd been afraid that they might sound grotesque, after being twisted and stored up for so long, like some strange parasite that had taken root in his body years before. And then I remember the anguish I'd felt as the tape rolled on and I glimpsed the boundary beyond which my father would always remain opaque.

Seated at my desk in front of the tape player now, I find this idea less terrifying than strangely consoling. I listen for the moment when my father's voice breaks off, followed by a distant muffled rustling in the background, the interminable whirring of the tape heads—louder and louder—and then the sound, brump-click, that signaled a button being depressed. Stop. Silence.

Afterword

In the years since I first learned about my father's racial background, DNA testing has become increasingly popular among genealogists as a way to uncover their more distant ancestry once the paper trail goes cold, and dozens of companies have sprung up to accommodate their interest. The types of available tests fall into two categories: lineage tests that trace the geographic origins of the person on the top of your maternal or paternal line—i.e., your great-great-great-etc.-grandmother was Welsh, or belonged to the Kru tribe in Liberia—and "ancestral admixture" tests, which determine the percentage of your ancestors who were Indo-European, sub-Saharan African, Native American, and East Asian.

The genetic markers used by the DNA ancestry companies to link a person to a specific population group were developed with the same technology that allowed scientists to map the human genome. This is ironic, because while one of the most trumpeted findings of the Human Genome Project was that "the concept of race has no genetic or scientific basis" since, in President Clinton's words, "all human beings, regardless of race, are more than 99.9 percent the same," the results of DNA genealogy tests tend to reaffirm people's notion that race is a biological fact. For me at least, they dangled the possibility of a definitive "scientific" answer to the question *How black am I?*

✳   ✳   ✳

I waited on the phone in Brooklyn while my mother pried open the little ceramic jar in which she kept the leftover ashes from my father's burial urn. Her willingness to sift through her dead husband's ashes for some sizable pieces from which his DNA might be extracted initially surprised me. But after a lifetime of being on intimate terms with death, my mother wasn't afraid to get her hands dirty with it. She even took some pleasure in the job. She'd put the phone down and I could hear her swearing in the background.

"What happened?" I asked when she returned. "You didn't spill them?"

She laughed wickedly. "I couldn't get the top off. But I have it now. Yup, there are some b-i-g pieces here."

"Are you sifting them through something? A colander?"

"Just feeling around with my hands."

"You're touching them?"

"Sure, why not?" She made some lip-smacking noises. "Yum, salty..."

"Mom, be serious."

"Oh. This one looks like Daddy's tooth."

My mother mailed off an assortment of chunks to one of the companies that provide DNA ancestry testing. But it turned out that the pieces were too small and charred to yield any insight into my father's genetic history. And even my mother—a hoarder who was particularly loathe to get rid of anything pertaining to my father— didn't still have a hairbrush or sweater lying around that might contain some of his stray hairs (with the root attached). I had to settle for testing myself and some of my family. Nevertheless, the results came as a complete surprise.

It's generally agreed among population scientists that, according to our DNA, human beings originated in East Africa. What we recognize as racial differences—skin color, hair texture, facial features, and body types—are mostly the result of adaptation to new climates as we migrated across the globe. For people living closer to the equator, darker skin helped to protect against potentially deadly exposure to the sun's ultraviolet rays. Alternately, the farther north humans wandered, the lighter their skin became, to aid the development of essential vitamin D, which required absorbing adequate ultraviolet radiation. Curly or frizzy hair was better suited for hotter climates, since it trapped sweat near the scalp, prolonging the body's natural cooling process.

According to the findings of the genome researchers, all these external differences only account for somewhere in the range of 0.1 percent of our genetic makeup, which is insignificant when compared with the thousands of genes that determine who we "really" are—our intelligence, our emotional sensitivity, our artistic talents—none of which can be sorted according to specific racial groups. Yet within precisely that 0.1 percent of difference also lie the clues about where our ancestors came from.

Two types of DNA that are exempt from recombination—the Y chromosome and mitochondrial DNA—pass down unchanged from one generation to the next, providing an unbroken link to our past, similar to the way a surname is passed down through the paternal line. However, just as the spelling or pronunciation of a last name sometimes altered slightly as a family moved through a region or across the globe, so did these normally static types of DNA undergo small copying errors as the human family ventured forth from its original home of Africa. These "spelling" variations—which usually reside on the "junk" portion of the DNA and don't affect our looks or character—function like passport stamps on our genetic code, allowing scientists to re-create the different migratory paths taken by human beings as they populated the earth and pinpoint where our ancestors lived thousands of years ago.

The Y chromosome is passed from father to son; therefore my brother's would lead me back to the region of origin for our very distant paternal great-grandfather. But I already knew from my genealogical research that the trail would almost certainly end in Europe. As with the vast majority of black Americans with European ancestry, the mixed-race pairings in our family tree occurred between white men and black women. I decided instead to test my father's mitochondrial DNA (which is inherited by both men and women from their mothers) to trace the geographic origins of my grandmother's maternal family tree.

Because men don't pass along their mitochondrial DNA to their children, I had to obtain a sample from my father's sister Shirley. She volunteered a swab of her cheek cells to send to African Ancestry, a company launched by a Howard University geneticist named Dr. Rick Kittles, which promised to connect her maternal lineage to a specific tribe in Africa. While at it, I collected another sample from her to send to DNAPrint Genomics, a company based in Florida that performed the ancestral admixture test.

Ignoring the Y-chromosome and mitochondrial DNA, DNAPrint analyzed the rest of the genome for variations called single nucleotide polymorphisms (SNPs) that could be sorted into the four basic population groups. Ideally these Ancestry Information Markers were present in all members of one group and absent in all members of the other groups. Again the markers don't typically appear on portions of our DNA that control specific traits, so the company wasn't considering genes for hair texture, skin color, or any of the other physical characteristics associated with race. At the same time, however, the degree of admixture does seem to affect physical appearance. According to DNAPrint, a person begins to exhibit recognizable traits of a population group at 30 percent ancestry.

Given that my father could pass for white, I expected him to fall somewhere below 30 percent African ancestry. By comparing Shirley's results to those for my mother, my brother, and me, the scientist at DNAPrint, Matt Thomas, was going to try to infer my father's ratio. It was strange to think that in a matter of weeks, I could have an answer to the question that I'd been grappling with for more than a dozen years.

News stories about DNA ancestry testing often include someone who didn't receive the results they were expecting. Richard Gabriel, the CEO of DNAPrint, told me that the mostly frequently disappointed group was people who expected to find Native American roots; about half the time, the results come back negative. The company had even coined the term American Indian Princess Syndrome to describe these customers' determination to prove this branch of their family tree. Their motivation might extend beyond an attachment to their family lore: with Indian gaming revenues reaching almost $20 billion annually, tribal membership can mean access to lucrative payouts. In 2006 the *New York Times* reported a story about an increasing number of individuals who hoped to leverage trace amounts of minority ancestry, discovered through DNA testing, to bolster their chances of obtaining college financial aid or new employment as a minority applicant. DNAPrint has found that about 5 percent of customers who self-identify as white show up with some African ancestry. More frequently people who think of themselves as black turn up with European and Native American roots.

In 2003 ABC's *Nightline* program featured a story about a Los Angeles high school principal who had recently obtained his "ancestral admixture" from DNAPrint. Like some of my Broyard cousins, the man's family were Creoles from Louisiana who had moved to California in the 1950s to escape Jim Crow segregation. He was very light-skinned, but he always thought of himself as black and raised his children to be proud of their black heritage. According to DNAPrint, however, he was 57 percent Indo-European, 39 percent Native American, 4 percent East Asian, and not black at all. The news program's requisite qualifications about margins of error and the estimated nature of the percentages notwithstanding, the principal told

Nightline that the results had "rocked my world." He even questioned his seventy-six-year-old mother about whether he was adopted. He said that he would mark off "Native American" on future census forms "because no one will doubt that I'm a native of this country or that my story is uniquely an American one."

I worried that I wouldn't show up with any African ancestry either. And in the first result I received from DNAPrint, I didn't. But then again neither did my aunt Shirley. I was 90 percent Indo-European and 10 percent Native American, and she was 94 percent Indo-European and 6 percent Native American. "But how can I not have any African?" asked Shirley. It didn't make sense, especially since we'd also received the results of her mitochondrial DNA analysis. According to African Ancestry, her and my father's maternal lineage traced back to the Hausa tribe, who could be found in present-day Nigeria.

The folks at DNAPrint suspected that my father and his sister's African ancestry may indeed have been little more than "one drop." It was certainly below the range for recognizable traits, perhaps even too negligible to be picked up. It was also possible that DNAPrint's current test wasn't always able to distinguish between Native American and sub-Saharan African ancestries. The accuracy of their Ancestry Information Markers depended on the purity of the people in their sample pools. Finding unmixed Native Americans presented a particular challenge, given a colonial history of the New World that not only wiped out many of the original inhabitants but also resulted in the frequent intermixing of natives with people of European and African descent. The absence of civil or sacramental records in most cases made it difficult to confirm the genealogy of Native Americans who believed themselves to be unmixed. DNAPrint decided to run our DNA samples again with a new version of the test that more than doubled the number of Ancestry Information Markers, which should significantly increase the accuracy of the results.

This time I showed up with 13 percent sub-Saharan African ancestry, which made more sense—until I compared my results to those for my brother and my aunt Shirley. Todd—who with his blond hair, blue eyes, and pale skin looked even less black than I did—had 18 percent African ancestry, while my aunt Shirley—who, although light-skinned, looked phenotypically black—turned up with only 9 percent African ancestry (and another 9 percent Native American). The results were too ambiguous to help in calculating my father's own admixture. It seemed that the inheritance of Ancestry Information Markers depended on the luck of the draw, which made these genealogical DNA tests feel more like a parlor game than the kind of hard science that I was hoping, against my better judgment, would unlock my family secrets once and for all.

Even so, both my aunt and my brother planned on mentioning the particulars of their admixture during their next visit to the doctor, in case the genetic hand they'd been dealt also contained a propensity for one of the diseases prevalent among members of their "invisible" ancestries. Shirley's cardiologist, for example, might want to take into account her majority European descent before prescribing BiDil, a heart medication that was approved by the FDA exclusively for black patients. And Todd's internist might want to consider screening Todd for prostate cancer at the recommended age of forty-five for black men versus fifty for white men.

The results of these genealogical DNA tests are destined to become more accurate and meaningful as the science evolves and the databases of sample pools grow larger and more diverse. The National Geographic Society is currently in the middle of a five-year, $40 million effort to collect 100,000 DNA samples from indigenous populations in order to create an atlas of humankind's migrations across the globe. The completed genographic database, which will represent "the world's largest collection of DNA samples," will allow scientific communities (and genealogical DNA companies) to greatly refine the genetic markers used to pinpoint a person's ancestral origins.

Perhaps then I'll be able to solve a new family mystery that arose during my DNA genealogical adventure. I had tested my mother in the process of trying to infer my father's ancestral admixture. She grew up thinking that she was Norwegian on both her maternal and paternal sides—a lineage that was no doubt particularly attractive to my father. But according to DNAPrint, she's 13 percent Native American, which could mean that one of her great-grandparents was a full-bloodied Indian. "How about that!" she exclaimed when I shared her results. "And you thought you got all your diversity from your father!"

My mother's father's family migrated from Norway to Minnesota in 1849, when the state was still a territory mostly populated by the Sioux and Ojibwe tribes. Although I haven't yet unearthed any genealogical records or buried family stories to support DNAPrint's findings, they do seem within the realm of possibility. But my mother doesn't attribute much significance to her newfound Native American heritage; she doesn't plan to acknowledge it on future census questionnaires nor has it affected how she thinks of herself. That her family's Indian ancestry—because of the particulars of the mixing or the attitudes of the surrounding culture—doesn't seem to have affected their lives whatsoever allows her to regard it as an intriguing but mostly benign revelation.

But obviously this wasn't the case in my father's family. History, law, and public opinion made the fact of his black blood matter, whether it was 50 percent, 13 percent, or only one drop.

Acknowledgments

Having the chance to express my gratitude has been a frequent and sustaining daydream during the seven years that I spent researching and writing *One Drop*. While the list of those who have helped me — from small kindnesses to crucial conversations — has grown too long to recall, let alone recount, there are a number of people and institutions without whom I could not have seen my way to the finish.

From the start, there has been the miraculous Jennifer Rudolph Walsh of the William Morris Agency, who conjured for me the time and freedom I needed to write the book that I wanted to write. I am also grateful to the Louisiana Endowment for the Humanities, the Ludwig Vogelstein Foundation, and the New York Foundation for the Arts for their financial support, to the MacDowell and Yaddo artist colonies for providing the opportunity for prolonged concentration, and to Donna Brodie and the members of the Writers Room in New York City for their fellowship.

I could not have completed my family history without the help of my newfound cousins. I am grateful to Sheila Prevost for reaching out that Christmas Eve so many years ago, for sharing the amazing research she had already completed, and for introducing me to her grandmother Rose and the rest of her family. Barbara Trevigne, Bernie

Cousins, and Gloria Golden also all shared their information about the Broyard and Cousin genealogies. Thank you.

My fellow researchers have provided welcome companionship and crucial assistance during what can be a long and lonely process. I am particularly indebted to Catherine Donnow, founder of the online discussion group New Orleans Gens de Couleur Researchers and my fellow members of the Creole Heritage, Education, and Research Society (CHERS). I am also grateful to Ingrid Stanley and Pat Schexnayder, founders of the Louisiana Creole Research Association, Inc. (LA Creole), whose tireless efforts to preserve the Creole culture in the aftermath of Katrina's devastation are an inspiration. I'm honored to donate a portion of the proceeds of this book to their cause.

In New Orleans, Richard and Kristina Ford introduced me to many people who were helpful to my project; chief among them was Curtis Wilke, who kindly offered me a place to stay time and again over the years. I am also grateful to Keith Weldon Medley for steering me through the labyrinth of New Orleans archives and to Beverly and Brandi Kilbourne for making me feel at home in my ancestral city.

At the New Orleans Public Library, Gregory Osborne, Wayne Everard, and Irene Wainwright expertly directed me through the Louisiana Division's archival material. Sally K. Reeves, Ann Wakefield, and Eleanor Burke made available the New Orleans Notarial Archives collection of historical acts. Dr. Charles Nolan allowed me access to the Archdiocese of New Orleans sacramental records. In St. Tammany Parish, Tom Aicklen, coordinator of the Lacombe Heritage Center, and Peter M. Cousin Jr. helped to fill in the blanks about the Cousin family. I am grateful to the following scholars of Louisiana history and the free people of color of New Orleans for their guidance: Rebecca Scott, Caryn Cosse Bell, and Diana Williams, and especially Mary White and Mary Gehman, for their careful readings of my manuscript. Thanks also to Dawn Logsdon for her helpful feedback and to Lawrence Powell for his editorial suggestions and the inspiring example of his masterly blend of narrative and scholarship.

During its long gestation, *One Drop* benefited greatly from the intelligence and generosity of many readers: Edward Ball, Catherine Dana, Ruth Davis, Roya Hakakian, A. M. Homes, Dana Johnson, Candy Shweder, Nina Siegal, Martha Southgate, Denyse Thomasos, Lynne Tillman, and Evelyn Toynton. I am particularly grateful to James Hanahan, Charles Graeber, and Michael Vincent Miller for their thoughtful comments on the completed manuscript and to Laurie Abraham for her invaluable contribution in making the book the best that it could be. My thanks also to Vincent Livelli, whose vivid memories enrich these pages, to the ladies at The Moth — Lea Thau, Catherine Burns, Jenifer Hixson, and especially Joey Xanders — who asked to hear the story in the first place, and to Tessa Blake, Amy Brill, Nell Casey, Elizabeth Condon, Sarah Haberman, Virginia Heffernan, Coleman Hough, Giulia Melucci, and Danzy Senna, whose friendship and enthusiasm have buoyed me over the years.

To illustrate *One Drop,* family members Mark Broyard, Beverly Broyard, Joyce Howard, Dionne Butler, Tony Broyard, and Jeanne Dominick shared with me their precious family photos, and Charlie Griffin of Griffin Editions carefully reproduced them. Computer genius Mark Winkler retrieved lost files, supplied new equipment, and literally kept me in business, all for the price of a few home-cooked meals.

At Little, Brown, I am grateful to Michael Pietsch for wanting the project, to Reagan Arthur for guiding it so patiently to completion, to Oliver Haslegrave for attending cheerfully to the endless details required to turn my tower of pages into a bound thing, and to Mario Pulice and Allison Warner of the art department for their help in making that bound thing beautiful. The exacting Peggy Leith Anderson made sure my words made good grammatical sense and Marlena Bittner helped to usher them out into the world. Thank you also to the fabulous Melodie McDaniel, for shooting an author's photograph in which I can truly recognize myself, and to the artist Lorna Simpson, who graciously took the time, during an eventful period in her professional life, to offer suggestions on the jacket design.

There are a handful of cherished friends who I suspect are as happy as I am that this book is finally done. My heartfelt thanks to Andrew Arkin for his fatherly presence, to Nina Collins for her wisdom and advice, to Laurie Girion for her big-sisterly ways, to Chinita Hard for her constancy and care, to Susan Epstein for showing me how to proceed again and again, to Lucinda Rosenfeld for her encouragement and commiseration, and to Joshua Wolf Shenk for inspiring me by his own example. I am also grateful to Mickey and Raye Israel for their support and affection.

I have no doubt that this story could have been told many different ways, and I'm honored that so many relatives entrusted me with their recollections so that I might offer this version. Thank you for welcoming me into your homes and for treating me as if I had always been one of the family. I am particularly grateful to my aunt Shirley Broyard Williams for her willingness to revisit a painful subject in exhaustive detail; to my brother, Todd Broyard, for remembering what I'd forgotten; and to my mother, Sandy Broyard, for demonstrating her love and faith countless times over. Finally, thanks to Nico Israel for his patience, for the precision of his insights, and especially for making with me a beautiful life to enjoy when I was finished: our daughter, Esme.

Notes on Sources

Wherever quotes from primary sources appear, the sources have been indicated in the text, unless their inclusion would intrude too awkwardly on the narrative, in which case they can be found in the notes below. Sources of quotes from my father's work have not been listed in every instance.

For the historical accounts of New Orleans, Louisiana, and Brooklyn, I am indebted to the scholarship of many historians and academics. The secondary sources upon which I relied most heavily are listed in shortened form by chapter in the notes section. Full references of works cited can be found in the bibliography.

The hundreds of genealogical sources I consulted have not been cited, except in cases where their mention is relevant. To complete my family history, I drew on records found in New Orleans at the Louisiana Division of the New Orleans Public Library, the New Orleans Notarial Archives, the New Orleans Archdiocesan Archives, the Historic New Orleans Collection, the Louisiana and Special Collections Department of the Earl K. Long Library at the University of New Orleans, the Xavier University Archives and Special Collections, the Amistad Research Center at Tulane University, and the Jackson Barracks Military Library; in Baton Rouge at the Louisiana State Archives and the Louisiana State University Libraries Special Collections in Hill Memorial Library; in Covington, Louisiana, at the conveyance office and the Historic Archives Department of the St. Tammany Parish Clerk of Court; in Washington, DC, at the National Archives' Compiled Service Records for the War of 1812 and the Civil War; and in Brooklyn, New York, at the Brooklyn Collection of the Brooklyn Public Library.

PART ONE

Chapter 1

My father's writings about the experience of being ill have been collected into *Intoxicated by My Illness*. That volume also contains his review of Ernest Becker's *Denial of Death*, which initially appeared in the *New York Times* in 1974.

I am grateful to the writer Leslie Garis for sharing with me notes she made during a visit to my father at the Dana-Farber Cancer Hospital.

Chapter 3

The chairwoman of the Southport Historical Committee, Margaret Zeller, provided information about the building guidelines in the historic village of Southport.

The details about the application process to the Pequot Yacht Club for my parents and Phil Donahue were based on the recollections of my mother, Sandy Broyard, and Edwin Gaynor, a former commodore for the Pequot Yacht Club.

Chapter 6

For more on the definition of Creole, see Kein's introductory essay in her anthology *Creole* as well as Domínguez's *Definition* and Hall's *Africans*.

Since I first visited the Boston Public Library in the early 1990s, the number of volumes concerning "passing" has increased dramatically. In addition to the reissued novel *Passing* by Larsen, the nonfiction works *Passing*, by Kroeger, and *Individualism*, by Pfeiffer, were particularly helpful.

Chapter 7

The quotes from my father about his father's character appear in an essay called "Growing Up Irrational" in *Men, Women, and Other Climaxes*.

For more about Gwendolyn Midlo Hall's slave database, see Firestone's "Identity Restored."

I am grateful to Major Jackson and Kathryn Friedman for directing me to the statistics about diversity at the University of Vermont in the late 1980s.

Ralph Ellison's observation about how African Americans are perceived comes from the opening passage of *Invisible Man*.

Chapter 8

Wayne Dawkins, author of *Black Journalists: The NABJ Story,* about the history of the National Association of Black Journalists, confirmed that my father is believed to be the first black staff member critic of a major U.S. newspaper.

The real names of Vivian Carter and her husband, Anthony, have been changed to protect their privacy.

Chapter 9

The scenes with my cousins Marchele, Robert, Erin, and Mark include some conversations that took place in an interview setting at a different time. These scenes have been condensed for narrative purposes.

PART TWO

Chapter 10

T. S. Eliot's reference to the Mississippi River as the "strong brown God" appears in "The Dry Salvages" section of *Four Quartets.*

Antonio Gramsci's quote about the "infinity of traces" comes from *Prison Notebooks.*

Chapter 12

Information about La Rochelle in the eighteenth century came from Clark's *La Rochelle.*

I am indebted to Hall's *Africans* for my account of life in French colonial Louisiana. The story of Louis Congo, the African native who received freedom after becoming the local executioner, and details about the slave revolt in Pointe Coupée both came from her book.

For more about the attitudes of French authorities toward race-mixing in French colonial Louisiana, see Johnson's "Colonial New Orleans" in Hirsch and Logsdon, *Creole New Orleans.*

For the description of Spanish colonial Louisiana, I drew mainly upon Hanger's *Bounded Lives.* Hanger's book was also useful in understanding the slave revolt in St. Domingue and its ramifications in Louisiana, as were Hall's *Social Control* and James's *Jacobins.*

I am grateful to my cousin Barbara Trevigne for her information on the history of the *tignon.*

Chapter 13

I am grateful to the Creole historian and genealogist Mary White for her assistance regarding street conditions and shoe styles in New Orleans at the turn of the nineteenth century.

The account of the 1803 transfer of Louisiana from France to the United States was based on *Memoirs* by Pierre-Clément de Laussat, the French colonial prefect for Louisiana.

The details about New Orleans's infrastructure problems during the early nineteenth century came from Fossier's *New Orleans.*

Bell's *Revolution* was crucial to my understanding of the political activism of Creoles of color during the American period, beginning with the agitation by the colored black troops on the question of citizenship.

The quotes from the letter to Claiborne describing the taunts of the black Haitians "eating human flesh" appeared in the Debien and Le Gardeur essay in Brasseaux et al., *Road to Louisiana.*

For more about General Andrew Jackson and the battalion of free men of color during the Battle of New Orleans, see Fleming's "Old Hickory's" in *Quarterly Journal of Military History.*

The petition of the Pointe Coupée property owners, including Etienne Broyard, requesting troops to control their slaves appears in Carter's *The Territorial Papers of the United States.*

The quote from Colonel Savary about the willingness of his colored troops to risk their lives for their country appears in Bell's *Revolution.*

See Johnson's *Soul* for more on the New Orleans slave market.

Tregle's essay "Creoles and Americans" in Hirsch and Logsdon's *Creole New Orleans* was very helpful in understanding Creole and American relations in New Orleans during the antebellum period.

See Domínguez's *Definition* for the historical application of the term "Creole" and its changing racial connotations.

I am grateful to Diane Williams, a PhD candidate in Harvard's American Studies program, for sharing her research on the term *plaçage,* namely that it also referred to relationships of unmarried white men with white women. Williams points out that the infamy of plaçage as solely an interracial institution seems to be mostly the product of accounts from visitors to the city rather than its natives.

The quote from the Englishman about mixed-race women appears in J. S. Buckingham's *The Slave States of America* (1842), as cited in Rankin's "Forgotten People."

The statistics about the imbalance between marriageable white men and white women appear in Paul LaChance's essay in *Revista/Review Interamericana.*

I drew upon Latrobe's *Southern Travels*, published by the Historic New Orleans Collection, for many of the details of New Orleans in the antebellum period, particularly the quadroon balls. Also, Mary White graciously shared her knowledge about plaçage relationships to counterbalance the many mythologies surrounding them.

Charles Gayarré's quote about the scene in the home of a white husband who kept a mulatto mistress comes from Rankin's "Forgotten People."

I am indebted to Sollors's *Neither* for its analysis of the history of understanding about racial difference, particularly the Curse of Ham and the theory of "mulatto sterility."

Chapter 14

I am grateful to Gregory Osborne, a former research assistant in the Louisiana Division of the New Orleans Public Library, for sharing his recollections of the range of reactions among white patrons on discovering evidence of black ancestry.

For more information on the Mardi Gras Indians, see Medley's "Mardi Gras Mambo" and "From Sire to Son" in the *New Orleans Tribune.*

Chapter 15

Reinders, *End of an Era,* provided details about the cotton industry in New Orleans and the continuing infrastructural problems.

I am indebted to Bell's *Revolution* for my account of the reaction in New Orleans to France's 1848 revolution. All of the quotes during the celebration at the St. Louis Exchange can be found in her book.

For more about the accomplishments of and restrictions on the free people of color during the antebellum period, see Desdunes's *Our People*, Rankin's "Forgotten People," Alice Moore Dunbar-Nelson's essay "People of Color in Louisiana" in Kein's *Creole,* Gehman's *Free People,* and Bell's *Revolution.* Logsdon and Bell's essay "Americanization" in Hirsch and Logsdon, *Creole New Orleans,* was also helpful in understanding the relations between free blacks and slaves.

The poem "A New Impression" originally appeared in *L'album littéraire* and was excerpted in Bell's *Revolution.* See Rankin's "Forgotten People" for more on the shift toward marriage among free people of color.

The proceedings of the Pandelly legal case during February 1854 were covered in most of the New Orleans newspapers.

Both Desdunes's *Our People* and Houzeau and Rankin's *My Passage* discuss *L'Union* editor Paul Trévigne.

See Nelson's "Free Negro" for more about the attitudes toward the free people of color by the New Orleans press. Louisiana governor Robert C. Wickliffe's appeal to the state legislature about removal of free blacks from Louisiana appears in Gayarré's *History*.

Schafer's *Becoming Free* was helpful in understanding the laws regarding free people of color prior to the Civil War, as was the chapter "Free People of Color of New Orleans" in the Christian manuscript at UNO.

For more about free blacks volunteering for the Confederate army, see Dunbar-Nelson's essay "People of Color in Louisiana" in Kein's *Creole*. My account of the New Orleans Creoles of color's participation in the Civil War draws mainly from Ochs, *Black Patriot*, and Hollandsworth, *Native Guards*. I am particularly grateful to Mr. Ochs for sharing his research about the racial makeup of my great-great-grandfather's company, Company C. McPherson's *Negro's Civil War* was also helpful.

The quote about the solidarity among black and brown Union soldiers comes from the Logsdon and Bell essay in *Creole New Orleans*.

Blassingame, in *Black New Orleans*, describes the doubt among whites and the white press about the fitness of black men as soldiers.

Chapter 16

I am grateful to Daniel Robert Samuels for sharing his thesis "Remembering North Claiborne: Community and Place in Downtown New Orleans" to help me understand the effect of the construction of interstate highway 10 on the Tremé neighborhood.

For more about the effect on crime of closing housing projects, see Young's "N.O.'s Murder Rate" in the *Times-Picayune*.

The murder of Durelli Watts and her daughter Ina Gex were covered extensively in the *Times-Picayune* during the summer of 2004.

The scene with my older cousin Rose condenses numerous conversations and an interview at her home. The information about Jeanne's home was obtained during a phone interview. Both Jeanne and Rose prefer to use only their first names for privacy.

For more on redlining and its effect on wealth accumulation for African Americans, see Adelman's documentary film *Race: The Power of an Illusion* and Conley's *Being Black*.

Chapter 17

Most of the quoted passages come from Ochs's *Black Patriot* and Hollandsworth's *Native Guards*, as do details about conditions in New Orleans during the Union occupation and movements of the Louisiana Native Guard throughout the Civil War. Blassingame's *Black New Orleans* also provided information about the privations in New Orleans, as well as the account of Paul

Trévigne's false arrest. Finally, Marcus Christian's "The Negro as a Soldier" helped to fill in the blanks.

Details about *L'Union*—including quoted material—and the Creole of color activists come from Bell's *Revolution* and her essay with Logsdon in Hirsch and Logsdon, *Creole New Orleans*. I also drew from Thompson's and Rankin's dissertations.

In addition to Ochs's and Hollandsworth's books, my account of the Battle of Port Hudson was aided by Hewitt's *Confederate Bastion*.

Chapter 18

During numerous interviews, both formal and informal, my brother, Todd, helped to confirm many details of my father's life, particularly his military service. Todd also readily supplied his own reactions to our family background throughout the course of my working on this project.

I am grateful to Michelle Olinger, Steve Lanusse-Siegel, Pat Schexnayder, and Kara Chenevert for sharing with me the stories of discovering their family histories.

The scene with Julie Hilla drew from my interview with her in New Orleans several years before she died. I am indebted to Mary Gehman for her help in confirming the chronology of Hilla's story.

An October 5, 1999, article in *Slate* magazine by Brent Staples drew my attention to Robert Stuckert's study. For more about Dr. Mark Shriver and his contribution to genetic testing for "ancestral admixture," see Gates's documentary series *African American Lives* (2006).

Chapter 19

See Donald's *Lincoln* for President Lincoln's aims and actions toward reconstructing the United States.

For Reconstruction in Louisiana and the Mechanics' Institute Riot, I am especially indebted to Hollandsworth's *Massacre*. Also helpful were Tunnell's *Crucible*, Bell's *Revolution*, Rankin's "Forgotten People," and Roussève's *Negro*.

For more on the *Tribune* newspaper, see Thompson's "Passing," the essay by Bell and Logsdon in Hirsch and Logsdon's *Creole New Orleans*, Rankin's essay "Black Leadership," and Houzeau's memoir, *My Passage*.

Lincoln's Reconstruction speech, the last speech he ever made, can be found in Basler's *Collected Works*.

For the reaction around the country to the Mechanics' Institute massacre and its effect on the congressional elections and the subsequent Reconstruction Amendments to the Constitution, see also Foner's *Reconstruction*.

Chapter 20

Baker's *Second Battle*, Klarman's *Jim Crow*, Harlan's "Desegregation," and Fischer's "Ascendancy" provided the background for the school integration fight in New Orleans during Reconstruction.

For more on George Washington Cable, see Turner's *Cable*.

The figures concerning the number of murdered Republicans in Louisiana during Reconstruction come from Chaillé's *Intimidation*, found in the Historic New Orleans Collection.

Thompson's dissertation was helpful in understanding the relations between Creoles of color and American blacks during Reconstruction, as were Bell and Logsdon's essay in Hirsch and Logsdon's *Creole New Orleans*, Rankin's "Forgotten People," and Bell's *Revolution*.

See Warmoth's *Reconstruction* for more on his political positions. Tunnell's *Crucible*, Foner's *Reconstruction*, and Woodward's *Reunion* provided background on Reconstruction in Louisiana.

Lieutenant Governor Dunn's quote about not seeking political equality comes from the Tureaud Collection at Amistad Research Center. Pinchback's quote about wholesale falsehood appeared in Bell's *Revolution*.

Chapter 21

I am grateful to my cousin Bernie Cousins for sharing with me the family history he completed about the Cousin family.

More on the history of the shifting definition of blackness in Louisiana can be found in Domínguez's *Definition*, Davis's *Who Is Black?*, and Diamond and Cottrol's "Codifying Caste."

Chapter 22

D'Antoni's *Chahta-Ima* provided some details about the Cousin family and the conditions in St. Tammany Parish during the Civil War.

Walton's *Black Republicans* and the dissertations by Webb and Uzee were particularly helpful regarding the black vote and the activities of black Republicans during the Reconstruction and post-Reconstruction periods.

The letter to Rutherford Hayes detailing the murders of black Republicans was written by Alfred Fairfax and appears in Webb's dissertation.

Pinchback's quote about looking "at things as they are" originally appeared in *The Louisianian* newspaper, and is cited in Bell and Logsdon's essay in Hirsch and Logsdon, *Creole New Orleans*.

Chapter 23

Reports of political meetings in the *Times-Picayune* and the *Crusader* aided my analysis of state and local political activity during the 1890s, including my great-grandfather's participation. Most quoted materials came from these accounts.

Details about Paul Broyard's building career and New Orleans architecture in general were drawn from the works by Friends of the Cabildo, Hankins's *Raised*, and *Louisiana Locals* for 1894.

Jackson's *Gilded Age* and her essay "Bosses" were helpful in providing information on the Louisiana state elections during the 1880s. For more on the 1896 gubernatorial election, see Howard's essay "Populist-Republican Fusion."

For more on Rodolphe Desdunes and the Citizens Committee involvement in the *Plessy* legal case, see the Bell and Logsdon essay in Hirsch and Logsdon, *Creole New Orleans*, and Medley's *Freemen*. Medley's book provided the quoted correspondence between Louis Martinet and Albion Tourgée.

Chapter 24

The story in which my father described his father dancing in his wheelchair is called "Anecdotes from the Hospital" and was published in the September 1982 *Atlantic Monthly*.

Chapter 25

Anthony's "Negro Creole" was very helpful for understanding the response of Creoles of color, including my family, to Jim Crow.

I drew biographical details about Paul Broyard and his family from interviews with his grandson Jimmy Broyard, granddaughter Rose, and great-nephew Irving Trevigne. My aunt Shirley Broyard Williams also provided background information about her parents' lives in New Orleans.

For more on the efforts to combat segregation by black leaders around the country, see Fairclough's *Better Day*.

PART THREE

Chapter 27

I am indebted to Wilder's *Covenant* for my account of the history of blacks in Brooklyn and the development of Bedford-Stuyvesant. Quimby's chapter on Bed-Stuy in *Brooklyn, USA*, Connolly's *Ghetto Grows*, and the *Brooklyn Daily Eagle* morgue at the Brooklyn Public Library were also helpful.

My father's recollections about his childhood are drawn from *Kafka*, the essay collection *Men, Women,* and his unpublished journals. In numerous interviews my aunt Shirley Broyard Williams also provided many details about her family's life in Brooklyn. In addition, Jimmy Broyard and my father's childhood friends Robbie King, Dr. Marjorie Costa, Lois Latte, and Elsner Horne all provided biographical data. For more about the Horne family, see Buckley's *The Hornes.*

I am grateful to Harold Chenven and Albert Gambale for sharing with me their recollections of my father during their years at Boys High School.

I'm grateful to the poet Michael Harper for drawing my attention to the memoir *I'm Katherine,* by his father, W. Warren Harper. I am also indebted to Sydney deLeon for sharing her memoir of growing up in 1930s Harlem, which helped to illuminate the experience of passing from a child's perspective.

Chapter 28

Quotes taken from Milton Klonsky's writing appear in his collected essays, *A Discourse on Hip.*

Vincent Livelli has been an invaluable source of information about my father's time at Brooklyn College and in Greenwich Village.

I am grateful to Gerald Gross for facilitating my interview with his late wife, Flora Finkelstein Gross.

Gale's *Contemporary Authors* provided the biographical details for Alfred Duckett's life.

Chapter 29

My father wrote about his recurrent dream for an essay called "Intoxicated by My Illness," which appears in his book by the same name.

For more on legal definitions of blackness and whiteness in the United States, see Davis's *Who Is Black?,* the Braman essay in the *UCLA Law Review,* and Lopez's "Social Construction."

I am particularly grateful to Daniel Sharfstein for sharing with me his essay "The Secret History of Race in the United States" and for his assistance in deciphering the decisions for the *Sunseri v. Cassagne* trials. The details of the case, *Sunseri v. Cassagne,* 196 So. 7 (1940), come from decisions published in *Southern Reporter* and from the trial transcript available at the Louisiana Supreme Court archives in New Orleans.

For more on Louisiana's racial laws and the career of Naomi Drake, see Domínguez's *Definition,* Trillin's "Black or White" from the *New Yorker,* and O'Byrne's "Many Feared" in the *Times-Picayune.*

Chapter 30

Klonsky's observation about the Greenwich Village streets appears in his *Discourse*.

For more on African American troops in World War II, including the quoted letters from white officers about commanding black troops, see Lee's *Employment*.

I am grateful to Edward Howard and Ellis Derry for sharing with me their recollections of the 167th Port Company. My father's military record and the historical record for the 167th also provided details about his service.

Enid Gort graciously shared her research and reflections on my uncle Franklin H. Williams, from which I gleaned many details of his life.

Chapter 31

Ross Wetzsteon's *Republic of Dreams* provided background on Greenwich Village of the 1940s and the quoted description of the San Remo bar.

Irving Howe's observations about the *Partisan Review* and political thought during the 1940s appear in his book *Margin*.

I am indebted to David Leeming's biographies of James Baldwin and Beauford Delaney for my account of their experiences in Greenwich Village.

W. F. Lucas's comment about my father's racial change during his subway ride into Manhattan appeared in Gates's article "White Like Me," as does the reference to my father in the correspondence between Arna Bontemps and Langston Hughes.

Details about the publication of Brossard's *Who Walk in Darkness* were drawn from correspondence found in the Laughlin Collection at Harvard, along with interviews with Anne Bernays, Tim Horan, and Vincent Livelli.

For more on the segregation of labor unions, see Hill's "Labor Unions."

The biographical details of Van den Haag's life come from the finding aid for the Ernest van den Haag Papers at the University of Albany. For more about his efforts to oppose integration, see Khan's *Separated*.

Chapter 32

I am grateful to my mother for sharing the correspondence between her and my father during their engagement. My numerous interviews and discussions with her also contributed greatly to my account of my father's life.

My father's essays on family life have been collected into *Men, Women*.

Chapter 33

For more on the effect of Katrina on New Orleans's black middle class, see Cass's article "Notable Mardi Gras Absences." Keith Medley is quoted on black Mardi Gras balls in Texeira's "Black Social Networks."

New Orleans East's uncertain future is discussed in greater detail by Howell and Vinturella in their *New York Times* piece and by Donze and Krupa in "Nagin Upbeat" in the *Times-Picayune.*

Afterword

For more on the significance of the findings by the Human Genome Project, see "Reading the Book of Life," a White House news conference on the decoding of the genome.

Wade's "The Human Family Tree" and Anger's "Do Races Differ?" were helpful in providing background about tracing ancestral origins in human genes, as was Cavalli-Sforza's *Genes, Peoples, and Languages.*

More information about DNAPrint's testing services can be found at their Web site, DNAPrint.com.

Bibliography

NEWSPAPERS

Cleveland (Ohio) *Gazette*, March/April 1894
The Crusader (New Orleans), 1891–96
Daily Picayune, 1892, 1894, 1896, 1898, 1900
New Orleans Tribune, 1864–68, 1869–70
New York Times, 1946–90

ARCHIVES

Biography—Duckett, Alfred A. 2004. In *Contemporary Authors (Biography)*, Thomas Gale, http://www.amazon.com/gp/product/B0007SBDW4/ref=ml_bd/102-8738840-8646560 (accessed July 17, 2005).

Brooklyn Eagle Morgue. In Brooklyn Collection, Brooklyn Public Library. Brooklyn, NY, 1938–45.

Chandler Brossard Correspondence. In James Laughlin Collection. Houghton Library, Harvard University, Cambridge, MA.

Compiled Military Service Records, Civil War. In National Archives. Washington, DC.

Compiled Service of Military Units in Volunteer Union Organizations, M-594. In National Archives. Washington, DC.

Family Note Cards [Bertha Neff]. Covington Courthouse, Covington, LA.

"History of the 167th Port Co." In War Department Records Branch, A.G.O. College Park, MD, 1944–46.

"Remarks of Lt. Gov. Oscar J. Dunn." In A. P. Tureaud Collection, The Amistad Research Center. New Orleans, LA.

BOOKS, ARTICLES, AND VIDEO RECORDINGS

Adelman, Larry. *Race: The Power of an Illusion.* Video recording. San Francisco: Independent Television Service, 2003.

Anger, Natalie. "Do Races Differ? Not Really." *New York Times,* August 22, 2000.

Anthony, Arthé Agnes. "The Negro Creole Community in New Orleans, 1880–1920: An Oral History." PhD diss., University of California, Irvine, 1978.

Baker, Liva. *The Second Battle of New Orleans.* New York: HarperCollins, 1996.

Basler, Roy Prentice, and Christian O. Basler. *The Collected Works of Abraham Lincoln.* New Brunswick, NJ: Rutgers University Press, 1990.

Bell, Caryn Cossé. *Revolution, Romanticism, and the Afro-Creole Protest Tradition in Louisiana, 1718–1868.* Baton Rouge: Louisiana State University Press, 1997.

Berlin, Ira. *Slaves Without Masters: The Free Negro in the Antebellum South.* New York: Oxford University Press, 1981.

Blassingame, John W. *Black New Orleans, 1860–1880.* Chicago: University of Chicago Press, 1973.

Braman, Donald. "Of Race and Immutability." *UCLA Law Review* 46 (1999): 1375.

Brasseaux, Carl A., Glenn R. Conrad, and David Cheramie. *The Road to Louisiana: The Saint-Domingue Refugees, 1792–1809.* Lafayette: Center for Louisiana Studies, University of Southwestern Louisiana, 1992.

Brossard, Chandler. "Letter to the Editor: Wake Up, We're Almost There," *New York Times Book Review,* May 2, 1971.

———. "Plaint of a Gentile Intellectual." *Commentary,* May 1950: 154–56.

———. *Who Walk in Darkness.* London: John Lehmann, 1952.

———. *Who Walk in Darkness.* 1st Herodias Classics ed. New York: Herodias, 2000.

Broyard, Anatole. "American Sexual Imperialism." *Neurotica,* Autumn 1950, 36–40.

———. "Anecdotes from the Hospital." *Atlantic Monthly,* September 1982, 81–86.

———. *Aroused by Books.* New York: Random House, 1974.

———. "For He's a Jolly Good Fellow." In *New World Writing, Tenth Mentor Selection.* New York: New American Library, 1956.

———. *Intoxicated by My Illness: And Other Writings on Life and Death.* New York: Clarkson Potter, 1992.

———. *Kafka Was the Rage: A Greenwich Village Memoir.* 1st Vintage Books ed. New York: Vintage Books, 1997.

———. "Letter to the Editor." *New York Times Book Review,* May 2, 1971.

———. "Mambo." *Neurotica,* Spring 1950: 29–30.

———. *Men, Women, and Other Anticlimaxes.* New York: Methuen, 1980.

————. "Portrait of the Inauthentic Negro." *Commentary*, July 1950: 56–64.

————. "Summer Madness." In *Summer*, ed. Alice Gordon. Boston: Addison-Wesley, 1990.

————. "Sunday Dinner in Brooklyn." In *Modern Writing*, ed. William Phillips and Philip Rahv. New York: Avon, 1953.

————. "Sunday Dinner in Brooklyn." In *Protest: The Beat Generation and the Angry Young Men*, ed. Gene Feldman and Max Gartenberg. London: Souvenir Press, 1958.

————. "A Truly Bad Book Just Doesn't Happen" (review of *Wake Up, We're Almost There* by Chandler Brossard). *New York Times Book Review*, April 4, 1971.

————. "Village Café." *Partisan Review* 17, no. 5 (1950): 524–28.

Buckley, Gail Lumet. *The Hornes: An American Family.* New York: Knopf, 1986.

Carter, Clarence Edwin, ed. *The Territorial Papers of the United States.* Vol. 14, *The Territory of Orleans, 1803–1812.* Washington: U.S. Government Printing Office, 1940.

Cass, Julia. "Notable Mardi Gras Absences Reflect Loss of Black Middle Class." *Washington Post*, February 25, 2006.

Cavalli-Sforza, Luigi Luca. *Genes, People, and Languages.* New York: Northpoint Press, 2000.

Chaillé, Stanford E. *Intimidation and the Number of White and of Colored Voters in Louisiana in 1876, as Shown by Statistical Data Derived from Republican Official Reports.* New Orleans: Picayune Office Job Print, 1877.

Christian, Marcus B. "A Black History of Louisiana." In Marcus B. Christian Collection, Earl K. Long Library, University of New Orleans. New Orleans.

————. "Free People of Color of New Orleans." In Marcus B. Christian Collection, Earl K. Long Library, University of New Orleans. New Orleans.

————. "The Mechanics Hall Riot." In Marcus B. Christian Collection, Earl K. Long Library, University of New Orleans. New Orleans.

————. "The Negro as a Soldier: 1861–1865." In Marcus B. Christian Collection, Earl K. Long Library, University of New Orleans. New Orleans.

————. "Negro Education: 1861–1900." In Marcus B. Christian Collection, Earl K. Long Library, University of New Orleans. New Orleans.

Clark, John Garretson. *La Rochelle and the Atlantic Economy During the* Eighteenth Century. Baltimore: Johns Hopkins University Press, 1981.

Conley, Dalton. *Being Black, Living in the Red: Race, Wealth, and Social Policy in America.* Berkeley: University of California Press, 1999.

Connolly, Harold X. *A Ghetto Grows in Brooklyn.* New York: New York University Press, 1977.

Corwin, Phillip. "Letter to the Editor." *New York Times Book Review,* May 2, 1971.

Coyne, John. "Letter to the Editor." *New York Times Book Review,* May 2, 1971.

D'Antoni, Blaise C., and St. Tammany Historical Society. *Chahta-Ima and St. Tammany's Choctaws.* Mandeville, LA: St. Tammany Historical Society, 1986.

Davis, F. James. *Who Is Black? One Nation's Definition.* 10th anniversary ed. University Park: Pennsylvania State University Press, 2001.

Desdunes, Rodolphe Lucien. *A Few Words to Dr. Du Bois, with Malice Toward None.* New Orleans, 1907.

Desdunes, Rodolphe Lucien, and Dorothea Olga McCants. *Our People and Our History: Fifty Creole Portraits.* Baton Rouge: Louisiana State University Press, 2001.

Diamond, Raymond T., and Cottrol, Robert J. "Codifying Caste: Louisiana's Racial Classification Scheme and the Fourteenth Amendment." *Loyola Law Review* 29 (1983): 255–85.

Domínguez, Virginia R. *White by Definition: Social Classification in Creole Louisiana.* New Brunswick, NJ: Rutgers University Press, 1986.

Donald, David Herbert. *Lincoln.* New York: Simon & Schuster, 1995.

Donze, Frank, and Krupa, Michelle. "Nagin Upbeat After Win." *Times-Picayune,* May 22, 2006.

Eakin, Sue L., and Solomon Northup. *Solomon Northup's Twelve Years a Slave: 1841–1853.* Gretna, LA: Pelican, 1998.

Eliot, T. S. *Four Quartets.* New York: Harcourt Brace Jovanovich, 1971.

Ellison, Ralph. *Invisible Man.* Modern Library ed. New York: Modern Library, 1994.

Fairclough, Adam. *Better Day Coming: Blacks and Equality, 1890–2000.* New York: Viking, 2001.

Firestone, David. "Identity Restored to 100,000 Louisiana Slaves." *New York Times,* July 30, 2000.

Fischer, Roger A. "Jim Crow's Ascendancy." In *The Louisiana Purchase Bicentennial Series in Louisiana History,* ed. Matthew J. Schott. Lafayette: Center for Louisiana Studies, University of Louisiana, 2000.

Fleming, Thomas. "Old Hickory's Finest Hour." *Quarterly Journal of Military History* 13, no. 2 (2001): 6–17.

Foner, Eric. *Reconstruction: America's Unfinished Revolution, 1863–1877.* New York: Harper & Row, 1988.

Fossier, A. E. *New Orleans: The Glamour Period, 1800–1840.* New Orleans: Pelican, 1957.

Friends of the Cabildo. "Line Item Index of Building Contracts in Orleans Parish." In Notarial Archives. New Orleans, LA.

Friends of the Cabildo, Samuel Wilson, Mary Louise Christovich, and Roulhac Toledano. *New Orleans Architecture.* Gretna, LA: Pelican, 1971.

Gates, Henry Louis, et al. *African American Lives.* Video recording. Hollywood: Paramount Home Entertainment, 2006.

Gates, Henry Louis Jr. "White Like Me." *New Yorker,* June 17, 1996.

Gayarré, Charles. *History of Louisiana.* New Orleans: A. Hawkins, 1885.

Gehman, Mary. *The Free People of Color of New Orleans: An Introduction.* New Orleans: Margaret Media, 1994.

Gramsci, Antonio, and Joseph A. Buttigieg. *Prison Notebooks, European Perspectives.* New York: Columbia University Press, 1991.

Hall, Gwendolyn Midlo. *Africans in Colonial Louisiana: The Development of Afro-Creole Culture in the Eighteenth Century.* Baton Rouge: Louisiana State University Press, 1992.

———. *Social Control in Slave Plantation Societies: A Comparison of St. Domingue and Cuba.* Baltimore: Johns Hopkins Press, 1971.

Hanger, Kimberly S. *Bounded Lives, Bounded Places: Free Black Society in Colonial New Orleans, 1769–1803.* Durham, NC: Duke University Press, 1997.

Hankins, Jonn Ethan, Steven Maklansky, and New Orleans Museum of Art. *Raised to the Trade: Creole Building Arts of New Orleans.* New Orleans: New Orleans Museum of Art, 2002.

Harlan, Louis R. "Desegregation in New Orleans Public Schools During Reconstruction." *American Historical Review* 67, no. 3 (1962): 663–75.

Hentoff, Nat. "Broyard & (More)." *Village Voice,* May 13, 1971, 19–20.

Hewitt, Lawrence L. *Port Hudson, Confederate Bastion on the Mississippi.* Baton Rouge: Louisiana State University Press, 1987.

Hill, Herbert. "Labor Unions and the Negro." *Commentary,* December 1959.

Hirsch, Arnold R., and Joseph Logsdon. *Creole New Orleans: Race and Americanization.* Baton Rouge: Louisiana State University Press, 1992.

Hollandsworth, James G. *An Absolute Massacre: The New Orleans Race Riot of July 30, 1866.* Baton Rouge: Louisiana State University Press, 2001.

———. *The Louisiana Native Guards: The Black Military Experience During the Civil War.* Baton Rouge: Louisiana State University Press, 1995.

Houzeau, Jean-Charles, and David C. Rankin. *My Passage at the New Orleans Tribune: A Memoir of the Civil War Era.* Baton Rouge: Louisiana State University Press, 1984.

Howard, Perry. "The Populist-Republican Fusion: 1896." In *The Louisiana Purchase Bicentennial Series in Louisiana History,* ed. Matthew J. Schott. Lafayette: Center for Louisiana Studies, University of Louisiana, 2000.

Howe, Irving. *A Margin of Hope: An Intellectual Autobiography.* New York: Harcourt Brace Jovanovich, 1982.

Howell, Susan E., and John B. Vinturella. "Forgotten in New Orleans." *New York Times,* April 20, 2006.

Jackson, Joy J. "Bosses and Businessmen." In *The Louisiana Purchase Bicentennial Series in Louisiana History,* ed. Matthew J. Schott. Lafayette: Center for Louisiana Studies, University of Louisiana, 2000.

————. *New Orleans in the Gilded Age: Politics and Progress, 1880–1896.* Baton Rouge: Louisiana State University Press, 1969.

James, C.L.R. *The Black Jacobins: Toussaint L'Ouverture and the San Domingo Revolution.* New York: Vintage Books, 1963.

Johnson, James Weldon. *The Autobiography of an Ex-Coloured Man.* Boston: Sherman, French, 1912.

Johnson, Walter. *Soul by Soul: Life Inside the Antebellum Slave Market.* Cambridge, MA: Harvard University Press, 1999.

Kahn, E. J. *The Separated People: A Look at Contemporary South Africa.* New York: Norton, 1968.

Kein, Sybil. *Creole: The History and Legacy of Louisiana's Free People of Color.* Baton Rouge: Louisiana State University Press, 2000.

Klarman, Michael J. *From Jim Crow to Civil Rights: The Supreme Court and the Struggle for Racial Equality.* New York: Oxford University Press, 2004.

Klonsky, Milton, and Ted Solotaroff. *A Discourse on Hip: Selected Writings of Milton Klonsky.* Detroit: Wayne State University Press, 1990.

Krim, Seymour. *The Beats: A Gold Medal Anthology.* Greenwich, CT: Fawcett, 1960.

Kroeger, Brooke. *Passing: When People Can't Be Who They Are.* New York: Public Affairs, 2003.

LaChance, Paul. "Were Saint-Domingue Refugees a Distinctive Cultural Group in Antebellum New Orleans? Evidence from Patterns and Strategies of Property Holding." *Revista/Review Interamericana* 29, nos. 1–4 (1999).

Larsen, Nella. *Passing.* New York: Modern Library, 2000.

Latrobe, John H. B., and Samuel Wilson. *Southern Travels: Journal of John H. B. Latrobe, 1834.* New Orleans: Historic New Orleans Collection, 1986.

Laussat, Pierre-Clément de. *Memoirs of My Life to My Son During the Years 1803 and After, Which I Spent in Public Service in Louisiana as Commissioner of the French Government for the Retrocession to France of That Colony and for Its Transfer to the United States.* Baton Rouge: Published for the Historic New Orleans Collection by the Louisiana State University Press, 1978.

Lee, Ulysses, and Center of Military History. *The Employment of Negro Troops.* Washington, DC: Center of Military History, 1994.

Leeming, David. *Amazing Grace: A Life of Beauford Delaney.* New York: Oxford University Press, 1998.

————. *James Baldwin: A Biography.* New York: Viking Penguin, 1994.

Lopez, Ian F. Haney. "The Social Construction of Race: Some Observations on Illusion, Fabrication, and Choice." *Harvard Civil Rights–Civil Liberties Law Review* 29 (1994): 1–62.

Louisiana Locals: The Commercial, Industrial, and Financial Outlook for New Orleans. New Orleans, 1894.

McPherson, James M. *The Negro's Civil War: How American Negroes Felt and Acted During the War for the Union.* New York: Vintage Books, 1965.

Mailer, Norman. "The White Negro." *Dissent* 4 (1957).

Malcomson, Scott L. *One Drop of Blood: The American Misadventure of Race.* New York: Farrar, Straus and Giroux, 2000.

Medley, Keith Weldon. "From Sire to Son—from Chief to Chief." *New Orleans Tribune,* January 2000.

———. "Mardi Gras Mambo." *New Orleans Tribune,* February 1989.

———. *We as Freemen.* Gretna, LA: Pelican, 2003.

Morning, Ann. "Multiracial Classification of the United States Census: Myth, Reality, and Future Impact." Paper presented at the International Union for the Scientific Study of Population. Tours, France: July 23, 2005.

Nelson, William J. Jr. "The Free Negro in the Ante Bellum New Orleans Press." PhD diss., Duke University, 1977.

O'Byrne, James. "Many Feared Naomi Drake and Powerful Racial Whim." *Times-Picayune,* August 16, 1993.

Ochs, Stephen J. *A Black Patriot and a White Priest: André Cailloux and Claude Paschal Maistre in Civil War New Orleans.* Baton Rouge: Louisiana State University Press, 2000.

Pfeiffer, Kathleen. *Race Passing and American Individualism.* Amherst: University of Massachusetts Press, 2003.

Podhoretz, Norman. *Making It.* New York: Random House, 1967.

Quimby, Ernest. "Bedford-Stuyvesant." In *Brooklyn, USA: The Fourth Largest City in America,* ed. by Rita Seiden Miller. New York: Brooklyn College Press, 1979.

Rankin, David C. "The Forgotten People: Free People of Color in New Orleans, 1850–1870." PhD diss., Johns Hopkins University, 1976.

———. "The Origins of Black Leadership in New Orleans During Reconstruction." *Journal of Southern History* 40 (1974): 417–70.

"Reading the Book of Life: White House Remarks on Decoding of Genome." *New York Times,* June 27, 2000.

Reinders, Robert C. *End of an Era: New Orleans, 1850–1860.* New Orleans: Pelican, 1964.

Roth, Philip. *The Human Stain.* Boston: Houghton Mifflin, 2000.

Roussève, Charles Barthelemy. *The Negro in Louisiana.* New Orleans: Xavier University Press, 1937.

Samuels, Daniel Robert. "Remembering North Claiborne: Community and Place in Downtown New Orleans." Master's thesis, University of New Orleans, 2000.

Sartre, Jean-Paul. "Portrait of the Inauthentic Jew." *Commentary,* May 1948: 389–97.

Schafer, Judith Kelleher. *Becoming Free, Remaining Free: Manumission and Enslavement in New Orleans, 1846–1862.* Baton Rouge: Louisiana State University, 2003.

Sharfstein, Daniel F. "The Secret History of Race in the United States." *Yale Law Journal* 112 (2003): 1473–1509.

Sollors, Werner. *Neither Black nor White and yet Both: Thematic Explorations of Interracial Literature.* New York: Oxford University Press, 1997.

Texeira, Erin. "New Orleans' Black Social Networks Hurting." Associated Press, April 8, 2006.

Thompson, Shirley Elizabeth. "The Passing of a People: Creoles of Color in Mid-Nineteenth Century New Orleans." PhD diss., Harvard University, 2001.

Toledano, Roulhac, and Christovich, Mary Louise. *New Orleans Architecture: Faubourg Tremé and the Bayou Road.* Gretna, LA: Pelican, 2003.

Trillin, Calvin. "Black or White." *New Yorker,* April 14, 1986, 62–78.

Tunnell, Ted. *Crucible of Reconstruction: War, Radicalism, and Race in Louisiana, 1862–1877.* Baton Rouge: Louisiana State University Press, 1984.

Turner, Arlin. *George W. Cable: A Biography.* Baton Rouge: Louisiana State University Press, 1966.

Uzee, Philip Davis. "Republican Politics in Louisiana, 1877–1900." PhD diss., Louisiana State University, 1950.

Wade, Nicholas. "The Human Family Tree: 10 Adams and 18 Eves." *New York Times,* May 2, 2000.

Walton, Hanes. *Black Republicans: The Politics of the Black and Tans.* Metuchen, NJ: Scarecrow Press, 1975.

Warmoth, Henry Clay. *War, Politics, and Reconstruction: Stormy Days in Louisiana.* New York: Macmillan, 1930.

Webb, Allie Bayne Windham. "A History of Negro Voting in Louisiana, 1877–1906." PhD diss., Louisiana State University, 1962.

Wetzsteon, Ross. *Republic of Dreams: Greenwich Village, the American Bohemia, 1910–1960.* New York: Simon & Schuster, 2002.

Wilder, Craig Steven. *A Covenant with Color: Race and Social Power in Brooklyn.* New York: Columbia University Press, 2000.

Williamson, Joel. *New People: Miscegenation and Mulattoes in the United States.* New York: New York University Press, 1984.

Woodward, C. Vann. *Reunion and Reaction.* Boston: Little, Brown, 1951.

Wright, Lawrence. "One Drop of Blood." *New Yorker,* July 25, 1994, 46–55.

Young, Tara. "N.O.'s Murder Rate Down in 2004." *Times-Picayune,* January 1, 2005.

Illustration Credits

PART ONE

Page 24: Todd, Anatole, Sandy, and Bliss Broyard. Mary Inabinet. **Page 53:** Bliss, Todd, and Sandy Broyard. Courtesy of Sandy Broyard. **Page 61:** Bliss and Anatole Broyard. Sandy Broyard. **Page 76:** Shirley Broyard Williams. Courtesy of Shirley Williams. **Page 80:** Lorraine Broyard. Courtesy of Shirley Williams. **Page 92:** Anatole Broyard's childhood home in New Orleans. Courtesy of Shirley Williams. **Page 121:** Los Angeles Broyards at Harold and Belle's. Collection of author.

PART TWO

Page 149: *A View of New Orleans from the Opposite Bank of the Mississippi, 1765.* Collection of the Louisiana State Museum. **Page 159:** *Hoisting American Colors, Louisiana Cession, 1803,* Thure de Thulstrup, c. 1903. Collection of the Louisiana Historical Society, courtesy of the Louisiana State Museum. **Page 165:** *The Battle of New Orleans,* John Andrews, 1856. Detail showing free black battalions. Collection of the Louisiana State Museum. **Page 167:** *Sale of Estates, Pictures, and Slaves in the Rotunda, New Orleans,* W. H. Brooke and J. M. Starling, c. 1860. Collection of the Louisiana State Museum. **Page 172:** *Fashionable African-American Women,* Edouard Marquis, 1867. Detail. Collection of the Louisiana State Museum. **Page 174:** *The Negro Gallery, July 15, 1871.* Reproduced from *Every Saturday.* Collection of the Louisiana State Museum. **Page 183:** Tootie Montana, Big Chief, Yellow Pocahontas, 1991. Michael P. Smith. **Page 192:** *Free Blacks from Saint-Domingue,* Labrousse, c. 1790. Collection of the Louisiana State Museum. **Page 220:** *Assault of the Second Louisiana (Colored) Regiment on the Confederate Works at Port Hudson, May 27th, 1863.* From *The Soldier in Our Civil War.* Collection of the Louisiana State Museum. **Page 246:** *The Riot in New Orleans. Harper's Weekly,* August 25, 1866. Collection of the Louisiana State Museum. **Page 253:** Paul Broyard. Courtesy of Joyce Howard. **Page**

272: Rosa Cousin. Courtesy of Joyce Howard. **Page 289:** Bliss Broyard and host at Plantation Revelers Ball. Collection of author. **Page 296:** Bliss Broyard dressed for Bunch Club Ball. Collection of author. **Page 303:** Paul Broyard and his two brothers standing, with two laborers seated. Courtesy of Joyce Howard. **Page 307:** Paul Anatole "Nat" Broyard. Courtesy of Shirley Williams. **Page 308:** Nat Broyard and Edna Miller Broyard. Courtesy of Shirley Williams.

PART THREE

Page 321: Lorraine, Shirley, and Anatole "Bud" Broyard. Courtesy of Shirley Williams. **Page 338:** Anatole "Bud" Broyard. Boys High School Yearbook, 1937. **Page 343:** Flora Finkelstein reclining on friends from Brooklyn College. Courtesy of Gerald Cross. **Page 351:** Ethel Broyard. Courtesy of Shirley Williams. **Page 354:** Application for social security number. Collection of author. **Page 373:** Second Lieutenant Anatole Broyard. Collection of author. **Page 377:** Anatole Broyard (left). Courtesy of Sandy Broyard. Franklin Williams (right). Courtesy of Shirley Williams. **Page 378:** First Lieutenant Anatole Broyard. Courtesy of Shirley Williams. **Page 383:** Sheri Martinelli. Courtesy of Steven Moore. **Page 402:** Anatole Broyard in *Time* magazine. Ben Martin for TIME. **Pages 408–9:** Anatole Broyard's girlfriends. Collection of author. **Page 422:** Anatole Broyard and Sandy Nelson cutting their wedding cake. Courtesy of Sandy Broyard. **Page 423:** Lorraine and Edna Broyard and Sandy Nelson at Anatole and Sandy's wedding. Courtesy of Sandy Broyard. **Page 425:** Todd and Bliss Broyard. Sandy Broyard. **Page 449:** Anatole Broyard. Sandy Broyard. **Page 466:** Bliss and Anatole Broyard. Sandy Broyard.

Index

About the Author

Bliss Broyard is the author of the collection of stories *My Father, Dancing*, which was a *New York Times* Notable Book of the Year. Her fiction and essays have been anthologized in *Best American Short Stories, The Pushcart Prize Anthology,* and *The Art of the Essay,* and have appeared in *Grand Street, Ploughshares,* the *New York Times, Elle,* and elsewhere. She lives in Brooklyn with her husband and daughter.